The Psychoanalytic Mind

Marcia Cavell

The Psychoanalytic Mind

From Freud to Philosophy

Harvard University Press

Cambridge, Massachusetts, and London, England   1993

Copyright © 1993 by the President and Fellows of Harvard College
All rights reserved
Printed in the United States of America

This book is printed on acid-free paper, and its binding materials have
been chosen for strength and durability.

Library of Congress Cataloging-in-Publication Data

Cavell, Marcia, 1931–
   The psychoanalytic mind: from Freud to philosophy/Marcia Cavell.
     p. cm.
   Includes bibliographical references and index.
   ISBN 0-674-72095-4 (alk. paper)
   1. Psychoanalysis and philosophy. 2. Subjectivity—Controversial literature.
   3. Philosophy of mind. 4. Freud, Sigmund, 1856–1939. I. Title.
BF175.4.P45C38 1993
150.19'52—dc20   93–7325
CIP

To my mother, Marcia Lee Masters,
and to Donald

Contents

Acknowledgments   ix

Introduction   *1*

Part One   *The Matter of Mind*

1   Meaning and Mind   *9*

2   Minding the Frontier   *43*

3   Mind, Body, and the Question of Psychological Laws   *57*

4   Telling Stories   *83*

Part Two   *Thinking about Children*

5   Behind the Veil of Language   *107*

6   Baby Talk   *121*

7   The Subject of Emotion   *137*

Part Three   *Irrationality*

8   Primary Process   *161*

9   Reasons, Repression, and Phantasy   *177*

10   Dividing the Self   *193*

       Conclusion: Valuing and the Self   *207*

       Notes   237
       Bibliography   255
       Index   271

Acknowledgments

In 1982–83 the National Endowment for the Humanities gave me a fellowship to write a work on psychoanalysis and philosophy, the theme of which was that the child comes to be a 'subject' or a 'self' only through its relations with other persons. (This was how I put it then.) In some form at least that was an idea familiar to 'Object Relations Theory' in psychoanalysis, and it struck me as philosophically right. I finished that manuscript, fearing even as I did that it was more gesture than argument.

Around this time I read Richard Rorty's *Philosophy and the Mirror of Nature,* which led me in turn to the work of Donald Davidson and a rereading of Wittgenstein. What I needed, I began to see, was the thesis articulated in different ways by all three philosophers that mind and language are interdependent; that as language is a communal activity, so is the mind a more interpersonal phenomenon than we are wont to think. But this way of arguing my earlier thesis implied that a lot of psychoanalytic ideas to which I had given allegiance could no longer stand. Tinkering with the manuscript, which I dismally tried for a few years, would not do; the thesis itself had to be thoroughly recast.

The present book, all of it new, rose slowly from the ashes of the old. Nevertheless that initial venture was invaluable to me, and I am grateful to the NEH for its support that first time around, as I am to a number of individuals for theirs. Richard Wollheim read a substantial number of pages and offered useful suggestions. Otto Kernberg, David Lewin, and Ruth Mathewson went through the manuscript line for line, and from all of them I learned a great deal, about friendship as well as writing.

The first piece in which I began to articulate some of the ideas developed here was printed in the *Journal of the American Psychoanalytic Association* (1988, vol. 36) under the title "Interpretation, Psychoanalysis, and the Philosophy of Mind." A companion article appeared by coincidence at the same time in *Psychoanalysis and Contemporary Thought* (1988, vol. 11) as "Solipsism and Community: Two Concepts of Mind in Philosophy and Psychoanalysis." Chapter 1 is a very much expanded discussion of the themes of those articles. Chapter 2 contains some material that appeared under the title "The Subject of Mind" in the *International Review of Psychoanalysis* (1991). A few remarks on Roy Schafer in Chapter 3 appeared in "The Self and Some Related Issues" in *Psychoanalysis and Contemporary Thought* (1985, vol. 8); and the second half of the Conclusion is revised from "Knowing and Valuing: Some Questions of Genealogy," in *Mind, Psychoanalysis and Art: Essays for Richard Wollheim*, ed. J. Hopkins and A. Savile (Oxford: Blackwell, 1992).

I have presented material that eventually found its way here at the New York Hospital–Cornell Medical Center, Westchester Division; the San Francisco Psychoanalytic Institute; and the departments of philosophy at Lehigh University, Princeton University, and the University of California at San Diego. Thoughtful responses from the audience on each occasion prompted needed corrections on my part.

Akeel Bilgrami, Arnold Cooper, Victoria Hamilton, Ernie Le Pore, Bruce Vermazen, Robert Wallerstein, and Richard Wollheim have each read a chapter or so of this book in manuscript, pointing out problems and possible solutions. All are astute critics and generous friends. Ariela Lazar read the entire manuscript, and in an extraordinary forty pages of comments helped push me to the finished version.

For their interest and their often inspiriting dissent, I am grateful also to students I have taught in courses on Freud and philosophy. I have in mind particularly Jim Greenwood at SUNY Purchase and Diane Klein at Berkeley. Conversations over the years with Allen and Dierdre Bergson, and with my daughter Rachel, helped teach me what dialogue at its best can be. And though neither of them has read what I have written, Drs. Ellen Simon and Louise Kaplan were in different ways indispensable sources of enlightenment and support, as was the Columbia Psychoanalytic Clinic for Training and Research, where I was a Special Research Candidate from 1970 to 1975.

Donald Davidson has been helpful beyond gratitude. I should add that I have undoubtedly missed subtleties in his arguments, unknowingly distorted his views, and put them to uses some of which he may not find entirely congenial.

Finally, I want to thank my editor at Harvard University Press, Mary Ellen Geer, whose advice was unfailingly tactful and judicious.

Writing was in its origin the voice of the absent person; and the dwelling-house was a substitute for the mother's womb.

— CIVILIZATION AND ITS DISCONTENTS

Introduction

Freud found the source of human neurosis in our long dependency on others and our capacity for symbolization. The conjunction, he saw, makes for deep longings, conflicts, and disappointments, breeding at the same time an imagination that can embroider reality for our short-term ease but our enduring pain. Psychoanalysis is essentially, and necessarily, a theory about creatures who have minds. But Freud's vision is continually in jeopardy. He himself, attracted as he was by mechanism on the one hand, biology on the other, and always passionate that psychoanalysis be a science, continually tried to reduce mind to something else. In this many analysts continue to follow Freud, when they have not fled in the opposite direction to 'hermeneutics'.

So what do we mean by 'mind'? What is it to interpret a mind? And what is this 'meaning' upon which both symbols and interpretation rely? Whether aware of them or not, every psychoanalyst must have assumptions about such traditionally philosophical questions, assumptions which inevitably color their approach both to theory and to practice. Freud knew that the path from theory to clinical detail goes two ways. Of course theory is guided by evidence. It also guides it, not only in that circular way that describes any discipline, but also because there are bound to be some assumptions, hidden or seemingly beyond reproach, which motivate the whole inquiry and so in a way come first. Many of Freud's assumptions clearly had this sort of a priori nature.

Inquiring into these assumptions is one of the projects of this book and more particularly of Part I, beginning with a discussion of meaning and mind. In Chapter 1, which sets the stage for much of what follows, I remark on Freud's vacillation between two different theories of meaning which he implicitly holds. Some of the confusions and problems in their discipline that psychoanalysts have diagnosed as originating in a conflict between mechanistic and non-mechanistic elements in Freud's concept of mind (G. Klein, 1976), or between a humanistic and a scientific understanding of psychoanalysis, reflect a conflict between a traditional, 'subjectivist' view of the mind, and another view, the one I believe to be right, which strains in a different direction. Many psychoanalysts may be surprised when the traditional philosophical view is laid before them to discover how heavily it shadows their own ideas on matters they may have taken to be just common sense. For on the model Freud was beginning to shape, the meaning of a thought or utterance is not the exclusive property, so to speak, of the thinker, and there is a sense in which one mind is inherently interpersonal in its very structure. This second model gives a key position to the concept of interpretation, which unlike introspection and soliloquy presumes a multiplicity of minds sharing a common language. It takes interpersonal understanding as a model for self-knowledge. It views the clinical setting less as an occasion for private catharsis than as providing space for a certain kind of dialogue in which transferential and counter-transferential relationships between patient and analyst are crucial. And it sees a dialectical relationship between subject and object, between a creature to whom we can attribute a subjective world and that creature's knowledge of an objective world it shares with others.

As I mean the anti-subjectivist model to be understood, its central claim is, at the most, only implicit in psychoanalysis. Many psychoanalysts have held that the individual is a medium for his culture, or that creatures with minds come into existence through communion and community. As usually stated, however, these are empirical generalizations; whereas the philosophical anti-subjectivist claim is not a merely empirical but a logical claim to the effect that meanings do not reside in the mind, free of any constraints imposed on them by the external world, and that acquaintance with other minds somewhere in one's past, at least, is a condition on the possibility of one's own mind. Though this view was hinted earlier in Anglo-American philosophy in the work of John Dewey and George Herbert Mead, it begins to be fully developed by Ludwig Wittgenstein, and later most notably by Donald Davidson.

Ours has been a century of philosophy devoted above all to the related questions of mind, meaning, and language, with which philosophy has made great headway. The view that I propose is widely held, but of course there are good philosophers who do not share it. This will ever be so with philosophy, as with disagreements of many other kinds: victory, which is in any case provisional, goes to the best argument, the most provocative insights, not to a view stamped 'True' for all time. I defend the view I propose. But I present it more as a frame than as an argument in its own right. To have done the latter would have entailed careful consideration of objections and criticisms, as well as alternative models of the mind like functionalism and connectionism, and would have been a project of an entirely different sort. I should add, furthermore, that my book is not meant to be a systematic account of principal psychoanalytic themes, but rather an exploration of those themes bordering philosophy and psycho-analysis to which I am led by my opening inquiry. For example, I speak very generally of sexuality, and scarcely at all of dreams.

I think the anti-subjectivist position I sketch in Chapter 1 is right. It is also peculiarly congenial to those ideas both of Freud's and of later psy-choanalysts that I think are the best. In particular it gives philosophical support to the various views that call themselves 'interactional'. My hope, furthermore, is that even those who are not persuaded by the position will find it illuminating both of the issues that any view of meaning and mind must consider, and of many directly related to it. In Part I, these issues are the nature of psychological explanation and psychoanalytic interpre-tation, the relations between mind and body, the status of psychoanalysis as a science, and the psychoanalytic 'narrative'.

Why, as a philosopher, do I take on in Part II questions about the minds of children? And what sort of questions are they? The answer to the second question is that they are primarily conceptual in nature; and I take them on because the anti-subjectivist position I defend commits us to certain views about when children can be said to think, even to have a 'subjective' world. In Part I, I have been asking: What are the necessary conditions for mind? Such a question will not be settled by empirical research. Take what on my view is a closely related question: What must a world be like in which it is possible for children to learn to use words to communicate their thoughts to others? Then ask, How far toward an answer will actual observations of children carry us? Well, we can cer-tainly note what children say at various points on their language-learning way, when they seem to have the hang of grammatical structure, and so on. But our views about whether or not they mean anything at all when they say something that sounds like 'apple', and if so what, will be guided by our concepts of meaning and mind. It is these about which the philos-opher wants to get clear.

Of course concept and observation are not independent of each other. Concepts change, partly in response to changes in our interests, in the world, and also to just the sort of ferreting out of hidden and perhaps unsup-portable assumptions that are the philosopher's business. And of course no philosophical position can be right that conflicts with observations, once one has freed them from the very assumptions one is challenging. Observations can indeed support the position by giving it the detail and texture which an a priori view as such always lacks. This is the relation, I believe, between my own picture of the mind and recent infant research. So (in Chapter 6) I appeal to the latter, just enough to indicate how this research fits in with and amplifies my philosophical views, suggesting some of the roots of both language learning and the development of thought.

At the beginning of Part II, in Chapter 5, I locate what I take to be the motivations of a primarily philosophical sort for certain presumptions about an infant 'sense of self'. And in Chapter 7 I take up that deeply tangled subject of affects and the emotions. My question is whether the connection between emotions and ideas—things like beliefs and desires— is merely contingent, as Freud thought, or rather essential and constitutive. Issues that are relevant to a theory of the emotions in general are the matter of this chapter; but because of its obvious relevance to questions about the emotional life of infants, my discussion seemed to fit best in Part II.

The direction of some of my remarks is from philosophy to psychoanalysis, what the latter might want to take from us. But the street goes two ways. Particularly in the area of how to think about irrationality, psychoanalysis has made a unique contribution to philosophical psychology, and this is my subject in Part III. Here I criticize the notion of 'primary process'; but at the same time, arguing that the explanation of symptomatic behavior calls for psychological 'mechanisms' which resemble but are not intentions, I give a partial defense of Freud's notorious vacillation between the languages of mind and body. I argue also that philosophical psychology has need for something like his ideas of repression, a divided self, phantasizing of a sort that is continuous with but slightly different from our everyday concept of daydreaming, and the legacy of childhood. Part III presented me with the most difficult problems of organization, for the concepts of primary process, phantasy, mental mechanisms, irrationality, 'the system Unconscious', 'ego', and 'id' cut across each other in ways that made straight lines of pursuit impossible. But more than any other sequence in the book, these chapters provide different aspects of a single argument and are best read with that in mind.

The Conclusion turns to questions about values and valuing. On the one hand, I don't think Freud explained some of the things he thought he did with the Oedipal complex; but I suggest a reading of it that, on the other hand, supplies some necessary detail to the view of mind and meaning outlined in the first chapter.

I hesitate to display more of my commitments at the outset, since they are bound to be misunderstood without the explanation which is the book itself. But I can say, quite generally, that they are certainly to Freud, for illuminating as he singularly did the psychological texture of our lives;

and because even when wrong, he was unfailingly interesting, as a philosopher as well as a psychologist.

Are my views Lacanian? No; though I think Lacan was right to conclude that mind and language are mutually interdependent. Here too I would have had to write a very different book were I to say how his route to that conclusion differs from mine and why I don't go along with him on other matters. An answer to these questions glims out from time to time, but readers looking for a disquisition on Lacan will not find it here.

What about 'object relations theory'? It comprises the body of psychoanalytic writings that I find the most interesting. But its central thesis, if it has one, is not very clear. Consider the definition given by Laplanche and Pontalis in *The Language of Psychoanalysis:*

> The reader unfamiliar with the psycho-analytical literature may easily be misled by the term 'object-relationship.' 'Object' is to be taken here in the special sense which it has for psycho-analysis in such expressions as 'object-choice' and 'object love' . . . 'Relationship' should be understood in the strong sense of the term as an *inter*relationship, in fact, involving not only the way the subject constitutes his objects but also the way these objects shape his actions . . . That we speak of the 'object-relationship' rather than of the relationship to the object serves to point up this connotation of interaction: to use the second formulation would imply that the objects predate the subject's relations with them and, by the same token, that the subject has already been constituted. (1973, p. 278)

What does 'subject' mean? Simply 'creature'? Or is 'subject' meant to single out specifically a creature for whom there is an inner, subjective world? Then under what conditions is there such a world? Perhaps when the creature is able to think, to have a view *of* or *about* the world rather than to be merely viewing the world. Then are pre-verbal infants subjects, or only potential subjects? And if the latter, what turns the trick?

And what is the import of 'constituted'? When a cat looks at a king, there is an object before the cat, and an object also of its looking. So then does the cat have an 'object' in the intended sense? If so, does it *constitute* the object? How? Simply by being in relation to it, the relation of 'looking at'? Or perhaps by thinking of it *as* an object? If the last is the sense of 'object' the authors have in mind, then perhaps there aren't objects for cats. In giving a way of answering these questions, the theory articulated in Chapter 1 (and supplemented in "Baby Talk") provides also a way of understanding the central thesis in object relations theory.

One last prefatory remark: many psychoanalysts are impatient with theory of any sort, wanting to get right away to the business of practice. They will ask: What are the clinical applications of what I say? There are some of a general sort. They have to do with things like the task of interpretation between analyst and patient and the role of external reality in one's 'inner', 'subjective' world. I believe the latter is far more important than either classical psychoanalytic theory or even current psychoanalytic practice holds, and that although the patient's thoughts are often distorted, they are generally responses to perceptions that are more or less veridical. But I am a philosopher, not a clinician, a philosopher with some psychoanalytic training and considerable acquaintance with the analytic couch. Without all of which I could not have written this book.

Part One

The Matter of Mind

1 Meaning and Mind

Meaning and mind are etymological cousins. Perhaps the thought goes something like this: you know what I mean by what I say or do when you know what I have in mind. So we might expect that a theory about one will presume or imply a theory about the other. The question is, which way to go? Should we start with mind, with what we think we know about the mind, and then work our way around to a theory of meaning, a theory about how we are able to communicate our thoughts to each other? Or should we start with language and head toward mind?

Strong intuitions have led philosophers for a long time to take the first route. So let's begin by following it, and ask, What is a thought? Take a simple example, my wishing that I had more coffee in my cup, which I believe to be empty. And again for simplicity's sake let's focus on belief, in this case, the belief that my cup is empty. Why do we want to talk about belief to begin with? one might ask. There are two related answers. First: It is through discovering the thoughts of another that we get to know her; it is through investigating and reflecting on our own thoughts that we get to know ourselves. Second: Knowing what someone believes and wants helps us to predict what she is going to do. Beliefs and desires play a role in action, a role so central that we can't imagine a world in which creatures had beliefs and desires but never acted on them.[1] For a while philosophers and psychologists in this century were persuaded that talk about mental states just was talk about behavior and dispositions to behave. But this ignores the fact that we want to explain why people do what they do; and an irreplaceably useful kind of explanation consists in telling us what they want and believe. Beliefs and desires stubbornly resist attempts to define them away, or reduce them to something else.[2]

With this initial plea for beliefs made, let's go on to say how we individuate them, how we distinguish one from another. Not, clearly, in the way we distinguish tables from chairs, or one table from another table. But beliefs are individuable for all that; Oedipus' belief that he killed a man at the crossroads is different from the belief that he killed his father at the crossroads—even though, unbeknownst to him, both are true descriptions of the same event. As my example makes clear, we identify a belief by stating the proposition at which it is directed. This is what gives the belief its content, tells us what it is about. So we might say that belief is a particular sort of attitude toward a proposition, since other attitudes toward the same proposition are possible: I can regret, be delighted, hope, wish, remember, intend it to be the case, desire, that my cup is empty. (Wish and desire are a little awkward; the grammarian will have us say that we wish the cup were empty, desire the cup to be empty; but the point is clear.) A propositional attitude has three variables: the believer, the attitude, and the proposition itself. Different persons can believe the same proposition; the same person can have different attitudes—belief, but also doubt, desire, regret, hope, guilt, and so forth—toward the same proposition; and one person can have many different beliefs.

We just noted, incidentally, that beliefs are *about* something; the proposition which identifies a belief tells us what it is about. Belief purports to represent some aspect of the world (which might be oneself, as when I believe that I went to Marienbad with you). Desire targets something in the world (real or imagined) as its satisfying object. Franz Brentano, Freud's professor at the University of Vienna, called this feature Intentionality.[3] It is a term philosophers continue to use, though most no longer hold with Brentano's account of it. A theory of the mental will have to tell us more about this relationship between thought and the world.

Something else it must take into account emerges when we ask how the believer knows what she believes. How do I know I believe my cup is empty? If someone were to ask me that in earnest, I'd be puzzled, because it's an obvious fact about belief that sometimes we just do know. But it's a fact we have to state carefully; for we are not always aware of what we are thinking. And we also want to leave open the possibility of various sorts of confusion about just what the attitude is, even what the proposition is toward which it is directed. (Do I believe there's a pot of gold at the end of the rainbow, or do I hope there is? Do I believe that we met in Marienbad, or in Trieste?) But carefully hedged, here is an intuition about mental states—an intuition often referred to as First Person Authority—that we should be loath to give up, and rightly so: When I have a thought of which I am self-consciously aware, I know its content on the basis of no evidence, indeed *on no basis,* non-inferentially; and this is a way that you cannot know what I am thinking. Your knowledge of what is on my mind does require evidence and can only be an inference from what I say and do. That mental states, like belief, can be known by their 'owner' without evidence is one of our criteria for calling something a mental state to begin with. It is important to note that even Freud did not deny this. An unconscious belief or desire is one of which the person can become conscious, in the right circumstances. These circumstances are what therapy is to provide. Furthermore, I can know what it is I believe, even though the belief itself should turn out to be false.

I   *The First-Person Point of View*

It is true that the first person provides a privileged perspective on some of the contents of one's own mind. Traditionally, philosophy has therefore taken it as the perspective from which to investigate the mental more generally. This was Descartes' strategy, but also that of Locke, Berkeley, Hume, Kant, Russell, and many in our own day, perhaps best known among them John Searle and Thomas Nagel. It's a starting point that easily leads to an interesting and disturbing place, to global skepticism about the senses, about the reality of the 'external' world (that is, the world that so many of our thoughts seem to be about), about the existence of other minds.

Here is Descartes, famously beginning his *Meditations on First Philosophy* by remarking:

> Some years ago I was struck by the large number of falsehoods that I had accepted as true in my childhood, and by the highly doubtful nature of the whole edifice that I had subsequently based on them. I realized that it was necessary, once in the course of my life, to demolish everything completely and start again right from the foundations if I wanted to establish anything at all in the sciences that was stable and likely to last. (1984, p. 17)

Sense experience seems to be the culprit, Descartes reflects. Yet surely the senses cannot be in error about certain very obvious things, "for example, that I am here, sitting by the fire, wearing a winter dressing-gown, holding this piece of paper in my hands, and so on" (p. 13). Only madmen could be so grossly deceived; " . . . and I would be thought equally mad if I took anything from them as a model for myself." Yet, he continues, even sane men have dreams. "How often, asleep at night, am I convinced of just such familiar events—that I am here in my dressing-gown, sitting by the fire—when in fact I am lying undressed in bed" (p. 13).

As Freud would do two hundred years later, though for different reasons, Descartes takes the ordinary phenomenon of dreaming as a challenge to some equally ordinary assumptions about the mind and its relation to the world. In Descartes' case the assumptions tested are that, in general, what we see is what there is; and that we are in direct, unmediated contact with the world around us. So the First Meditation closes with the possibility that I might be mistaken in all my beliefs. Yet this skeptical possibility shows me—Descartes concludes in the Second Meditation—that there is indeed something of whose existence I am certain, namely, myself as a self, as the subject of my thoughts, as thinker. (At this point in the *Meditations* the belief in oneself as embodied has not yet been justified.) I am certain also that I have mental states, whose content I know by an act of mental inspection. The possibility of error enters the mind, Descartes sees, when it makes judgments to the effect that its perceptions correspond to things as they are in the external world. But the perceptions themselves, the *ideas* or mental states, are free from error.

> What was it about them ["earth, sky, stars, and everything else that I apprehended with the senses"] that I perceived clearly? Just that the ideas, or thoughts, of such things appeared before my mind . . . even now I am not denying that these ideas occur within me. But there was something else which I used to assert . . . This was that there were things outside me which were the sources of my ideas and which resembled them in all respects. Here was my mistake; or at any rate, if my judgement was true, it was not thanks to the strength of my perception. (pp. 24–25)

Notice that Descartes' doubts about the existence of the things his ideas *purport* to represent in no way jeopardize—so he thinks—their ability to represent, nor his to know what they represent. So then Descartes must implicitly hold that the Intentional character of a thought is internal to it, that mental content depends on nothing external to the mind that entertains it. Presumably his ideas of earth, sky, stars, and so on, go on being just those ideas—and he can know that they do—whether or not there are earth and sky, indeed whether any of his beliefs about the external world is correct. This is the assumption Putnam (1975) calls 'methodological solipsism', that "no psychological state . . . presupposes the existence of any individual other than the subject to whom that state is ascribed" (p. 220).

In the recent literature it has also been called *internalism* about mental content. The interaction between brain and outside world may determine what beliefs we have; but given that we have the beliefs we do, their *content*, according to the internalist, is determined by things from the skin inward. A mental state is some particular kind of structure—perhaps a syntactical structure, an inscription in a 'language of thought' (Fodor, 1987), a picture, or a representation—in the brain. How do I know the contents of my thought on those occasions when I do? Clearly not by looking at the external world, nor by asking others, but by an act of intro-spection. So we might imagine that an omniscient Being could at any point in a creature's life know what was on its mind, conscious or uncon-scious, by looking into it. The Being need know nothing about the crea-ture's relations to its surrounding world. Of course none of us is such a Being. Our minds are transparent to ourselves only in occasional shoals of self-awareness; and hidden forever—the internalist goes on—are the minds of others.

Internalism can seem, incidentally, to be a necessary consequence of the belief that there are minds only where there are bodies, one mind, fur-thermore, to each body. My brain states are internal to me; so if my thoughts are a function of the states of my brain, presumably my thoughts must also be in principle describable in terms of things going on in me alone. If we hold an externalist view of the mental, this is an apparent consequence we will have to confront (see Chapter 3).

Internalism seems to be part and parcel of that First-Person Authority we noted earlier, that on those occasions when I do know what I am thinking, I know it without appeal to any evidence. If this is so, then surely these thoughts, at least, must wear their contents on their face. But notice that while this is so in a certain sense for the thinker himself, and given that he is already a thinker, we have said nothing yet about how content gets attached, as it were, to belief. If I make this point in relation to language it may be clearer: how do I know what I mean when I say, 'I believe my cup is empty'? Here too the answer is, 'I just do'. For me, the meaning of that sentence is literally self-evident. Yet we would not be content to say that the meaning of a sentence is simply contained within it. Clearly it has to do with the meaning of other words in the speaker's language, with the rules, or conventions, or whatever it is that allows one person to communicate something to another, and so on.

Notice something else about Descartes' argument from error: It is one thing to say of any particular idea that it might be mistaken, even invented more or less out of whole cloth; another to say that all our ideas might be. Often the move from *some* to *all* loses a grip on sense. For example, some-times I deceive myself; can we imagine coherently that I might always? (Then how do we understand what it is we are being deceived about?) Every particular event must have a cause; must the class of all particular events also have a cause? (And what is the cause of that?)

Furthermore, if we sever in this way the representational content of a mental state from the world it purports to represent, we are apt, like Des-cartes, to be led to an analysis of perception according to which we do not see trees, smiling faces, real objects in the world, but our *ideas* of these things. For in this way of thinking about the mind, *ideas*, or alternatively, *experiences*, are interposed between mind and world. In the subsequent history of philosophy these ideas are construed as propositions, mental images, or sense-data, depending on whether the philosopher in question is Descartes himself, or Locke after him, a later empiricist, or Brentano, or indeed many contemporary philosophers. But for them all, the objects even of our veridical mental acts are not the ordinary things of a familiar physical world, but private, subjective entities. (If one does not push the analogy too far, on such accounts we are like those prisoners in the cave Plato describes in *The Republic,* mistaking shadows in the interior of our minds for the real world.)

Some ambiguity in the psychoanalytic concept of an 'object' can be traced, I believe, to such a Cartesian theory of perception: it is easy to slide, for example, from saying, truly, that our perceptions of reality are influenced by our phantasy life as well as by much else that is personal to each of us, to a dubious theory according to which what we directly perceive is always and necessarily some 'inner object'. There is a perfectly ordinary sense of 'representation' in which my belief that there is a tree outside my window is true just in case there is a tree outside the window. So we can say that my belief represents the world in this way. But it doesn't follow that representation takes a detour through some mental object.[4]

Something like this, however, may be what Freud has in mind in the following passage:

> In psycho-analysis there is no choice for us but to assert that mental processes are in themselves unconscious, and to liken the perception of them by means of consciousness to the perception of the external world by means of the sense-organs . . . Just as Kant warned us not to overlook the fact that our perceptions are subjectively conditioned and must not be regarded as identical with what is perceived though unknowable, so psycho-analysis warns us not to equate perceptions by means of consciousness with the unconscious mental processes which are their object. Like the physical, the psychical is not necessarily in reality what it appears to us to be. (1915, p. 171)

That is, the object of either conscious or unconscious mental processes is not the world itself but a mental representation of it, outer world or inner as the case may be.

The point I am making is easily misunderstood, and I won't be able to clear it up until later. But here is a promissory note: Only a certain assumption about meaning—the internalism mentioned a moment ago— makes us think we must choose between either the Naive Realist's view that the world is just as we perceive it to be, or the Idealist's view that the objects of our perception and thought are subjective entities of some kind. A theory of mind must of course acknowledge that perception may go astray in various ways. But the theory can do so while allowing that our beliefs and perceptions are (often) directly about the world and not about some mental intermediary.

The first-person perspective inevitably leads to skepticism about the material world. The existence of other minds poses a double problem, since even if we could believe our senses about the existence of another body in a given case, the fact that the mental is held to be ineradicably private, only contingently expressed in behavior, and knowable only to the mind whose it is, means that our belief that another body is inhabited by a mind is yet a further inference. (As Descartes puts it, what we take to be another person might be an automaton.)

This is not to say that a philosopher who makes these assumptions must settle for skepticism ever after. Descartes, for one, thought that through his proofs for the existence of a benevolent God we could be certain of the existence of an external world, our own body, and the correspondence between certain of our ideas and reality.[5] But the authority with which Descartes speaks for his first-person experience puts the knowledge of everything else in peril. His task—and that of philosophers who follow in his steps—is then to find in first-person experience some privileged beliefs, ideas, or data of sense which are for one reason or another immune to error and which can serve as a base for knowledge. Cartesianism is unable to make sense of the intuitive idea that I can truly claim to know there is a tree outside my window only if that belief is both consistent or coherent with other things I think I know, and if it also corresponds with things as they are, since checking for correspondence between belief and reality is exactly what Cartesian subjectivism rules out.

Kant thought to answer skepticism by conceding that we cannot know the 'noumenal', things as they are in themselves or as they are for God. To believe otherwise is to think we might transcend the limits of the knowable, the knowable for us, which can only be the phenomenal world of appearances, things as they are *for* creatures like us. But if knowledge of the phenomenal world is possible—and it seems it is—it can only be, Kant argued, because the human mind, not merely my mind, spontaneously and pre-consciously organizes the data of sense always in the same way, casting it, for example, in spatial and temporal form. Knowledge is an interplay between the innate or the a priori, and stimuli that come from without. It is because what we know has been shaped by the mind itself that knowledge of the phenomenal world is possible. There is knowledge, Kant assures us, because the human mind imposes a conceptual scheme on the data of sense, and this conceptual scheme—since it is of the mind's own making in the first place—renders the data intelligible or knowable.

Kant is surely right that external stimuli are met by something within the 'knower'; that knowledge cannot be construed either as entirely given from within, or as passively received from without. Such an insight is crucial, furthermore, to contemporary research in cognitive psychology.

Struck, then, by what is valid in Kant's attempt to bridge internal and external, historians may think of Kant as making the decisive move beyond Descartes. But note that Kant is still working within the received problematic; for he accepts the Cartesian assumption that what we are immediately in touch with, even in those states we call 'knowledge of the world', is something private and subjective; Kant calls it 'experience'. Like Descartes, Kant begins his investigations into the nature of the mind, thought, and knowledge from a first-person view, trying to work his way from the inside out.

Consider in this context the distinction David Rapaport draws between the materialist and the Kantian traditions:

> It may seem surprising that Freud was . . . tardy in bringing the psychological significance of the real outer world into the structure of . . . [his] theory. Therefore it will be important to remind ourselves of some historical relationships. Philosophical psychology, the ancestor of scientific psychology, was a subsidiary of epistemology. Its major query was: How do we acquire our knowledge of the world of reality? . . .
>
> Freud's point of departure was different: he was concerned with the evaluation by the psychic apparatus of *internal stimuli* (drives, needs) rather than *external stimuli* . . . Thus it occurred that only after considerable exploration of psychic reality and in the wake of observations concerning maladaptations to external reality did Freud have to face the problem of reality adaptation . . .
>
> For the theory of thinking, it may be of some advantage to note that his manner of facing the problem . . . shows some similarity to Leibniz' formulation of the problem of epistemology. Leibniz asked: How is it possible that reasoning arrives at conclusions which coincide with the outcome of processes occurring in reality? or in other words: How can there be a correspondence between *verité de fait* and *verité de raison*? Freud's problem was: How can the apparatus regulated by the pleasure-principle (drives) be also adapted to reality? (Rapaport, 1951, pp. 316–317)

Rapaport, like Freud, accepts a first-personal formulation of the problem; and he thinks that only an answer along Kantian lines, bridging rationalism and empiricism, can solve it.

But Kant's distinction between the noumenal that we cannot know and the phenomenal—organized by us—that we can has struck some philosophers less as justification of knowledge than as a voiding of the very concept. Our reservation amounts to this: Since Kant gives us no way of knowing that our conceptual scheme is in fact shared among knowers, he unwittingly opens the door—through which many have rushed—to the possibility that other cultures have conceptual schemes that are unintelligible to us, not merely now but forever and in principle. In that case knowledge is relative to a conceptual scheme, itself not subject to revision; and the 'truth' of a proposition is merely its consistency with a system of beliefs which is possibly incompatible with other systems, no one of which then can claim to be true in the ordinary sense. Of course I have said nothing yet to suggest the incorrectness of this idea. The criticism will come later when I sketch the third-person or externalist view.

Beginning with his quest for a first foundation for scientific knowledge, Descartes set out some of the assumptions of modern philosophy: (1) The First-Person View: that introspection provides the perspective from which to investigate the nature of the mental. (2) Objects of the Mind: that there is a kind of mental object present to or before the mind which mediates between the subject, or the knower, and the object known. The mind's knowledge of the external world is through private, internal 'ideas', which, when veridical, *represent* reality. (3) The Transparency of the Mental: that the meaning of a word or a sign is immediately present, unmediated, and transparent to the mind. This view is usually a corollary of the idea that there are Objects of the Mind. (4) Internalism (about meaning): that the content of thought can be severed from any connection with the real world, including other persons; in other words that our ideas might be just as they are though the world be different. Contemporary functionalist and language-of-thought accounts of the mind, for example, hold that thoughts are a kind of inner representation which can be viewed as computational states of the brain. The content of these thoughts is in no way constituted by relations between thought and world.[6] (5) Mind-Body Dualism: that mind and body are two different substances; or that the mind has no necessary dependence on the body.[7] (6) Foundationalism: that certain of our ideas or beliefs or experiences are immune from error, and in being so provide a foundation for the rest.

Since Descartes, epistemology has vacillated between conceptions of truth as correspondence and as coherence. Before considering either, let's say more generally that by 'knowledge' we mean something like justified true belief. Justified belief alone won't do, since a belief for which I have evidence and reasons may yet not be true. (Ptolemy had the best of reasons for thinking the sun moved around the earth.) Nor is truth itself enough, since someone might espouse a true belief without having good reasons for thinking it true—say he makes a random but lucky guess, or that what he has managed to persuade himself is true because he wishes it were, turns out to be the case. The correspondence theory captures our intuitive idea that a belief is true only if things are as it says they are. It reminds us that though we may have good reasons for holding a belief true, yet it may be false. But the theory makes for problems about knowledge; for if the mind is acquainted, as modern philosophy has traditionally said, only with subjective entities in the form of 'ideas', then checking for correspondence between the mind's objects and the things to which they presumably correspond is ruled out.

Alternatively, we can view truth as coherence, a system of mutually supportive beliefs. A true belief, on such a view, is such simply in virtue of its coherence with other beliefs. This view allows for knowledge, since we can have reason for thinking that a belief coheres with others, but at the cost of severing truth from the world. For nothing guarantees that an internally coherent system will tell us how things in fact are. Furthermore, like the idea that knowledge is relative to a conceptual scheme and for the same reasons, the coherence theory is compatible with the possibility of there being two equally coherent but mutually incompatible systems of belief.

I have promised to offer a theory of meaning which doesn't force us to choose between the naively realist view that everything is just as we think it is, and the idealist's view that the objects of our perception are not things in the world but in us. At the same time it will suggest a way around the dilemma of coherence or correspondence. For now, let me remark on the way in which the issue crops up for psychoanalysis. The coherence theory has its parallel in the view that the truth of a psychoanalytic interpretation is a matter of its fit with the narrative pattern created so far. This position has been championed, among others, by Lussier (1991), Schafer (1983, 1990), Wallerstein (1988), and Spence (1982). A correspondence theory lies behind the belief of many psychoanalysts, Freud included, that a good interpretation corresponds with the patient's psychic reality.[8] How to judge the validity of analytic interpretations is a sticky matter—but not, as I will discuss in Chapter 4, because of some dilemma about truth in general.

Freud obviously rejects certain Cartesian assumptions, but he less obviously accepts others. He rejects the Cartesian bifurcation of mind and body. Human beings are first of all organisms, striving like others to adapt to the environment and to perpetuate the species. However murky the concept of instinct, it is here that Freud most specifically tries to deal with the problem of how the mental arises out of something organic and material. Freud obviously also rejects the 'transparency' thesis, the idea that the meaning of one's thoughts or words is fully present and immediately apparent to introspection. But he is tempted by the view I have called Objects of the Mind. In a passage quoted earlier he speaks of consciousness as a kind of psychical eye; elsewhere he calls consciousness "a sense organ for the apprehension of psychical qualities" (1900, p. 615). And he also assumes, like the functionalist and language-of-thought accounts referred to earlier, an internalist view about meaning. Clark Glymour remarks that "exactly like the cognitivists of our day, Freud held the brain to be a machine, and although he did not use the word, a machine that computes . . . Further, like many of our contemporaries, Freud held there to be a private, innate language of thought in which propositions are expressed" (1991, p. 60).

In a passage that echoes Descartes himself, Freud writes:

Consciousness makes each of us aware only of his own states of mind; that other people, too, possess a consciousness is an inference which we draw by analogy from their observable utterances and actions, in order to make this behavior intelligible to us . . . the assumption of a consciousness in them [our fellow men] rests upon an inference and cannot share the immediate certainty which we have of our own consciousness. (1915, p. 169)

The passage is ambiguous between the idea that consciousness makes each of us aware of having a consciousness, or that it makes us aware of its contents. I read it as saying both. So Freud is led to the traditionalist's skeptical view that all knowledge begins and ends with first-person experience:

In our science as in the others the problem is the same: behind the attributes (qualities) of the object under examination which are presented directly to perception, we have to discover something else which is more independent of the particular receptive capacity of our sense organs and which approximates more closely to what may be supposed to be the real state of affairs. We have no hope of being able to reach the latter itself, since it is evident that everything new that we have inferred must nevertheless be translated back into the language of our perceptions, from which it is simply impossible to free ourselves. (1940a [1938], p. 196)

Like the Cartesian, Freud draws here a radical distinction between the 'internal' and subjective world, which we can know, and the real, external world, which he claims we cannot.

In a panel discussion on the nature of psychic reality, R. Michaels (1985) refers approvingly to the view that "only the world of subjective experience is knowable" as the view "in accord with most modern philosophic notions of reality" (p. 517). It is in accord with philosophic tradition, but not with the influential movement in modern philosophy that I will describe shortly. Psychoanalytic therapy depends, furthermore, on assuming that knowing what someone means (or thinks, believes, wants, intends, and so on) is a matter to be determined only in part and only sometimes by asking her; it is revealed as well in other sorts of behavior and in the way in which one utterance, act, or thought hangs together with others of the agent's utterances, acts, and thoughts.

Let me summarize the difficulties with the first-person approach.

First: Construing the contents of a belief as internal to it inevitably leads to skepticism about the external world, not the healthy sort that reminds us of human fallibility, but global skepticism. Such a skepticism suggests to many of us a flaw not so much in the human condition as in our own reflections on meaning and truth. For consider: We have seen that it is the character of belief, for example, to be about something beyond itself: the belief that the world is round represents the world as being round. That representation is the meaning of the belief. But if there is no way, even in principle, of ascertaining whether or not the world is round, how can we even know what it means to say it is? What entitles us to use a language of material things to describe our thoughts? How do we know that our thought is a world-is-round-sort-of-thought? How do I know the content of any of my own mental states? 'I just do', the internalist rightly answers. But that doesn't absolve us from asking how a mental state acquires its content in the first place. And that is a question an internalist is going to have difficulty answering.

Second: Language is clearly a public phenomenon. We communicate with language the very things we have been talking about: beliefs, desires, perceptions, hopes, intentions, and so on. The first-person view begins with the private, internal, and subjective, and will have to account for meaning by somehow matching public words to these private states or objects. I don't say it can't be done. But the fact that we do succeed in communicating with each other more or less successfully some of the time is a clue that perhaps we have taken the wrong starting point in investigating the mind.

And third: the first-person approach is going to have a hard time accommodating beliefs and desires which are unconscious. One of our criteria for a mental state is that it is a phenomenal datum of consciousness. But if we want to posit unconscious mental states there must be another criterion as well, one which sometimes takes priority.

Now there is a fact about mental talk I noted at the beginning that suggests a very different approach to mind and meaning from the one we've been considering. Concepts like 'belief' and 'desire' are at least as useful in describing and explaining what other people do as in our descriptions of ourselves. What is John doing? 'Building a bird-cage'; 'Buying tickets for the opera'; 'Leading his troops into battle'; 'Trying to seduce you'; or just 'Talking'. Note that the very description of John as building a bird-cage imputes to him certain beliefs, desires, and intentions, namely the wish to build a bird-cage and the belief that he is doing so. Any theory about the mental must recognize that it enters into our accounts of action in this central way. 'Internal' or 'subjective' states are more public than we may think, as the public often has an 'internal' or 'subjective' side. The concept of an action faces two ways, toward the mind and toward the external world.

II The Interpreter's Perspective

For reasons just outlined, the second, anti-subjectivist approach to mind and meaning begins to look more attractive: Whereas Descartes and the Cartesians believe that first there is thought or Intentionality, or as Hobbes puts it, "mental discourse," and then, as a matter of convenience, speech (Hacking, 1975), we will assume that we cannot divorce the activities of thinking and speaking. As language is public, anchored in a shared external world, so, in a way, are the thoughts which it expresses. Akeel Bilgrami puts it this way: "If another's meanings . . . are determined by items in a world external to her, then it is neither surprising nor avoidable that they are available to one who lives in the shared environment" (1989, p. 64). The strategy is to look to the process of interpretation to tell us not only how we know the minds of others but also how we are able 'to mean' ourselves.

The interpreter's or the third-person perspective which I will be developing rejects both Descartes and Skinner (or Ryle), both *defining* the mental in first-personal terms as what is available for introspection, and *reducing* the mental to dispositions to behavior. But the interpreter's perspective accepts from behaviorism this much, that the human organism, mind included, is a part of the natural world. Intention (with a small 'i'), for example, is not some invisible mental nugget; it has conceptual links to action. And as behavior is public, so in a way is the thought which motivates and explains it. (At his most original, it is this perspective which Freud anticipates.)[9] While the third-person perspective grants that one can sometimes know her own thoughts in ways no one else can, it denies that their contents can be entirely captured by first-person reflection. And though it holds that intentions are not mysteriously private, it insists that attributions of 'subjective' attitudes like belief and desire cannot be reduced to statements about atoms, brains, and neurons. Introspection is not adequate to capture the mental; but neither are observations stripped of the terms in which the first person speaks.

In arguing for the interpreter's perspective I will be paying attention primarily to Ludwig Wittgenstein, W. V. O. Quine, and Donald Davidson; but Hilary Putnam, among many others, would belong in an account which aimed for historical completeness.

WITTGENSTEIN

No text has had a greater impact on twentieth-century philosophy than Wittgenstein's *Philosophical Investigations* (1953), which, remarkably, is a repudiation of his own earlier *Tractatus Logico-philosophicus* (1922). In both books, Wittgenstein's primary concern is with meaning: How do words mean? How does a sentence say something? How does language connect with reality? At the time of the *Tractatus* Wittgenstein thought that if we understand the elements of which a factual proposition is composed, then we will understand the sentence without further explanation; and he thought this could be so only if a sentence shows or pictures what it refers to. The idea, then, is that if we know what 'cat' and 'mat' name, for example, and we understand how the 'is on' of predication works, then for us the sentence 'The cat is on the mat' pictures the cat on the mat; and this picture is the sentence's meaning. The fundamental unit of meaning is the word; and words hook onto the world by picturing a piece of it.

In Wittgenstein's later view, words come to have meaning only as used in sentences, by actual speakers, in particular contexts, in the course of carrying out all sorts of communal enterprises. Wittgenstein begins the *Philosophical Investigations* by quoting Augustine: "When they (my elders) named some object, and accordingly moved toward something, I saw this and I grasped that the thing was called by the sound they uttered . . . Thus, as I heard words repeatedly used in their proper places in various sentences, I gradually learnt to understand what objects they signified" (p. 2). Though he himself holds that ostensive definitions are important pieces of information for an interpreter, Wittgenstein denies Augustine's suggestion that the meaning of a word is simply what it names; and he argues that ostensive definitions cannot *explain* language learning, for they presuppose too much. In an early formulation of the concept of language games, Wittgenstein says they are "primitive forms of operating with signs that reveal their implication in activities" (1958, §17). Reflection on this interaction reveals, for one thing, that it is the sentence, not the word, which is the unit of linguistic meaning. For it is sentences (or single words understood as sentences, like 'Fire', or 'Mama', or 'Come') that figure in such activities as playing games, solving problems, or going places. So we might say that meaning is constrained by relations between language-user and world.[10]

Even if this were not the case, words—and concepts—are meaningful only as defined by their place in sentences and by their relations to other concepts and sentences. 'What do you mean by tree?' 'An object like that', I say, pointing to a tree. Yet it has an infinite number of properties; so which particular properties—what aspect of my visual field—do I have in mind? Or as philosophers put it, under what description am I singling out this object? Will I also call a telephone pole a tree? A rose bush? A pointy tent? Explicating the concept 'tree'—with the meaning most of us give it—requires explicating certain relations between sentences about trees and sentences about growing things, perhaps also about wood, and so on.

Whereas on the earlier analysis meaning began with naming, now Wittgenstein points out that before we can know what a name stands for, we must already know how the name is used in the language game of which it is a part. For example, only if we have some idea of how to order colors, or some grasp of the language of gestures (say, pointing) through which sensations are expressed, can we learn the meaning of 'yellow'. As there is no one and only 'right' use, but many, depending on the occasion, so there is no one determinate meaning to be given to each sign.

Attention to the ways language is actually used in daily life will free us from the temptation to hypostasize language and meanings. We use words in a great variety of ways—to tell stories and jokes, describe, advise, prescribe, give orders, make poems and love, evaluate, and so on. We have a word, 'language', to refer to all these different forms of communication; but it is no more true that there is only one language than that there is only one kind of thing people do together, or one sort of game they play. This is the point of Wittgenstein's famous remark that "to imagine a language means to imagine a form of life" (1953, 8e). So to come to understand a language is to be initiated into that form of life. And by the same token, attention to our language, our ordinary language, may reveal to us aspects of our human forms of life we had not noticed, or had taken for granted.

According to the traditional view, words are meaningful because of their relationships to mental images, or states of mind like wishing or intending, and these are prior to language. The relation between real bricks and 'brick' is only incidental to meaning; for after all I can talk about bricks though none are around. The word 'brick' refers to the material object via a concept or an image for which 'brick' stands. But, Wittgenstein now points out, mental images and concepts, in the form of private ideas 'in the head', are no less problematic than the phenomenon they are supposed to explain. When someone says to me, 'Brick, please', must I first refer to a picture of a brick in my head? If so, how will that picture, even assuming there is one, tell me what is wanted? By the resemblance between pictured ('inner') bricks and real (external) bricks? But similarity is neither a necessary nor a sufficient condition for representation. It isn't necessary because a gesture can convey an insult, a configuration of colors a country, without bearing any similarity to what it represents, or at least none that doesn't itself require interpretation. Nor is similarity sufficient, as Hilary Putnam (1981) brings out by asking: If an ant, crawling on the sand, happens to trace a line that looks like Winston Churchill, will we say that the line depicts, or represents, or refers to Churchill? Does a cloud that looks like a castle represent a castle? An artist can intend us to see his cloud as a castle. But then, given the right context, a squiggle or a dot might serve the same purpose.

For x to represent, or depict, or describe, or symbolize, y, a necessary condition is that someone intend that it will; x must mean y to that same someone. But Intention (meaning) and intending (to do something) are the very notions we wanted to elucidate. We invoked mental concepts or images to explain how it is I can know that 'brick' means or represents those red objects over there. The answer was: The word gets linked to a mental image or concept of brick, and it is the mental image which does the representing. But how? If similarity isn't sufficient in the case of images in the external world, neither does it suffice for ones in the internal world. All we've done is push our question back one step.

Wittgenstein does not deny the existence of mental images; his point is that they do not have the explanatory force we may have thought. For it is the ability to mean something by what one says, or to represent one thing by another, or to understand *x* as *y*, or to have a belief in mind one knows to be the belief that her white car is in the garage, that needs clarification. Take, for example, the ambiguous picture which can be seen as either a duck or a rabbit, but not both at the same time. The change can be brought about at will, and can be experienced. But seeing the picture *as* a duck is not an experienceable inner process. We show how we see the picture by what we say and do. There is a parallel here with meaning (Wittgenstein, 1953, pp. 194–214). One can use the word 'till' now with this sense, now with that. An observer can infer which sense someone has 'in mind' from what she does with the word, what 'language game' she plays. Yet meaning by 'till' 'a tray for keeping money' is, again, not an experienceable inner process for the user of the word.

So now we can say against an internalist view of meaning: As physical pictures and images do not bear their meaning on their face, neither do mental pictures and images.

Perhaps our idea that the meaning of a sign is a state of mind comes about this way, Wittgenstein suggests:

> We think of the meaning of signs sometimes as states of mind of the man using them, sometimes as the role which these signs are playing in a system of language. The connection between these two ideas is that the mental experiences which accompany the use of a sign undoubtedly are caused by our usage of the sign in a particular system of language. (1958, p. 78)

They are caused by it, Wittgenstein agrees; but they do not explain it.

Descartes and philosophical tradition held that public discourse follows private; words frame, but in no way help to create, the ideas they communicate. Wittgenstein's revolutionary move was to undermine the notion that we can divorce the private from the public in this way. In his passages about thought as silent speech he warns against the idea that language is a veil cast over thoughts which simultaneously hides and partially reveals them (1953, 220e). He urges that on the contrary silent speech is derivative from heard speech. As we learn to calculate in the head by calculating on paper, so we learn how to single out something in our minds, how to think of it as a face, a farce, a seduction, from telling things and being told.

Augustine wrote:

> Little by little I began to realize where I was and to want to make my wishes known to others, who might satisfy them. But this I could not do, because my wishes were inside me, while other people were outside, and they had no faculty which could penetrate my mind. So I would toss my arms and legs

about and make noises, hoping that such few signs as I could make would show my meaning, though they were quite unlike what they were meant to mime. (1961, p. 25)

First there is private thought—including wish and desire—Augustine supposes; then a fitting of that thought to public speech. This is a picture, we notice, that only a creature who can both think and talk might have. In the picture Wittgenstein draws the direction goes the other way: first there is the child's induction into a form of life, which at the same time is its learning of a language, and with this induction an entry into thought. A language of symbols that is used in thinking must also of necessity be a language that is used to communicate. As for reference, it is socially fixed, not determined by private entities in individual minds/brains.

QUINE, DAVIDSON, AND THE RADICAL INTERPRETER

The philosopher John Austin once remarked that if someone asked him for the meaning of a particular word he would tell him. But if someone asked for the-meaning-of-a-word he would kick him downstairs.[11] Quine and Davidson share something of this spirit. But whereas Austin seems to be saying that there is no philosophically interesting question about meaning, this is not Quine's and Davidson's view. Austin was right that meaning can't be defined. The attempt will fail because, as Quine shows in "Two Dogmas of Empiricism" (in Quine, 1980), in appealing to the notion of synonymy or something like it, it is bound to presume the very thing we are after. But if we are willing to give up the quest for a definition, then something general and interesting can be said.

Quine's argument in "Two Dogmas" depends on rejecting a venerable distinction in philosophy between questions of fact and questions of meaning, between sentences some of which are true (or false) both because of what they mean and because of their empirical content (like 'All bachelors are neurotic'), and sentences which are true (or false) because of what they mean alone (like 'All bachelors are unmarried males'). Knowing the truth of any so-called 'empirical' sentence obviously depends both on knowing what it means and knowing the way the world is. But it doesn't follow that we can separate these elements out from each other. Nor can we separate data from the theory we bring to it. For example, our coming to understand what "wavicles" are just is our mastery of what the theory says about them. By the same token, it is not clear whether two physicists, discussing whether neutrinos have mass, are discussing the same objects. "To discern two phases here, the first an agreement as to what the objects are (viz. the neutrinos) and the second a disagreement as to how they are (massless or massive) is absurd" (Quine, 1980, p. 41).

The doctrine now known as meaning holism which Quine articulates was in part a reaction to logical positivism, which held, among other things, that all meaningful descriptive terms must be definable in terms of some basic vocabulary (the favorite candidate consisted of sensation terms); and that the meaning of every sentence is given by the conditions under which it might be verified.[12] (It followed that any proposition which was unverifiable, not in fact but in principle, had no literal meaning.) As Putnam remarks, much of the philosophy of science in the twentieth century has consisted in undermining these reductivist theses (1988, p. 6). The verificationists were right, Quine argued, that the meaning of a sentence is to be explicated in terms of experience. And they were right also to take the sentence as the unit of meaning over the word. Yet the grid has still been too finely drawn; for even the meaning of a sentence cannot be given in isolation from its connections to other sentences. "Our statements about the external world face the tribunal of sense experience not individually but only as a corporate body," Quine famously said (1964, p. 41). This implies that the hope of finding some basic vocabulary from which all other terms can be derived is also misguided. The idea of meaning holism is relevant, incidentally, to the current psychoanalytic quest for a common ground, the hope of finding among all the different schools and theories some essential core they share. Wallerstein (1990) suggests that it consists in the clinical phenomena of transference and resistance, which he claims are the common referent for all analysts, whether their training is Kohutian, Classical, or Kleinian. Everything else is metaphor. But the differences in theory cannot be dismissed so easily; for 'transference' and 'resistance' are terms clearly laden with theory. What one analyst sees as transference another may not, and so on. If there is no common theoretical ground on which Kohutians and Kleinians stand, there is no reason for thinking that they 'see' the same phenomena in their consulting rooms.

Like Wittgenstein, Quine insists on a naturalistic approach to meaning. Quoting Dewey, Quine says: "'Meaning . . . is not a psychic existence; it is primarily a property of behavior.' Once we appreciate the institution of language in these terms, we see that there cannot be, in any useful sense, a private language . . . Semantics is vitiated by a pernicious mentalism," he continues, "as long as we regard a man's semantics as somehow determinate in his mind beyond what might be implicit in his dispositions to overt behavior. It is the very facts about meaning, not the entities meant, that must be construed in terms of behavior" (1969, p. 27).

The examples of meaning holism given earlier were drawn from science. But Quine intends the theory to apply to language generally. We can approach an account of linguistic meaning from two directions: we can ask how the child learns to talk about objects and to acquire knowledge of the world; or we can ask how a field anthropologist, armed with nothing but her own common sense, might go about trying to understand the language of the tribe she wishes to study. Quine is an empiricist; he thinks all knowledge begins with experience. But his arguments do not require multiple observations of actual children, nor surveying the methods of practicing anthropologists. It will serve his purpose to show how it might be that, beginning with nothing but her own experience, a child or an anthropologist could learn about her strange neighbors at home or in the larger world.

Learning a word has two parts: it requires becoming familiar with the sound of it and being able to reproduce it, which the child does by observing and imitating others; and it requires learning how to use the word, which is the semantic part. Even in the paradigm case the second is by far the more difficult. Quine (1969) describes a process in which the child is taught to associate words with "patterns of sensory stimulation," which must be imagined to be similar enough from individual to individual so that from these patterns a world of objects can be constructed.

We are to imagine a field translator who also goes about the project of understanding her subjects from the ground up, unaided by any manual of translation. (Quine calls this, therefore, a process of *radical* translation.) Making such a manual is one of her goals. The difference between child and anthropologist is that the child is learning a first language; the anthropologist is discovering how to translate a foreign language into one that is familiar. But like the child, the anthropologist is guided by her own patterns of sensory stimulation—which in her language she has learned to call 'rabbits', 'trees', 'inanimate objects', and so on—and by her observation of the circumstances under which her subjects utter the sounds they do. If, predictably, they say 'Gavagai' when a rabbit goes by, the anthropologist has some evidence for inferring that for them 'Gavagai' means 'There's a rabbit'. But every such conjecture stands ready to be revised in the face of other observations that call the translation into question. Even when the anthropologist is far enough along to be fairly sure that she is tracking something to do with rabbits, 'Gavagai' might be better translated as 'There's a rabbit-part', or 'A rabbit's hurrying by'. How the anthropologist translates any one sentence will have implications for how she translates others; and since the whole thing has to fit with the ongoing evidence she is acquiring, she must remain flexible about the meaning she assigns to any one term or sentence, or any group of the sentences. As Quine says, "Our boat stays afloat because at each alteration we keep the bulk of it intact as a going concern" (1964, p. 4).

Davidson accepts the view that meaning must show itself in dispositions to behave in certain ways. Like Quine's and Dewey's, this is a view not only about how we understand what another says, but about what he means; for the conditions for translating or interpreting others will turn out to be constitutive of the cöntent of words and thoughts themselves. Davidson accepts also meaning holism and the idea that meaning is in a certain sense indeterminate, that is, that in theory it is possible for there to be two equally good translation manuals of another's language. Meanings are not entities, neither in the mind nor in some Platonic heaven. And for the kinds of reasons given both by Wittgenstein and Quine, Davidson believes that an appeal to meanings as somehow prior to words, sentences, and utterances is doomed to fail. In any case, it would leave us "stranded further than we started from the non-linguistic goings-on that must supply the evidential base for interpretation" (1984, pp. 126–127). Yet we don't want to abandon the quest for meaning altogether, understood as a theory about how interpretation is possible. Davidson sketches a field, or builds a model, on which Belief, Desire, Meaning, Truth, World, My mind, Other minds, Action, and Language are situated. To understand how they hang together is to say all about meaning there is to say.[13]

Where Quine constructed a model of translation which would tell us how to translate sentences of another's speech into our own, Davidson's model focuses more explicitly on what it is to understand another's thoughts, hence the move from 'radical translation' to 'radical interpretation'. Quine tells me how to connect another person's utterances with mine; Davidson tells me how to connect his utterances with the world. It is a theory addressed to the fundamental question of semantics, namely how words relate to things. Davidson's strategy too is to ask how an interpreter without the help of dictionaries and translation manuals might go about trying to understand another creature or community. "Like the traditional philosopher who wants an answer to the skeptic," Richard Rorty writes, Davidson "wants us to step outside of our language game and look at it from a distance," not, however, by moving to some metaphysical standpoint outside all language games (say by imagining some perfect and God-like knower), but "from the mundane standpoint of the field linguist, trying to make sense of our linguistic behavior" (1985, p. 339).

Why a thought experiment? If what we want is a theory of interpretation, why not investigate what travelers and linguists and interpreters of other sorts actually do? Because, as with Quine, the inquiry isn't empirical but 'grammatical', or conceptual. There is an empirical observation at its base, namely the familiar fact that we manage to communicate with each other. (One could balk the argument by refusing this premise.) Then we are to ask what must be the case for this mutual understanding to be possible.[14] We are attempting to uncover those broad features of reality which the activity of understanding others presumes.

Why 'radical' interpretation? Why not just think about ordinary interpreters, you and me, talking together? Because those broad features of reality that we're after may be obscured when we think about language, meaning, and mind against a backdrop of others speaking our own tongue, others who are, like us, already accomplished speakers and thinkers. Because it has taken the adult first person as the position from which to raise questions about mind, these are just the features that internalism, too, must overlook. How, then, might a radical interpreter, someone who knows nothing about another speaker, get started? Davidson's theory assumes first of all that we can sometimes know that we are observing a creature who is engaged in the activity of asserting something or holding something true, even if we have no clue as to what is being asserted.[15] (A different though related assumption is that a child who is beginning to learn a language, but not yet herself a speaker, may be able to tell when someone is communicating with her. Current infant research warrants both assumptions, as I say in "Baby Talk.") And it assumes, second, that some of what is asserted is true. Given these assumptions, we can begin to get a perch on what the speaker means and what she believes. For example, if she is a German speaker, she holds 'Es regnet' true if she believes that it's raining. For surely if we know that 'Es regnet' is held true if and only if it's raining, then in a perfectly ordinary sense of the word 'meaning' we know what 'Es regnet' means for that speaker. And we can come to know the conditions under which she holds utterances true if we assume that events in our common world are sometimes causing her to say and believe what she does. Successful communication presumes at least this: that we inhabit a common world, and that there is a causal connection between world and speaker/believer which helps to constitute both meaning and mental content.

And just at this point Davidson's theory takes a pivotal turn from Quine's. In both, the concept of cause plays a crucial role in meaning. But how the critical variables in this causal story are picked out makes for the difference between an internalist (Quine's) and an externalist (Davidson's) account. Quine's account ties meaning to patterns of stimulation at nerves' endings. So if the patterns that cause an interpreter to think 'There's a rabbit' are the same as the patterns that cause the speaker of an alien language to cry 'Gavagai!', the interpreter can provisionally assume that the alien's 'Gavagai!' can be translated as 'Lo, a rabbit!' Thus rabbits and other worldly objects may be viewed, Quine says, as 'posits'. All that matters to meaning are the proximal stimuli, what occurs within or on the skins of speaker and interpreter. There is nothing to guarantee, furthermore, that the same stimuli correspond to the same events and objects in the world. Substitute 'mind' for 'skin' and Quine's view of the mind is as first-personal as Descartes'.

Quine is right that for communication to succeed some things must already be shared. He locates one of them: which objects we focus on, and how, reflects our interests. So we can say that communication rests, among other things, on shared interests. This is a necessary but not a sufficient condition for meaning. Undoubtedly there must also be innate similarity responses. But stimulations of nerve endings cannot be shared; nor can they be easily observed. And even if they could, how might we infer from them, in a non-circular way, just what in our shared world is causing them? How could the interpreter locate the common stimulus to which she and the speaker are responding? Routes from nerve endings to brain are a necessary part of the story of any act of speech. But our problem was how to account for interpretation, and the fact that some of the time, communication succeeds. What this requires is two people responding to each other and to objects in a public space.[16]

It is important to notice that the causal relation between world and sentence which Davidson posits is not merely contingent. He does not say that *probably* many of our utterances are caused by events in the outside world, but that such a causal relation—contrary to the internalist's view—somewhere in the system of a person's beliefs is determinative or constitutive of meaning itself. The thesis must be carefully put. For of course not every utterance or belief is so caused. Speakers do not always, or even typically, use language to make assertions or express beliefs. We play games, joke, tell riddles, bemuse ourselves, intentionally deceive others, phantasize, mis-remember, speak in metaphor. But if as your interpreter I could never figure out what you believe to be the literal truth, I could not understand your metaphors, nor what it would be for you to be telling a lie.

So a great many of our beliefs are related only distantly to the external world. (Examples of ones likely to be nearer are 'It's raining', or 'People have just come into the room', said when it is, or they have.) Many of a child's beliefs about what will happen when he goes for the first time to the dentist, for example, may hang by a slender thread from some event that has nothing to do with dentists, at least in anyone's mind but the child's. And even when there is a direct causal relation, meaning holism reminds us that what a speaker means in saying what he does is a function not only of his relation to the world, but also of what other things he holds true. A bolt of lightning may cause Demeter to believe that Zeus has struck Mt. Olympus with his spear. But the meaning of that belief for Demeter can be fleshed out only through discovering what else he believes.

The externalist view about meaning requires only that there be a causal relation between world and mind *somewhere* in the network of a speaker's beliefs. This relation spreads over the network as a whole in ways to be determined by the process of interpretation. Charles may not mean by 'weather' what I think he does, even though he and I apparently share many other terms. And he may express his feelings of hurt not with angry words but withdrawal, or extreme self-control, or by changing the subject. Inferring from what a speaker says and does just what he thinks took place in the external world, and what has taken place in fact, is as hard as we always thought it was. Eliminated is the difficulty neither of discovering from a person's words and actions his subjective states, nor of making inferences from them about the objective world, but only the possibility that his 'inner' 'subjective' world has nothing to do with an external and inter-subjective reality.

I have said that the circumstances under which a sentence is held true provide a key to what the sentence means.[17] True by whose lights? Certainly the speaker's. But the interpreter's as well. It is because the interpreter sees that it is raining, or sees a rabbit going by, and at that very moment sees the speaker apparently responding to the same event, that the interpreter is able to hazard a guess, forever subject to revision, about what it is that causes the speaker to assert what she does. A condition of interpretation, then, is that speaker and interpreter hold in common certain beliefs to be true. If we think this is not the case, it is because we are overlooking and taking for granted all the many beliefs we share. A Trobriand Islander and I may disagree, for example, about why someone became ill. He thinks witchcraft, I think amoebic dysentery; his ontology includes demons and gods, mine does not; and so on. But beneath the differences in our names for things we will find, for example, that we both believe that the man became ill; that men have bodies; that things grow in the ground. As Davidson says, "We can make sense of differences all right, but only against a background of shared belief. What is shared does not in general call for comment; it is too dull, trite, or familiar to stand notice. But without a vast common ground, there is no place for disputants to have their quarrel" (1984, p. 200).

So a first constraint on meaning is a causal relation between mind and external world. A second is that speaker and interpreter share this world, and many beliefs about it. Then there is the constraint of *holism* I talked about earlier. To know what you mean in saying 'I see a tree outside my window', I have also to know what you mean by saying things like 'That's a tree, not a flower', and 'There are windows in my house', 'Here is a pane of glass', and so on; for a concept acquires its meaning only through its place in a web of other concepts. There is no particular list we can supply of the things that must be believed if someone is to believe there is a glass of water on the table, but unless there is some appropriate network the attribution of any particular belief lacks sense. If you and I speak the same language and have histories that are roughly similar, I shall often know what other beliefs are implied by any one belief, and something about what has gone on in fact in your—our—world. To the extent, however, that our histories or circumstances or language are different, my difficulty in understanding you makes me more aware of the contextual nature of all thought. We jump into what some call the 'hermeneutic' circle, making guesses that lead us progressively to revise our understanding of what any individual sentence means.

An application of these ideas to psychoanalytic practice is the following. What is the psychoanalyst assuming when she uses the patient's free association as a guide to interpretation? Certainly this: that if her patient is following the analytic 'rule' not to censor any of his thoughts, those that are unconscious and repressed will out. But also this: that we come to understand the meaning of any one of a person's sentences or thoughts through discovering its connections to others, thus lighting up the larger network in which it is enmeshed. And this is just the thesis of meaning holism.

That the network of beliefs must be 'appropriate' is a way of saying that meaning is a *normative* notion.[18] Meaning and interpretation are both governed by a standard, namely that of rationality in a broad and general sense of the word. The idea is that the place a belief occupies in a mental network has a *logical* character, and must if it is a *belief,* something that has sense. Imagine thinking that for all you know I believe that 'The seas are salty and it is not the case that the seas are salty'. What, then, could you understand me to mean by the words 'sea' and 'salty'? In what sense could you even attribute to me the state of belief in the first place? Or what if I say that I believe Mary and John went to the circus, then deny that John went to the circus?

To make sense of someone we must exercise a principle of charity which attributes to her certain rational norms, norms like: believe only those propositions you think true; do not believe propositions that are contradictory; draw inductive inferences on the basis of all available relevant evidence; do not act contrary to your own best judgment.[19] These are not norms that people consciously hold, but ones implicit in their thought and their behavior. Charity in this context has nothing to do with generosity, nor with a parochial imposition of our own standards on others. It specifies some necessary conditions for making sense of another's behavior, conditions that are constitutive of the concepts of belief, desire, and action. The principle makes explicit the fact that it is the nature of what we call thought to be intelligible, both to oneself and to others. David Lewis makes the point by saying that a creature "might have no beliefs, desires, or meanings at all, but it is analytic that if he does have them they more or less conform to the constraining principles by which the concepts of belief, desire, and meaning are defined" (1983, p. 112).

There are exceptions, like unintelligible mutterings. But we would have no reason to describe mutterings that were unintelligible not just to us now but in principle as expressing thought. And often one holds conflicting beliefs; does not learn from the past; acts contrary—or so it seems—to her own most considered intentions; and so on. Such forms of irrationality are the psychoanalyst's daily fare. How to account for them is a subject we will come to in later chapters. But irrationality is such only against a background of rationality, and it is discovering this which makes sense of apparent non-sense.

The fact that interpretation presumes a common world, the sharing of many particular beliefs, and some very general norms of rationality rules out the skeptical possibility that you and I are guided by different and mutually incomprehensible conceptual schemes. The scheme-content distinction has been given many formulations. One is the idea that language organizes experience, that it provides, in Whorf's words, "a classification and arrangement of the stream of sensory experience" (1956, p. 55). Another is the idea of Kuhn and Feyerabend that scientific revolution produces a new language which is incommensurable, or not intertranslatable, with the old. And another is Quine's: "We talk so inveterately of objects that to say we do seems almost to say nothing at all; for how else is there to talk? It is hard to say how else there is to talk, not because our objectifying pattern is an invariable trait of human nature, but because we are bound to adapt any alien pattern to our own in the very process of understanding or translating the alien sentences" (1969, p. 1).

Of course different languages have different vocabularies and grammars; and as anyone knows who has tried translating from one language into another, different languages inflect different attitudes toward the world. Furthermore, some revisions in scientific theory may be so fundamental as to make it seem as if the terms involved have entirely changed their meaning. And finally, as we have learned from Quine, meaning can never be determinate; therefore translation will never yield synonymy. Yet, Davidson argues, if the language of another person, time, or culture were so alien as to defy translation altogether, how could we recognize it as embodying a conceptual scheme to begin with? How could we identify it as a form of *speech* rather than a meaningless babble, or, like the parrot's, the sounds of speech without the sense? How, if we did not share some beliefs, could we get a grasp on the idea that there are other beliefs, perhaps a great many, about which we disagree? "The dominant metaphor of conceptual relativism, that of differing points of view, seems to betray an underlying paradox. Different points of view make sense, but only if there is a common co-ordinate system on which to plot them; yet the existence of a common system belies the claim of dramatic incomparability." The short line to take against all such relativistic arguments then, is that "nothing . . . could count as evidence that some form of activity could not be interpreted in our language that was not at the same time evidence that the form of activity was not speech behavior" (Davidson, 1984, pp. 184–186). To know that you have such a scheme to begin with, I would have to find some of what you believe and say intelligible, which means I would have to find some of it true, by your lights and mine; for we have made convergence in the conditions under which we hold beliefs true a condition of intelligibility. Though of course we may describe them differently, your world and mine cannot be worlds apart if we are able to attribute not just some particular sense but any sense to each other. Davidson writes:

> The truth of an utterance depends on just two things: what the words as spoken mean, and how the world is arranged. There is no further relativism to a conceptual scheme, a way of viewing things, a perspective. Two interpreters, as unlike in culture, language and point of view as you please, can disagree over whether an utterance is true, but only if they differ on how things are in the world they share, or what the utterance means. (1986, p. 309)

If this is right, then we can say the following two things about psychoanalytic practice. First, 'empathy' cannot be a matter of my getting somehow outside my own mind and into yours, but rests rather in discovering and widening the common base we share, exercising my imagination in regard to the beliefs and desires you may have in respect to which your behavior seems more or less reasonable to you. Even with strangers from a strange land, whose talk is at first unintelligible to us, we can assume something common in the way of a world, though just how common remains to be explored. We even take for granted, quite rightly, that in some general ways we share certain experiences of this world: fatigue and hunger; moods of relative elation and sadness; objects that get in our way and cause us pain or frustration, and so on. Again, just how much we share, and where we differ, is at the beginning of our conversation, and to some extent forever after, an area of darkness perhaps never completely to be filled in. But it cannot be all dark.

And the second follows from the first, namely that the psychoanalyst and even her maddest patient, if, that is, she can be understood at all, must hold many beliefs and desires in common. From these as her base, the psychoanalyst works toward understanding those that are not common, even at first incoherent. Indeed this seems to be one of the lessons to be drawn from Freud, that the insane are not just biologically human, but mentally so. They have beliefs and desires which serve to explain what they do, and in ways that are generally familiar.

But how does Freud, or indeed any interpreter, know for sure which beliefs he shares with a speaker? How does he know when the speaker's thoughts are fully rational and when not? How does he know which parts and aspects of their common world have struck them both? It is crucial to keep in mind that the interpretive procedure is a *process,* of necessity ongoing and open-ended. Interpretation aims at the best fit between coherence and correspondence. We have to fit what the speaker is saying both to what we know (or presume) to be the case in our shared world, and to the rest of her utterances and beliefs, while being prepared at any point to revise the narrative we have been making. This doesn't mean that coherence is our only guide, for interpretation has to keep in mind as well the constraints on meaning of causality and mental holism.

I spoke earlier about difficulties for theories of truth and knowledge either as correspondence or as coherence. The problem is that each says something right and something wrong. If we are genuinely in a state of knowledge, we want to say, then what we believe must be the way the world is. This is what's right about correspondence theories. But we also must have good reasons for thinking this is the way world is, reasons which can only take the form of other beliefs. This is what's right about coherence theories. But how, if our knowledge about the world is built up out of ideas, or percepts, or sensory stimulations, will we ever be in a position to check for the relation between ideas or stimulations and world? How can we get past the ideas or stimulations to see if the correspondence relation holds? The dilemma seemed to open up a gap between justified belief and knowledge: we can have justified belief without any guarantee that what we believe is true. We can insist on truth as correspondence, but at the cost of saying that knowledge is impossible.

The problem, we can now see, arose from a view of meaning as something private and internal, mediated by internal entities. The dilemma between truth as correspondence and truth as coherence was thrust on us by our attempt to divorce meaning from truth. But it is just the connection between them that guarantees the connection between truth and knowledge. The traditional, internalist view sunders the content of idea or belief from real events in the world that may or may not have caused me to hold it. Meaning is internal to belief, the view says, and has nothing essential to do with the believer's causal relations to the world. But if the meaning of a sentence is given in general by the conditions in the world which cause a speaker to hold it true, then meaning is constrained by circumstances in the external world, just the circumstances about which knowledge wants to make claims. Knowledge is both correspondence and coherence, in the sense that the sentence 'Snow is white' is true if and only if snow is white. And this is the very relation that, together with meaning holism, allows the sentence to mean what it does. The relation between sentence and external world in virtue of which the sentence is true (when it is) is not something tacked on to it but essential to its meaning. Yet I can be said to know that the sentence is true only if it is supported by my other beliefs. So the only thing that can justify a belief is other beliefs; this is the insight that coherence theories of truth and knowledge have going for them. The event of a rabbit's going by causes my belief that a rabbit just passed by. And my belief that a rabbit passed by may both cause and justify my belief that there are small animals in these woods.[20]

Which of my beliefs or yours are true? We can't know the answer to that for certain—just as we saw a moment ago that while the psychoanalyst can be assured that both he and his patient have some true beliefs, and share some of them in common, he cannot say for sure just what beliefs they are. But then we should be skeptical of any theory that said we could. What Radical Interpretation tells us is that in the network of any person's beliefs it must be that some are true, if she is to have any mental states at all; no particular beliefs can be counted on now and forever to stand fast to challenge. So in this sense the reality to which knowledge aspires is always just beyond us. This too is something we have known all along. The mistake, however, has been to infer from this inescapable uncertainty that what we know—when we do—is not the world itself but something of our own making.

I come now to a final constraint on meaning, the one that shows the generally interpersonal character of the mental; for we have not yet fully answered Wittgenstein's question: How is my meaning rain when I think 'rain' accomplished? The event of rain causes my belief—when it is true—that it is raining. But how do I know it is *rain* that my belief is about? Any creature, if it is the right size and has the right bodily equipment, can hide from the rain, climb a rock, eat an apple. But only a creature with a mind can be in the state of hoping to climb the rock or thinking about the rain, thinking about it *as* rain. There are some who deny that the concept of mind plays any necessary role in our stories about human affairs. But even Freud abandoned this line.[21] So we need to distinguish instinctive, programmed, wired-in, tropistic responses (like the sunflower's turning toward the sun), and even a lot of highly intelligent behavior on the part of species other than ourselves, from responses and behavior whose explanation demands the attribution specifically of beliefs and desires.

To see what is missing from our account of the mental so far, let's turn to a primitive learning situation. The mother hands the child an apple, saying 'apple' as she does. Mother and child are together interested in the apple, and interested also in each other's response to it. The child babbles, and at some point, in this or a similar transaction, the child hits on a sound close enough to 'apple' so that the mother rewards the child—with a laugh, intensified interest, more play, or any of the other kinds of responses that infant observers have described. No doubt creatures of various sorts have innate similarity patterns. And it is probably the case that infants and mothers couldn't communicate with each other at all unless they were cued to things in the world in roughly similar ways.[22] So in time, given the similarity patterns that the mother finds between apples, that the child finds between apples, and that the mother finds in the child's proto-linguistic responses to apples, we can give content to the mother's saying that the child is responding specifically to apples.

So far, however, there is nothing to distinguish our response to the child from our response to a trained dog. A dog is fed when it hears a bell, and in time the bell causes it to salivate. The same triangulation pattern allows us to say that the dog's salivating, or barking, is a response to the bell. The mother has in mind the apple when she says 'apple', and apple is what she means by the word. Our question is the point at which we can say that this is also what the child means. The question is not epistemological, how we know what the child means, but what must be the case for us to attribute any meaning to the child at all. Presumably we are not tempted to say that the dog *means* 'bell' when it salivates or barks. So our story about the child needs a more complex form of triangulation than the one we have so far described.

What it needs is precisely the interaction itself between child and mother. If we are going to call the child's response to the apple *linguistic*, we must impute to the child the intention to communicate. The child must be knowingly and intentionally responding to a specific stimulus, and it must know that the mother is responding to that same stimulus. So it must be something public, discernible by both mother and child, to which, furthermore, they can give a name that will allow them both to speak of it even in its absence. They must be responding to the same object in the world; they must be responding to it in similar ways; and they must observe that they do. (Davidson's interpreter is not in the first instance a child learning to speak. But a reader familiar with Trevarthan's observations of early mother-infant reactions—to be discussed in Chapter 6—may be struck by the similarity between his account of 'triangulation' and Davidson's.) Such an interaction not only allows the mother, or an interpreter *A*, to say of *B*, 'he is discriminating *x*'; it allows *B* to say of himself, as it were, 'I am seeing an *x*' (or 'I want an *x*', or 'I am thinking about an *x*').[23] The belief that there is an apple on the table draws a line to the world, or seems to. But what fixes the terms joined by the line? If we say, 'I and the thing itself', then the thing is at the mercy of my whim. There is nothing to give me the idea of it as an external *object* which can be seen from different perspectives and which I may have right or wrong. Not just something but someone is needed to give content to this idea:

> To have the concept of a table or a bell is to recognize the existence of a tri-angle, one apex of which is oneself, another a creature similar to oneself, and the third an object (table or bell) located in a space thus made common. The only way of knowing that the second apex—the second creature or person—is reacting to the same object as oneself, is to know that the other person has the same object in mind. But then the second person must also know that the first person constitutes an apex of the same triangle another apex of which the second person occupies. (Davidson, "Second Person," unpublished)

Notice that there is no point of view except *A*'s from which *B* can be said to be responding to something in the same way. Sameness is our category, not, so to speak, the world's.

We can make the point in a slightly different way. A creature cannot be said to believe in what we might call a 'hard' sense of that word, one that distinguishes reflexive and instinctive behavior from intentional behavior, unless it has the concept of belief as something which can be true or false. (Of course one need not know which of one's beliefs are true and which false.) It is a grasp of these concepts that is needed to distinguish discrimi-natory reaction—which adult thinkers share not only with babies but also with sunflowers and thermostats—from Intentionality. The concepts of belief, of truth and falsity, in turn presume the concept of an objective world that one's beliefs are about. Under what conditions can one be said to have the concepts of belief and of an objective world? Under the condi-tions of agreement and disagreement with another speaker/believer. (So the psychoanalyst might say that the child is on its way to a concept of reality when it encounters, and tolerates, a 'No'; which can happen only within a context of much 'agreement' and sympathy.) As Carol Rovane (1986) puts it:

> The basic idea is that one cannot recognize that one's beliefs constitute a sub-jective point of view on something objective, or independent of one's beliefs, except insofar as one also recognizes other subjective points of view. Hence self-conscious believers must also be self-conscious communicators, i.e., interpreters of others. (p. 423)

So if in attributing a 'subjective' 'inner' world to a creature, we attribute to it Intentional states, then such a creature must have the concept of an objective world. Moreover, there must be an objective world, and in it people with whom the creature is, or has been at one time, in interaction. As thought and talk are interdependent, so too are subjectivity and objectivity.

I am incidentally, then, in agreement with Lacan on two fundamental points: that language is a necessary condition for the unconscious, and that language is necessarily social. But all I mean by the first is that lan-guage is the condition for the mental in general, whether conscious or unconscious. Whereas on Lacan's view language separates the child from its 'subjective' experience, creating the unconscious in the process, on mine there is nothing we can speak of as 'subjectivity' prior to language.

It is often objected to a third-person view that while it may tell us how I can come to know your mental states, that is not the same thing as telling us about those states themselves. But remember: our inquiry has been guided by the premise that we are able to communicate with each other some of the time. Furthermore, while my beliefs are inalienably mine, yet their content is in a sense public. You and I, believing that Columbus discovered America in 1492, or that the coup in Russia has been defeated, have the same belief. They aren't identical, for yours is lodged in your mental network, mine is lodged in mine. But they are close enough for us to agree or disagree and to know perfectly well what the other is talking about. This conviction, about the publicity of language and what it presumes, led us to an externalist account of meaning and mental content. So the point is "not that interpretation constitutes content. Rather, it is because content is externally determined that it is a public phenomenon. And, because it is a public phenomenon, interpretation and the constraints we put on it will help shed light on intentionality" (Bilgrami, 1989, p. 71).[24]

In linking the mental to language, do we imply that only that which can be spoken, aloud or in the mind, can be thought? No. A creature may have thoughts that it has not and cannot put into words. Nor are we denying cognitive powers to animals and infants. If one likes one can call those powers 'thought' in a weak sense of that word. We are saying that a crucial point in mental development comes with language; that language is social; and that thought in a hard sense, the sense that allows us to say that a creature is thinking *about* something, is also in a sense social. We imply that thoughts in the strong sense can be attributed only to a creature who can articulate some of them.

And now it might look as if we are in a circle: A creature can be said to have beliefs only if it shares a concept of truth with other creatures. But to know the conditions under which a sentence held to be true would be true is to know what it means. And only if one can interpret the speech of others, that is, if one can some of the time make successful guesses about their beliefs, can one be said to have beliefs oneself. So what comes first? Belief? Meaning? Or the concept of truth? Does the child first have beliefs, then meaningful beliefs? Does the child first have the concept of truth, then acquire beliefs?

None of these; the idea is that meaning, truth, and belief are inseparable. As Wittgenstein said about beliefs: "When we first begin to *believe* anything, what we believe is not a single proposition, it is a whole system of propositions. (Light dawns gradually over the whole)" (1972, §141).

Light dawns gradually over meaning, truth, and belief, and all together. They are as inextricable from one another as the knowledge one has of some of the contents of one's own mind is inextricable from the knowledge one has of some of the contents of the minds of others.[25] The illumination is not momentary; it is an activity, or a process. To give a Wittgensteinian sort of example: in learning how to play baseball one does not first learn about first base, then second, then third, then what it is to be up at bat, and so on. One learns them all together. There is no one point at which a child can suddenly be said to have the hang of language. There is no one point at which it can be said to think.

The view of the mental sketched in this chapter gives a way of reading the central thesis of object relations theory mentioned in my Introduction; for the implication of the interpersonal view of the mind is that thinking in the hard sense is conditional on the child's real relations with others, and that this thinking is in turn a presupposition for phantasizing about 'objects' of any sort.[26] The child is 'constituted' as a subject—by which I mean a creature with interpretable mental states—through his communications with other persons.

R. G. Collingwood writes:

> The child's discovery of itself as a person is also its discovery of itself as a member of a world of persons . . . The discovery of myself as a person is the discovery that I can speak, and am thus a *persona* or speaker; in speaking I am both speaker and hearer; and since the discovery of myself as a person is also the discovery of other persons around me, it is the discovery of speakers and hearers other than myself. (1938, p. 248)

On the first-person, Cartesian view of mind, first I know what I think and mean; then using your language as my data together with other sorts of your behavior, I make inferences that you think, and about what. Casting meaning as an entirely internal affair, it is a picture that inevitably concludes with skepticism, generating at the same time that quest for certainty or for first foundations that has nagged Western philosophy since Plato but that became even more urgent in the seventeenth century. We have stood Cartesianism on end: only a creature who can interpret others can be said to think itself. Subjectivity arises along with inter-subjectivity and is not the prior state. To make the motions of Descartes' first meditation, doubting the world and other minds, one must be in possession of all one needs to put the doubt to rest.

Let me end this chapter on a rather more psychological note. Descartes wanted to anchor knowledge vertically, building it up from something indubitably known. He took that to be one's own internal mental states. Beyond the pale of certainty and in question, then, are the existence of one's own body, the external world, and other minds. Mind and the self depend on nothing beyond themselves save God. This is not so much a qualification on our self-sufficiency, however, as further evidence of it. As Heidegger said, the Cartesian quest for certainty is yet another expression of the Western desire to construe knowledge as an instrument of power and to escape contingency; for the other side of Descartes' apparently modest avowal that without divine assistance knowledge would be impossible is his assurance that he most resembles this omnipotent Being, and it is in the very shadow of His embrace that he knows and doubts.

Philosophy begins in the only place it can, *here,* in the midst of things, with thinkers who are already accomplished at thinking and whose thinking takes time and the world for granted. Without our abilities to move around objects and to see, both of us, the same physical object from different perspectives, to move our tongues and mouths and to make sounds, to remember the past in such simple acts as my recognizing this as the same object we saw a moment ago, to enter into countless forms of communal life, there could be no beginning for those acts of communication that we have said are basic both to interpretation and to thought. Knowledge is not anchored vertically, and by that token no particular piece of it can be given a lifetime guarantee. It is held in place by the very contingencies it takes for granted, as are one's mind and one's existence as a self. Neglect these contingencies and we lose a grip on the very idea of meaning.

But there are powerful motives for 'neglecting' them. For if we sail past global skepticism, we also abandon the quest for certainty that puts skepticism on the map.

2 Minding the Frontier

Like modern philosophy in its Cartesian turn, psychoanalysis began with reflections on error. Freud's early seduction theory traced neurosis to real traumatic interactions between the child and others. But Freud came to think that what he had taken for memories were instead phantasies, stories reflecting 'internal' desire rather than events in the external world. Whether the early seductions reported to Freud were illusory or not, surely he was right that what we regard as belief is often the visualization of a wish fulfilled; memory, desire passing as history. So it has become an axiom of clinical practice that psychoanalytic interpretation is concerned with uncovering 'psychic reality', or the patient's subjective world. But one has to go carefully here; for this idea of psychic reality can falsely seem to presuppose an internalist view of meaning.

A view closely allied to meaning internalism has it that subjectivity in the form of an inner, private world comes first, followed by some knowledge of external reality or what we take to be external reality. Subjectivity is thought to be first in both an epistemological and a genetic sense. Only the genetic version interests me here. It holds that the subjective—in the form of 'impressions' for Hume, 'sense data' and 'raw feels' for others, and for Freud, instinctual wishes (though as will emerge, Freud's commitment to internalism is never wholehearted)—is first in the order of time, providing the seeds from which later thought and knowledge flower. I will call this the assumption of genetic priority.

In this chapter I want briefly to introduce several key and interrelated Freudian themes to which we will return for extensive discussion in later chapters—the unconscious, instinct (or drive),[1] phantasy, and the child's earliest 'mental' states. For it is particularly in his handling of these themes that Freud grapples with three of the main philosophical problems discussed in the last chapter: the sense in which thoughts are 'inner'; the conditions for assigning mental content; and how to think about the ground from which the mental arises, or the relation between mind and body.

Let's begin with Freud's first systematic exploration of the unconscious, *The Interpretation of Dreams* (1900), noting that interpretation is a form of explanation appropriate only to texts or doings or utterances that are meaningful, meaningful not only to an interpreter but also to the creature who is their author. Wet streets, thunder, a sore throat, a suspicious-looking rash are meaningful to us. So in a different sense are the words of a parrot. But since in none of these cases is there an agent who might mean something by them, interpretation is not in order. The idea that dreams can be interpreted implies, then, Freud's basic premise that dreams are mental phenomena, and that as such they have meaning to the dreamer.[2]

On Freud's view, every dream represents a particular state of affairs as one wishes it were; and the meaning of the dream is just the wish that it visualizes as fulfilled. "*Thus its content* [is] *the fulfillment of a wish and its motive* [is] *a wish*" (1900, p. 119).[3] The first dream Freud analyzes, the one he gives us under the heading "Analysis of a Specimen Dream," is the famous Irma dream in which a patient who had in fact ended her therapeutic work with him only partially cured is being received as a guest of the Freuds' in a large hall. Freud reproaches her for not having accepted an interpretation that he had given her and says that if she still gets pains it is her own fault. When Irma protests that her pains are more intense than he appreciates, he notes that indeed she looks pale and puffy and thinks that perhaps she is after all suffering from organic trouble. He calls in a Dr. M. and his friend Otto, who confirm that she is suffering an organic illness, one that stems from an injection Otto had given her earlier with an unclean syringe.

Associating to the dream, Freud recalls a visit the day before from Otto, who had been staying with Irma and her family in the country. Freud had asked Otto how Irma was, and had received the reply: 'she's better, but not quite well'. Freud was conscious of being annoyed by the reproof he detected in Otto's words, and that evening wrote out Irma's case history with the idea of giving it to Dr. M., a mutual friend of Freud's and Otto's. Freud interprets the dream as motivated by two wishes, to relieve himself of responsibility for his patient's lingering illness and to revenge himself on his friend Otto for having implied that Freud is at fault. The dream satisfies both wishes in picturing Irma's illness as somatic in origin, and as having been caused by a carelessness of Otto's.

As interpreted by Freud, the Irma dream thus aptly illustrates the thesis that dreams are wish-fulfillments. But so stated we do not yet have the crucial qualifications to his theory, namely that every dream is the disguised fulfillment of an unconscious, repressed, sexual, infantile wish. This qualified concept of wishing is key also to his views about unconscious phantasy, symptom formation, and neurosis in general. And it is to provide a model of mental processes which will accommodate such infantile wishes that Freud writes the famous concluding chapter to his *Interpretation of Dreams*. There he speaks of the wish as a 'primary process' wish, meaning, in part, that it is 'instinctual'.

Greenberg and Mitchell (1983) claim that the distinction sometimes drawn between psychoanalysis as a natural science and as an interpretive discipline is spurious, for "the drives are not only the *mechanisms* of the mind, they are also its *contents*" (p. 23). Freud's drive theory, they say, is also a theory about meaning. Consider his reflex arc model of early mental functioning according to which the psychic apparatus is directed toward keeping itself free as far as possible from stimuli. "Its first structure followed the plan of a reflex apparatus," Freud says, "so that any sensory excitation impinging on it could be promptly discharged along a motor path" (1900, p. 565). How does the apparatus handle pressing somatic needs? In the earliest stages of development, by motor activity, for example, by thrashing and crying. But this solution doesn't work for more than minutes at a time. A somewhat better solution becomes available once the organism has had an experience of genuine gratification, the memory of which becomes associated with the need; for now when a similar need arises, the organism summons up ('cathects') the remembered perception and 'hallucinates' satisfaction. Freud calls such a primitive need a 'wish'; and he thinks that hallucinatory wish-fulfillment is the model for phantasizing, at whatever age. The content of the unconscious, he says, is made up entirely of such 'wishes'. And he claims that "nothing but a wish can set our mental apparatus at work" (1900, p. 567). Greenberg and Mitchell comment: "From the perspective of mechanism, the wish of 1900 has the same status as the drive of later theory. Both create the internal tension which, experienced by a psychic apparatus which operates under the rule of the constancy principle, moves the mind to action" (1983, p. 29).

The reason for saying that drive theory concerns mental contents as well as mechanisms is that the concept of a wish, like that of belief and desire, has built into it reference to something beyond itself. Freud does not call the very first need a 'wish', but only need which can recall an experience of gratification. In doing so he acknowledges that wishes are Intentional states; and in claiming that first wishing comes about through a causal interaction between the organism and the external world, he has part of what is necessary for an externalist view of meaning. But we need more for Intentionality than this.

Here is the problem I see: If an instinct can be said in any sense to be *a wish,* then it must have at least some minimal meaning or content to the dreamer.[4] What gives the infantile, unconscious wish its meaning, its content? The content of a painting, in this sense, is what it pictures or represents; of a belief, the proposition to which it is directed, say *that there is a tree in front of the window.* If, to take an example of Wittgenstein's, someone doodles on a piece of paper in a way that suggests to me a particular 'interpretation', or even suggests it to the doodler after the fact, it does not follow that it had that meaning or that content to him at the time. For that to be the case he must have had it consciously or unconsciously in mind. The difficulty I am raising, then, is not how we can know what the dreamer was thinking when he dreamed his dream, but that in the case of the very early 'wishes' Freud invokes as essential to his theory, the conditions for assigning any *specific* mental content to the infant are not yet present. So there is justice in Robert Holt's remark (1976) that 'wish' functions in Freud's theory merely as a psychological name for something which has not been given the appropriate characteristics.

Freud's model of cognition assumed that the infant has the capacity for veridical perception of specific objects, and for recalling those objects in moments of need. But both philosophical argument and infant research agree that this model is mistaken, and that there cannot be representation of absent objects before the age of about eighteen months. There is evidence, furthermore (see Piaget, 1962), that rather than being a substitute for action in the world, as Freud believed about hallucinatory wish-fulfillment, representational thought arises gradually out of action patterns together with global experiences of satisfaction.[5]

Minimal as it is, the implicit externalism in some of Freud's early views is lost in his later drive theory, according to which mental development is primarily determined by things going on within the organism. Many of Freud's views about 'the unconscious' either go in the direction of meaning internalism, or betray an underlying reductivism according to which 'the unconscious' is a pseudo-psychological name for what would be better described in strictly bodily terms. As for internalism, let's look at Freud's remark that "What we have . . . called the conscious presentation of the object can . . . be split up into the presentation of the word *and the presentation of the thing*" (1915a, p. 201). The difference between a conscious and an unconscious presentation is that the first consists both of the thing and the word belonging to it, while the second is the presentation of the thing alone. By 'presentation of the thing', also 'object-presentation', Freud means a mnemic residue. ('Presentation' in such passages is a translation of 'Vorstellung', alternatively translated by his editors as 'idea'.) By 'presentation of the thing' I take him to mean the mental image or the concept of the thing.[6] He goes on to say that "a word . . . acquires its *meaning* by being linked to an object-presentation" (p. 213).[7]

The context of the passage is not a philosophical disquisition on the relations between words and world; it is a reflection on the peculiar quality of schizophrenic speech and thought. But in "The Ego and the Id" (1923) Freud makes the distinction again, saying that "the difference between a *Ucs.* and a *Pcs.* idea (thought) consists in this: that the former is carried out on some material which remains unknown," while the latter "is brought into connection with word-presentations" (p. 20). So I read these passages as expressing an internalist view according to which the role of language is to give expression to 'ideas' that are prior to and logically independent of it, ideas that are entirely subjective and internal. More particularly, Freud sometimes says that language makes thought visible:

> The part played by word presentations now becomes perfectly clear. By their interposition internal thought-processes are made into perceptions. It is like a demonstration of the theorem that all knowledge has its origin in external perception. When a hyper-cathexis of the process of thinking takes place, thoughts are *actually* perceived—as if they came from without—and are consequently held to be true. (1923, pp. 20–23)

(Here, incidentally, is Freud's subjectivist idea of the mind as a kind of Inner Eye before which ideas occur as 'presentations' [Rorty, 1979].) In the order of development, Freud claims, first there is private wordless thought; then words, which somehow provide the lens through which the thinker perceives his thoughts.

The idea of a pre-linguistic, imagistic form of thinking plays a central role in Freud's early account of repression (1915b). He describes a three-stage process in which the clinical phenomena, namely the various symptoms to be explained, are the final stage. The second is what he calls 'secondary' repression or 'repression proper', which simply names the obvious fact for which any theory of the mind must account, that we are able in a more or less purposive way not to know the contents of our own minds. Secondary repression is a fate that befalls what Freud calls 'secondary process thought', which presupposes one's being in possession of 'the reality principle'. In other words, secondary repression presupposes the agent's capacity to make assertions which she realizes are evaluable for their truth and falsity, acquaintance with external reality as such, and a grasp of the distinctions between past and future, real object in the world and thought about it. This is not the case with primary repression, on which Freud says secondary repression depends.[8]

Primary repression is described as a condition in which "the psychical (ideational) representative of the instinct [is] denied entrance into the conscious" (1915b, p. 148). A closer look at how Freud speaks of such representation reveals an ambiguity similar to the one we noted in the idea of instinctual wishing. Are instinct and that which represents it two different things? In which case representation is an entirely internal matter. Or does the instinct itself do the representing? If so, then the instinct may point somehow to the external world. Freud takes both lines. He says in one passage that instinct is "the psychical representative of the stimuli originating from within the organism and reaching the mind, as a measure of the demand made upon the mind for work in consequence of its connection with the body" (1915c, pp. 121–122). In other passages he distinguishes instinct from its ideational representative: "An instinct can never become an object of consciousness—only the idea [*Vorstellung*] that represents the instinct can" (1915b, p. 177). Why, apropos of the second passage, would Freud maintain that instinct can never become an object of consciousness? The only answer I can think of is that instinct is, as he defines it, *not* an idea or a representation of any kind, but a biological process.[9]

The same idea seems all but explicit in Freud's interesting but strange claims "that everything conscious has an unconscious preliminary stage" (1900, p. 612), and that "mental processes are in themselves unconscious" (1916–1917 [1915–1917], p. 21). Presumably Freud intends both conscious and unconscious to refer to orders of the mental. But what can the content of these passages be other than a reductivist thesis that mental processes are 'really' merely organic, or neuro-physiological? It is this idea, in fact, that seems to lie behind his hopes for psychoanalysis as a natural science:

> Whereas the psychology of consciousness never went beyond the broken sequences which were obviously dependent on something else, the other view, which held that the psychical is unconscious in itself, enabled psychology to take its place as a natural science like any other. The processes with which it is concerned are in themselves just as unknowable as those dealt with by other sciences, by chemistry or physics, for example; but it is possible to establish the laws which they obey and to follow their mutual relations and interdependencies over long stretches. (1940a [1938], p. 158)

It seems plain here that Freud sees nothing to distinguish psychology from sciences like chemistry and physics, and this because he thinks that 'psychological' laws will one day be statable in thoroughly non-mental terms. (The argument against this possibility will be made in the next chapter.)

Such passages may express not only a conviction that the mental can be reduced to the non-mental, but also a confusion between the different ways in which mental and bodily states are both 'inner'; for it seems to be partly in virtue of their innerness that Freud calls instincts quasi-mental. They are, he says, "representative of an endosomatic, continuously flowing source of stimulation" as contrasted with 'stimuli', which are "set up by *single* excitations coming from *without*. The concept of instinct is thus one of those lying on the frontier between the mental and the physical" (1905, p. 168).

Here is the distinction to be drawn between the innerness of bodily and mental states: the first are 'inner' in that they can in general be identified without reference to their causal interactions with things external to themselves. (It depends on how they are described. Describing a patch of skin as 'sun-burned' makes reference to the cause, but presumably the state of the skin could be described in other ways.) But this is not the case with mental states. For if externalist theories of meaning are right, then hidden in what we call an inner mental state are relations at once causal and logical, somewhere in the mental network, between it and the external world. Freud taught that internal and external do not carry self-authenticating stamps; examined in isolation, the content of a thought does not reveal its history. It is because this is so that phantasized seductions may present themselves as memory. But the lesson works both ways; for the sense in which mental images and phantasies are inner does not preclude a relationship with reality that determines them as the particular inner events they are.

Inner and outer, 'internal' mental event and external world, is a dialectic Freud returns to again and again. In "Instincts and Their Vicissitudes" (1915c) he distinguishes between stimuli impinging on the organism from the external world and those arising from within. The latter—instincts—pose a difficulty for the organism, since unlike threats from outside, those from within cannot be evaded by flight, that is, literal flight. At first, Freud says, the organism has a relatively accurate gauge for distinguishing internal from external reality in the difference between those stimuli which it can avoid by muscular action, and those which it cannot. But in time it learns to defend itself against instinctual dangers in ways that deflect this gauge. Now such defense typically requires judgment, which Freud again assimilates to entirely inner processes:

> The function of judgment is concerned in the main with two sorts of decisions. It affirms or disaffirms the possession by a thing of a particular attribute; and it asserts or disputes that a presentation has an existence in reality. The attribute to be decided about may originally have been good or bad, useful or harmful. Expressed in the language of the oldest—the oral—instinctual impulses, the judgment is: 'I should like to eat this', or 'I should like to spit it out' . . . the original pleasure-ego wants to introject into itself everything that is good and to eject from itself everything that is bad. The other sort of decision . . . is a concern of the definitive reality-ego, which develops out of

the initial pleasure-ego . . . It is, we see, once more a question of *external* and *internal*. What is unreal, merely a presentation and subjective, is only internal; what is real is also there outside. (1925, pp. 236–237)

Freud tells us that "the study of judgment affords us . . . an insight into the origin of an intellectual function from the interplay of the primary instinctual impulses. [It] is a continuation . . . of the original process by which the ego took things into itself or expelled them from itself, according to the pleasure principle" (ibid., p. 239).

In assuming that judgment can be reduced to its causal antecedents, Freud is making the mistake Locke and Hume made in thinking they could account for knowledge and understanding in terms of (private, first-personal) sense data. In the absence of certain sensations there would be no knowledge that there is a tree outside my window. But beyond this, knowing or believing that there is a tree requires concepts, including that of the objectively real. The infant would never get to beliefs and desires without its native endowments, which just apropos of language and thought must be enormous. But judgment is not in play when it takes its mother's milk, any more than it is for a plant turning toward the light. Judgment presumes a complicated repertoire that includes grasp of what it is to justify a belief and to make assertions about the true and the false. Assimilating instinctual or discriminatory response to judgment passes over the crucial question of what that space is between 'mere' organism and thinking organism; or it assumes there is no space, no logical space. Nor does it help to posit 'autonomous' ego functions.[10] For if judgment does not develop out of instinct alone, neither is it present from the beginning.

But perhaps there is a continuum—we might suggest on Freud's behalf—from the instinctual to the fully mental, along which range representations of different kinds. We might try saying, for example, that like beliefs and desires, instincts are identified by reference to objects beyond themselves, and so in that sense satisfy at least one of the requirements for the mental. As human actions require a teleological explanation in the form of the agent's goals and her beliefs that certain behavior will serve her goals, so instincts too are teleological. Ego instincts, for example, serve the goal of self-preservation or adaptation; the sexual instincts serve the goal of reproduction. Organic processes in general may be given teleological descriptions: the sperm seeks the ovum; the plant turns toward the light.

Ronald de Sousa argues along these lines, calling such teleological behavior a form of representation. He claims there is an Intentional spectrum, which he notes incidentally gives Freudian instinct theory philosophical support (1987). At the low end is "quasi-" or "nonmental intentionality," where stimuli are translated into stereotypical sequences of "T-

instinctual" behavior by automatic mechanisms; at the high end, full mentality or Intentionality (he does not capitalize this word for this sense). De
Sousa's reason for calling T-instinctual behavior a quasi-mental grade of
Intentionality is that it involves feedback, the testing and evaluation of
which, he says, must already have some characteristics in common with
representation. These characteristics are "generality" and "intentional
inexistence," namely that "the condition 'represented' in the testing mechanism may never occur" (p. 97). They therefore resemble the human mind
in what many have taken to be one of its essential features, de Sousa says,
its ability to entertain thoughts of things which do not exist.

The main problem with this account is that it isn't clear whether the
representational characteristics of "T-instinctual" behavior refer to anything other than a capacity for discriminatory response to the environment. We do describe the behaviors of creatures other than humans
teleologically; but if teleology of this sort involves some kind of representation, it doesn't seem to be the right kind to illumine meaning and mental
content. For the sense in which a thermostat, or the dance of the bee, 'represents' has little to do with the sense in which we can mean something by
what we say, or think about golden mountains, or the mother we had, or
wished we'd had. The infant responds selectively to cues in the environment; so do bees and even plants. (On a related point, Lichtenberg
comments [1983, chap. 4] that while infant research shows the infant to
have far more complex differential responses than we had thought, at the
same time psychoanalysts underestimate the perceptual-cognitive steps
necessary to form an intrapsychic representational world. Lichtenberg
adds that complex behaviors which psychoanalysts have explained via
psychic representations can be explained perfectly well without them.)

Some theorists think there is a kind of explanation which is different
from, on the one hand, (1) describing behavior in terms of selective
responses to stimuli, and explaining it in terms of responses that are
'wired in'; and, on the other, (2) describing behavior as intentional action
and explaining it in terms of motives involving desire and belief. This
third kind of explanation is said to be mentalistic, or quasi-mentalistic, in
attributing goals to creatures and behavioral systems, where this is a distinct mode of description from (2).[11]

I think that this 'third' kind is not truly distinct from but parasitic on
(2); but arguing this fully would take me too far afield. The gist of the
argument is this: It is natural for us to explain the behavior of many
things, including heat-seeking missiles, as we do our own, by saying what
they want or think, or that they behave *as if* they wanted or thought *that*
such and such were so. Of course the missile is crucially different from the
infant. For one thing, while we can precisely specify the 'goals' of the
missile, strictly speaking they are not its goals at all but those of the

person who designed it. And this difference is related to another, that while the infant, being much more like us than the missile is, has something very much like goals, nevertheless we cannot be very specific about what its goals are. Our trouble, oddly enough, is that the language of beliefs and desires which we must use to describe purposive infant behavior is far too precise and complex, so that we can easily end up saying more than it makes sense to say. Here is an analogy: when we assign numbers to the players on a team, we are using only a few of the properties of numbers and disregarding the rest.[12] If Mary is player number 6 to Jim's number 12, she may precede him in the order of playing, but she is neither half of him nor divisible by two, and so on.

Think how finely the language of beliefs, desires, and intentions allows us to home in on another's Intentional states and the behavior we describe in terms of them. We can distinguish between, for example, my wanting to hold the book that Robert Redford just held, the book that is a copy of *Pride and Prejudice,* the book that entertained my brother in the hospital, the book my sister grabbed from me, the book on which I spent my last dollar, the book with the shiny red cover, and so on. Though these may all be descriptions of the very same object, they are not necessarily all true descriptions of my *wanting.*[13] And this suggests one of the ways in which a description of a mental state or an action that is at first ambiguous and open to multiple interpretations can in theory, at least, be rendered increasingly both more precise and more complex as interpretation proceeds.

The situation is different with infants. The baby burrowing into its mother's lap may be described equally well as 'wanting to get back to the womb', 'to scoop out the mother's "good" insides', 'to feel safe', 'to take the place of its sibling', and so on; and there is nothing to rule any of these interpretations out. The analyst may reply: 'But the burrowing infant wants all these things; its wants are over-determined and ambiguous'. Notice, however, that the ambiguity, say, of Shelley's intentions in writing "Adonais," or of a line of his poetry, or of a pun or a 'slip of the tongue', is typically a matter not of some intrinsic indeterminacy of meaning but either of a multiplicity of meanings, or of the fact that literal meaning is being used in a way which cannot itself be fully captured in words.[14] (Wittgenstein is said to have abandoned the picture theory of language when a friend made the Neapolitan gesture of brushing his chin with his fingertips and asked: 'What is the logical form of that?' [Monk, 1990, p. 261].)[15]

Or when we say that the Rat Man (Freud, 1909), inspecting his naked body in the mirror, wants to reassure himself that he is physically intact, to defy his father whose presence the man phantasizes, to give himself sexual pleasure, to show his father how much better endowed he himself is, and so on, each description calls for a somewhat different line of defense. All may be true, but all need not be, since they are not simply different ways of accounting for the same phenomena. If we then say that the Rat Man's intentions in performing this action are ambiguous, we mean that he has consciously or unconsciously in mind a multiplicity of different meanings, and that each of our interpretations is supportable (and falsifiable) in detail. But again this may not be true of rival interpretations of the baby's behavior.

I suspect some infant theorists of mistaking what are essentially limits in our mentalistic descriptions of infant behavior for an inherent fuzziness in the thoughts we attribute to them. But if we want to posit a psychological continuum, we might think of it this way: At the near or infant end is behavior for which there will be a great number of equally 'accurate' psychological descriptions between which there is nothing to choose; from there on, behavior which is interpretable in ways that are increasingly precise; and at the far or adult end, behavior which can in principle be given a highly articulate description, one incompatible with other descriptions, at the same time as it may be exceedingly complex. The reason for drawing a line between animal intelligence and the fully mental would then be that at some level of complexity new terms begin fully to apply (see the discussion of 'emergent properties' in Polanyi [1958]).

It is important to keep in mind in this context that the analyst's speculation about her patient's early mental 'representations' relies almost entirely on his post-verbal phantasies and behavior. This is not to say that the adult's phantasy of castration, for example, is radically discontinuous with things that went on with him as a pre-verbal child. Long before we have reason to credit them with a network of concepts, children are acquiring fears, habits, styles of interpersonal relating, that are part of the causal history of their later thoughts. But we would want to try to spell out the continuity in terms appropriate to what that child might have been doing, experiencing, and learning at the time.

What, then, should we make of all the clinical data that suggest the recalling of very early phantasies? Lewin (1950), for example, claims that the idea of an oral trend—the wish to devour, the wish to be devoured, and the wish to sleep—together with its links to many of the phobias, can be repeatedly confirmed in analytic patients, that is, in individuals expressing their wishes and fears in the form of symbolic representation. If infants are unable to represent their oral experiences in this way, then how and when does this oral trend come about? And what is the relation between these 'later' symbolic forms, and experiences that occur during the 'oral' phase (the first twelve to eighteen months)?

Lichtenberg's suggestion is that very early experiences which are not coded symbolically may yet "cast their shadow," becoming embedded in modes of interacting with the world that can be activated even in adulthood.

> The toddler of about 18 to 24 months is in a position similar to Pirandello's six characters in search of an author: The infant has memories, affects, organized states (with transitions between them), preferences, and complex interactional patterns, all in search of a form of symbolic representation. (1983, pp. 168–169)[16]

Our talk about pre-verbal phantasies is then our mentalistic way of describing these increasingly complex modes of early interaction, and all the learning of which they are a part.

A last word on phantasy before I take it up again in later chapters: Susan Isaacs calls phantasies the psychical representatives of instinct of which Freud spoke, and she comments:

> Experience has already proved that throughout every aspect of mental (no less than of physical) development . . . any given phase develops by degrees out of preceding phases . . . This general fact of genetic continuity [has] a specific bearing upon an important question: are phantasies active in the child at the time when the relevant impulses first dominate his behavior and his experience, or do these become so only in retrospect, when later on he can put his experience into words? The evidence clearly suggests that phantasies are active along with the impulses from which they arise. (1952, pp. 74–75)

Isaacs says that these phantasies are not reducible to impulses; they are *mental accompaniments* of impulses. She notes, however, that "in attempting to give . . . examples of specific phantasies we are naturally obliged to put them into words . . . This is clearly not their original character and inevitably introduces a foreign element" (p. 84).

The argument rests on shaky ground. Every organism must have all the genetic equipment it needs for whatever functions it develops. In this trivial sense, genetic continuity is a "fact." But the equipment is only the necessary condition, as having a body is a necessary but not a sufficient condition for mind.[17] The ovaries of a female infant have all the eggs they will ever have; but the infant is not yet able to reproduce. The child that will learn to speak must be wired for speech; but it cannot speak prior to its communications with others. And depending on how hard one wants to press the concept of thought, prior to such communications it may also not be able to think. Between discriminatory behavior and the mental, something crucial intervenes. That something has to do, I have argued, with the learning of a language. But in line with my earlier suggestion, a more charitable interpretation of the continuity Isaacs is referring to might be this: We use a psychological vocabulary to describe infant striving and learning because it is the best available, and because as the child develops it becomes increasingly apt.

In any case, the fact that the infant will come to have thoughts, phantasies, and desires of very complex kinds means that experience may later acquire a meaning it didn't have at the time. So Freud suggests in saying that childhood traumas operate in "a deferred fashion." Past and present are woven together in the human mind in ways that defy the drawing of any clear line between now and then, the linguistic and the pre-linguistic.

Psychoanalysts have been struck by the fact that widely divergent views about early development all seem equally compatible with observable data, and equally effective in clinical application. In his presidential address to a 1988 meeting of the International Psychoanalytic Association, Robert Wallerstein said that "all our theoretical perspectives . . . are but our chosen explanatory *metaphors*," heuristically useful in making sense of the clinical data. He alludes to articles by Joseph and Anne-Marie Sandler (1983, 1984) that distinguish between "the past unconscious and the present unconscious." The Sandlers write: "It is our firm conviction that so-called 'deep' interpretations [i.e. into the infantile past] can have a good analytic effect only because they provide metaphors that can contain the fantasies and feelings in the second system [i.e. the present unconscious]" (1983, p. 424). Talk about very early infant experiences may capture with poignant accuracy how the adult feels now, or how he thinks he might have felt earlier. It is for us as adults that Winnicott's descriptions, for example, of the infant's earliest anxieties—falling forever, coming apart, being in bits—are so evocative.

We might now extend this point a little, saying that the attribution of thought to babies is itself metaphorical.[18] There are good reasons for such metaphorical talk; for one, projecting our mental lives onto infants allows us to treat them as potential members of the human community, with all its responsibilities and privileges; and treating them so is undoubtedly one of the ways in which we open this community to them. For another: the infant makes his way into the world of concepts, language, communication, the idea of an objective reality, and so thought, only slowly. And surely there is no sudden illumination when body, equipped for thought in all the ways that the human body must be, flashes into mind. The infant doesn't first learn one concept, and then another and another. Nor does he first learn concepts, or about the objective world and the minds of others, or first have a sense of himself, and then master the other things; for all are interdependent. When does the infant have enough of the whole picture for us to say he has a mind? Clearly no tidy answer can be given.

A final reason is that we have, as I have said, no alternative. One way of putting the mind-body problem is to say that we are forced to choose between explanations in which Intention and intentions figure, and those which call on nothing more than causal mechanisms of one sort or another, however complex; for many behaviors elude both grids. Instinct is Freud's weasel word, the courier for negotiating the dark passage between body and mind. If neither 'wish' nor drive/instinct makes it to the border, perhaps it is because there just isn't some third terrain, some third sort of explanation, for which a special vocabulary is appropriate. Understandably, then, Freud vacillates between mentalizing the biological, on the one hand, and reducing the mental to something else, on the other. We will confront this problem again in the next chapter in addressing the explanation of action; again in Chapter 6, "Baby Talk"; and yet again in Chapters 9 and 10, where we will see how uneasily some of the phenomena we call repression fit the available explanatory frames.

3 Mind, Body, and the Question of Psychological Laws

Both from within and beyond the bounds of psychoanalysis, Freud's insistence that it is a science has been much disputed. Typically the argument has centered around worries that psychoanalysis is essentially an interpretive discipline in which reasons play a key explanatory role, that science demands causes, and that reasons are not causes.

I think it is true that Freudian interpretation depends generally on the everyday reason-explanation model—sometimes called 'folk psychology'—which it then expands in various ways, and that precisely this is one of its strengths. (These are points I will take for granted until I return to them in Chapter 9.) One of the claims of this chapter is that although reason-explanations are causal explanations, nevertheless no psychology which treats mental states *as* mental can be a science in the sense that Freud claimed for psychoanalysis.[1] This qualification, however, is crucial; for my thesis does not free psychoanalysis from the need to support its clinical hypotheses in ways that have been called for by Adolf Grünbaum (1984), and explored by Benjamin Rubinstein (1976) and by Weiss, Sampson, and the Mount Zion Psychotherapy Research Group (1986). Freud's more ambitious hopes are my target. Their interest lies in the way they mesh with a number of larger philosophical issues, among them the nature of psychological explanation and the relations between mind and body. My discussion of these issues will have implications, furthermore, for psychoanalytic metapsychology, for the concepts of agency and freedom, and for Adolf Grünbaum's critique of psychoanalysis.

I Reasons, Causes, and Explaining Actions

There are, in general, two kinds of explanations with which we are familiar. We say that the troops got scurvy *because* they lacked vitamin C; that the crystal shattered because of the cannon blast; that Mary's skin cancer was caused by excessive exposure to sun. Or we say that someone did *x for such-and-such a reason*—John hit the man over the head because he thought he was a robber; Mary collected the twigs because she wanted to build a bird-cage; the Rat Man removed the stone from the road because he believed it might injure his beloved. (All the complexity of that story, as Freud [1909] tells it, qualifies the reasons that explain the man's behavior; it doesn't replace reasons with some other explanatory idea.)

The second is the one we ordinarily use for actions, or behavior we think is intentional. Actions—like tying your shoe, building a bird-cage, practicing an *entrechat*—are an interesting class of phenomena.[2] Brian O'Shaughnessy remarks that we may be "insufficiently surprised at the fact that we ask of an action that is clearly visible, '*What* is he doing?' Such a question lines the action up with portraits, arrows, hieroglyphs, sentences, and in a sense also with mental images and even with thoughts" (1980, p. 18). An action is something done to satisfy a desire, given certain beliefs of the agent about how the world is, about the object of desire, and about how it may be achieved. It is this belief-desire nexus we have in mind when we say that actions, unlike mere twitches, are meaningful.

This sort of explanation that we use for actions understands the behavior in question teleologically. (Though not all teleological explanations are reason-explanations. For example, functional explanations are not.) It has an aim or a purpose, which is specified by the agent's beliefs and desires. If Sam intentionally turned left at Market and Vine, then he desired to do so, and believed that was what he was doing. (Often, as in this case, spelling out the relevant belief is otiose. But that is not always so.) The belief in question need not be of a means-end sort. If I am whistling, it may be in order to catch your attention or to send a signal; but it may be because I just feel like whistling (and think that is what I am doing.)

For obvious reasons, Aristotle called such reasoning 'practical reasoning'; and with some refinements, the model of it he provided continues to serve very well. The implication, however, is not that the agent must know at the time just what desires and beliefs are motivating her, nor that every action is preceded by a conscious piece of deliberation. C. I. Lewis made the point this way:

> If in walking I turn right instead of left at a certain junction, you will attribute
> that motion of my body to me as my act; and so will I. Though it may be that

neither of us could find indication of deliberate decision or explicit prevision or any definite assessment of values in the initiation of it. If you ask me why I took this turn, I shall doubtless reply by indicating an objective which lies in this direction; "This street will take me home." I consider that the course taken was something which I did; and did for the reason assigned; even though from the time I took the turn until you made inquiry I had not thought of the matter at all . . . I took no thought upon alternatives and made no judgment; the process might well be said to have done itself. (1946, p. 7)

The beliefs and desires that make an action intelligible must be available for a retrospective analysis; the agent needn't have gone over them in her mind beforehand.

Interestingly, to say *what* someone did is at the same time to say something about *why* she did it. (This is not usually the case with causal explanations. Describing something as the breaking of the crystal tells us nothing about why it happened.) For the description of an action has conceptual links to statements about the agent's beliefs and desires. If it is true that John is building a bird-cage (rather than a rabbit hutch, or building a bird-cage rather than designing a puzzle, or just 'messing around'), then he must believe he is building a bird-cage, and that must be what he wants to do as well. And these very beliefs and desires begin to explain why he is doing what he is. He may be building a bird-cage because he hopes to win a prize at the State Fair, and that, because he wants to prove he's cleverer than his sister, and so on. Any theory of mind must reckon with the fact that beliefs and desires play at least as important a part in our account of the observable doings of other people as in our first-person accounts.

As for causality, we presume that where a singular causal proposition is true ('On this day, in this park, the lighted match caused the fire'), there must also be a general proposition of the form, 'Whenever *x*, then *y*'. Singular causal relations seem to presuppose the existence of causal laws of which these relations are instances. Just here lies one of Wittgenstein's arguments, persuasive to a generation of English and American philosophers, that reasons are not causes.[3] For things like beliefs and desires, he thought, cannot be formulated in terms of laws:

'Determinism applies to the mind as truly as to physical things' [he imagines someone saying]. This is obscure because when we think of causal laws in physical things we think of *experiments*. We have nothing like this in connexion with feelings and motivation. And yet psychologists want to say: 'There *must* be some law'—although no law has been found. (Freud: 'Do you want to say, gentlemen, that changes in mental phenomena are guided by chance?') Whereas to me the fact that there *aren't* actually any such laws seems important. (1967, p. 42)

This un-lawfulness of reasons is connected with another way in which they seem to differ from causes. The proposition that an action has such and such a cause is a hypothesis, for which a number of experiences are needed as evidence. But if you tell me that your reason for going to San Francisco is to see the ballet, I don't ask you how you know. What makes something a reason, Wittgenstein thought, is just the fact that it can be acknowledged as such. For it is a distinctive feature of mental states like belief and desire that the agent is able to avow them.

He concluded that on this issue, as so often in philosophy, we are misled by grammar. The fact that we use one word, 'why', to inquire after both cause and motive gives rise to the confusion that a motive is a cause of which we are immediately aware, a cause seen or experienced, as it were, from the inside. Freud in particular, treating unconscious motives as both purposes and causes, was a victim of this confusion, Wittgenstein held.[4]

The Wittgensteinian argument apparently challenges psychoanalysis on two fronts. First, if reasons are the sort of thing that are in principle avowable, then the concept of unconscious reasons seems to be in trouble. This is not my primary concern in this chapter. But in brief, my answer is that to say that reasons are the sort of thing we can acknowledge implies nothing about when, or under what conditions. As I noted in Chapter 1, Freud himself held that beliefs and desires are in principle avowable. He insists on the difference between a merely 'intellectual' assent, or arriving at an unconscious belief as a 'likely' possibility, and a full-blooded memory or acknowledgment. As Cioffi says, what Wittgenstein calls Freud's 'confusion' may have shown more "grammatical flair than grammatical muddle" (1969, p. 195). For reasons might be said to constitute causes precisely when the subject can ignore the reasons for his action, yet acknowledge them as his reasons at some point. (Bouveresse [1991] comments that Freud treats reasons as causes in supposing that they can be conjectured by a scientific type of reasoning and confirmed at the end by the agent's acknowledgment; he treats causes as reasons in supposing that causes can be known in the second fashion.)

Wittgenstein was right that one criterion by which we assign a belief or desire to someone is that he avows it. But there is another, the role of beliefs and desires in explaining action. In the typical case, the two criteria come together. My belief that there is coffee in this cup and my wish to have some coffee explain my lifting the cup to my mouth, and of this belief and this desire, also of their motivational force, I am or can easily be fully aware. But sometimes there is a gap. There seems to be no way of explaining Becky's wounding remark without imputing to her an intention to wound, which she denies; no way of accounting for the fact that Graham repeatedly sabotages his own sincere intentions without assuming he has other intentions of which he is unaware. The Cartesian, holding that first-person avowability is the one and only criterion of the mental, digs in his heels; he says that either these two are grossly deceiving themselves, or else they do not have these intentions. The behaviorist digs in his heels, replying that only behavior counts. Freud insists rather that there are two criteria, neither of which we can abandon; and he closes the gap which sometimes opens between them with the concept of unconscious mental states.

The second Wittgensteinian challenge to psychoanalysis is the idea that causes instance laws while reasons do not, not laws, anyway, which are known in the same way. (Compare 'Excessive exposure to sun can cause skin cancer' with 'Someone who desires to cross the road and believes it is possible, will try to cross the road, if he has no countervailing desires'. The latter requires no evidence; and it is trivial.) Wallerstein invoked the reason/cause distinction in a recent address on the subject of psychoanalytic diversity. He describes as hermeneutic "a psychology that is based only on reasons, on the 'why' of behavior, and not at all like a science, which is based on causes, or the 'how' of behavior" (1988, p. 69). Accepting this formulation, psychoanalysts then tend either to claim that in addition to a clinical theory in which reasons figure, psychoanalysis needs also a metapsychological theory; or they abandon hope that psychoanalysis can be a science.

I believe that Wittgenstein's second challenge stands, though not for the reasons that he and others gave and that Wallerstein as well assumes. The difference Wittgenstein marks is not an ontological difference between reasons and causes, or between mental events and physical events, but a difference in the ways in which events are described. Actions are events that have causes as do all other events; but describing an event as an action, in which motives and reasons play an explanatory role, locates the event on a special kind of map. I believe this map is essential to psychoanalytic explanation, and that for reasons that will emerge later it does exclude psychoanalysis from the circle of the 'hard' sciences. First, however, I want to establish that reasons are indeed causes, a position now so widely accepted among philosophers that I will only briefly rehearse first the negative, then the positive arguments.

(1) Beliefs and desires are not events, it is said, but states, or dispositions; and only events can cause events. There is no good reason for thinking so. Even dispositions, for example the fragility of my heirloom crystal, can certainly enter into causal accounts.

(2) The cause of an event, it is held, must be logically distinct from the effect it explains; yet my reasons for an act are not logically distinct from my action, as when the cause is said to be wanting to turn left at Market and Vine and the effect is turning left at Market and Vine. But surely *wanting* to turn left and *turning* left are logically distinct. For better and for worse, the human condition is such that not all our wantings materialize

the object of desire. In any case, not all reasons have this sort of grammatical relation to their effects: wanting to rescue the bird, or noticing that it has struck the pane, causes me to get up and go to the window. It is true that typically in a reason-explanation there will be a carry-over in the description from cause to effect. This is an important fact about such explanation, for our description of something as an *action,* something done intentionally (under some description or other, a qualification I come to in a moment), is constrained by the intentions with which we think it was done; and intentions are described in terms of the effects which the agent envisions. This teleological feature of reason relations doesn't put them beyond the reach of causal relations, however, but specifies the particular kind of causal relations which they are.

(3) If actions have causes, then we are helpless victims, it is thought; agency drops out of the picture. But whether or not I have helplessly done what I did depends on the sorts of causes that moved me, not on whether there were any. Think of the ideally rational case as follows: I want x (or to have x, or to have it be the case that x) above all my other wants; I have taken the trouble to investigate how best to achieve it; and I believe with good reason that I am most likely to achieve it by doing y; and so y is what I will be moved to do. This description of the ideally rational act seems also to be a description of the freely volitional act, one that I do under neither internal compulsion nor external constraint. Some sorts of desires, those we call impulsive, or repressed, or infantile, or somehow split off from the desires and values which represent me best, make inroads on my autonomy. But in general the fact that I do something because I truly want to do it is a good reason for saying that the act is autonomously mine. If so, then reason and freedom are best served, as Spinoza argued, not by an absence of causality, but by a structure of reasons that is the cause of my act. That psychological structure of beliefs and desires which is ideally rational and that psychological structure which causes me to act as I do, will be one and the same.

(4) Reasons not only explain an action; they also sometimes justify it. And this is not the case with the causes that physics or even biology speaks about. This is a genuine difference. But in itself it doesn't argue that reasons are not causes, only, once again, that they are a particular kind of cause, namely one which sometimes justifies.[5]

What's going for the idea that reasons are causes is the fact that reasons do sometimes, but not always, effect the action for which they are reasons. When they do not, it is because we have other reasons by which the first are outweighed or with which they conflict; or circumstances beyond our control interfere; or we do what we have reasons to do, but not because of them. For example: Nathan had reasons for getting to the church on time, and he did, but because he was—coincidentally—kidnapped; not because of his desire, or his reasons. Driving to Corleone's house with the intention of killing him, Giacomo accidentally hit a man who turned out to be Corleone. Giacomo did what he intended to do, but that intention played only a wayward role in the causal story. So to capture the link between one's reasons for doing something, and doing it *because* of them, we need to insist, with common sense, that the 'because' is the ordinary 'because', that reasons can after all be causes.

A reason-explanation explains an action in two ways, both of which are necessary if the explanation is genuine. First, it 'rationalizes' an action in showing how, given a certain desire or end of the agent, and certain beliefs (often implicit) about how that end may be achieved, the action in question 'made sense' or was rational in the light of just those beliefs and desires, even if it was irrational in the light of others. We understand why someone who adores chocolate indulges in a hot fudge sundae, even though that isn't so reasonable a choice given her conflicting desire to lose weight.

Second, the beliefs and desires that explain the action must in fact be among the ones that moved the agent to action; in their absence she would not have so acted. It is this second aspect that requires us to say that the reasons which explain an act must also have caused it. For I might want to give my friend Jane a hard time, and believe that inviting her to dinner with Tom will do it, yet not invite the two of them together *because* of that belief/desire pair. Of course an action may be 'over-determined', in either of two senses. In the first, a multiplicity of belief-desire combinations were together necessary to produce it; in the second, a multiplicity of belief-desire combinations were present, but not all of them were causally efficacious.

Beliefs and desires are not explanatory if they are outweighed by other beliefs and desires of the agent; or if circumstances beyond his control interfere; or if, as in the example about Nathan, though he has done what he had reasons to do, he has not done it *because* of them. Then too the agent may be fooling himself in thinking he has certain beliefs and desires on which he would act 'if only he could'. Or it may be that he had these beliefs and desires, genuinely thinks that he acted because of them, but was in fact moved to action by others, or even by something beyond his control. Wishful thinking may be at work here, but not necessarily; for though the content of my states of mind may be in principle avowable by me, this does not mean that their status as cause also is. In the easy and typical case, a reason is, as Wittgenstein mockingly put it, a cause "seen from the inside." How do I know that I am drinking this cup of coffee because I want to—that it is *because* of my desire for coffee that I am putting the cup to my lips, and so on? I just do. In such easy cases the content of a desire is so wedded to its causal role in behavior that we no more ask how we know about the one than about the other. But this is not so in cases which are more complex. Susan thinks she gave up the ballet because she was told she had a heart condition; but on later reflection she may begin to suspect that the reasons which actually motivated her lay altogether elsewhere. Just this complexity of reasons, incidentally, that they have both an introspective first-personal aspect and also one that is impersonal and explanatory, helps to explain those cases of self-ignorance, even self-delusion, in which the agent is not 'deceived' about the contents of her beliefs and desires, but only about which ones are actually at work, and how, in her actions.

The concept of 'rationalization' in the specifically psychoanalytic sense is appropriate for, among other things, reasons which fail either of these two criteria for a reason-explanation. The reasons the agent gives would show his action to be rational, if they were in fact reasons he holds; but they are not. Or they are reasons he holds, but are not among the causes of his action. The obverse can also happen: A belief may cause an action without rationalizing it in the sense that explanation requires. For example, believing she sees a ghost at the window causes Emma to spill coffee on the rug; desiring to win the race causes John to have a heart attack. Neither of these causes is a reason for what it explains.

Of course only some behavior is intentional. And only some behavior counts as action, something that reveals a person's agency, what he has done rather than what has befallen him. Beliefs and desires are not always part of the explanation of human behavior. Even where they are, and even where I have acted on an intention, what came of my action may not have been something I intended. Something is an action only if it is intentional under some description, as philosophers put it, a description which specifies how the agent saw the action, whether consciously or unconsciously. Furthermore, as we saw earlier, a doing can be intentional under one description, yet not under others that also apply to it. Oedipus intended to hit the stranger at the crossroads (even though he did it without plan and forethought); but he may not have intended to kill him, even though that is what he did. In any case he didn't intend to kill his father, simply because he didn't know it was his father he was hitting. The shots fired at Sarajevo brought on the First World War; but that was not the intention with which they were fired. Turning on the light (intentionally) to look for his glasses, John (unintentionally) surprises his wife in the arms of another man. Intending to play the considerate guest, Janet carries her cup of coffee to Jane's kitchen, (unintentionally) spilling it on Jane's new rug.

Each of these stories reveals somewhat different vicissitudes of action. The first illustrates the fact that what we do has an endless number of true descriptions; and only those which tell us how the agent saw the action, either consciously or unconsciously, are relevant to determining his intentions. If we describe his action as the action of hitting someone, Oedipus meant to do what he did. If we describe it as killing his father, he did not. The second and third stories both inform us that the consequences of our actions far outrun what we intend and often what we might have foreseen; for the world is wider both in time and space than we can at any moment know. All the stories remind us that we are purposive agents who are also subject to accident, nature, chance, and fortune. And all might call for further investigation of a more psychoanalytic kind. Oedipus might not have intended to kill his father, but may have wanted to (unconsciously or consciously). He might have intended to kill his father (at some later time), though might not have known that this was in fact what he was doing. He might not have known it was his father, yet foreseen that such a happening was within the realm of possibility had he taken more thought than he did. John may not have had his wife's whereabouts consciously in mind; but he might nevertheless have heard sounds that awoke his subliminal suspicions. Janet might not have (consciously) intended to spill her coffee on the rug; but she may have had motives for doing so, motives that operated on her in a less than fully intentional way. Law courts and psychoanalytic consulting rooms are rich fields in which to study such ambiguities of intention.

To affirm the causal role of reasons in human behavior of course does not deny the indispensability of the body. Without the requisite neurophysiology, the body's cooperation, and so on, reasons could never take effect. That doesn't mean they play no crucial role in the explanatory story. As Freud writes:

> Anything that is observable in mental life may occasionally be described as a mental phenomenon. The question will then be whether the particular mental phenomenon has arisen immediately from somatic, organic, and material influences—in which case its investigation will not be part of psychology— or whether it is derived in the first instance from other mental processes. (1916–1917 [1915–1917], pp. 60–61)

Perhaps we can gloss the why/how distinction in the earlier quote from Wallerstein this way: If I have done what I did because I thought I was drinking a glass of water and that is what I wanted to do, then these reasons are the 'why'; the 'how' would tell a story about the conditions of my arms, my larynx, my brain. These are not explanations between which we have to choose.

In the *Phaedo*, Socrates makes fun of Anaxagoras for saying that he will explain how the universe is ordered by mind for the best, and then giving a physical account of it.

It seemed to me [Socrates is speaking] . . . as if one should say that Socrates does with intelligence whatever he does, and then, in trying to give the causes of the particular thing I do, should say first that I am now sitting here because my body is composed of bones and sinews . . . Or as if in the same way he should give voice and air and hearing and countless other things of the sort as causes for our talking with each other, and should fail to mention the real causes, which are, that the Athenians decided it was best to condemn me, and therefore I have decided that it was best for me to sit here . . . If anyone were to say that I could not have done what I thought proper if I had not bones and sinews and other things that I have, he would be right. But to say that those things are the cause of my doing what I do, and that I act with intelligence but not from the choice of what is best would be an extremely careless way of talking. (Plato, 1952, 98c–99a)

Here I might note in passing that recent work in cognitive psychology does not have the significance some have claimed for it. Morris Eagle (1980) cites an experiment, for example, in which subjects were asked to choose a piece of clothing from among a number of items. Though their choices showed a clear bias for the item on the right, none of them mentioned position when asked the reasons for this preference. Eagle concludes that the best explanation of the subjects' behavior is not through unconscious motives, but non-motivational terms of external stimuli (for example, the position of an item on a table). He doesn't consider the possibility that people tacitly believe that the object on the right is somehow superior, not unlikely in a culture that, for whatever reasons, assigns honor to the right hand. A more important line of objection asks whether we can without incoherence replace all motivational explanations or reason-explanations with ones that are non-motivational. This is the question of reducibility. As an installment on the answer which is coming, we might notice that if beliefs and desires never played a genuine causal role in human behavior, then the reasons that experimenters offer in explanation for their experiments would be idle; so equally would be the claim that experiments support their conclusions.

The trouble with reason-explanations—the check they impose on psychoanalysis as a science—lies elsewhere than in the reason-cause distinction per se.

II   Interpretation and the Unlawfulness of the Mental

According to Franz Brentano (1924), the mental is defined by "reference to a content" or "directedness" toward objects. Brentano held that mental phenomena differ from physical phenomena in being directed toward a special kind of private, immaterial, mental or 'Intentional' object. This must be the case, he thought, if I can contemplate golden mountains, dream about a debut in Carnegie Hall, lament the loss of Paradise, even though none of these objects or events exists.

In 1956, Chisholm remarked on a characteristic of mental terms that reflects the important facts about them noted by Brentano, but that does not presuppose a peculiar class of mental objects. Chisholm revived the notion of Intentionality to refer to this feature: Whereas typically we can substitute co-referring terms without changing the truth value of a sentence, this is not necessarily so in sentences containing mental predicates. 'Laius', 'the father of Oedipus', and 'the old man with whom Oedipus had an argument at the crossroads' refer to the same person. And if we are interested only in whom Oedipus killed ('to kill' is not a mental predicate), then we can say with equal truth that he killed the king of Thebes, his father, the old man at the crossroads, and so on. But we cannot make these substitutions *salva veritate* in a sentence about whom Oedipus *believed* he killed, or *meant* to kill, or *wanted* to kill, or *felt remorse about having killed*. Such terms are then said to be 'semantically opaque'. If Mary ate (another non-mental verb) a piece of salmon that happened also to be the last piece of salmon, and the very piece John planned to give his starving child, then Mary ate the piece of salmon that John planned to give his starving child.[6] But since she might not have known what she was doing under all these descriptions, it is not necessarily the case that she meant or wanted to eat (or believed she had eaten) the salmon John planned to give his starving child. 'Believe', 'intend' (in the sense in which we speak of doing things intentionally), 'desire', 'hope', 'feel guilty about', 'lament', 'mean' are all mental verbs by this criterion of semantic opacity, in contrast to 'kill', 'eat', 'hit', 'pick up', 'run toward', and so on, which are not mental verbs.

Taking Chisholm's lead, contemporary philosophers are apt now to think of a mental verb as specifying an attitude toward a proposition and as featuring typically in a sentence in which the usual rules of substitution break down. To describe someone's pain we can simply say that her left foot hurts; to describe her states of believing or remembering we have to say she believes or remembers *that p*. (If we don't ordinarily speak of desire or wish as propositional in this way, nevertheless its content too can usually be rendered in a proposition or a set of propositions: Oedipus desires *that the murderer be found, that he be punished,* and so on.) Not all mental verbs fit this scheme; but most do.

Now we can ask about the possibility of psychological laws in this way: First, could there be laws—laws with the same kind and degree of universality as in physics—linking events described in the language of mind to other events so described? Second, could there be laws linking events described in the language of mind to events described as physical? Because of the holistic and essentially normative nature of reason-explanations, I shall answer No to both questions.[7]

Explanations in the physical sciences also invoke norms, the scientist's conception of what is the best explanation—the most warranted, or elegant, or fruitful. But my explaining your action invokes norms in an additional way, since I must assume norms on the part of the thing to be explained, namely you. Like the natural scientist, I am guided by my norms in explaining your action; but as a social scientist I am also guided by the norms I attribute to you, and that I must, when describing what you do as action; for the cogency of a psychological explanation depends on its ability to make sense of the attitude or behavior to be explained, which means, as we have seen, that it must be shown to be reasonable in light of some set of beliefs and desires one attributes to the agent (though of course it may not be reasonable in the light of other beliefs and desires the agent also has). This is the 'principle of charity' invoked in Chapter 1: Your evaluating all those of your beliefs and desires that are relevant to a given decision presumes norms on your part. And my understanding why you do what you do presumes my taking your norms into account. Even a paranoid does what he intentionally does because, given his anxieties, beliefs, and desires, his actions seem to him to be—at least in relation to just those mental attitudes though perhaps not to others—the appropriate or the justified or even the right thing to do.

The following passage reveals that Freud is onto the normative and holistic character of psychological explanation:

> So long as we trace the development from its final outcome backwards, the chain of events appears continuous, and we feel we have gained insight which is completely satisfactory and even exhaustive. But if we proceed to reverse the way, if we start from the premises inferred from the analysis and try to follow these up to the final results, then we no longer get the impression of an inevitable sequence of events which could not have been otherwise determined. We notice at once that there might have been another result, and that we might have been just as well able to understand and explain the latter. The synthesis is thus not so satisfactory as the analysis; in other words, from a knowledge of the premises we could not have foretold the nature of the result.
>
> It is very easy to account for this disturbing state of affairs. Even supposing that we have a complete knowledge of the etiological factors that decide a given result, nevertheless what we know about them is only their quality and not their relative strength. Some of them are suppressed by others because they are too weak, and they therefore do not affect the final result. But we never know beforehand which of the determining factors will prove the weaker or the stronger. We may say at the end that those which have succeeded must have been the stronger. (1920b, pp. 167–168)[8]

'Quality' and 'quantity' are key terms in Freud's early *Project for a Scientific Psychology* in which he proposed to represent "psychical processes as quantitatively determinate states of specifiable material particles" (1950 [1895], p. 295). He hypothesized a division of the neurons into three classes, differentiated according to function. The first two classes were said to be concerned respectively with external and internal stimuli, and to operate on a purely *quantitative* basis. The third was correlated with the *qualitative* differences which individuate conscious ideas and feelings. In the passage quoted above Freud says that we know only the "quality" of the etiological factors and not "their relative strength. Some of them are suppressed by others because they are too weak." This description of the matter neglects the fact that when we are talking psychology, some of the "etiological" factors are beliefs and desires; and determining their strength and quality differs crucially from determining the strength and quality of two viruses, say; for we cannot determine the quality, the content, of a person's beliefs or desires independently of determining their relative strength in the holistic network. This is the idea that, despite the mechanistic talk of the *Project* in the passage quoted earlier, Freud acknowledges. An interpreter arrives at the strength of a belief or desire and its content simultaneously, playing one off against the other, keeping in mind the mental network as a whole and what is going on in the external world. We aim for the best fit between behavior, coherence, and correspondence; for a belief or desire that is senseless in the context of one mental structure may reveal its sense when I see it in the light of another, or when I discover an event in the world that has caused you to think and act as you do.

To be sure, an interpreter can hold constant the meaning of some statements, the content of some beliefs. Suppose that you and I are both speakers of English, and looking out the window you remark that it's raining. If I see that it is, I know without having to think about it that you believe it's raining. Then when you go on to say something puzzling, I am not likely to think I need revise my understanding of this belief of yours. But suppose you tell me that you know your father died, yet you behave (like the Rat Man) as if you believed he were still alive. Or you say that you want above all to be with your mother in Atlanta for Christmas, yet I see you making plans to go to Rome. Now, as your interpreter, I have to do some juggling. And in my juggling I will try to determine how some of your desires win out over others; how some desires win out even over your beliefs (as in repression, or self-deception, or denial). I will be trying to determine which desires are 'stronger', and the relative 'strengths' of your commitment to the truth, for example, versus your need (wish) to escape into phantasy; and so on. Assessment of the content of one thought or desire is inseparable from that of others; and assessment of content is inseparable from determining which ones win out, and how.

The upshot of all this is that while we can often close in on a description of behavior well enough for all practical purposes, there is no point at which we might legitimately say, 'Nothing more we could learn would affect our description of what the agent has done'. This is why there can be no hard-and-fast laws linking mental states and events to other mental states and events, laws of the sort 'Given a desire x and the belief that y is the way to achieve it, an agent will attempt to do y'. Laws can be at best probabilistic, for example, 'When insulted, a person is likely to feel hurt' (Rubinstein, 1976). Nor can there be some more complex predictive law, since in my search for a cogent explanation there is in principle no end to the adjustments in interpretation I will be prepared to make. This is why explanation of human behavior is *ex post facto* and not in any stringent way predictive.

Summarizing some of Robert Waelder's conclusions on the role of prediction in psychoanalysis, Wallerstein writes:

> The existence of regularities in nature is after all but one of the conditions necessary to prediction; others are the awareness of the regularities, and the having in hand information about *all* relevant parameters . . . Waelder then states that this third prerequisite of prediction . . . may be lacking for two different reasons. The first is a practical obstacle: that we do not yet have the techniques for their assessment. The second is a theoretical obstacle: that it "would run counter to what *we believe* are inherent and therefore unalterable limits of observation, as in the case of the impossibility of measuring both the location and the impulse of an electron with an accuracy greater than that indicated by the Heisenberg uncertainty principle." (1964, p. 677)

The limit to which I am calling attention is neither a practical obstacle of the sort Waelder names, nor an observational limit. It *is* a theoretical difficulty; and it affects psychoanalysis on two fronts: as a clinical theory about the nature and limits of interpretation, and as a general model of the mind.

What about laws linking mental states with physiological states? At this point one might say: 'All right, we'll grant that reasons are a kind of cause; and also that psychological explanations differ from explanations in the physical sciences. But why isn't this a good reason for trying to reduce one kind of explanation to the other, mind to body? Who's to say such a reduction can't be made?' Here are the three things that might be meant by the reducibility of the mental to the physical: (1) that every mental event or state is a material event or state, though the converse is not the case (not every material event or state is mental); (2) that there are laws correlating all the explanations stated in a psychological language with explanations stated in the language of physical science; (3) that science will one day be able to get along without the language of mind altogether.

I believe (1) is true. And this is all we need, by the way, to avoid metaphysical dualism, Descartes' idea that mind and body are distinct substances. But there is a problem already with (2). It is the difference between saying on the one hand that every mental event is identical with some physical event or other—the theory of 'token-token identity'—and on the other, that all mental events of a certain *type* can be correlated with all physical events of a certain type. There are notorious problems with such correlations, and without them we can't make generalizations of the sort science demands. Daniel Dennett argues the point as follows:

> Suppose Mary thinks about *pi* at noon, and the identity theorist claims that Mary's thought is identical with her noontime brain process *p* (having defining physical features F, G, H, . . .). It is not remotely plausible to suppose that every *thought about pi* is a brain process with features F, G, H, . . . , if only because there is no reason to suppose intelligent creatures elsewhere in the universe would need to share our neurophysiology or even our biochemistry in order to think about *pi*. It is not even plausible that every *human thought about pi,* or even every *thought of Mary's about pi* is identical with a brain process falling into a class specifiable solely in terms of the physical features of its members. (1978, p. 253)

For such reasons most philosophers think that token-token identity is the best sort of mind-body identity theory we can have.

We can now take up Wittgenstein's principal objection to the idea that reasons are causes. Recall his claim that where two events have a causal relation, there must be a general law of which this particular relation is an instance. We have just denied the existence of laws linking events described as mental and as physical. Do we then deny that actions fall under causal laws? As agents, are we, though part of the natural world, yet somehow exempt from the lawfulness which governs it? And what about the reasons themselves, those reasons that are causes? Mustn't they also instance causal laws?

Earlier I suggested that the answer has to do with the difference between describing an event as merely a physical event and as an action, also between causal relations and causal laws.[9] As a relation between individual events, causality holds no matter how these events are described. If Oedipus' action at the crossroads caused the death of an old man, and that man happened to be Laius, and the father of Oedipus, and the king of Thebes, then whether he meant to or not, Oedipus caused the death of his father and the king of Thebes. As Davidson puts it, "The principle of causal interaction deals with events in extension [what a term in fact picks out] and is therefore blind to the mental-physical dichotomy" (1980, p. 215).

But something is an action only under a certain description; so also causal laws hold between events under certain descriptions, as instances of floods, or famines, or decisions. Laws are linguistic affairs; they typically relate statements. And it is the possibility of laws linking Intentional states to other Intentional states, or Intentional states to physical events, that we deny. Davidson continues: "The principle of the nomological [lawful] character of causality must be read carefully; it says that when events are related as cause and effect, they have descriptions that instantiate a law. It does not say that every true singular statement of causality instantiates a law" (1980, p. 215). The famine in Bangladesh may have been caused by the flood. But the laws backing that causal connection may have to do with the conditions under which crops and people flourish, rather than directly with floods and famines. And the laws that lie behind reason-explanations may have to do with neurophysiology; for example: 'Whenever nerve reflexes x and y are in such-and-such a state, a movement z (all other things being equal) will follow'; but not 'Whenever a creature's nerve reflexes x and y are in such-and-such a state, it will try to commit a murder', or tell a lie, or feel remorse, or *believe* or *want* or *intend* z. (Of course there might be laws of the following trivial sort: 'Whenever someone intends to do x, then he will do x, his body and the world willing', since to say that someone intends to do something is exactly to say that he will do it if nothing interferes.)

So far our opposition to the claim that psychology can be a science on the order of physics, or even biology, has turned on the nature of folk-psychological explanation. So now that claim might shift ground, contending that folk psychology is just, as Freud thought, a temporary expedient which can be gotten rid of without loss someday.

Loss of what, to whom? The obvious answer is: of everything that interests us as persons, as members of a world in which marrying, feeling guilty, promising, disavowing and repressing, committing murder, joining the baseball team, believing that the earth is round, and so on, have the importance they do. These are the things we want to understand about our enemies and friends; and such a project necessarily invokes mental states like beliefs, desires, and intentions. For as we saw earlier, even to describe an act as promising or joining the baseball team we have to use the language of beliefs and desires. Of actions it is both explanatory and constitutive. If our interest is in what Oedipus meant to do, or what Maisie knew, or what Little Hans saw, then nothing but the language of mind will satisfy. Reductionists refer disparagingly to reason-explanations as 'folk psychology'. But if reduction isn't possible, then folk psychology is the best we can do, and good enough. Now if we put this together with what else we've said about psychological explanation, the implication is that we might have laws predicting all the events in the universe, physically described, yet not know how to predict them once they are cast in the language of mind.

This needn't be so bad. I can understand why you want to go to Paris, even be able to predict rather reliably, under some conditions, whether you will, without being able to cite some general law of which this is an instance. There are rough-and-ready laws on which we rely all the time: if I think you are signaling because you want to turn right at the corner and there is no obvious reason why you can't, I will expect you to move to the right of the road. I do this only on the basis of implicit, often very ready inductive generalizations, in this case relating arm movements in specific kinds of situations to behavior. This is prediction of a boringly simple sort. But we also make more complex predictions all the time, and must in order to judge how to behave ourselves. The psychoanalyst asks herself things like, 'Why is John suddenly so silent?' Speculating that John is angry about her imminent departure, she then tries to put together what else she knows about John so as to decide on her own best strategy. The psychoanalyst can also arrive at rough predictions about how a child raised in such-and-such a way is likely to behave in certain circumstances, and so on. And certainly psychoanalytic interpretations and hypotheses, whether about how children develop or about why someone acted as he did, are empirical, requiring validation and evidence.

So here is where we are: mental states are supervenient on physical states; for every mind there must be a brain, though the reverse is not true. And every mental state is a material state, though not merely so; for what makes a particular mental state count as a state of hoping to meet Sarah, or intending to eat the salmon, is not anything that might be smoothly mapped onto physical events *described as such*. Some physiological state *A* correlates with the belief, 'Sarah will be at the corner of Market and Vine'. But *A* may not hook up with other physiological states in ways that reflect either the holism of the mental or its anchor in the external world. Davidson's name for this view, 'anomalous monism', aptly summarizes its essential theses: Cartesian metaphysical dualism is wrong, for reality is one; yet Mind and Body articulate one and the same realm of material processes and events in different and irreducible languages that may never mesh, with the result that no system of causal laws can capture psychological states.

Wittgenstein was right that reasons and actions, described as such, do not institute causal laws of any interesting generality, whether these are laws relating mental events to each other or to physical events. He may also have been right that if *x* causes *y*, then it instances a generalization; but the generalization—we have said—will position *x* and *y* in the language of body.

Something like this may be what Benjamin Rubinstein has in mind in distinguishing talk about persons considered as organisms on the one hand, and as residents of our ordinary human world, on the other. In the case of colors, he says, we require special instruments to discover that a red object in our ordinary world is an object that reflects wavelengths of a certain length. "In the case of a person, on the other hand, we do not need particular instruments to discover that he is also an organism. What we require is merely a different way of looking at him, namely, the way we look at things from the point of view of natural science" (1976, p. 251).

Here is an analogy: every painting is entirely composed of material bits of pigment in a certain spatial arrangement on a material surface. But we wouldn't expect a knowledge of chemistry to yield information about whether or not the painting is graceful, or original, or even about its representational content. Or another: a written presentation of an argument in physics, say, consists of molecules on paper. But knowing their chemical constitution won't tell us how sound the argument is.

So long as psychoanalysis hopes to understand human actions, it will always be, and must be, an interpretive discipline. It will attempt to find out what we have meant by what we have said, what obscure desires, what strange beliefs—yet beliefs and desires for all that—give both cause and sense, or reason for, our more-or-less intentional doings. The so-called hermeneuticists are wrong in saying that interpretations do not uncover links that are causal in nature; but they are right in insisting that our explanations of actions are interpretations, and that as such they can be incorporated only in a 'softer' science than physics.

One of the things that psychoanalysis means in calling itself a science is that analyst and patient may make genuine discoveries about how the patient sees things, what she wants, phantasizes, believes, remembers, and so on, consciously *and* unconsciously. Nothing I have said here throws this into doubt. In fact, the view of meaning on which I am relying strengthens this idea; for it says that the very possibility of one person's interpreting another rests on the fact that they share norms, many beliefs and desires, and a material world in common. Interpretation is not 'subjective' in a sense that leaves truth up for grabs, or that makes it merely a matter of one person's opinion, or that potentially places all narratives on an equal footing. If 'objectivity' describes what is in the public domain and intelligible according to norms that are also public, then human thought and behavior can be understood only on the assumption that they, together with our interpretations of them, are objective in this sense.

III   Implications for Metapsychology

None of this answers the question: Does psychoanalysis need a metapsychology? (See Klein, 1976; Gill, 1976; Rubinstein, 1976; Holt, 1989.) And if so, in what vocabulary should it be couched? Freud used metapsychology to raise a large and important group of questions, including the following: Is repression an intentional process? Once a thought or memory is repressed, how does it manifest itself in the person's mind and behavior thereafter? In what sense are the so-called 'mechanisms' of defense 'mechanisms'? Are unconscious contents organized differently from those which are readily conscious? How are events in a pre-verbal infant's life recorded in memory, and how do they affect the behavioral patterns the infant is developing?[10]

It may well be that, as Gedo has argued (1979), psychoanalysis requires explanations running the gamut from a language of full-fledged intentions at one end, to talk of neurophysiology and pre-intentional behavior at the other. The distinction between mechanism and intentionality may well be one of degree. 'Repression', for example, may sometimes refer to an act that is fully intentional, sometimes to one that is mental but less than fully intentional, and sometimes to behavior that takes place entirely below the level of introspectible beliefs and desires. As for the infant, even though his early experiences cannot be rendered in a mental language of belief, desire, and phantasy, they may nevertheless play an important role in later development, as may behavioral dispositions acquired in infancy. So this amounts to a minimal plea for pluralism.

However, there are clear and negative implications for Freudian instinct or drive theory, the form that metapsychology most characteristically takes. Consider it in its most general form, as the claim that all human motivation arises from an underlying state of excitation. In attempting to say something more specific about what this excitation is, Freud always postulates two groups of instincts. In his first instinct theory (1905) they are ego-preservative and sexual instincts; in the revised theory (1920a) they are life instincts and death instincts. Most of the analysts who remain faithful to drive theory tend now to think of the two groups of instincts as sexuality and aggression.

The *Standard Edition* translates both Freud's *Trieb* and his *Instinkt* as 'instinct'. A number of writers, however, insist on the distinction between instinct and drive, and on the value of the latter concept:

> An instinct is an innate capacity or necessity to react to a particular set of stimuli in a stereotyped or constant way . . . What we call a drive in man, on the other hand, does not include the motor response but only the state of central excitation in response to stimulation. The motor activity which follows this state of excitation is mediated by [the] 'ego' . . . which permits the possibility that the response to the state of excitation that constitutes drive or instinctual tension will be modified by experience and reflection. (Brenner, 1957, pp. 17–18)

But this qualification doesn't make the instinct/drive theory more useful; it rather suggests what is wrong with it. For that 'mediation' which 'the ego' allows is precisely the 'mediation' of beliefs and desires. Consider the claim that all human behavior is driven by "a state of excitation." If true, it is trivial. It is trivial in the sense that a desire, one might say, just is a state of excitation. As an un-trivial claim it amounts to the following: (1) All human behavior is in principle—though not in practice yet—explicable in terms of brain functioning. This is false, if the mental is irreducible to the physical. Or, (2) All human motivation is derived, and derivable, from two kinds of innate responses to stimuli (according to a dualistic theory). This also rests on the reducibility of mind to body (plus a good number of other highly implausible assumptions). Surely it is the case that all motivation has a neurophysiological component. Surely also this neurophysiology, together, perhaps, with things like behavior conditioning, is all that is required to explain some human behaviors. For many others, however, the bodily, described as bodily, is insufficient.

Drive theory is in trouble in other ways. For one, to the extent that it contains propositions which are empirically testable (for example: that the nervous system is passive and functions only when stimulated from outside itself, or that all stimulation is inherently noxious), it has been disconfirmed (Holt, 1976). For another, what is supposed to differentiate drives from other less primary motivations is that (a) drives are universal in all human creatures and (b) they have an innate component. But drive theory does not countenance all such innately determined behavior as the expression of a drive, for example, the needs for stimulation, warmth, and human contact of various sorts (Bowlby, 1969; Harlow and Harlow, 1962). Call all this the life instinct and 'drive' becomes so general as to lack content. Call the needs for human contact the 'sexual instinct' and the difference between a drive theory and an object relations theory is lost.

Brenner says, "It cannot be emphasized too strongly that the division of drives that we use is based on clinical grounds and will stand or fall on those grounds alone" (1957, p. 22). A great number of facts about human motivation have been observed by clinicians who adhere to drive theory, and any challenge to it will of course want to preserve these facts. One of them is that sex and aggression play an even larger role in human behavior than we had thought, often showing up in unexpected garbs and places. This is the important truth that drive theory encodes, and psychoanalysts rightly insist that it not be minimized. But to defend the view that every desire is 'really' either sexual or aggressive would require some extra-clinical, a priori assumption about what desires 'really' are.[11]

IV   Schafer's Concept of Agency

The discussion of action leads directly to the concept of agency, of what sorts of things human agents are responsible for and in what sense.

What one means to do is a function of what one knows, or believes. We interact with the world, and what we have been calling actions are among such interactions. But the world in which we act is the world as seen by us under certain descriptions. (This is one of the important truths behind the psychoanalytic notion of 'psychic reality'.) Since an action is something done with an intention, which is a mental term, the linguistic behavior of 'action' is like that of belief and desire. And since responsibility is assigned on the basis (partly) of what actions we have done, responsibility too is partly a matter of what we thought we were doing. One can intend to kill someone—and so be guilty, perhaps, of murder—yet not intend to kill one's father—and so be morally innocent of parricide. One can want to kill one's father—consciously or unconsciously—yet not intend to, even while doing so in fact (if one mistakes one's father for someone else, or doesn't know it is one's father).

Two senses of 'intentional' have figured in this chapter. In the first, 'intentional' means 'purposive' in a strong sense of that word. In the second, Intentionality is the defining feature of the mental. A memory, a hope, a belief are all Intentional states in this second sense. There is a connection between the two senses. It is this: in the sense in which we say that someone *intentionally* hurt someone's feelings, or said (with unconscious design) 'I hereby declare the meeting closed', or did something not merely purposeful (a chicken's crossing the road may count as that) but *on purpose*, intention is a purpose of a specific kind, one constituted of an interlocking belief and desire. It is intention that distinguishes action from mere behavior, my raising my arm from my arm's (helplessly) rising (as it might if I suffered some disease), a 'Freudian' slip of the tongue from a mere neurological disturbance. Intentional behavior is goal-seeking behavior of a kind to be explained in terms of beliefs and desires. So intentions are a function of Intentionality.

This is an important point because there is a weak sense of 'purpose' according to which any biologically adaptive behavior is purposive, a cat's yawn as well as the Rat Man's attempt at undoing. Not everything which is purposive is done *on purpose*. Furthermore, many things that we do which are intentional under some description are not intentional under others. (Your marrying the widowed Queen and your marrying your mother may be one and the same act; and both are your doing. But only under one of these descriptions is it something you intended to do, if you are Oedipus.) And a great many living things—worms and neonates among them—to which we wouldn't want to attribute either kind of intention can be said to be goal-seeking or purposive in some weak and general sense.

One of the most momentous discoveries of psychoanalysis is that far more behavior than we had thought is expressive of intentions in both senses. What we had insouciantly attributed to a malfunction of memory or vision, to happenstance or constitutional inadequacy, we now often acknowledge as purposeful, if not fully intentional. The psychoanalyst may rightly suggest we will learn more by assuming that behavior has a specific goal than that it doesn't, and that no categories of human behavior can be ruled out in advance as immune to his professional curiosity. But it is easy to slip—as Freud often does—from talking about behavior as purposive in the weak sense, or as adaptive, or as serving a function of the species or the organism, to talking about it as purposive in the strong sense.[12]

Some years ago Roy Schafer proposed what he called "a new language for psychoanalysis." Its fundamental rule was to "regard each psychological process, event, experience, or behavior . . . as some kind of activity, henceforth to be called action" (1976, p. 9). He then defined action as "human behavior that has a point; it is meaningful human activity; it is intentional or goal-directed performance by people; it is doing things for reasons" (p. 139).

The proposal, like some others in recent years, was motivated by the idea that Freud's mechanistic vocabulary has little to do with what goes on in the consulting room, and that an important part of the therapeutic task, furthermore, is getting the patient to take responsibility for her behavior. Schafer's proposal neglects, however, the differences between activity and action, purpose in the weak sense and intention. It neglects also the important connection between intention and Intention. Schafer writes:

> For Brentano (1874), intentionality was a way of defining mental phenomena as distinct from physical phenomena. It is not a casual [causal?] framework for explaining actions in general; it is a priori or definitional rather than empirical. The project of discovering the motive of an action, which has been an essential aspect of psychoanalysis as an empirical psychology, can have little to do with this established sense of intentionality. (p. 200)

But it is Intentionality as the distinguishing mark of the mental that allows us to speak of "doing things for reasons." How does the agent see what he is doing, or under what description? What did Oedipus think was happening at those crossroads? Did he see the man he killed as a threat to his life? As an impediment to his will? As a stranger? As his father? All of these? None? How we answer these questions bears on how we describe what Oedipus did.

Schafer goes on to say:

> Unreflective action does not lose the name of action. Consequently, attribution of responsibility may be carried out on the basis of whether one has done the action or on the basis of how one has done the action, or both. How includes the notions 'deliberately', 'impulsively', 'accidentally', 'vengefully' and so forth, and thus takes in situations and reasons or the 'why' of the

action. Be that as it may, *that* and *how* should not be confused, and, in any case, the decision to waive responsibility is a separate matter to be settled in the terms of personal or societal rules adopted for that purpose. (p. 233)

This skates too fast over the relations between, as he puts it, the *how* of what I've done and the fact *that* I've done it. If we are describing an action in the sense that has been our focus here, then the accuracy of our description varies with the accuracy of the reasons we attribute. Someone may have felled a lion; but he wasn't *going on a lion hunt* unless he wanted to hunt lions and believed that was what he was doing.

V *Grünbaum's Critique of Psychoanalysis*

Grünbaum (1984) has recently taken a number of psychoanalytic theorists to task for insisting that psychoanalysis is not a natural science, and that Freud may have misunderstood his own theory in claiming it was. Against such theorists Grünbaum makes the following arguments (among others).

(1) Freud's mature understanding of what is scientific does not require reduction to the laws of physical science but is based on methodological features. (Grünbaum cites Freud, 1935, pp. 32–33; 1914, p. 77.)

(2) Habermas is mistaken in claiming that explanations in the natural sciences always rely on "context-free" laws of nature and so differ categorically from explanations derived from a patient's narrative.

(3) Observations in any science are theory-laden; so Ricoeur, for example, is mistaken in thinking that the fact that the analyst "interprets" puts his activity beyond the pale of science.[13]

(4) Reasons *are* causes. Furthermore, so Freud himself maintained in claiming that both conscious and unconscious motives qualify as causes (Grünbaum cites Freud, 1909, p. 199; 1910, p. 38). George Klein and Schafer both then contradict Freud himself, the one in saying that psychoanalytic explanations provide reasons rather than causes, the other in denying that unconscious reasons are causes.

Grünbaum is right on all these accounts. Yet the argument I have given here does discern a categorical difference between explanations in the natural sciences on the one hand, and in any science, on the other, which deploys irreducibly mental terms.[14] The difference is rooted in the holistic and normative nature of the mental, not in some spurious distinction between reason and cause, or interpretation and observation.

Grünbaum also criticizes a number of Freud's causal hypotheses on their own ground. Arguing that Freud (rightly) viewed mental states as both reasons and causes, Grünbaum goes on to say that Freud had insufficient evidence for his claims that repression causes symptoms, and that undoing it brings symptom relief. One might reply that the causal connection between repression and symptoms is fundamentally the same—though more complex and less obvious—as that between desire and action, action and belief. If this were so, then no inductive evidence of some special kind would be needed to establish a causal connection in any particular case.

Grünbaum tries to block this response by arguing that repression and symptom-formation cannot be related as reasons to action; for while the reasons that explain an action need not be conscious, in the nature of the case they must be rational. And this implies that if the agent

> who harbors certain repressed aims . . . were made conscious of them, he/she would *believe* his/her neurotic conduct to be a means to their fulfillment and would engage in that maladaptive conduct. For example, on this construal of the psychoanalytic explanation of paranoid comportment, the attribution of such thought and behavior to repressed homosexual impulses would be held to license a subjunctive conditional as follows: If the homosexual feelings *were* conscious, they would combine with [a means-end belief] . . . to yield *motivating* reasons for the agent's paranoia. (1984, p. 79)

But surely the paranoid does not believe even unconsciously—Grünbaum objects—that his delusional conduct is a way of satisfying his homosexual longings. Furthermore, while the explanation presumes that, conscious or unconscious, the homosexual feelings provide reasons for the paranoia, psychoanalytic theory claims on the contrary that their motivating power evaporates as they become conscious.

While I don't think that repression can be understood as a straightforward instance of acting for reasons,[15] nevertheless I see several misunderstandings in Grünbaum's argument. First, the wish that repression and symptom-formation satisfy on Freud's later instinctual model is not itself erotic, but rather the wish not to acknowledge an erotic wish, or to avoid something that makes one anxious. Second, if repression did display the full intentional structure, the repressed aims *would be* rational, from their own point of view: If I thought (consciously or unconsciously) that I might be less anxious if I had a certain belief, I would have a good reason for acquiring it if I could. I would have a reason for being a believer in *x*, though I would not have evidence in the light of which it was reasonable to think *x* true.

Of course since there is a sense in which belief aims at the true (Williams, 1973a), and since believing something because it makes one happy subverts this aim, belief arrived at by the route of pleasure subverts its own nature. In that sense it is irrational. Furthermore, an action might be reasonable from the point of view of one specific desire, but irrational from the point of view of the agent's desires overall. One goal of psychoanalytic insight is to replace reasons for belief that do not warrant it with reasons that do; and desires that are reasonable from only a partial perspective with desires that more of one's self can endorse.

What kind of predictive power do psychoanalytic causal hypotheses have? No more than folk-psychological explanations, but no less. James Hopkins writes:

> Grünbaum himself stresses that we know motives to have a causal role, which he does not claim that we establish by neo-Baconian means: 'If an agent is actually moved to do A by having a certain reason or motive M . . . the agent's having M qualified as being *causally relevant* to what he did, *regardless of whether M is conscious or repressed*' (72). Still, he invokes this same notion, causal relevance, in claiming that a psychoanalytic view that repression is pathological 'lacks the sort of controls that are needed to establish *causal relevance*' (185). So a question arises as to why controls should be required for psychoanalytic but not commonsense judgments on the role of motives. (1988b, pp. 37–38)

We neither expect nor look for 'controls' with respect to our causal hypotheses about motivation. But they are causal nonetheless.

Mere thematic similarity, Grünbaum has argued, is not sufficient to establish a causal connection between one event and another. For example, the similarity that Crusoe finds between marks in the sand and human footprints does not entitle him to infer that he has company on his island. (He must help himself as well to the inductive generalization that such shapes are rarely, if ever, caused by a choreography of sand and air.)[16] This is so. But Grünbaum ignores the special role that thematic similarity plays in ordinary reason-explanations. If you have a desire that is accurately described as 'wanting to cross the road', and it is contravened neither by circumstances in the world nor other desires of yours, I will expect you *to cross the road*. Or working backwards: if you cross the road, and I have reason to think you did so intentionally, then I will assume you wanted *to cross the road*. Actions are identified by the beliefs and desires that motivate them; beliefs and desires are identified, in part, by the actions they cause. And to this extent, wishful thinking, daydreaming, and phantasizing have a logic similar to that of action: If Cinderella daydreams of a handsome prince coming to rescue her, we assume she wishes he might, *and* that the wish has caused the daydream.

Why does 'lifting repression' remove symptoms? Here is a highly schematic answer, based on the extent to which the explanation of neurotic symptoms does resemble reason-explanations. If one is doing x because one wants y, then discovers that one had made some kind of mistake and it isn't really y one wants but z—or that though one does want y, one doesn't want it on the whole, or given what now one sees to be its price in terms of other things one values—then presumably one will no longer do or want to do x.

A neurotic symptom expresses a desire or a wish of which one is unaware either of the content, or of its motivating force in one's behavior. Typically, as well, the desire is left over from an earlier period in one's life when it was more appropriate. Suppose one becomes aware not only of the wish, but also of its inappropriateness to the world as one now understands it. Suppose one sees also that the wish is discordant with others of one's desires which, on reflection, one finds one values more highly. I take this to be the sort of complex and unfolding insight that 'lifting repression' signifies. If so, it would be remarkable if it did not sometimes shift the causal valences of belief and desire, altering behavior along the way.[17]

Freud thought that science demanded causal determinism; and because of his materialist convictions, he thought causal connections were incompatible with choice. But his own behavior as a psychotherapist belied these assumptions. What he hoped to do for his patients was to open a space between infantile wishes and action (or 'acting out'), a space in which those wishes could be considered, overruled by other desires, perhaps revised or left behind altogether. The outcome would be that one's actions would still be 'determined' by desire. But this is a sense of determinism which, rather than being incompatible with cause, requires it.

4 Telling Stories

Is the narrative which emerges from the analytic dialogue a reconstruction of the past, or a new construction in the here-and-now? Do analytic interpretations aim to be true? Or is the analyst hoping merely to construct, as Donald Spence (1982) and others have argued, a kind of internally coherent narrative? In either case, how does this new story effect change? And what, in the dialogue between analyst and patient, is being 'transferred'? Something from the patient's past onto the present? Or merely something now between analyst and patient?[1] The issues here are tangled and complex.

Let's begin by setting the historical stage. Early in his case history of the Wolf Man, Freud (1918 [1914]) recounts a dream of his patient years earlier on Christmas Eve, the eve as well of the child's fourth birthday. He went to bed, then, hoping for many gifts. Though the manifest content of the dream is oddly tranquil—six staring, white wolves, sitting immobile on the branch of a wintry tree—the man recalls having awakened in great terror.

Freud interprets the dream as a highly condensed and disguised allusion to a wish by the patient for sexual intimacy with his father (a 'gift'), which revives a forgotten "memory trace," Freud thinks, of an act of parental intercourse observed by the child at the age of a year and a half. At the time, Freud speculates, the observation had caused the child no anxiety. But by the occasion of the dream he has learned that women are 'castrated', as Freud puts it; so now the wish to be sexually gratified by his father as his mother had been means to be castrated like her as well.

Memory, reinterpreted in the light of subsequent events, becomes part of the fabric of the present wish, coloring it with anxiety. Understandably, the dream causes terror even as it gratifies desire.

On behalf of an imagined skeptic, Freud goes on to suggest that this 'primal scene' is not the content of a genuine memory but of a later phantasy. He remarks that a number of facts support such a view: "And above all there is this one: so far as my experience goes, these scenes from infancy are not reproduced during the treatment as recollections, they are the products of constructions . . . [they] have to be divined—constructed— gradually and laboriously from an aggregate of indications" (1918 [1914], p. 51).

So now we have several possibilities: (1) the primal scene took place when and more or less as Freud says it did; (2) it took place only in the patient's phantasy; (3) it was a phantasy the patient constructed later; (4) it happened neither in fact nor in phantasy but is the analyst's construction entirely.[2] (The Wolf Man never does acknowledge either the memory or the phantasy, a fact that can easily get lost in the course of Freud's discussion.) To this last—dire—possibility Freud responds: "An analyst, indeed, who hears this reproach, will comfort himself by recalling how gradually the construction of this phantasy which he is supposed to have originated came about, and, when all is said and done, how independently of the physician's incentive many points in its development proceeded" (p. 52). But Freud closes the discussion by saying that the verdict is not clear; the evidence is, even for him, inconclusive.

In "Constructions in Analysis" (1937) Freud returns to these problems of history, asking again, first, if the analyst can hope to date accurately what he has unearthed, and second, if he can know whether a 'historical' find is make-believe or memory. In either case, though, it will have to be dealt with seriously, since "*in the world of the neuroses it is psychical reality which is the decisive kind*" (1916–1917 [1915–1917], p. 368).

Now he mentions yet a third problem: though still convinced that it is by the path of 'constructing' the past that health is restored, Freud acknowledges that "if the analysis is carried out correctly, we produce in [the patient] an assured conviction of the truth of the construction which achieves the same therapeutic result as a recaptured memory" (1937, pp. 265–266). Freud doesn't explain why this should be so; but we may presume he is invoking transference. In any case the suggestion seems to be that the truth of an interpretation may not always be essential to its curative power.

One of the most interesting of Freud's discoveries is the 'Nachträglichkeit' (or 'deferred action') that he postulates in the Wolf Man case and elsewhere, that the mind interprets not only the present in terms of the past—this is not news—but also the past in terms of the present. If this is so, then of course there is little hope of constructing a reliable chronology from the patient's remarks alone. The more general implication is that the clinical data of adult psychoanalysis provide a very poor basis for developmental hypotheses.

About the psychoanalytic narrative, Schafer writes:

> It is a story that begins in the middle, which is the present: the beginning is the beginning of the analysis. The present is not the autobiographical present, which at the outset comprises what are called the patient's presenting problems or initial complaints together with some present account of the past . . .
>
> Those traditional developmental accounts, over which analysts have labored so hard, may now be seen in a new light: less as positivistic sets of factual findings about mental development and more as hermeneutically filled-in narrative structures . . . The time is always present. The event is always an ongoing dialogue. (1983, pp. 238–239)

For the reasons Freud himself suggests, this strikes me as both eloquent and right. (The circularity of psychological time is a theme to which, speaking about phantasy and what Freud calls 'acting out', I return in Chapters 9 and 10.) But saying so leaves unanswered a number of questions about the enterprise of interpretation which are lurking in these woods.

Legitimate worries about what we can know of another's experiences and mental states, or for that matter our own, arise in different ways for different sorts of interpreters. The historian knows that reconstructing her subject's intentions is hampered by the often gaping differences in their perspectives and by an absence of much relevant data. The psychoanalyst recognizes, for one thing, that she has imposed on herself constraints of confidentiality that prohibit her from consulting outside sources; for another, that her patient himself often cannot tell present illusion from past event; and for yet another, that she, the psychoanalyst, is in the process, she hopes, of changing the very subject she wants to understand. Finally, literary critics and readers of all kinds know that setting words free from the context of action in which they are normally uttered and understood makes interpretation of any sort of written text difficult. These are all fairly particular worries, some having to do with history, some not.

Now we come to skeptical questions often raised by historians, psychoanalysts, and readers alike, questions provoked not by the nature of history or the phenomena of transference, but addressed to meaning itself. For some post-modernists declare that the notion of a reality in relation to which an utterance may be true is a thing of the past. They say that every interpretation is necessarily a creative act, whose value is independent of the author's intentions, assuming in the first place that there were any.

I want to argue, first, that within the limits imposed by the therapeutic situation itself, the psychoanalyst can arrive at true, objective interpretations of her patient's states of mind: there is no choice to be made between a story that is coherent and one that 'corresponds' to the facts;[3] and further, that the truth counts, both in knowing why the patient behaves as he does and in helping him to change. Then, in section II, I will return to the issue of reasons and causes; for our stories about ourselves need to incorporate causes that are not reasons as well as causes that are. Finally, having argued the case for truth, I want—in section III—to make a modest case for the 'constructivist' position, a case that will go something like this: the analyst is interested in freeing her patients from old and rigid ideas that get in the way of his responding sensitively and with all his available resources to what is happening now. This is sometimes but not always a matter of speaking the literal truth, or unearthing something already there. There is a kind of story in between the true and the tall, a sort of illumination partaking of both creation and discovery.

I Interpretation and Truth

Perhaps some of the things that happen to a person leave no mark. They are not registered at all; or if they are, they are truly not repressed but forgotten. If there are such events, they are of no interest to the psychoanalyst. She wants to know about things that were experienced, whether or not and how they are now remembered; and this interest defines a very general sense in which only *psychic* reality—beliefs, desires, phantasies, memories—counts in explaining human behavior generally.

This sense can easily get confused with another, however, according to which what really happened, and what the person really saw and thought and felt at the time, is said not to matter. Surely this cannot be. A real sexual assault on a child by an adult, for example, has an effect that a merely imagined sexual assault does not. Both the real and the phantasied assault may arouse conflict; but they will not be defended against in just the same ways, and will weave themselves differently into the child's mental network.

The psychoanalyst may never be able decisively to tell genuine memory from defensive distortion, but it is a discrimination to which her interpretive ear must be continually alert. For she knows that often when events are 'forgotten' or mis-remembered there is a psychoanalytically interesting reason: a defensive purpose is being served; some memory or painful self-recognition is being screened. Resistance and repression, Freud always said, go hand in hand. The first is the clue to the other; and though repression may have been a necessary means of defense against trauma at the time, its persistence can be psychologically costly. Truth comes obviously into the picture here in that the intelligibility of the notion of a defensively distorted memory depends on the notion of a memory which is more or less veridical.

So let's now take up some of those general skeptical questions alluded to earlier. The fact that the reality about which psychoanalysts want to discover truth is 'psychic' in the sense defined is not itself problematic. It is as much a fact about someone that she believes (mistakenly, wishfully) that she resembles Ingrid Bergman as that she heard thunder last night; that she phantasized her father's beating her mother as that she (truly) remembers that he did. Clearly a sentence attributing a belief to someone might be true whether or not the belief itself is the product of hallucination, phantasy, or whatever. If we think of reality as that about which truths can be told, then it includes minds as well as bodies; so if minds are nevertheless beyond the reach of truth, it must be for reasons we haven't yet mentioned.

Perhaps one holds that the truth of any proposition is in any case nothing more than its coherence with other propositions. Or one holds that people, in particular, cannot be 'objects of knowledge'. In a passage quoted earlier, Hanly writes as if these assumptions were one and the same, and he links them to the issue of reasons versus causes:

> The ideas of truth as coherence, of the intrinsic indefiniteness of persons as objects of knowledge and of voluntarism, are logically interconnected in the following way: If a person's actions are motivated by reasons which are neither causes nor caused, if a person freely chooses his motives, then his actions become at once immunized against the influence of his past and unpredictable. (1990, p. 376)

In previous chapters I talked about how interpretation must marry coherence and correspondence. Neither by itself is a sufficient constraint on meaning, nor an adequate criterion of truth. Let me briefly summarize the argument.

Coherence comes into interpretation this way: describing someone's action—making a chariot from a pumpkin, murdering his father, recalling or phantasizing an act of parental intercourse—imputes to him certain beliefs and desires; it tells us something about how he sees the world, or "under what description." And the content of any one belief or desire, any one description, is a function of its place in a network of others.

But correspondence comes in as well; for in our encounter with someone we want to understand, we must be able to find a relation between his words and what we can see going on in our common world. If we cannot at some point tie words to a shared material reality, understanding can't get started. This is the fact about interpretation that deconstructivist theories typically deny.

Many thoughts do not have any obvious or direct causal relation to the external world, and for this reason the psychoanalyst may think he can set material reality aside. If so, he neglects the fact that unless we are anthropologists starting from the ground up, our interpretations begin *in medias res*: Freud can take for granted, for example, that his patient the Rat Man knows he lives in a city called Wien in a country called Österreich, that they are speaking German together, that water is wet and the desert dry, that no man lives much more than a century, that birds sing and lions roar, and so on. Freud knows also something about how the man is using the words 'father', 'mirror', 'guilty', 'razor', 'little girl', 'death' (think of all this in German, of course), and so on.

In their attempt to clarify some very basic questions about interpretation, philosophers tend to focus on less problematic cases. This may make their accounts lopsided. Yet the psychoanalyst, faced with speech that is somehow displaced or distorted, is apt to neglect the background against which disfigured speech can be recognized as a form of *speech*, that is, as communicating mental content. A man complains of the nuisance created by "miracled birds," which he says are composed of "the fore-courts of heaven." A woman says that someone is making a hubbub in her stomach.[4] Finding out what they mean comes with tracing lines of sense to other of their utterances that are less puzzling. Freud's genius was to show how, by making adjustments in a familiar model of interpretation, we can fit to it behavior we had thought unintelligible.

The psychoanalyst might reply, 'But even the kinds of things you say I can confidently know about my patients' attitudes often turn out to be wrong'. True. All our certainties about another's mind are provisional, but not all equally so, nor all at the same time. If you had no clues about what I think is the case, you couldn't raise questions about my possible lies, my phantasies, my self-deceptions. You begin by making certain assumptions which may have to be continually revised.

'Nor can I assume', my hypothetical analyst continues, 'that my patient and I inhabit the same world. Oh, perhaps the world out there is the same; but what matters is the world in here. And that often turns out to be very different'. Again, we could never know about these differences unless we could begin with something shared.

Applying the point to historiography: the historian's particular perspective is typically very different—temporally, culturally, psychologically—from that of his subjects. Does this mean that he has no hope of discovering the truth about what they thought, that he is necessarily imposing on them his own perspective, his own conceptual scheme? How are we ever to understand those odd beliefs, Carlo Ginzburg asks about his heretical miller, Menocchio, who told the Inquisition that angels emerged from an original milky chaos? Still, Ginzburg must assume that Menocchio's conceptual scheme is not so alien from Ginzburg's own as to beggar description, since a premise of his investigation is that he can describe at least some of Menocchio's beliefs, namely those that are odd.

Freud worried greatly about Fliess's accusation that he, Freud, was a "thought reader" who read his own mind into the minds of others. Freud was so defensive that even a year later he wrote to Fliess: "In this you came to the limit of your penetration, and take sides against me and tell me that 'the thought-reader merely reads his own thoughts into other people', which deprives my work of all its value. If I am such a one, throw my every-day life [the parapraxis book] unread into the wastepaper basket."[5]

Freud was too quick to see himself damaged by the charge. Of course we know what Fliess may have had in mind, that Freud mistook his own phantasies for his patients'. If so, Freud was cutting the process of interpretation short, a liability to which any interpreter is subject. But in a certain sense, reading one's mind into the mind of another is the right and only way of understanding him. No other light can discover the Intentionality of his behavior. This fact about interpretation is problematic only if we think of a particular mind as more peculiar and more private than it is. Any act of interpretation rests on certain fundamental assumptions only rarely explicit in the mind of the interpreter. About a large realm of human behavior we assume that the agent has her reasons, reasons that would be intelligible to us if we knew enough about the world she lives in and how she saw it. The notion of rationality on which the interpreter relies is his, but not merely his.

What about the matter of meaning indeterminacy, Quine's idea that it is theoretically possible for two different translation manuals to render equally adequate accounts of every sentence in a language? Doesn't this possibility indicate "the intrinsic indeterminateness" of other persons as objects of knowledge, as Hanly has put it? I don't think so. It doesn't really compromise the idea that there are facts of the matter about what is going on in someone's mind, facts that can be discovered and related. Davidson suggests the following analogy: Centigrade and Fahrenheit are equally good ways of measuring temperature. Assigning a number on either scale registers very many different relations, all of which can be precisely captured by both scales. Yet we don't say that therefore how hot or cold it is outside is 'indeterminate'. Just so, though the business of interpretation is far more complex: putting words to a mental state specifies relations between it and others, as well as between these states and the world. There are then an extraordinary number of relations which any two equally good interpretations or translations will have to preserve.

Indeterminacy of meaning or translation does not represent a failure to capture significant distinctions; it marks the fact that certain apparent distinctions are not significant . . . indeterminacy is important only for calling attention to how the interpretation of speech must go hand in hand with the interpretation of action generally, and so with the attribution of desires and beliefs. (Davidson, 1984a, p. 154)

Often two accounts of what someone has done are equally good only because we know so little. Here indeterminacy is a function of our ignorance, not an intrinsic property of interpretation; and typically, as we learn more we see that one interpretation is better. Is it in theory possible that no matter how much we were to learn, two interpretations would do equally well? Yes. But this would mean that the difference between them was now a purely verbal matter. So neither the requirement on interpretation that it be coherent nor the indeterminacy of meaning is a good reason for saying that the psychoanalyst is after something other than 'correspondence' between interpretation and psychic fact, or that he is concerned with 'truth of a particular kind' (Spence, 1982).

Can the analyst decisively distinguish phantasy from memory? Often not; but the reason, I am insisting, isn't some general problem about the possibility of knowing another's mind, or the unavailability of an external world to tell our tales about.

It is the nature of the mind to tell stories. Some go 'Once upon a time in a faraway land there was a wicked witch . . . '; others go 'Because I was angry with him for what he said about Jose, I hit John over the head . . .', or 'I went to Agra to see the Taj Mahal'. Stories of the latter sort are subject to errors of various kinds, including self-deception, but they are not necessarily make-believe; for the explanation of an action links up means and ends, sees present behavior as aimed at fulfilling purposes conceived in the past, looks for contingencies of various sorts that deflected our intentions, and less than explicit purposes that somehow had their way. Yet if it is the literal truth we're after, then these stories must respect the same constraints that govern any psychological account: causal relations between mind and world, interpersonal relations between my mind and other minds, conceptual relations between one thought in my mind and all my other thoughts.

The narrative nature of the mental is intimately connected to Freud's crucial discovery that telling and retelling our stories can free us in certain ways from the past, at the same time bringing present purposes, intentions, actions, and their consequences into greater harmony.

II Reasons, Causes, and the Importance of the Stories We Tell

I have three things in mind. The first has to do with the fact that reasons are only one kind of cause in the working out of our lives; the second with the differences between reasons and other kinds of causes; and the third with the way in which we may be captive to old stories, old reasons.

(1) Even when we do what we mean to do, inevitably our actions also have some consequences that we didn't intend. *Oedipus the King* is the classic example in more ways than one: Oedipus answers the riddle of the sphinx, so saving Thebes from a plague, but unwittingly cursing it anew; the shepherd who saves the infant from death unknowingly prepares his ruin; the messenger who brings the 'good' news that the dead king was not Oedipus' father inadvertently informs Oedipus that he may indeed have married his mother. Sophocles' play continually illumines the way in which our designs on the future are completed by forces beyond our control, as we ourselves are shaped by history in the act of giving it shape. For what then, if anything, was Oedipus responsible?

A superficial reading of the play answers, 'For nothing; it was Fate'; just as a certain approach to the mind-body question blames genes and brains. So let's briefly see what this argument amounts to before taking up more interesting problems. Clearly we are not responsible for our genes and brains, the argument goes; and since these givens are the matter of our doing what we do, it is out of our hands.

My answer is that moral responsibility demands only a causal connection between our behavior, on the one hand, and our beliefs, desires, character, motivations, intentions, and so on, on the other. If the world were such that none of these had any connection whatever with what we do, that our minds were spinning always out of gear with world and body, there would be no such thing as responsibility. Nor would there be if there were no beliefs and desires in the first place. Freedom and responsibility have their sense only within a vocabulary of mind.

Sophocles' play clearly does assume a causal connection between Oedipus' psychological states and his killing of his father. For a start: had Oedipus not fled Corinth—which he did with full intention—and had he not allowed his temper to get the better of him on the road when an old man ordered him out of the way, then he would not have killed his father; or at least not at the time and in the manner that he did.

The more interesting question about Oedipus' freedom has to do with the discrepancy between what he intended and what he accomplished. I noted in an earlier chapter, taking Oedipus as the paradigm case, that actions are intentional only under a description. Under the description 'killing my father' Oedipus' deed at the crossroads was not intentional. Yet kill his father he did, and that because there was something else—smiting the old man who barred his way—which he did intentionally. So while it would be a mistake to hold Oedipus responsible for an act of (intentional) parricide, it would be equally a mistake to describe his killing his father as something which befell him through no will of his own.

What is to be learned from this? What might an Oedipus learn? A just answer would need a detailed reading of the play. Let me assume, what I think is the case, that Sophocles' Oedipus learns something about his own pride, about a certain tendency to overestimate the power of reason and to bully if necessary to have his way, traits that are not necessarily faults but that can cloud judgment. So there is a point to Oedipus' taking responsibility even for what he didn't do intentionally, since it is by coming to see the tendencies of our behavior, to anticipate unwanted consequences of our actions, to discover what causes were at work in us or the world that made things come out in the surprising ways they did, that we become better able to match consequence to intention.

To return now to the historian: What does Ginzburg want to discover? At least two different kinds of things: on the one hand, what was going on in Menocchio's mind, his beliefs, desires, intentions, how he saw the world, or under what descriptions. These are things of which, in principle, Menocchio could have been aware. But on the other hand there are things of which he could not, like the impact on his life of the printing press or the Reformation. For this second sort of thing, the historian's different temporal perspective allows him to see more that is relevant to understanding his subject rather than less, to notice features of his subject's world for which the subject lacked the relevant concepts, or features so pervasive as to be virtually invisible to him. Even so discerning a man as Freud, for example, was not able to conceptualize the prevailing sexism in Europe and America at the turn of the century and its effect on his own attitudes. The historian is a kind of hindsight fortune-teller, seeing the causal role in his subject's life of events beyond his ken.

Michael Baxendall (1985) makes a similar point about art history, though he blurs in doing so just the distinction I am noting:

> Intention is the forward-leaning look of things. It is not a reconstituted historical state of mind, then, but a relation between the object and its circumstances. Some of the voluntary causes I [as critic] adduce may have been implicit in institutions to which the actor unreflectively acquiesced: others may have been dispositions acquired through a history of behaviour in which reflection once but no longer had a part. Genres are often a case of the first and skills are often a case of the second. (p. 42)

Discovering someone's intentions *is* 'reconstituting a historical state of mind'. It attempts to articulate the sorts of things of which an agent was or might have been conscious. But the impact of commercial mathematics on Piero della Francesca's painting, or of the Reformation on Menocchio's heretical behavior, was in neither case part of the agent's intention, nor a force of which he could have been aware.

In this sense the concept of an act is larger than that of intention. Think how many answers there must always be to the question 'What is *x* doing?'

Imagine Thelma, knowingly making a fuss with a man behind the airline ticket counter. She is trying to get him to put her and her family on the plane to Carolina that she has been told is oversold; raising her voice because she thinks otherwise she won't appear forceful enough; attempting to go to her sick father; and so on. All of these are among her conscious intentions, though some are more at the forefront of her mind than others.

She is also, perhaps, behaving as she thinks her mother might have behaved in similar situations; expressing anxiety; embarrassing her children; damaging rather than improving her chances with the ticket agent; providing her husband with the push that will finally carry him out the marital door; starting a small riot among the passengers behind her; and so on. Any or all of these may be descriptions that for one reason or another are not available to her, perhaps because she genuinely does not observe the facts that warrant them. So we are in the realm of causes that are not reasons, effects that are not among those one intends. Yet becoming aware of them can affect her behavior, even what reasons she forms, in the future.

Harry Frankfurt has suggested that just as we distinguish bodily movements which I initiate from those which are mere happenings in my body, so we should distinguish thoughts and passions which I initiate and with which I identify myself, from those which are mine only in "some gross literal sense." Under certain circumstances, why may not a desire "be an event in the history of a person's mind without being that person's desire? Why may not certain mental movements, like certain movements of human bodies, in this sense belong to no one?" (1976, p. 242).

An important difference between the involuntary movements of one's body, on the one hand, and on the other his involuntary pleasures, desires, and thoughts, is this: When he becomes aware of the latter, that awareness itself may change their significance in his psychic life, that is, in the structure of his consciousness as a whole. The disclaimer that some feelings and thoughts are not really 'mine', or no more so than the beating of my heart, is given the lie by the fact that acknowledging something as 'mine' for which I was not responsible in the sense defined by intention may change the person who makes such an acknowledgment, changing his relationship to just such thoughts and feelings. Where before they acted upon him, he may now be in a position to choose whether to act on them or not.

(2) I noted earlier that unlike causes, reasons enter into a network which is rational and normative. Causes are neither good nor bad in relation to the things they effect. But our reasons call for evaluation in various ways. This means that when I cite reasons as the cause of my behavior, I open it to a special kind of inquiry, since it will always be relevant for me to ask whether or not my reasons justify my action in the light of other things I want or value or know.

This is obviously so when one is weighing one set of reasons against another, as in a case of (conscious) conflict: on the one hand Thelma wants to go to Carolina to see her sick father; on the other to greet friends arriving from out of town. It is less obviously so when explaining what we do calls for reasons from a more distant past. Then a slightly different kind of evaluation may be called for. Suppose May has been feeling vaguely hostile to John for some time. She might actually have forgotten the cause of her hostility, or she might have been pinning it on some recent event which, once considered, doesn't seem to account for her feelings and behavior. So, reflecting, she recalls something John did a long time ago, and discovers the source of her hostility there. Now she is in a position to ask herself if she thinks this source justifies her present anger; if her behavior toward John now is consistent with her overall desires and values; if the beliefs and desires that motivated her earlier response are in keeping with her present view of things; if she wants to be the sort of person who acts on motivations like this; and so on.[6]

Note that it is because May interpreted John's behavior in the way she did that it made her angry. So in this sense her beliefs were both cause and reason for the hostility. (This does not imply that 'material reality' as distinct from 'psychic reality' is irrelevant. Her story includes whatever happened to her in fact. And it will be in going over this that she may come to see it differently.) Clearly the stories we tell ourselves about the events of our lives play a critical role in their effects on us now. So may new stories free us from old patterns.[7]

It does not take much redescription to understand Freud's therapeutic goals—undoing the patient's *resistance, bringing repressed material into consciousness, releasing energies that have been inhibited,* allowing them to find *new aims*[8]—in the terms of reason-explanation. Freud is saying that some of our maladies come from a certain fixity of the descriptions under which we see ourselves. Call this fixity 'repeating the past', or 'transferring the past onto the present', or being 'obsessive', or suffering the consequences of 'repression'. Any interpretive strategy that makes available to us descriptions that were unavailable before may be all to the good. Freud wants to open his patient to new ways of seeing himself and the world, so freeing him from behaviors, even passions and motivations, that have previously constricted him.

One understands her own life as a whole in terms of certain critical experiences; one conceives her experiences in terms made available by the way she understands her life as a whole. A change in meaning of any part of this can affect the rest. In this respect Schafer's account of analysis as working in a temporal circle is apt. But Schafer misstates his own point in saying that "the facts are what the analyst makes them out to be" (1983, p. 255).

Speaking for the hermeneutic position, Hanly remarks: "If a person's actions are motivated by reasons which are neither causes nor caused, if a person freely chooses his motives, then his actions become at once immunized against the influence of his past and unpredictable" (1990, p. 376). Reasons *are* causes, and themselves have causes, which are sometimes again reasons: Mary is putting these sticks together in this way because she wants to build a bird-cage; and she wants to build a bird-cage because she wants to best her sister of whom she is envious. (The reasons may also have causes that are not reasons: for example, Sam believes there is a fire next door because there is.)

What would it be to 'freely choose one's motives'? My motive for yelling 'Fire!' is my perception of the fire, plus my wish to alert my friend to emergency action. I choose neither this perception, this belief (that there is a fire), nor this wish. I simply have them and I act. As the story is told so far, there is no 'free choice of one's motives', nor any compulsion either.

But perhaps my 'Fire!' example is unfair: choosing one's motives comes into play only when we have time to deliberate, or when there is a conflict. Susan is envious of Mary's prize, and tempted, she finds, to say something that will tarnish Mary's pleasure. And since this isn't a motive in herself which Susan wishes to honor, she resists and says the generous thing instead. Here a motive is evaluated and rejected. But the rejection is in turn motivated, by the desire or value which, on reflection, Susan finds more pressing, more important. It is the moment of self-awareness, accompanied by reflection, that makes such a choice possible. Now this moment doesn't in turn require a cause, a motive, or a reason; it is simply an aspect of consciousness itself, though things like repression can get in its way.

Hanly goes on to say:

> Present choice determines the meaning of the past and the motives of actions. Psychic life ceases to be sufficiently determinate to be a suitable object for descriptions whose truth resides in their correspondence with an objective state of affairs.
>
> Bound to this view is the hermeneutic, phenomenological, existential, and idealist idea that self-consciousness involves the capacity for self-transcendence. Self-transcendence allows for the abrogation of causality. (p. 376)

This much is true: How I *now* understand events in the past determines what meaning they have for me *now,* and this understanding is open to new influences, including my own acts of reflection. Self-consciousness of the sort that allows one to be aware of the reasons for his reactions and actions and to reflect on them can transform the meaning of an event.

When it does, it may affect one differently. This isn't an abrogation of causality but a making room for new causal connections to come into play.

The nature of meaning, I have said, constrains interpretation in ways that allow us to speak of it both as increasing narrative coherence and as aiming at truth in the more ordinary sense of informing us about the world, the real world. I have so far neglected the peculiarities of the psychoanalyst's interpretive task. Sometimes it resembles the philosopher's, as Wittgenstein thought the philosopher himself a kind of psychoanalyst. Sometimes it resembles the art critic's; sometimes the parent's, or the priest's.

III   Truth and Beyond

Wittgenstein remarked that the philosopher wants to understand something already in plain view which is nevertheless somehow puzzling; this was the similarity he saw between the philosopher and the psychoanalyst. But how can we say something to someone worth hearing—John Wisdom asks—if we don't know anything he doesn't know already?

> Well, of course, there are those who manage this. They say 'You look lovely in that hat' to people who know this already. But under these circumstances the words reveal nothing to the hearer except, possibly, something about the speaker. However, suppose now that someone is trying on a hat. She is studying it in a mirror. There's a pause and then a friend says 'My dear, the Taj Mahal'. Instantly the look of indecision leaves the face in the mirror. All along she has known there was something wrong with the hat, now she sees what it is. And all this happens in spite of the fact that the hat could be seen perfectly clearly and completely. (1953, p. 248)

Of course the woman might look uncomprehendingly at her friend; the metaphor leaves her cold. So the analyst's interpretation may truly fall flat. He may not be able, though, to know immediately whether resistance is at work or not, since such things are revealed only in the ongoing process of interpretation. But resistance is no part of Wisdom's story, and it is his story that raises the question of how to describe what the friend has done. For without stating a fact he has said something that the woman takes as illuminating an object in plain view. He has not stated a fact but spoken metaphorically, in doing so giving shape to his friend's yet vague impressions, allowing her to see something that, once seen, she realizes was there to be seen.

It is tempting to think of a metaphor, as many have, as ellipsis for a set of propositions, ones with a certain sort of meaning. But it seems rather that metaphor works by prompting us to see one thing *as* another, or in a certain light. Think of Wittgenstein's duck-rabbit picture, the picture that can be seen as either a duck or a rabbit. When I say to you 'It's a duck', is my action best described as telling you *that* it's a duck, or even that it's like a duck? No. It's more a matter of calling something to your notice or attention, only a part of which may be propositional in character. If this is so, then for all their illumination metaphors are neither false nor true; their value can no more be rendered in propositions than can a picture's.[9]

So the analyst's insightful remarks may sometimes be more a matter of speaking in metaphor than saying the literal truth, may more resemble the kinds of interpretation a critic gives of a painting or a poem or a piece of music than the kind in which you attempt to discover the literal meaning of my words. There are poor interpretations of a painting, ones that focus exclusively on certain features at the expense of others that are equally important, or, on my view, ones that altogether ignore the artist's intentions. But there is no one right interpretation, and in theory, there are as many good interpretations as observant readers.

Now let's change Wisdom's story slightly. Suppose the lady with the hat tearfully attacks her friend's good will, says defensively that the hat reminds her of one they had both admired in a painting of Monet, yet after a while ruefully acknowledges that what she now sees as a plainly foolish object she had earlier seen as a grand gesture. In fact she realizes that the grandness, no, the grandiosity of the hat was the source both of its appeal to her and her uneasiness in wearing it. Here we have something like resistance, and with it, apparently, the idea of knowledge possessed yet denied.

The solution has two parts. The first is the idea that since the content of a thought is partly constituted by its relations to the network as a whole, an idea just entering it may be relatively indeterminate, in a sense other than that discussed earlier in relation to Quine; for there are many possible connections which will give the idea more content and which take time to be made. The second is the fact that while repression may take the form, as Freud held, of putting a fully formed thought out of consciousness, it need not. One can also find something painful, and avoid thinking about it, without knowing just what makes it painful. (This is an idea I develop in Chapters 8 and 9.) Discovering what this is may be like seeing something familiar in a new light. The Taj Mahal lady may now be able to go on to say, and to see more clearly, what before she had only glimpsed in the hat.

Like the critic, the analyst too gathers up the patient's behavior into themes, or styles, or repetitive patterns; the critic points out, for example, how often the characters in a painting by Manet aren't looking at each other, seem somehow estranged; the analyst tells her patient that he seems often to cast people in the role of an authority which he then tries to evade. This may not be something he *intends* to do in the narrow sense, more a matter of habit and style.

Literary theory has made much in recent years of the response of the reader to the text. It is in part because critics are speaking to readers who are different at different times and places that different critics will want to say, should say, different things about the same text. This in turn is because, or so one might argue, criticism aims to make the best, the most coherent, the most exciting work out of the text for its readers that it can. And this means taking their perspective into account. In a similar way, it will matter how the psychoanalyst's interpretations speak to the imagination of this patient: when an interpretation is made, in just what language, with what feeling. How the interpretation is made matters as much as its intrinsic insightfulness.

Many happenings in the mind are not propositional attitudes at all; they are not reasons, but perceptions, moods, mental images, patterns of salience, illuminations on the road to Damascus, styles of attention, surges of emotion, habits of attending, and so on. But they can play a causal role in our forming the thoughts we do, and in the valence of desire and belief as they enter into the forming of intentions. All these mental happenings are food for thought, and thinking about them may change the beliefs and desires we have. Other persons can play a crucial role in the making of the mind in bringing such happenings to our attention and creating new concepts with which to think about them.

We have so far neglected two quite special things that set the psychoanalyst apart from other historians: the fact that he postulates beliefs and desires that pre-date his patient's history as an articulate creature, and the phenomenon of transference. The psychoanalyst does not merely report on his subject but interacts with her, and relies on that interaction for the construction of his narrative. Let's talk first about this interaction.

In "Remembering, Repeating, and Working Through" (1914), Freud writes:

> We may say that the patient does not *remember* anything of what he has forgotten and repressed, but *acts* it out. He reproduces it not as a memory but as an action; he *repeats* it, without, of course, knowing that he is repeating it.
>
> For instance, the patient does not say that he remembers that he used to be defiant and critical towards his parents' authority; instead, he behaves in that way to the doctor. He does not remember how he came to a helpless and hopeless deadlock in his infantile sexual researches; but he produces a mass of confused dreams and associations, complains that he cannot succeed in anything and asserts that he is fated never to carry through what he undertakes. He does not remember having been intensely ashamed of certain sexual activities and afraid of their being found out; but he makes it clear that he is ashamed of the treatment on which he is now embarked . . .

> [The physician] celebrates it as a triumph for the treatment if he can bring it about that something that the patient wishes to discharge in action is disposed of through the work of remembering. (pp. 150–153)

Freud may be pushing too hard here on the idea of *remembering*, and implicitly on the idea of narrow intentions. One can only remember what he once knew, while the patient may never have known that he was defiant of his parents' authority, and so on. Defiance may have been more a style of behavior that he never noticed, perhaps because he lacked the necessary concepts. But he is in a position now to learn about what goes on in his interpersonal relations by seeing how this particularly observant person, namely the analyst, reacts to him. If the analyst becomes agitated, or worried, or vaguely feels he should be taking care of this patient, or that he is responsible for all the patient's woes, or becomes bored, or begins to see himself as a tyrant, or if his mind begins to wander, it may not be in response to something the patient is doing, either intentionally or unintentionally. But it also may.

The phenomena of transference and counter-transference—Freud discovered—put the analyst in a uniquely privileged position, as historian, as teacher, and as healer. For the patient acts out with him roles, conflicts, and passions elicited only by the most important people in his life, the ones who symbolize early parental figures. The analyst, in turn, accepts and understands this, and encourages in his patient those attitudes that allow what Freud calls 'remembering' to take the place of acting out. Freud suggests what they are in saying that the patient's illness "must no longer seem to him contemptible, but must become an enemy worthy of his mettle, a piece of his personality, which has solid ground for its existence and out of which things of value for his future life have to be derived" (1914, p. 152).

Take the case of the Rat Man. In their fifth session together, Freud explains that the tormenting and apparently senseless feelings of guilt from which his patient suffers must be appropriate only to mental contents of which he is still unconscious. The Rat Man wants to know what guarantees that once its cause is discovered, the tormenting guilt will wear away. He goes on to say himself that self-reproach can only arise from a breach of one's own moral principles, and that a "disintegration of the personality" must be already present.

Freud agrees. But he explains that the contrast between the moral self and the evil self coincides with that between the conscious and the unconscious self: the latter is the infantile, that which has been split off and repressed. The tormenting guilt will wane when the situation that originally evoked it has been discovered; for in the working through of that discovery it will also have become clear that there is no longer the reason for the guilt there was once. It is caused, Freud suggests, by the Rat Man's (repressed) hatred for his father and has its source in childhood. Freud points out that only someone who loved his father would feel guilty about having hostile impulses toward him. And he reminds his patient that wishes and feelings are not full-blown intentions: One can have conflicting wishes, no one of which is by itself an intention; one can in moments, and from the perspective of certain of one's desires, hate the person one also loves.

As Jonathan Lear (1990) has remarked, Freud's own favorite picture of the analyst as scientist leaves out the attitudes we have just seen Freud adopt: a sort of acceptance of his patient that makes possible his self-forgiveness, a new confidence in himself as someone who can escape the prison of the past and who is larger than the passions which terrify him. Lear calls this attitude of the analyst's a kind of love. So encouraged by Freud, the Rat Man begins in the sixth session to assemble memories of childhood incidents, thoughts, and hostile impulses that were not so much repressed as omitted from his 'story'. Now he begins to realize that from an early age he had regarded his father as an impediment to his libidinal wishes. We can imagine that the Rat Man also comes to realize that he is no longer the impotent creature in relation to his father that he once was; and that he no longer need choose between gratifying himself and his father.

In drawing a picture of how the Rat Man might have seen the world as a child, Freud allows him to feel sympathy for that child. But since the world for him is now very different, the picture also allows him a certain distance. The child can come into play. Freud writes:

> The main instrument . . . for curbing the patient's compulsion to repeat and for turning it into a motive for remembering lies in the handling of the transference. We render the compulsion harmless, and indeed useful, by giving it the right to assert itself in a definite field. We admit it into the transference as a playground in which it is allowed to expand . . . The transference thus creates an intermediate region between illness and real life through which the transition from the one to the other is made. (1914, p. 154)

The analytic situation is constructed so as to restrict the expression of 'repressed' impulses to talk; and just for this reason it leaves the patient free to explore them in relative safety. One is also more likely to acknowledge his wishes if he realizes that by themselves they are neither acts of will nor subject to the will. (The Rat Man says at the beginning of the sixth session that he had always believed, and still does, that his parents could guess his thoughts. And it is the Rat Man who acts as if he believed that wishes had the efficacy of deeds.) If someone confuses wishing *a* might happen with making *a* happen, then in his mind denying himself permission to do *a* may be confused with denying to himself *that* (in some moments) he would like to do *a*; 'repression' will be the only 'moral' way out.

Schafer remarks that apropos of the analytic situation "there is no sharp split between subject and object" (1983, p. 255). If this is so, the reason is not some general epistemological condition, but the peculiar relation between psychoanalyst and patient we've been talking about. The 'object' under interpretation in psychoanalysis is not a material object— painting, book, score—which is expressive of the author's intentions, but a person on the way to forming new intentions, new thoughts, new ways of going about things. The psychoanalytic 'object' is the painting already on the canvas *and* the painter still in the act of painting it; the text *and* the author writing the text. Or we could say that where the critic speaks normally *about* the painting and *to* its viewers, the psychoanalyst speaks about his patient's life, to an audience who is also both author and changing patient.

Does the analyst resurrect old experiences, Schafer asks, or rather help his patient to constitute and develop new ones (1983, p. 190)? Surely both. Which brings us back to the Wolf Man's childhood dream. Freud speculates that the child 'remembered' an earlier event in terms of the meanings it could only subsequently acquire. But what about that earlier event itself? Construction or reconstruction? Repression—the patient's— or invention—Freud's?

Serge Viderman (1979) has suggested that some analytic constructions give retrospective significance in the following way: there are very early experiences which never were nor could have been expressed in propositional form. Through his interpretations the analyst 'creates' these experiences in a way that allows them now to be understood. I would put this slightly differently: Many things happen to an infant before it has thoughts in any real sense of that word; causes of all sorts have been operating on him from the beginning, affecting his ways of going about things in ways we can only guess. Over the course of time these causes also helped shape both the content and the style of his beliefs, for example his sharp eye for detail and his myopia for the total picture.

The psychoanalyst may sometimes be called upon to address these sorts of causes as well as his patient's conscious and unconscious reasons, and to help him understand how reasons and causes have interacted. This is how I read Gedo's suggestion that analytic interventions may occasionally have to go beyond interpretation, trying to satisfy basic needs rather than wishes (1979). An organism has needs, but only a psychological organism has wishes; and only such psychological states are up for interpretation. As an infant the patient had needs, say, for a 'holding' environment that would keep stimulation below the level of trauma, needs that were not met. So an adult patient who never learned to handle his own response to over-stimulation, say, nor even to recognize when a situation was likely to have that effect, may need to be taught such skills.

The analogy of parent and language-learning child is both an apt and a misleading model for the aspects of the relation between analyst and patient on which I have focused in the third section of this chapter. The model is misleading because the infant has no thoughts to speak of prior to some fairly systematic communication with other persons. The model is apt because concepts themselves are not discovered, or rediscovered as Plato thought, but forged, typically through dialogue. (I include in dialogue listening to a symphony, looking at a painting, going to the ballet.) The upshot is that the mind is continually in the making, a process in which other persons play an indispensable part.

And just this insight, or this cluster of insights, is what the constructivist position has going for it: that the mind is better conceived as a network of ideas, ever expanding and re-weaving itself, sometimes in response to stories that cast large ranges of the old network in a new light, than as a Cartesian homunculus; that dialogue plays a constitutive role in such re-weaving; and that this dialogue proceeds only some of the time along the way of reasons and of truth.

The Freud many of us love knew all this and was himself among the bearers of the message. It is one of the things we hear in the concepts of transference and counter-transference. But there is another Freud who was under the spell of a very different picture, a metaphysical picture which is difficult to discern behind the following unexceptionable ideas that Freud also held: that the human mind is not exempt from the rule of causality; that the causes that explain human action are typically also reasons; that these causes/reasons often have a history much older than the agent herself acknowledges.

But now Freud attempts to derive history and narrative in general from something prior to history. (Wittgenstein remarked that many of Freud's ideas have the appeal of the mythological, "explanations which say this is all a repetition of something that happened before" [1967, p. 43].) Both the creative and the irrational act are to be understood, Freud says, as expressions of a pre-linguistic, pre-social, pre-historical form of mentality that is unfamiliar with reality, with logic, and with time. Freud calls this original mentality primary process, and he sometimes holds it the basis not only for neurosis and art but also for language and thought in general, hiding even in adults just behind or beneath reason, to surface in symptoms and in dreams. In the realm of primary process are very early memories of the sort Freud postulates in the Wolf Man case, and a primary form of repression which is responsible for the memory's being 'forgotten'. Primary process is ineffable from the point of view of 'secondary' process thought, though not, Freud believed, from that of the psychoanalytic scientist.

I will consider primary process in Chapter 8. For now let me make a rough suggestion, taking a path marked out over a number of essays by Richard Rorty.[10] In his continuing polemic against the ideas that there is some essential human nature, that there could be such a thing as a foundation for knowledge, that there are any simple entities which are the source or guarantors of thought—Platonic Ideas, sense-data, God, mental images—and that are what they are independent of other entities, Rorty has put the early Wittgenstein and the late Heidegger on the wrong side of the fence just drawn, as looking for something 'primordial' (in Heidegger's case), for that which can be shown but not said (in Wittgenstein's), for the hidden or the ineffable at the source of the unhidden and the effable. My suggestion is that it is in part something very like this quest for a primordial unconditioned just beyond the edge of the sayable which drives Freud's archaeology.

Part Two

Thinking about Children

A language owned in the root of the tongue is loved without being the object of love: there is no sense of separateness from it. Do I love my eyeballs? No; but sight is everything. CYNTHIA OZICK

5   Behind the Veil of Language

Do infants have a sense of self? A subjective life? Are they selves? Is there *something that it's like to be* an infant?[1] Feelings about these questions go strong and deep.

The questions—we want to say—are empirical. Of course there are countless empirical questions in the neighborhood, many of which I will discuss in the next chapter. For example: To what extent, and to what things, do infants respond in specific and differentiated ways? (A great many.) Are neonates enclosed in an 'autistic' or 'narcissistic' cocoon, or are they alert to the world around them from the beginning? (Observation overwhelmingly indicates the latter.) Are there behaviors indicating that infants perceive a three-dimensional world? (Yes.) At what age does the infant begin to track an object? (Right away.) When does the infant begin to smile specifically as a social response? (Opinion varies. But surely by the age of two and a half months.) Are the needs to eat and sleep, the urge to eliminate, paradigmatic of the infant state (as psychoanalytic 'drive' theory would have it)? Or does this paradigm neglect a lot of other things that seem to be equally important? (The latter.) How does the infant interact with its mother? With its father? What affects seem to be available to it? How does it respond, and how differently at different ages, to the absence of its mother? To her non-responsiveness? To her intrusiveness? To the absence of its father? And so on.

But the empirical questions get mixed with assumptions that are not empirical and that may affect both what is seen and how it is described.

I   The Question of Infant Subjectivity

In his recent and very interesting *The Interpersonal World of the Infant* (1984), Daniel Stern says it will be one of the basic assumptions of his book that

> some senses of the self do exist long prior to self-awareness and language . . . Self-reflection and language come to work upon these preverbal existential senses of the self and, in so doing, not only reveal their ongoing existence but transform them into new experiences. If we assume that some preverbal senses of the self start to form at birth (if not before), while others require the maturation of later-appearing capacities . . . then we are freed from the partially semantic task of choosing criteria to decide, a priori, when a sense of self *really* begins. (pp. 6–7)

It is clear in this passage that Stern is himself making an a priori decision. No matter. Both he and I are staking out positions in the philosophy of mind. What interests me about his position is how uneasily it fits his own observations: though the picture he draws is thoroughly interpersonal, still he gives it a subjectivist frame. That testifies, I think, to the hold on us of the sorts of subjectivist assumptions I spoke of earlier.

Stern acknowledges that we are not certain what we mean by 'a self'; but it is something like this, he hazards: "the agent of actions, the experiencer of feelings, the maker of intentions, the architect of plans, the transposer of experience into language, the communicator and sharer of personal knowledge" (p. 5). Of course infants do not have intentions, make plans, put their experience into words; nevertheless we can attribute to them

> the sense of agency . . . the sense of physical cohesion . . . the sense of continuity . . . the sense of affectivity . . . the sense of a subjective self that can achieve intersubjectivity with another . . . the sense of transmitting meaning . . . In short, these senses of the self make up the foundation for the subjective experience of social development, normal and abnormal. (pp. 7–8)

The virtue of the locution 'sense of *x*' is its very ambiguity. It suggests, first of all, something of which we are not aware, but might be. So Stern says that normally the adult's senses of herself as "the agent of actions, the experiencer of feelings, the maker of intentions," are, like breathing, out of awareness. Yet we can become aware of them.

Here is the problem I see: When an adult becomes aware of himself as the agent of actions, and so on, he becomes aware of himself as *the one who* told a lie, for example, or knocked over the Steuben glass vase, or moved his left arm. Can the infant also become aware of such things? Presumably not. It has neither the concepts for those actions, nor, more important, a concept of self; so it can have no awareness of itself *as* a self.[2] And if it can't yet be said to mean something by its cries, it's hard to know how it can have a sense of transmitting meaning. In time, of course, it will learn to connect the things it does with the behavior of people around it. This is one of the necessary conditions for its learning how to mean.[3]

The locution 'sense of self' is ambiguous in yet another way: one can have a sense of impending disaster, for example, without the belief that disaster is coming, or any ideas about what its specific nature will be. Here having a sense of *x* is rather like apprehending the world in the color of a certain mood. Yet even though the apprehension cannot itself be fleshed out in terms of specific beliefs, it requires some beliefs as background. 'A sense of impending disaster' for a creature lacking a concept of disaster and some beliefs about disasters and the world could be nothing more than an agitated state.

We might contrast having a sense of *x* with *sensing x*, say the heat of the room or another's agitation. An infant can, I think, sense its mother's anxiety, her love, her anger. We say so because it responds differentially to them. There is good biological reason, furthermore, why an infant would be tuned in to the grosser emotions of the persons on whom its life depends. (Though of course these descriptions for what it senses—*the mother's anxiety, love,* or *anger*—are ours.) Animals are said to be able to feel vibrations deep in the earth that we cannot, and to become nervous just before an earthquake. They sense the quaking of the earth. But to say that they know there is about to be an earthquake or have a sense of an earthquake in the making would be projecting our mental states on them. 'Having a sense of', like 'seeing', 'being aware of', and 'having an experience of', and unlike *sensing,* suggests Intentionality.

When an infant and I are both looking at a red ball, are we seeing the same thing? It depends on how much or how little we want to claim. If a chicken pecks at the ball, or if the baby reaches for it, then we might say they see the ball, meaning there is something there *we* call a ball that they're responding to, or that the retinas of their eyes are receiving ball-like images. (I am using 'see' in a way that is not semantically opaque.)[4] But then do we also want to say that they see the ball that I bought at the dime store, or the ball that I had been looking for all morning? If we are still talking about what in the world provokes their response, or what is going on at the surface of their retinas, the answer will be yes. But this 'Yes' doesn't entitle us to say anything about what the creature in question sees the ball *as,* or how it thinks about it even in a rudimentary way. Seeing *x* as *y* does presume concepts, among them the concept of *y.* Seeing *as* is a mental verb or predicate (and so, as we saw in Chapter 3, the usual rules of substitution break down).

Talk about an experience, or experiencing, often carries with it the Intentionality of experiencing *as,* at the same time as such talk may not want to be committed to whatever Intentionality presumes. Take an experience as rudimentary as pain. The infant *has* pain and is *in* pain. Is it *aware of* having pain, or even aware of *pain?* What is the force of saying so if not to say that it is aware of pain *as* pain, or of itself as in or as having pain? Freud is surely right that the fact of pain, and its lessons to the child about what it means to be a person, separate from other persons, are crucial for the nature of the inner, subjective world that human beings develop. In time the child learns that it can hide its pain, that even when it is not hidden others may be indifferent to it, and that even when they care, they cannot remove pain from the child as they can a scratchy sweater or a pesky dog. If soliloquy is a source of pride, proof of our autonomy and independence of mind, the knowledge of other minds as *other,* which more sharply than most experiences pain brings home, can be a source of such acute distress that the imagination will go to great lengths to deny it. But all this is about the significance of pain for someone who knows she is in pain, a knowledge which the pre-verbal infant doesn't have.

If by attributing to the infant 'awareness of' pain, or a red ball, or its mother's presence, we think we mean more than that the infant has pain and expresses it in its behavior, that it sees the red ball (though not that it sees it *as* red), and that it responds to the presence of its mother in special ways, then Wilfred Sellars offers the following reflection:

> When we picture a child . . . learning his *first* language, we, of course, locate the language learner in a structured logical space in which we are at home. Thus, we conceive of him as a person (or, at least, a potential person) in a world of physical objects, colored, producing sounds, existing in Space and Time. But though it is *we* who are familiar with this logical space, we run the danger . . . of picturing the language learner as having *ab initio* some degree of awareness—"pre-analytic," limited and fragmentary though it may be— of this same logical space. We picture his state as though it were rather like our own when placed in a strange forest on a dark night . . . [we] take for granted that the process of teaching a child to use a language is that of teaching it to discriminate elements with a logical space of particulars, universals, facts, etc. of which it is already undiscriminatingly aware, and to associate these discriminated elements with verbal symbols. (1956, p. 290)

In a similar vein, Rorty remarks: "If we think of the Eye [of the mind] simply turning inward and spotting a raw feel, the whole complex of social institutions and behavioral manifestations which surround reports of such raw feels seems irrelevant" (1979, p. 108). Unless there were such a thing as pain behavior we could never teach a child the meaning of 'toothache'. But it follows from this neither that the pain just is the behavior, nor that the infant 'knows' pain before it has a concept of it.

The mistake that Wittgenstein exposed, Rorty continues, is the idea that we learn what pain is in the second sense by casting language over the first, "clothing our direct acquaintance with special felt, incommunicable qualities in words (thus rendering ourselves forever skeptical about whether the same incommunicable quality is being named when our friends use the same word)." The raw feels may well be a necessary causal antecedent for a knowledge of pain, but no more than that.

> As long as it is thought that the Naturally Given is known through and through simply by being seen by the Inner Eye, it will seem odd to suggest that the behavior and environment which we must know about in order to *use* the word 'pain' in ordinary conversation should have anything to do with what 'pain' means. (1979, pp. 110–111)

The child will come to be able to notice that she has pain and to be aware of pain as pain. When she does, it will be because she will have acquired the concept of pain. At this point the child will be able to let us know about her pain in a variety of ways, one of which is by telling us about it. (If plants could learn to talk, we might call their gentle cringings pain behavior.)

Stern remarks that what we call "the observed infant" is

> a description of capacities that can be observed directly: the ability to move, to smile, to seek novelty, to discriminate the mother's face, to encode memories, and so on. These observations ... reveal little about what the 'felt quality' of lived social experience is like ... As soon as we try to make inferences about [that] ... we are thrown back to our own subjective experience as the main source of inspiration. But that is exactly the domain of the clinical infant. (1984, p. 17)

The passage ends with the demurrer that "a degree of circularity is unavoidable" in the fact that "the subjective life of the adult, as self-narrated, is the main source of inference about the infant's felt quality of social experience." This amounts to an acknowledgment that attributing subjective experiences to an infant is necessarily projecting onto it our own, including, of course, our present phantasies and memories.

If one thought that all imagining of what the world is like for another person is projection, and necessarily so—a view I'll call 'projectivism'— then one might think that projecting one's own mental states onto an infant is just an extension of the same sort of thing. So the argument I am attributing to Stern goes like this: We think ourselves justified in making such projections with adults; more than that, as their potential communicants, friends, and psychoanalysts, we feel it incumbent on us to understand them as best we can. So why not project our states of mind also onto infants?

As a view about how we understand others, I think projectivism is mistaken, a holdover from the Cartesian idea that first one knows one's own mind and then makes guesses about the minds of others. We sometimes speak of empathic identification as a matter of 'putting myself in your place'; but it's a misleading image, suggesting that what I imagine is myself, seeing the world as it looks to you. Instead, I imagine the world from the point of view I think is yours.[5] Using my own beliefs and desires as a base, I try to see where yours differ. (Of course words are not our only medium for knowing the minds of others. Think of what Fred Astaire learns about his partners when he dances with them, or a conductor about the musicians in his orchestra. And long before they can speak, infants are obviously learning an enormous amount about the people around them.) Normal adult empathy presumes a sense of oneself as separate from, so like—not literally one with—the other person. Perhaps the best image for this is dialogue itself: in speaking to you—if I want to be understood—I use words I think you will understand, I talk loudly enough for you to hear me, and in your direction. If I want you to look at something in particular then I point, or gesture in some other way; and so on.

But even if knowing another's mind were aptly described as a kind of projection, whether the infant has subjective states to begin with remains in question. It's one thing to use our own very rich subjective experience as base for imagining the inner world of little Hans, or Dora, or a Samoan adolescent, that is, someone to whom we know we can attribute an inner world in the first place. Inferences about the world as it is *for* others are always in order because we know that it cannot be exactly the same as it is for us, that no two subjective worlds are alike, that people's beliefs and desires differ in some respects even in circumstances that are outwardly much the same. Inferences are possible because these others are like us in very general respects: they have beliefs, concepts of the objective world which their beliefs are about, of truth and falsity, concepts also of themselves as selves. They anticipate the future and remember the past, catch themselves making mistakes, and so on. Interpretation requires us to learn what we can about their beliefs, what they remember and anticipate. And surely in all this we use our own first-person experience of believing, desiring, planning, and so on, as an essential guide.

It's quite another thing to use our own subjective experience as the base for trying to imagine the experience of a creature to whom we have no reason for attributing this mental repertoire. The first sort of imagining may or may not be a matter of projection; the second can be nothing else.

Summmarizing a lot of data strongly suggesting that early infantile agitations and excitements are only much later symbolized and represented, Lichtenberg writes:

> This formulation casts a doubt on the assumption that as adults we regularly make empathic contact with infants and young toddlers. If we define 'empathy' as entering into the state of mind of another person, then an adult has a very difficult, almost impossible, task to empathize with the infant. As

adults, in the very attempt to enter the infant's state of mind, we use, at least in part, an adult symbolic mode of cognition; that is, to the extent that we put thoughts in the head of the baby in order to understand him or her, we miss the nonsymbolic nature of the infant's state of mind. (1983, p. 173)

What behavior would show us, could show us, that the infant has a sense of self? And why do we want to say it does? Stern's justification, as we saw, is that it frees us "from the partially semantic task of choosing criteria to decide . . . when a sense of self *really* begins." The passage continues: "The task becomes the more familiar one of describing the developmental continuities and changes in something that exists in some form from birth to death" (1984, pp. 6–7). But surely this is the task in any case. Something exists, and perhaps continues to exist as *the same thing,* from birth to death, namely a sentient organism. But we may or may not want to call that thing a self. (Similar questions arise about whether or not the fetus is a person.)

Stern may think we have to choose between saying: (a) prior to self-consciousness, the infant is a self and has a sense of self; and (b) prior to self-consciousness, the infant senses itself as merged with another (for the latter view see Mahler, Pine, and Bergman, 1975). Finding no evidence for the second, Stern opts for the first. But there is no such choice to make. Or rather, both alternatives presume just that order of the mental which self-consciousness presumes. To say that the infant senses itself as merged with another is not the same as saying that it recognizes no distinction between self and other. The first makes sense only for an infant that has already recognized itself as a self.

The idea that, prior to language, there is an initial subjectivity carries with it the idea of an unknowable state of unmediated at-oneness with the world from which language has forever separated us. As Stern says, with language "the infant gains entrance into a wider cultural membership, but at the risk of losing the force and wholeness of his original experience" (1984, p. 177). And again: infants "become estranged from direct contact with their own personal experience" (p. 182).

Jacques Lacan (1977), incidentally, may also hold such a view: language, or "the Symbolic order," gives us thought, self-consciousness, the ability to speak and think in the first person; but at the same time, he says, it alienates us from "Truth," from "the Real," from our primordial experience, which thereafter we can never know. Language introduces a "split" between the conscious self and another order of 'being' which from then on is unconscious and repressed. What we know as ourselves is our experience as altered by language, by "the discourse of the Other," by self-estranging identifications. First there is experience, one's *own* experience, the Given, and then the world as articulated by culture.

According to Lacan, the child enters the Symbolic order through his Oedipal identification with his father; but this identification, this alienation, has been preceded by earlier identifications, in particular with the child's own image in the mirror. (Lacan means us to understand this as metaphor for whatever experiences give the infant the sense of itself as whole, a unified being, a center of agency.) Prior to language the infant has anxiously experienced itself as broken, fragmented, in parts—an 'hommelette', Lacan puns. It latches onto its image of itself as intact and whole as appeasement to this anxiety.

So then Lacan must attribute to the infant in the "imaginary" pre-symbolic stage a sense of itself *as* fragmented, *as* being one with the mother, jubilance at seeing itself *as a unified whole,* and so on. But if we mean these words in anything like their ordinary sense, then we impute to the infant also ideas or concepts of part and whole, self and other; and if we do not mean them in their ordinary sense, then in what other?

Lacan sees that if "drive" is to be a psychological term, if it is to describe mental states, then, as Freud said in an insight he did not pursue, drives must *represent.* They must yield to a theory of meaning that will give them content in something like the sense that beliefs and desires have content. Lacan sees also that the way to do this, perhaps the only way, is to posit a pre-linguistic stage which is nevertheless language-like. So he introduces the idea of Signifiers—words conjoined with images—which have no signifieds, or which signify nothing. But so far as I can see, this is a kind of double talk, motivated, perhaps, by the assumption of genetic continuity questioned in Chapter 2, the idea that if intention, thought, and the ability to mean something by what one says and does are not reducible to something non-mental, then they must be present in a rudimentary form from the start.

On my view, as on Lacan's, the unconscious comes with language; but that is because language, or something very like it, is the condition for the kinds of complicated intentions that Freud's interpretations via the unconscious call for. With the ability to be aware of x as y comes also the ability to deny that it is, or to notice that it is z and to ignore that it is also y, to turn away from what one doesn't want to see, to misdescribe what one knows, and so on. There is no way of having recognition, awareness *of,* knowledge *of* or knowledge *that,* without having also the possibility of misrecognition and error.[6]

The idea I impute to Stern and Lacan—call it the 'behind-the-veil-of-language-idea'—is this: 'The Truth in the form of some purely subjective experience, untrammeled by others, by convention, by repression, is prior to thought, knowledge, and the idea of an *object* as something public and in principle shareable. It is in virtue of this priority that subjective experience is truer than anything we can ever know'. The problem is that the concepts of truth, knowledge, and objectivity have what meaning they do only in their connection with each other.

Another version of the 'veil' idea may go this way: 'I know that some of the things I think I believe and desire are not really *my* beliefs and desires, but borrowed from others, or adopted because I thought I might so please them better. Furthermore, all my beliefs and desires are conditioned by language, for which others are again my source. So far so good. Now the idea continues: language is therefore an imposition on me of society, of its rules, of the whims and conventions of others. So none of what I call my beliefs and desires is purely mine. If I could undo language—which of course I can't—I would be restored to my own mind, to the world as it looked *to me*'.

But what was this *me* prior to language? And what would it be to recover or return to it? To forget how to talk? To lose my mind? There is a perfectly good sense in which many of the things I think I believe are not really my beliefs: I mouth those of others out of laziness or admiration or fear; or I haven't really thought about what I think I believe, yet if pressed would dig in my heels, and so on. But this is not the case and could not be the case with all my beliefs.[7]

The idea of an unknowable reality which is the really real has for companions the idea of a really real and so unknowable self, and the phantasy of a self totally unconnected with, independent from, invulnerable to, all other selves. Freud half voices this phantasy for us when he says that "the liberty of the individual is no gift of civilization. It was greatest before there was any civilization" (1930 [1929], p. 95). But if there is no such thing as an individual—a *human* individual—prior to civilization, then while other people may in particular cases impose on me, a fundamental connection between my mind and other minds is no imposition on mine but its very condition.

The lament for a world lost to us through language must assume, contrary to what Lacan explicitly says, that there is thought before language, that language is a veil cast over a mental world which already exists. For otherwise there can be no such thing as *how the world looked to me* before I learned how it looked to others. So it is not surprising that, belying the genealogy he has himself given us, Lacan must attribute thoughts to the pre-verbal infant. And it is not surprising that Stern speaks approvingly of the idea that thought is already present for the infant,

> ready to be linked up with the word. The word is given to the infant from the outside, by mother, but there exists a thought for it to be given to. In this sense the word, as a transitional phenomenon, does not truly belong to the self, nor does it truly belong to the other. It occupies a midway position between the infant's subjectivity and the mother's objectivity. (1984, p. 172)

Something like this is true of the relations between some thoughts and words when thought is already well on the way. It is also true, of course, that names are in the beginning arbitrary, and that they are given to the child by adults. But the belief that something is a dog, or an apple, or a face, is not arbitrary; and such beliefs rest on a grasp of the distinction between private and public, what is mine and what is ours.

The idea that there is an original order of uninterpreted experience prior to language invokes the Kantian dualism of content and scheme that I talked about in Chapter 1. The empiricist, thinking he is being modest in his claims to knowledge, postulates first of all sensory data, the 'content' on which language will make its constructions. The sensory data are not interpretations of reality; they are simply givens, the empiricist thinks, and as such, as close to an apprehension of reality as we can come. In organizing the data language makes 'knowledge' possible, at the same time as it estranges us from the very thing knowledge is supposed to be about. Reality in this picture is as unknowable as it was for Descartes.

On the view I have been championing, the world itself is what we have been in touch with all along. It is neither behind (or beyond) talk, nor constituted by it. This is what it means to get rid of the dualism of content and scheme. By the same token, the way we are in touch with the world admits the possibility of mistakes about it—not a *big* mistake, the mistake of thinking, for example, that there is a world out there at all, or that the world which is there is in every particular different from how we think it is—but particular mistakes.

But the scheme-content dualism can be prised apart, as John McDowell points out, from another idea of Kant's that is right, and that helps to account for the fact that inner, subjective experience reaches out to public, objective facts. This other idea is that experience is a cooperative exercise of spontaneity, drawing on our conceptual capacities, and receptivity to the larger reality of which we are a part. We can abandon the view that spontaneity operates on some pre-conceptual 'given', while keeping in mind that experience is an interplay between the world's acting on us in causal ways and our acting on the world. As for the child, I said in Chapter 1 that she learns concepts, so acquiring the capacity for subjective experience, in interactions with objects and people in a real objective world, a fact which itself begins to close the presumed chasm between the subjective and the objective.

McDowell writes:

> Acquisition of concepts involves initiation into behavioural repertoires which at first mean nothing to the subject; this initiation takes place in the context of impacts from the world, in a way which makes it intelligible that when light dawns, what comes into being is awareness of oneself as enjoying a course of experience: that is, as tracing one subjective route, among many

possible subjective routes, through an objective world that reveals itself in different regions and aspects according to the changing perceptual opportunities which one's particular route through it affords . . .

What it is for an episode or state to be subjective, in a strong sense that becomes applicable with what I spoke of as the dawning of the light, is for it to be an element in a stream of consciousness, something that its subject could appropriate into a subjective biography. We can begin to understand the subjective continuity which the idea of a stream of consciousness involves by taking it to be the subjective aspect of a continuity which also has an objective aspect: the continuity of the history of a perceptual point of view on the world. (1989, pp. 7–8)

Put it this way: A creature that can tell a story about itself, and only such a one, is a self, someone to whom we can attribute subjectivity.[8] And the coherence of this story requires innumerable points of contact between storyteller and an outside world, which is going on its way quite independently.

II   The Concept of Subjectivity

On the view just set out, subjectivity is a relational property that logically presumes objects external to the subject. This view contrasts sharply with another, according to which subjectivity is a property entirely internal to an experience. Proponents of this second view hold there is an ineffable something that *it is like to be* an infant, or a bat. The subjectivity defies description, since it is said to accrue to any mental state or to any experience, *over and beyond its content*. It is a quality unique to every experience, yet not merely a function of all the elements that make that experience what it is.

Nagel (1979) assumes that bats, for example, have experiences, and he thinks that because our sensory equipment is categorially different from theirs, we will never know *what their experience is like*:

We believe that bats feel some versions of pain, fear, hunger, and lust, and that they have other, more familiar types of perception, besides sonar. But we believe that these experiences also have in each case a specific subjective character, which is beyond our ability to conceive. (p. 161)

Presumably we can know what it is like to be a person more or less like ourselves, because we can, after all, know what the subjective quality of our experience is like, and we can conceive hers to be like ours. Thus our 'bat' problem also arises, Nagel thinks, apropos of human beings whose sensory relation to the world is different from ours in certain important ways, say if they are deaf or blind from birth while we are 'normal'.

Here is one of those basic intuitions on which people divide. To some Nagel's intuition is sensible and right; others, I among them, can't make much sense of it. Words are not likely to persuade in either case, though they can perhaps deflate the conviction that the assumption is inescapable. So I will say why I take the tack I do, and suggest that something like this subjectivist intuition is behind views such as Stern's and Lacan's.

To begin with, we might ask how we go about knowing what it is like to be another creature who is more or less like us, but who comes from a different culture, or who, unlike us, is blind, or deaf, or schizophrenic. We find out as much as we can about the world in which that person lived, how she or he behaved or behaves, or about the neurophysiology of deafness and how the other senses compensate. As Kathleen Wilkes (1988) remarks in response to Nagel, a congenitally deaf scientist who had devoted his research energies to the phenomenology and psychophysiology of auditory perception would know far more than most of us do about hearing. As for bats, we can discover quite a lot about 'what it is like' for them just by learning what we can about bat perception and behavior.[9] Note that all this is in principle describable.

Do we indeed know what the subjective quality of the experience of seeing this red ball is, beyond everything we can see and say about what *the ball* itself is like, and what we see when we see the ball? Is there something else I am familiar with, and only I, that is *the subjectivity* of this experience? Not that I can see. Or if there is, then it seems it prevents me also from knowing what anybody's experience is like.[10]

Summarizing a similar line of objection, Norman Malcolm says:

> The bafflement that one feels about the undertaking of trying to describe the 'inner quality' or 'subjective character' of seeing, arises from the impression that a sighted adult not only displays normal visual discrimination, and a normal use of the word 'see', but *also* knows what seeing is like. As if there were tucked away inside seeing, the inner quality of what it is like. But in so far as 'knowing what seeing is like' has any meaning at all, it refers to nothing other than the ability that a sighted adult has of making visual discriminations, reports and judgments. This accounts for Nagel's confidence that a sighted adult 'knows what it is like to see': for what this amounts to is the tautology that such a person is not only able to make visual discriminations, but also can employ the language of sight in the normal way. (1984, p. 54)

Nagel is not alone in his commitment to an unspeakable kind of subjectivity. Here is how Richard Wollheim describes it:

> The subjectivity of a mental phenomenon is how the phenomenon is for the subject: it is, in a phrase that I owe to Thomas Nagel, what it is like for the subject to have that particular mental phenomenon.
>
> An initial difficulty with subjectivity that has far-reaching consequences is that by and large subjectivity cannot be described in any direct fashion. We get nowhere when we try to say either what subjectivity is in itself or what it is in the case of a given mental state—unless we do this obliquely. But for me to have said this much is to reveal two features of subjectivity as I see it. The

first feature is that subjectivity is a determinable attribute of mental phenomena, so that every mental phenomenon that has subjectivity has its own particular subjectivity. In this respect subjectivity is like colour, for every object that has colour has a particular colour. But, just as two objects can have the same colour, so two mental phenomena can, I presume, have the same subjectivity. (1984, p. 38)

Wollheim then says that the best way of appreciating subjectivity is to ask ourselves whether we think it's conceivable for there to be two mental states that have the same thought-content, "no matter to what degree this is specified, but that seemed somehow different." He thinks the answer is Yes. But the thought experiment Wollheim asks us to make isn't possible. Saying why will give me another way of responding to Nagel as well. The catch is the phrase "no matter to what degree [the thought-content] is specified." Of course I can imagine John's having said to me what he just did and my being amused rather than angry, or wondering what to say to him that might calm him down, and so on. But Wollheim says that in these cases I am not imagining subjectivity as he means it, and the problem I find is that there is no way to do that; for any one experience (or thought) is infinitely complex, enmeshed as it is in the network of thoughts, desires, memories, hopes, regrets, and so on, which is uniquely mine. I suggest that if we think we are imagining two mental states which are somehow different, though their mental content is identical, it is because we haven't imagined these mental states—nor could we do so— with all their content explicit.

It is important to keep in mind just what Nagel and Wollheim are claiming: not merely that the experience of each of us is different; nor that each experience has its own quality; nor that my access to some of my experiences is privileged in a certain way. With all this most would agree. It is that over and above the content of each experience, complex as it may be, there is something else, this ineffable and inescapable private quality.[11] To make connections with my first two chapters: such a view can only be supported, if at all, by an internalist view according to which the content of a mental state is determined entirely from within.

I have a suggestion, however, about something we might want to say, something that may sound like Nagel's and Wollheim's idea but isn't. Call the 'content' of an experience what is in principle available to conscious and articulable awareness (even though one may not be conscious of it in the moment). Now the following seems highly possible: a present experience, say of agitation, might recall very early experiences of agitation that were not and could not have been symbolized at the time, and that have been stored in memory in a special 'affective' way. Then these memories might give a special quality to the present experience, something that could not be put into words.

A last note on subjectivity in infants: 'But how do you know they don't have mental images? representations? beliefs? desires? interpretable states?' someone may ask. Of course it will never be possible to look inside the mind of an infant and discover, No representations! That—looking inside the mind—and only that, it seems, would satisfy the person who persists with this How-do-you-know question. And that idea, that were we able to look into the mind we would find its contents entirely *there,* is just the internalist idea I've been criticizing.

The empirical question asks: 'What is the mind like?' the philosophical, 'How can we best elucidate our concept of mind?' Of course the questions reflect each other. All the things we think we know about the mind have helped to shape our concept of it. And it is only by its light that we know what we do, or think we do, about the mind. If the line of argument I have given is right, the answer to the How-do-you-know question would be: The reason for saying that infants don't have representations is that we wouldn't know what *we* mean in saying they do. Furthermore, we can explain everything we need to explain without positing them. Of course we might discover all kinds of things that in time would cause a shift in our own deepest concepts. That is the empirical part of the possibility. But the empirical discoveries we've been making about infants and about how they learn have been leading away from the idea which opened this chapter, that the infant has from the beginning a sense of itself, a sense of itself *as* a self.

In his meditations on civilization and its discontents, Freud says that "the infant at the breast does not yet distinguish his ego from the external world." He learns to do so only through discovering that some of his gratifications come to him from outside. "In this way there is for the first time set over against the ego an 'object'" (1930 [1929], p. 67). Substitute 'self' for 'ego' (Freud's own word was "das Ich," or the I) and the passage says that the sense of self and awareness of others are interdependent. I suspect Stern would agree with this. But taking the thought seriously requires a different picture of the self from the one he paints. I would draw it this way: the concept of self has awareness of self *as* a self built into it, an 'I' who can tell stories about its passage through the world. This means both awareness of oneself as *the one who* is doing this or saying that, and awareness of others as ones with whom one shares a world and from whom one is separate.

6   Baby Talk

If it is true that subjectivity, in the form of interpretable states of mind, is something a creature achieves, then how shall we describe what goes on before? Light dawns gradually over the whole, Wittgenstein remarked. So how might we envision this gradual dawning? In linking thought and language he gave us an important clue; for children learning language is a phenomenon we can study.

It will be helpful to distinguish first, and very roughly, between three different aspects of language: grammar (structure, or syntax); semantics (reference, or meaning); and pragmatics, or the purposes to which any given use of language is being put.[1] Noam Chomsky (1975), for instance, focuses primarily on the first. Reacting against the behaviorist's claim that language learning can be accounted for through stimulus-response conditioning, Chomsky argues that no empiricist story could begin to explain the child's ability to infer, on the basis of very little data, complex grammatical rules. For that, he said, we have to posit an innate 'knowledge' of linguistic structure.

Many linguists believe that while there may be some built-in Language Acquisition Device (as Chomsky called it), it can't work in the absence of fairly extensive human interaction.[2] In any case, structuralist theories of language, like Chomsky's, Saussure's, and also Lacan's, don't tell us about what the philosopher is most likely to be interested in: how the child learns the meaning of words, how the child learns *to mean* something by what it says. If, as Wittgenstein insisted, meaning is inextricable from the purposes to which language is put, and these from larger social activities, then this is where we will need to look to discover the child's entry into the semantic dimension of language.

Now I want to recall a distinction mentioned in an earlier chapter, between natural and non-natural signs. Spots are a 'natural' sign of measles, the child's crying of its distress. The cry has meaning in the non-natural sense only when we can say that the child itself *means* us to understand something by its crying. Paul Grice (1957) has argued that for this we need something like the following: An utterer U means something by uttering x if and only if he intends to produce a particular response in his audience A, and if he intends to produce it by means of the audience's recognition of this intention. And U can intend to produce a certain response in A by saying x only if U thinks it possible for it to have that effect. (If I intend you to fly when I say 'Fly!' I must believe it possible for you to fly.) So included in U's intentions are some beliefs about A. Asking what responses U intended to produce will be a way of asking what he meant in uttering x.

If this is right, then the path the child travels in learning *to mean* will be the same as that which teaches her something about the responses of another, about how to elicit those responses, and to know that something she has done is the reason why the other is responding as he is. We will want to investigate how child and caretaker come to have common foci of attention, how in time the child comes to use sounds to stand for something in a shared world.

The idea is not that thought originates with language, for that way of putting it overlooks the fact that language learning itself probably starts with the beginning of a child's life, prepared for from early on by many kinds of responsiveness to the world and to other creatures that are wired in. A great deal of empirical research into infant development has been going on in recent years, and while it would be inappropriate to try to summarize it here, I want to report on it selectively in section I, to indicate how it supports and is supported by the philosophical line I have been taking. At the end of the chapter I make some brief remarks on possible connections between communication and mental illness.

I   Seeding the Mind

From the start the infant is equipped for attachment to its mother (Bowlby, 1969). It responds preferentially to the smell of her milk, the feel of her breast, the sound of her voice. It has a propensity for eye-to-eye contact, and to be soothed by human holding, rocking, and touching (Emde, 1981). It knows how to disengage itself from a gaze or an attention that is apparently too insistent or too demanding (Stern, 1977). At around six months it looks to its mother's face and to objects in the world in ways that suggest it is wired for the sharing of visual reality (Scaife and Bruner, 1975).

From infant research we get the picture of the infant as a complexly perceiving, feeling, responding, and acting creature in virtue of preprogrammed response patterns—at once affective, perceptual, and motor—that long before the advent of mental images are increasingly inflected by learning and experience. These response patterns include memories, primarily in the form of motor activity and its links to pleasure and pain.[3] The baby cries with hunger, it sucks the breast or bottle, and it experiences relief. What is the hungry baby remembering, if anything, when in the future it sucks contentedly on a pacifier or its own thumb? Psychoanalysts have traditionally said the infant has a memory in the form of an image of a breast or a bottle, and the pleasurable sensation of being fed. As hunger approaches, the image is activated. Now psychoanalysts familiar with infant research are suggesting an alternative explanation, one that also posits memories, but of motor sequences with their accompanying affect. The sequence in the example above begins with a painful sensation of hunger, which is then tied in memory to a motor activity, say sucking. It is the motor activity itself which triggers or is associated with a pleasurable affect (Lichtenberg, 1983).

According to Piaget (1952), thought is rooted in action—an idea in harmony with Wittgenstein's and Davidson's that a study of language and meaning cannot be divorced from the activities in which they figure. In Piaget's theory the mental development of the young child goes through three principal stages, each building on the one that precedes it. The first is the Sensori-motor Period, from birth to approximately 18 months. The infant learns by transforming objects in the world through his activity, which on the one hand attempts to 'assimilate' and adapt the world to himself, on the other to 'accommodate' himself to the world. So the inborn sucking response, for example, gets embedded in a wider pattern involving infant, activity, and world. Before this period is over the infant's own behavior will have transformed rigid reflexes into flexible patterns of response. (Bruner [1985] has discovered, for example, that an infant as young as five or six weeks is capable of learning how to control a visual display by the speed of his sucking on a pacifier. The display goes into sharper focus as the infant sucks harder; and when he is sucking to produce clarity, the infant looks as he sucks.) The infant is developing the concept of an object in this period—Piaget thinks—but he does not yet have the capacity to form images or representations.

Piaget divides the second stage—the Concrete Operational Period (from approximately 18 months to 11 years)—into two sub-periods, the preoperational period (roughly 18 months to 7 years, though authors date it differently) in which the child is developing the capacity to represent things, and the period of Concrete Operations proper, in which he is learning to think about things at greater levels of abstraction. Piaget calls the final period, in which intelligent adult thinking is consolidated, the Formal Operational Period.

Piaget is concerned with general questions about how we become knowers. Like all such inquirers, he must begin with some at least tacit assumptions about what sort of thing the mind is. Whereas Vygotsky (1978) focuses on the social basis of mind, Piaget takes the individual as his starting point, and studies the child in relative isolation. Given this focus, it is likely that although Piaget never addresses questions about meaning per se, had he done so his view would have been internalist. (And since the children whose behavior he studied had of course been in intimate contact with other human beings from the beginning, there is no way of telling from Piaget's work what part those interactions played in his observations.) If, however, one sees language and thought as essentially social in character, then to catch them in the making one will want to observe the infant in interaction with other human beings.[4]

Recall that whereas on the traditional view, the direction of explanation goes from the private to the public, I have argued that the direction of explanation must go the other way. It is because the meaning of a term is fixed by things in the world that different people can mean the same thing by a word even though they are in different psychological states. In Hilary Putnam's way of putting it (1988), reference is a form of social interaction that links an initial referring event to later ones of a similar kind. The child learns to mean something by a sound or a string of sounds through learning that he and someone else are both using those sounds to talk about the same thing.

Bruner's hunch is that "language acquisition 'begins' when mother and infant create a predictable format of interaction that can serve as a microcosm for communicating and for constituting a shared reality" (1985, p. 18). I would put this only slightly differently, saying that there must be a shared reality to begin with for communication at any level to get going. What has to be 'constituted' is the two individuals' mutual understanding of each other as having the same thing in mind. Influenced specifically by Putnam, Bruner suggests that "the problem of how reference develops can . . . be restated as the problem of how people manage and direct each other's attention by linguistic means" (p. 68). Since bringing the attention of another to a common focus is widespread in the primate order, it is not surprising that six-month-old human infants will follow another's gaze. "What is surprising is that even during their first year, they begin redirecting their attention in response to subtle conventional cues that are features of adult language, such as characteristic upward changes in intonation" (p. 69).

Bruner's observations track two infants and their mothers over a period of some twenty months, beginning when the infants were five months and three months old. His conclusion is that "reference is dependent . . . not only upon mastering a relationship between sign and significate, but upon using social procedures in concert with one another to assure that the sign and the significate that become linked overlap in some negotiable way with the uses of others" (p. 88). If we then assume, as such observations suggest we should, that the child begins to develop "the concept of semanticity," that patterned sounds stand for particular things or classes of things in experience, it will not be particularly puzzling that sounds which at first accompany ostensive referential gestures eventually may replace them (pp. 68–69).

Summarizing a number of observations of interactions between mothers and very young infants, Colwyn Trevarthen also reports a mutual responsiveness that has some of the character of reference:

> For all its resemblance to conversation between adult friends, this remains, in one respect, a very strange form of human communication . . . Language is flowing only one way, from mother to infant . . . Almost no reference to topics outside the person-to-person engagement can be detected from what the baby expresses . . . I say *almost* no reference advisedly, however, because there is a sense in which even a two-month-old does make incipient comment about outside reality, a kind of hint at description of surroundings, by way of orientations, pointings and signs of curiosity, interest or puzzlement . . . This very rudimentary germ of a referential activity, foreshadowing reference in language, depends, we notice, on the systematic way the baby's attention is periodically transferred from the mother and focussed to some outward destination, pin-pointing a locus in their potentially shared world. (1987b, p. 4)

L. Sander (1975) has noted, more generally, that infant and mother are biologically predisposed to mesh their behaviors in a rhythmic way; and Stern observes that even within the first six months the child

> has 'got' the temporal patterning of human behavior and the meaning of different changes and variations in tempo and rhythm . . . He has learned the social cues and conventions that are mutually effective in initiating, maintaining, terminating, and avoiding interactions with his mother. He has learned different discursive or dialogic modes, such as turn-taking. (1977, pp. 5–6)

Consider what Stern (1984) calls "affect attunement," the infant's capacity to recognize another's gesture as an appropriate response even when it is in a different sensory modality. In two of Stern's examples— drawn from the first six months of infancy—the child lets out a cry of delight that has a certain aural curve, and the mother spontaneously does a shimmy whose intensity reflects that curve; the child beats a rhythm on the table which the mother unthinkingly answers back in the way she nods her head. The child's contentment with her appropriate responses, and his surprise with her inappropriate ones (as measured, for example, by the intensity and the dynamic shape of her behaviors) are indications that he treats what they are doing as communication. Through such experiences the child is learning about what it is to have and to signal an intention, and about how communications can succeed and can fail.

Even before speech infants can make jokes and laugh at those of others. They can recognize when they are being asked to cooperate on a joint venture, and how to do so. By the time an infant is nine or ten months old, he can engage in a triangular relationship with his mother and an object in their shared world of the following sort: the baby gives an object to his mother and shows pleasure when it is accepted; or the mother shows the baby how to do a task, the baby accepts, then looks at the mother, and both are pleased. Trevarthen writes:

> When a 10-month-old offers an object to the extended palm of another, makes a vocal and gestural utterance in the form of a command or declaration, responds with precise co-operation to a request expressed by facial signs and in gesture and speech, plays a give-and-take game, or obeys learned instructions of speech or gesture to choose objects or perform specific manipulations with them, the expressive manner of what the infant does gives these acts a co-operative form seen in the behaviour of no other species. (1978, p. 214)

Trevarthen thinks the detailed evidence of his tapes suggests that developments of the baby's brain at around this age (nine or ten months, or 40 weeks) "cause the infant to accept persons in a new way." The change seems not to be primarily a reflection of environmental input; and it seems voluntary, not reflexive: the infant's reaction to persons may not be forthcoming even though appropriate stimuli are present, and the infant tries to interact when the circumstances aren't congenial:

> The behaviour that starts at 9 months is a rudimentary outline of exceedingly complex cognizance-sharing acts of adults that we normally consider to be both consciously intended and bound by rules of cultural origin. For example, it includes prototypes of pointing to an interesting event and addressing a comment on it to another, giving and taking with acknowledgment of the shared intention, and accepting a word as specifying a particular experience. (1978, pp. 183–184)

While younger infants perceive objects and use them to communicate with persons, at nine months these 'intentions' come together. Now the response of the baby takes in the mother's response and comments on it in a way that resembles adult conversation: you hear and understand what I have said to you, though it is nothing you have heard me or anyone else say before, and perhaps not quite what you expected me to say; you respond, intending that your response will be taken by me in a certain way, and knowing enough about me to be able to form such an intention. At nine months we seem to see for the first time that sort of triangulation I spoke of in the first chapter, where I said that if we are going to call a child's response to an apple, say, a specifically *linguistic* response, then we must impute to the child the intention to communicate. The child must be knowingly and intentionally responding to a specific stimulus, and it must know that the mother is responding to that same stimulus.

Both Stern and Trevarthen emphasize the mutuality of these mother-infant interactions. Trevarthen reports a study done with a two-month-old infant and its mother in which they were communicating with each other affectionately, but by video screens in separate rooms. When the mother's baby talk was replayed to the baby, he started to react with smiles and happy babbling, then within a few seconds became distressed and withdrawn. Trevarthen concludes "that the contingent responsiveness of the mother's behavior is essential to the maintenance of a positive emotional state in the infant" (1983, p. 153).

In a famous article comparing the mother's face to a mirror, Winnicott asks:

> What does the baby see when he or she looks at the mother's face? I am suggesting that, ordinarily, what the baby sees is himself or herself. In other words the mother is looking at the baby and *what she looks like is related to what she sees there.* All this is too easily taken for granted. I am asking that this which is naturally done well by mothers who are caring for their babies shall not be taken for granted. I can make my point by going straight over to the case of the baby whose mother reflects her own mood or, worse still, the rigidity of her own defences. In such a case what does the baby see? (1971, p. 112)[5]

Winnicott answers by saying that the mother's face is then not a mirror; that the baby's creative capacity begins to atrophy; that what could have been the "beginning of a significant exchange with the world" is blocked.

We might distinguish two different ways in which the mother may 'mirror' her baby. According to the first, she sees her anxieties about herself reflected in the child's behavior, or her desires to have a certain sort of baby lead her to recognize him only in those moments when he is gratifying this need. When he frustrates her desires, she ignores him or reacts with anger. Such a baby may then become sensitive to the mother's demands that he be a baby of a certain sort, trying to be the child she seems to want him to be. In time he may himself become confused about who he is, about whether or not he is as he appears. In a second sort of interaction between mother and child, the baby often initiates the dialogue; the mother responds to him as this particular child, and so sees and responds appropriately to him. Such a child is encouraged to see the world directly rather than as a stage or mirror for his performance, or a set of signs that he is approved.

Winnicott speaks of the mother's face in the language of subjectivism, as mirroring the baby's self. But we can keep what we need from his metaphor if we say that, literally, the mother does not mirror the baby's self but projects a self (not necessarily *her* self) onto him, treating him as a human creature in the making. Over time the baby learns what he is doing through seeing its effects on her; and the more sensitively, the less absent-mindedly, she responds to what he does, the more he is able to discriminate one thing he does from another.

In a passage that incidentally echoes Winnicott's theme, H. M. Southwood says that what the mother "gives back" must largely determine what the child attends to and how:

> When one considers that the learning of a language must be based on . . . this reciprocal feedback of facial expressions and sounds, and that [the baby's] awareness of himself . . . must be almost entirely a consequence of mother's teaching, then there . . . is a good case for constructing a somewhat different model of mental life [than Stern's]. This should not start from a retrospective extrapolation from our concept of the self-aware and language-using individual further and further back into babyhood . . . but rather from the mother and her allies who initiate the baby into the world of communication and language. (1988, pp. 238–239)

What the baby learns through its interactions with its mother shapes its view of the human world, of communication, and of itself as a communicator. Is it able to get the attention of the other? Under what conditions? Does it get back something appropriate to what it has given out? I don't mean that the child is able to ask such questions, but that its early communications set up pathways for thoughts, set in motion behaviors—of trust, avoidance, openness, spontaneity—that thought will come to inhabit, and reinforce.

Of course, as we've noted already, only some of these communications are verbal. Parents convey their attitudes toward their infant through the way they hold her, their tone of voice, the tempo in which they do things, and so on. And the infant, in responding to these messages, lays down action patterns that may stay with her for the rest of her life (see Basch, 1976b).

Years ago George Klein (1976) noted that the erotic zones Freud singles out to mark sexual development are just the bodily areas across which the child's most important communications with others—her learnings about their intentions toward her, her first interpersonal pleasures and pains—take place: the mouth in feeding (and of course in speech); the anus, first in the way the child is handled and later in the processes of socialization;

the genitals, from the beginning in the pleasure the child receives from being touched, and because the child's sex—in ways Freud may not have sufficiently appreciated—determines how the parents hold her, talk to her, their demands, desires, and expectations in regard to her.

"If a lion could talk, we would not understand it," Wittgenstein remarks (1953, p. 223), for we wouldn't know how to hear what a lion's mouth does as 'talking'. Virgil Aldrich comments: "One learns the primary use of the term 'talk' in talkative association with other people. It is this that determines (defines) the concept of talking, where the sense of the speaker's utterance is 'bodied forth' and grasped without perplexity, thanks to its being in the right place" (1973, p. 361). The speaker shows us what he feels—smiling, frowning, smiling in a strained way, pretend-frowning—and what he thinks, and what he intends to do about it.

Derrida teaches that writing, not speech, is the primary form of communication. His point is that language of any sort does what it does by evoking something absent. We take speech as primary because we are under the illusion that words reveal (rather than distance us from) reality. But Derrida is silent about an obvious and stunning fact: we learn to communicate and to think through talking (or for children who are deaf-mutes, through some other form of intimate human contact), in the presence of specific human others, whose faces and bodies and voices cannot help expressing emotion, and which we see, and hear, and touch. The shapes and sounds of these others talking to us and thinking aloud in our presence must be our first acquaintance with language; so also with mind and other minds.

Think then of the mother not just as *an* 'object' for the baby but his first object, because the first he cares about, and the one through whom he will himself become a subject, directing himself to the world in all the ways of thought. What beliefs a person has are obviously to some extent a function of what is in front of him, but also of his reasons for looking in just this direction, his interests and the manner of his looking. I am not speaking of wishful thinking, but the fact that only a person who cares or has been made to care about mountains, or jazz, is going to know about the relative heights of the Karakorams and the Andes, or when Billie Holiday sang with Lester Young. By 'the manner of looking' I mean whether one feels confident in her ability to see what is there, to stand it if it is painful or disappointing, to ask the right questions.

II   *The Practice of Belief*

A researcher on the subject of children learning to talk remarks that experiments showing that children are egocentric can't be right, for then language learning would be truly mysterious. Instead it is apparently the case that children understand social situations first, perhaps especially those involving intention, and then use this to help make sense of what is said to them (Donaldson, 1978).

Philosophical reflection and infant observation both tell us that long before it can actually speak the infant is learning a lot that prepares it for language, and that much of this learning is of a specifically interpersonal nature. This is one implication of Wittgenstein's idea that learning a language is learning a form of life, which I read as saying that much about the ways of a community must already be shared before one can interpret others and be interpreted to them; and that these shared ways cannot themselves be put into words, though nothing could be said without them. Writing about Wittgenstein, Stanley Cavell remarks:

> We learn and teach words in certain contexts, and then we are expected, and expect others, to be able to project them into further contexts. Nothing insures that this projection will take place (in particular, not the grasping of universals nor the grasping of books of rules), just as nothing insures that we will make, and understand, the same projections. That on the whole we do is a matter of our sharing routes of interest and feeling, modes of response, senses of humor and of significance and of fulfillment, for what is outrageous, of what is similar to what else, what a rebuke, what forgiveness, of when an utterance is an assertion, when an appeal, when an explanation—all the whirl of organism Wittgenstein calls 'forms of life'. Human speech and activity, sanity and community, rest upon nothing more, but nothing less, than this. It is a vision as simple as it is difficult, and as difficult as it is (and because it is) terrifying. (1969, p. 52)

Wittgenstein (1953) asks us to imagine a very simple use of language, a primitive "language game":

> I send someone shopping. I give him a slip marked 'five red apples'. He takes the slip to the shopkeeper who opens the drawer marked 'apples'; then he looks up the word 'red' in a table and finds a colour sample opposite it; then he says the series of cardinal numbers . . . up to the word 'five' and for each number he takes an apple of the same colour as the sample out of the drawer.—It is in this and similar ways that one operates with words.—"But how does he know where and how he is to look up the word 'red' and what he is to do with the word 'five'?"—Well, I assume that he *acts* as I have described. Explanations come to an end somewhere. (§1)

If we think of language use as a kind of rule-following, then explanations come to an end somewhere in the sense that understanding a word, or a request, or a command, or how to continue a mathematical sequence, cannot be rendered as the visualizing of a formula, or the application of a rule, for formulas and rules are themselves in need of interpretation. Following a rule is of course not the same as doing something mechanically: the sense in which persons follow rules will not be illuminated by our knowing the mechanics of an adding machine. Even if we imagine the rule-follower as having a slip of paper in his pocket or an image in his head, what is crucial to our being able to attribute to him an understanding of the rule in question is his membership in a community in which there are practices of certain sorts, practices that teach him what a rule is in the first place.

Wittgenstein gives us an idea of the sorts of practices he has in mind in asking us to consider the multiplicity of language games; for example:

Giving orders, and obeying them—
Describing the appearance of an object . . .
Constructing an object from a description . . .
Reporting an event
Speculating about an event
Forming and testing a hypothesis—
Presenting the results of an experiment . . .
Making up a story; and reading it
Play-acting
Singing catches—
Guessing riddles—
Making a joke; telling it—. . .
Asking, thanking, cursing, greeting, praying.
(1953, §23)

I am adding to Wittgenstein's theme the idea that many of these 'games' rest on earlier learnings that take place in language only minimally, and that begin to teach the child what to do with the words she will learn. The infant who has learned to speak has already learned something about the difference between a request and a command, a Yes and a No, pointing at an object with one's finger and playfully wagging it, a hug of consolation and a smothering hug, a string of sounds that asks a question and one that scolds, a friendly tease and a humiliating rebuff, an invitation and a refusal. We learn something about the force of words before we learn what they mean.

One might respond to this by saying—in something like the spirit of Freud's quest for a mind-body frontier—that representations, beliefs, language learning, Intentionality, meaning, all rest on a 'background' of pre-Intentional understanding.[6] The problem would be how to understand this 'understanding'. One might try calling it, vaguely, a matter of practices or capacities. But that wouldn't justify the claim that the phenomena in question are mental. Or one might say, equally vaguely, that the understanding is a matter of 'assumptions' and 'presuppositions'. But since these are themselves Intentional states, they will need explaining just as representations did.

Why not just say that there must be many capacities which are temporally prior to the having of Intentional states and without which the latter would not be possible? We can include these capacities in some larger sense of 'the mental', if we like. But if we press the question: 'Mind or body?' we are apt to get into trouble. Here the question simply doesn't apply.[7] (Is the week-old infant's ability to recognize the special smell of his mother's milk a mental ability? And how about these: The infant's wail of pain? His throwing his rattle furiously on the floor? His smile of recognition at the sight of his mother and his special way of greeting her? His gesturing to an object in their shared environment?)

The idea that the mental has its life, and necessarily, within a context of activity and practice suggests something else: that the practices and capacities in question are not something over and beyond believing, representing, and desiring, but a part of those attitudes themselves. Psychoanalysts may be unhappy with philosophical talk about beliefs and desires because such mental states seem more particular, more nugget-like, than their own concept of thinking suggests. I believe the difference is not so great as it appears, and that 'belief' and 'desire' are even for the philosopher abstractions. 'Practices' and 'capacities' tell us more about what it is to represent or to believe in the first place.[8]

III   Communication and Mental Illness

Stern says that a reason for placing the sense of self at the center of his inquiry "is the clinical one of understanding normal interpersonal development" (1984, p. 7); so he will focus "on those senses of the self that if severely impaired would disrupt normal social functioning and likely lead to madness or great social deficit" (p. 7). But if it is true that thought is dependent on interpersonal relations, then things may to an extent go just the other way around: the developing sense of self falters if the child's communications with significant others are impaired.[9] Of course inborn deficits in the child's ability to set up pathways of communications with others may contribute to later 'madness'. But the problem would lie in the impairment of those abilities.

Communications go astray in a number of ways: The adult may be routinely unresponsive to the child, or, like the 'wrong' kind of 'mirroring' mother, consistently mistake what is going on in the child for what is going on in her. She may use the child to serve her own needs, at the same time frustrating his; or exact agreement from the child, not acknowledging his separateness from her. Or she may deny that her words mean what they do; or that she has done what she has done; or that the world is as both she and the child can see it to be. Doubtless all adults do all of these things occasionally. It is a question of how, and how much.

Ferenczi (1933) begins a famous article titled "Confusions of Tongues between the Adult and the Child (The Language of Tenderness and Passion)" by remarking on the "clairvoyance" with which some of his patients detect his hypocrisy, his vanity, or his secret dislike for the patient. He tells us that when honest self-examination convinced him they were right, he encouraged them to express their anger and criticism openly, but at first to little avail.

> Gradually, then, I came to the conclusion that the patients have an exceedingly refined sensitivity for the wishes, tendencies, whims, sympathies, and antipathies of their analyst ... Instead of contradicting the analyst or accusing him of errors and blindness, the patients *identify themselves with him.* (p. 226)

Eventually, however, the analyst's "renunciation" of his "professional hypocrisy" leads to an easing of the patient's condition. "Tragic events of the past" can be recollected without loss of equilibrium, and the "traumatic-hysterical attacks" become milder.

> Now what brought about this state of affairs? Something had been left unsaid in the relation between physician and patient, something insincere, and its frank discussion freed, so to speak, the tongue-tied patient; the admission of the analyst's error produced confidence in this patient ... *It is this confidence that establishes the contrast between the present and the unbearable traumatogenic past,* the contrast which is absolutely necessary for the patient ... to re-experience the past no longer as hallucinatory reproduction but as an objective memory. (p. 226)

By this path of transference and counter-transference Ferenczi is led to the matter of infantile seduction.

> A typical way in which incestuous seductions occur is this: an adult and a child love each other, the child nursing the playful phantasy of taking the role of mother to the adult. This play may assume erotic forms but remains, nevertheless, on the level of tenderness. It is not so, however, with pathological adults. (p. 227)

So this communication between parent and child is a confusion of tongues: one partner in the dialogue understands the play between them as tenderness, the other as passion. What happens next, Ferenczi says, is that just as in analysis the patient "identifies" with the analyst, so the child "identifies" with his seducer, "introjecting" the seducer's feelings of guilt.

How should we gloss the notion of identification here? Each strand in Ferenczi's account yields a slightly different sense. The child feels physically and morally helpless. If his anxiety reaches a certain pitch, it compels the child to subordinate [himself] . . . to the will of the aggressor, to divine each one of his desires and to gratify these . . . The fear of the uninhibited, almost mad adult changes the child, so to speak, into a psychiatrist and, in order to become one and to defend himself against dangers coming from people without self-control, he must know how to identify himself completely with them. (pp. 228–229)

So 'identification' in the first sense simply refers to the child's ability to understand the adult's intentions. The child, that is, is a remarkably good interpreter. The confusion of tongues occurs in a context in which the child knows quite well how to interpret the adult. It is the adult who misunderstands.

Second, the child takes on the burden, partly out of the wish to be taken care of once again himself, of putting to rights "all disorder in the family" (p. 229). The child wishes to protect the adult from his guilt feelings, and to protect also his own image of the adult. So the child may come to think of his real past as a phantasy and of himself as the guilty seducer.

Then, since the child is still in the position of learning about the world, he comes to understand the meaning of his play by what it calls out in the adult, and knowing that the adult feels guilty, he learns that what had seemed harmless play is instead "a punishable offence": "The playful trespasses of the child are raised to serious reality only by the passionate, often infuriated, punitive sanctions and lead to depressive states in the child who, until then, felt blissfully guiltless" (p. 229). That is, the child comes to view what has happened in the adult's terms.

But the child also has another view, the one that describes his original intentions; so he is confused. He thinks of himself as simultaneously innocent and culpable. The pathological consequence is a 'split' in the child's personality: on the one hand an accurate view of things; on the other the phantasies he is motivated to construct. Furthermore, the child's confidence in the testimony of his senses, Ferenczi says, is broken: his confidence in his senses, and also in other persons, or in the mutuality of dialogue. Ferenczi is presumably describing a child who has already been initiated into language. Even so, the confusions he is talking about take place so early, in relationships so crucial to the child, that we can imagine their having a lasting impact.

Ferenczi does not comment on the implications of these views for a theory of repression; but one implication would seem to be that in some instances the repressed is what cannot be said to the other, and what the other forbids one to say even to oneself. What the adult taking care of the child does not want to know, he does not want the child to know. And given the extreme vulnerability of the child, she does not want to know it either. Perhaps introjection, projection, and identification can be understood as ways, similar to those in Ferenczi's account, in which early personal interactions shape the child's ideas about itself, ideas that are necessarily reciprocal with its ideas about others.

The usual psychoanalytic view of schizophrenia traces it to a pre-verbal period in which self and 'object' are not yet distinguished or are confused. But schizophrenic symptoms are best understood in quite the contrary way, Sass argues (1987), as a result of heightened self-awareness. Thinking, judgment, reflection, the concept of self, and self-reflection are all in place. But the schizophrenic's worries about the very existence of his self are extreme. So he tries through acts of introspection to catch himself, the one who is watching, not the self in the mirror, so to speak, but the self looking at the reflection. And to his despair, all he finds—like Hume (1951), whom Sass does not mention—are fragmentary impressions. Ironically, then, the schizophrenic's desperate attempt to find himself convinces him of the truth of his darkest fears, that neither he nor anything else is real; for the sense of self hovers at the edge of active engagement with the world, just that engagement from which the schizophrenic has withdrawn.

Sass does not deny that schizophrenia is often characterized by subject-object confusions. But are they remnants—as Mahler, Pine, and Bergman (1975) postulate—of a particular period of cognitive-emotional development? Or are they rather the product of a phantasizing which rests on a fairly accurate perception of reality, and a hyperactive consciousness of self rather than a lack of it? If the latter is true, as Sass implies and as Stern (1984) himself suggests, these phantasies might express the wish (or the fear, or both) that another could read one's mind, or that their two selves were forever fused, or that just by wishing one could make another think what one wished him to, or that all one's own pains and pleasures were the direct consequence of the other's desire, and so on. These are complicated thoughts that one couldn't attribute to someone without attributing to him at the same time concepts much like ours of self, other, mind, body, and world.

7 The Subject of Emotion

Of course infants *feel*, for example pleasure, pain, excitement, tension, contentment. But whether to say they experience emotions like sadness, shame, pride, and so on, depends both on our knowledge of infants and on a conceptual analysis of what sort of thing emotions are.

The most important question such an analysis confronts is the relation between emotion and thought. Clearly some such relation exists in the typical case: Sophie feels guilty because she holds herself responsible for her daughter's death; the Rat Man was afraid that his parents knew his murderous thoughts; Prufrock is proud because he dares to wear his trousers rolled. But just what relation is it? Is the thought somehow tacked on to an emotion that is more or less what it is with or without the thought? Or are emotions themselves cognitive through and through?

Freud follows a long tradition which divides reason from passion, as it divides mind from body. The tradition also tends to make us think that belief is necessarily 'cold', and passion blind. It is the failure of psycho-analysis to confront these assumptions squarely which is responsible for its lack of a coherent theory of the emotions;[1] for most theorists have not truly abandoned Freud's attempt to derive mental life from instincts, or drives, while half acknowledging that concepts, experience, and interpersonal relations play a more essential role in the emotions than either drive theory, or its modified version, the structural theory, allows.[2] Edith Jacobson, for example, begins by questioning the extent to which affect corresponds to either instinctual or ego processes. Nevertheless, accommodating her views to Freud's, she suggests that some affects arise from tensions within the id, the ego, or the superego, and some from tensions between two or more of these structures. She then points out the severe limitations of her analysis, noting that the affects it cannot reckon with include, among others, "kindness and heartlessness, sympathy and cruelty, loving and hostility, sadness, grief and happiness, depression and elation" (1953, p. 47n). Such a limitation is surely sufficient proof that something is fundamentally wrong with her scheme. We might give a recipe for boeuf bourguignon if we made enough substitutions in one for chicken fricassee. But the dish would likely turn out better if we started the recipe from scratch.

In this chapter I weigh in with those many philosophers who have argued that emotions are mental phenomena irreducible either to physical states or to behavioral dispositions, though both would enter into any comprehensive account; that thought is a necessary condition for emotion, not its accomplice but part of its very constitution; that emotions are therefore neither beyond nor beneath reason but, like beliefs, the sort of thing which can be said to be both rational and irrational. Cognition is more passional than it is typically held to be, and passion more informed. I will call this the cognitivist view.[3] Let me make clear that the issue is not merely terminological, for example about when and how children learn to call their experiences sadness, shame, or pride. If we lacked linguistic labels for peaches and nectarines, there would still be differences between them, though we would be unable to name and even, perhaps, to notice them. But if thought is constitutive of the emotions in the sense I have in mind, then without the appropriate thoughts we lack the emotions themselves.[4] The implication is that infants come equipped with certain material that time, the world, and early pre-verbal communications with other people will shape into emotions, but that they do not experience emotions per se.[5]

Freud's official view is that emotions are nothing but physiological processes, or epiphenomena of them. "Affects and emotions," he writes, "correspond to processes of discharge, the final expression of which is perceived as feeling" (1915a, p. 178). Or in the slightly different terminology of the *Project,* the affect is said to be a quantity, a charge of energy, which becomes 'qualified' by being bonded with any number of different 'ideas'. Quantity and quality form a complex which can then be split, or repressed and converted into a somatic symptom. In hysteria, for example, "the incompatible idea is rendered innocuous by its *sum of excitation* being *transformed into something somatic*"; in obsessional neurosis the idea is separated from its affect, which now *"attaches itself to other ideas which are not in themselves incompatible"* (1894, pp. 49–53). The implications of this view are both that in relation to emotions there is no essential difference between adults and infants, and also that while rationality and irrationality can be predicated of beliefs and thoughts, they are not applicable to the emotions.

The following sorts of clinical data might seem to support Freud's analysis: one can feel consciously triumphant about having done *x*, when unconsciously one feels no triumph at all about *x* but rather about *y*, and not triumph but guilt about *x*; one can, under the influence of repression, feel only anxiety where before one felt desire; one can consciously entertain thoughts that might be expected to be accompanied by certain feelings, though (consciously) there are none at all; and so on. But is Freud's analysis right? Are the ideas imported from some other system—say 'the ego'—and somehow attached to an affect that is itself qualitatively colorless? Is the relation between affect and idea merely contingent, such that the affect is what it is with or without the idea, as an ivory bead remains an ivory bead even when it has fallen from the necklace, or as a red truck remains a truck when we paint it white? Or is the bond more like the relation between the concept of trucks and the belief that there are trucks, or between color and sunsets? If the latter, then the 'idea' is an essential constituent in the identity of an emotion, and emotions are in the domain of the rational along with desires and beliefs.

Interestingly, just this is one of the assumptions consistently underlying Freud's own interpretive practice. "When there is a mésalliance," he says to his patient the Rat Man,

> between an affect and its ideational content [in the instance at hand between the intensity of his patient's self-reproach and the occasion for it], a layman will say that the affect is too great for the occasion—that it is exaggerated—and that consequently the inference following from the self-reproach (the inference that the patient is a criminal) is false. On the contrary, the [analytic] physician says: 'No. The affect is justified. The sense of guilt is not in itself open to further criticism. But it belongs to some other content, which is unknown *(unconscious)*, and which requires to be looked for'. (1909, pp. 175–176)

The Rat Man consciously believes he feels suicidally guilty about some current omission which he judges to be trivial. Hence his puzzlement and Freud's. Unconsciously, however, his guilt is about his murderous wishes against his father, together with his infantile conviction that wishing amounts to doing. The 'displacement' of the guilt still needs explaining. But once these wishes and the constellation of beliefs and desires surrounding them have come to light, the feelings become intelligible; they are, as Freud puts it, justified. The point of view from which an emotion seems to be inappropriate is that of one's conscious beliefs, and perhaps one's more grown-up self. Guilt may be premised on false or illusory 'ideas', or 'ideas' one consciously denies; but 'ideas' must be in the background. So the interpretive task is to find the *unconscious* ideas that explain the emotion, precisely by showing its rationality. Freud writes: "Psychoanalysis can put [neurotics] upon the right path by recognizing the emotion as being . . . justified and by seeking out the idea which belongs to it but has been repressed and replaced by a substitute." Exactly so. But now Freud continues:

> A necessary premise to all this is that the release of emotion and the ideational content do not constitute the indissoluble organic unity as which [*sic*] we are in the habit of treating them, but that these two separate entities may be merely soldered together and can thus be detached from each other by analysis. (1900, pp. 461–462)

About this passage Lear rightly remarks: "The deeper point, which Freud ought to be making, is that an emotion and its appropriate idea *do* constitute an indissoluble organic unity" (1990, p. 91). It is precisely because they have an essentially rational structure that Freud was able to talk of neurotic and repressed emotions which have been deflected from their natural shape. This can happen in many ways, one of which is suggested by the case of the Rat Man: an emotion that is rational in a certain limited context, say a fret of certain childhood beliefs and desires, is somehow preserved, becoming discrepant with one's beliefs and desires as a whole.[6]

Recognizing the essentially rational connection between 'ideas' and emotions clears up a puzzle Freud himself acknowledges. He asks whether instinctual impulses, emotions and feelings—which he lumps together—can be unconscious, answering that "the antithesis of conscious and unconscious is not applicable to instincts. An instinct can never become an object of consciousness—only the idea that represents the instinct can" (1915a, p. 177). Yet he grants that emotions and instincts are not equivalent in a couple of relevant respects. For one, unlike instincts, emotions seem to be in the domain of the phenomenal: "It is surely of the essence of an emotion," he writes, "that we should be aware of it" (ibid.). For another, there is a sense in which an emotion can be unconscious, namely when it has been linked to the wrong idea, or when the associated ideas have been repressed altogether. What may present itself in consciousness as free-floating anxiety, or restlessness, or as annoyance with your brother because he treats something you have given him lightly, may be unconscious guilt, or fear, or fury because the fellow exists at all.

The way around Freud's puzzle lies in saying, first, that while emotions, like all other mental states, are no doubt identical with neurophysiological states—which as such are neither conscious nor unconscious—yet emotions are not reducible to them; and second, that emotions are complex in the way that other mental states are, and consciousness is not a necessary feature of any of them.

Let's explore the nature of the logical connection between emotion and cognition by expanding on Freud's own remarks. How should we understand 'ideational content'? What Freud is onto is the fact that typically emotions refer beyond themselves, have the character of 'aboutness', are directed toward 'objects'. In short, in line with our earlier analysis of Intentionality we can say that emotions are attitudes toward propositions, though not necessarily ones of which the agent herself is conscious. While we often do know what our emotions are about, there is a spectrum of cases with transparent self-knowledge at one end and various sorts of errors and self-deceptions at the other; the propositional component that identifies the emotion's content belongs to our analysis of it and is not necessarily a content of the subject's present or past conscious awareness.

The following account of the Rat Man is vastly over-simple, but it serves as an example of emotional Intentionality. The man feels guilty because he believes *that* he is in some way responsible for his father's death, and because he has a negative evaluative attitude—I will sometimes refer to such an attitude as 'desire'—toward the belief. The belief distinguishes this feeling of guilt from others; the evaluative component tells us why the emotion is *guilt* rather than some other response, say glee.[7]

To take another example: Sophie's feelings of guilt over the death of her daughter are different from the guilt she feels about the lie she told her lover, though between these two feelings there may be deeper underlying connections of the sort that psychoanalysis often investigates; and *guilt* over the death of a daughter is not the same as *sadness* about that same event. In complicated cases, questions crowd in. Is Sophie feeling guilty more specifically about having chosen to let the Gestapo kill her daughter rather than her son? Is she feeling guilty perhaps about the wish to be alone with him? Does she think of what she has done as an act of terrible betrayal or even of murder because it reverberates with memories of other older betrayals, perhaps other and only imagined murders? The possibilities are many; they point, however, not to an absence of ideational content but its complexity.

Emotions are dependent on beliefs in yet another way; for members of an emotion type share some general beliefs or concepts. Necessary to guilt, for example, but perhaps not to other unpleasant emotions like shame and embarrassment which guilt resembles, is the belief that one is in some sense responsible for having done something wrong by one's own lights. Someone who feels guilty must have the concepts of right and wrong, of self, of agency, and must be able to differentiate doing something which he himself holds wrong from doing something which is merely disapproved of by others. (Freud recognizes this condition for guilt when he distinguishes it from what he calls guilt-precursors, such as fear of the loss of love.)

Take another emotion, gratitude. If Mary feels grateful to Sarah, then Mary must believe she has been given something by Sarah, and Mary must have some pro-attitude toward that gift. But since gratitude is different from a feeling of obligation, and from pleasure in the receipt of something without regard to the donor, our analysis needs in addition something like the following: Mary desires *x*, or believes that *x* is desirable (I am not sure what to say if Mary does not think *x* is desirable but believes that Sarah believes Mary will find it so); and Mary believes that Sarah is responsible for giving Mary *x*. I think the following are conditions as well: Mary believes that she could not have procured *x* by or for herself, or at least not easily. (If she thinks otherwise, then she will not feel grateful; though she may think that what Mary has done is generous or kind.) And Mary believes that Sarah intended to give her *x*. (If Mary stole *x* from Sarah, or if Sarah accidentally left it at Mary's house, and so on, then Mary may be delighted with *x*, perhaps grateful to her lucky star, but not to Sarah.) Mary believes that Sarah believed that Mary would find *x* desirable. (Brer Rabbit is delighted that the fox, falsely thinking that rabbits hate briar patches, threw him into one; but Brer Rabbit is not grateful, at least not to the fox.)

To test this out, suppose the gift Mary has received is a round-trip ticket to Paris, and she believes that her very generous friend Sarah has sent it to her. If Mary now discovers it was not Sarah but Jack, then her gratitude turns instead to him; or if she learns that she has won the ticket herself because hers was the winning answer in a contest, she no longer feels *gratitude* but perhaps pride; or if she finds out that Sarah plans to put a bomb on her airplane, outrage replaces gratitude. (These are points not merely about the actual contingencies of her feeling but about the nature of the feelings themselves.) Of course it's possible that when Mary learns that the ticket has come to her through her own doing, or that Sarah's 'gift' is booby-trapped, Mary still feels grateful to Sarah on its account; it's possible for her to discover that it was the gift of Jack and not Sarah, yet to feel angry with Jack, even though she would have felt grateful had the gift been Sarah's. But in such cases we'd be puzzled; we would know something is missing from the story.

This point about the cognitive character of guilt and gratitude embraces most if not all of the emotions. Think of fear: typically one is afraid *that* one has insulted one's best friend, that there will be an earthquake, that one will slip on the ice, and these are things one doesn't want to do; shame: one believes he has done something that diminishes his esteem; grief: one thinks she has lost something or someone she loves or values; pride: one believes she has or has done something that brings honor to herself. It is because emotions have a logical relation to beliefs and desires that they can be said to be rational and irrational: My belief that I have done something shameful or estimable, that something is dangerous or that someone is intentionally making my life miserable, is my *reason* for feeling as I do.

In the passage quoted earlier Freud says something else that our own analysis needs. He speaks of the 'ideational' content of an affect as its 'occasion', by which I take him to mean its cause. What we have called the 'object' of Sophie's guilt, namely her belief that she is to an extent responsible for the death of her daughter whom she loves, is a partial cause of her guilt; she feels guilty *because* she believes this. If she didn't, she wouldn't feel guilty, not about this. The Rat Man feels guilty *because* of his wish to harm his father, combined with his conviction that such a wish is dangerous and wrong. Just as earlier we saw that the beliefs and desires which move one to action are in the typical case also causes, so beliefs and desires are both the reasons for one's being in the emotional state one is, and an essential part of its causal story.[8]

Why should we say so? The answer is somewhat different for emotions than for actions. About the latter we noticed that one may have reasons for doing *x,* and may do *x* in fact, yet not because of those reasons. Giacomo intended to kill Corleone and was on his way to do so when he ran down a stranger in the road, who turned out to be Corleone. It was the very failure of the coincidence of reasons and causes in such an instance that led us to see the point of saying that 'normally'—when there are no such wayward causal chains—the agent does what he does *because* of his reasons. In the case of action, we intend to do *x* as a means of doing *y,* and this means-end relation can fail in a number of ways. But since there is no means-end relation of this sort in the case of emotions, no such slippage is possible.

Yet obviously Freud was right to insist that emotions have causes. What might they be? Hormonal imbalances, surges of testosterone, neurological firings are part of the total causal story. But if we were to find in any given case of what we had been calling shame or pride that bodily business is all that's going on, we would withdraw our description of the person as truly feeling ashamed, and so on. Even William James in reducing affect to physiology posited a perceptual stimulus in explaining the affective response. For example, the snake in the road causes a visceral response which registers in consciousness as fright.

But the idea of a 'perceptual stimulus' is more complex than this example suggests; for one can be frightened about a snake in the road even though none is there. We who have beliefs and desires share with creatures who do not a number of built-in responses; so we are apt to overlook the fact that the causal story in our case is much more compli-

cated, that we do not react to the world directly but only as apprehended
by us in certain lights, under certain descriptions. I say that I am pleased
because I inherited a house, ashamed at having behaved foolishly, jealous
because you betrayed me, suggesting that the causality in each case goes
straight from a 'stimulus' or event in the world—albeit in these examples
of a complexity that could only inspire feelings in cognitively sophisticated creatures—to me. But of course I can experience pleasure at the
thought of having inherited a house though no house is in the offing,
think I have done something shameful when I have only dreamed it.
Tragic Othello makes the case most clearly: that Desdemona has betrayed
him is the content of his jealousy, though she is innocent in fact. So an
analysis of these reactions must pedantically say that I am pleased because
I believe I have inherited a house, angry or jealous because *I believe* I have
been betrayed, and so on. The story that explains my emotions remains
fully causal, and the real external world still hovers in the background.
But the immediate causal agents of my emotions are my desires and
beliefs.[9] And this is precisely the insight we honor in saying that the affect
is occasioned by its ideational content.

Like perceptions, and more patently than beliefs and desires, emotions
show us in our guise as organisms interacting with the world around us,
which makes for confusion about both perception and emotion. We say of
the infant, 'Susan sees a dog'; but only of the older child, 'Susan sees that
there's a dog'. The first is a kind of seeing that doesn't presume Intentionality, the second a kind of apprehending or knowing that doesn't necessarily presume visual seeing; for a blind person too can see *that* there's a
dog. Yet we understand wanting to say in both cases 'Susan sees the dog'
since it may be the dog that causes the state in question.

The situation is similar for affects. The barking dog frightens the baby,
and the dog also frightens me. The baby's fright, attested by its cries and
pulse, is not banked by beliefs and desires; mine, which is, does not necessarily have either a sensational or a behavioral component. So it might be
helpful to think of both perceptions and emotions as on a spectrum, going
in the case of the latter from affects that lack mental content to emotions
as such.

Many philosophers have objected that the object of an emotion cannot
also be its cause. Since their arguments are very similar to the ones cited
earlier against the identification of reasons with causes in the case of
action, I will discuss them only briefly. The first objection holds that the
object of someone's emotion is the sort of thing about which he cannot be
mistaken and which is known at first hand, by introspection. If I am angry
about your rude remark, that is something I know without any evidence,
whereas causal connections are contingent and knowable only by
induction. Earlier we answered that avowability is one of our criteria for

the mental, but only one. And what is avowable in principle may not be avowable now, in these circumstances. Emotions are more complicated than actions in a way relevant to the argument. Though an elaborate skein of thoughts may be necessary to identifying my emotion as just the state it is, there is no reason why I should be aware of all of these thoughts, and under just that description which reveals their logical connection to what I feel. John's anger over Mary's remark may be partly caused by the fact that he confusedly assimilates it to something offensive said by someone else, or that he still holds a grudge against Mary for something she did a long time ago. When he becomes aware of this he will understand why he is angry; and he may at the same time see that his way of understanding the remark is inappropriate, that the reasons for his anger aren't very good reasons, or ones he now wants to honor.

The second objection and my answer to it are implicit in these last remarks. It is said that since the link between the description of my act as building a bird-cage and my desire to build a bird-cage is logical in nature while causal connections are contingent, desire cannot be a cause of my action; just so—the argument goes on—since the link between my feeling of shame and my belief that I have done something shameful is logical, again the relation between the two cannot be causal. The answer is this: Of course if x is described as something I believe I have done and that I find shameful, if y is described as something you have done intentionally to make me suffer, then the connection between my action and my shame, your action and my anger, is logical and apparent, to whoever is describing things this way. But so identifying x or y is not a merely conceptual matter. If I know that Laius is my father then I know that I am Laius' son; but I may have to discover that Laius is my father, hence that I am Laius' son. All that is necessary to the contingency of the relation between two things is that there be some way of describing them which does not make the relation logical.

So we can now say that the explanation of emotion resembles that of action in that there are reasons why the agent feels or acts as she does, and these reasons specify those beliefs and desires in the light of which we can see the emotion or the behavior as rational, appropriate, or justified. The emotion also gives us a partial causal explanation of why the agent felt or acted as she did. Of course emotions are unlike actions and intentions in important respects, since we don't decide, or plan, or choose to feel angry, while action is typically (but not necessarily) the outcome of some such process. Furthermore, the role of belief is different in the two cases; for if I learn that a belief of mine is mistaken, then in the ordinary case (when the belief is not itself, for example, a product of wishful thinking) I give it up, and whatever intentions were premised on it are changed accordingly. But reassessing an emotion may not have so straightaway an effect. If Lear is in a state of high indignation because he believes he has been mistreated and he then discovers his belief was wrong, it would now be incorrect to describe him as indignant. But his emotional fever may burn a while nevertheless, perhaps even (mis-)leading him to look for an appropriate object.

Yet it is easy to exaggerate the differences between the structure of action and that of emotion; for one may willfully, perhaps even intentionally, focus on the thing she knows will make her angry, or induce in herself the provoking belief, or 'whip herself up' into an emotional state. And sometimes we can see that if we really believe and want what we say we do, then we 'ought' or ought not to be angry, or grateful; that is, we see that another emotional state would be more appropriate. If it is yet not ours, then perhaps we are deluded about our beliefs and desires.

We tend to think of actions as initiating in us, emotions and perceptions in the world. So thinking, we regard passions as things we undergo or passively suffer. But there is a mistake here. When we are ashamed, what acts on us is not shame itself, but a situation in the world construed by us in some particular way; and in this construal we have some agency (Gordon, 1987). As Spinoza said, the differences between acting and being acted upon are less a matter of category than degree.

A full-blown theory of the emotions would have to articulate more carefully the ways in which emotions are and are not like actions. It would also want to address the following:

(1) If an emotion is an attitude toward a proposition or a set of propositions, what attitude is it? Belief is the attitude of holding true; desire, of wanting to change the world so that the proposition which is the object of desire will be true. And as compounded of belief and desire, intention is (I'll assume) the making of an all-out judgment to the effect that one will do x because one believes it a means to y, which one on the whole desires, or desires to be the case. Emotion is also, I have said, a meshing of belief and desire. So in the case of emotion can we say something more general, as we can for the other propositional attitudes, about what attitude this meshing yields? I don't think so. No single attitude seems to cover all the emotions. If this is right, then here is another interesting respect in which they differ from beliefs, desires, and intentions.[10]

(2) How should we group the emotions, and which affective responses are built in?

(3) What are the relevant sorts of beliefs and desires in each important emotion type? How do they mesh? And to what behavioral dispositions do they give rise?[11]

(4) Are emotions reducible to certain belief-desire constructions? Or does something else enter in?[12]

I have not attempted to answer these and other questions about emotions but only to establish their generally rational character. The subject came up, we remember, because the connections we found between thought and talk, interpretation and the mental, led us to conclude that infants do not have subjective states in a philosophically interesting sense of that phrase. We were forced then to an unseemly conclusion, that if emotions are mental, infants do not have emotions. But we have now reached that point by an independent route, not via a theory of the mental but of emotion itself. So putting the two together, we can say that infants acquire an inner mental world as they acquire concepts, which they do through interacting with other creatures, learning at the same time to inhibit certain of their responses to the world. Inhibition of behavior precedes the having of feelings which one may learn to keep to oneself or to avoid acknowledging altogether.[13]

Having agreed that emotions are subject to rational appraisal, we must now ask, in what ways might an emotion be said to be irrational? This is a large and interesting subject which would require a book in itself. I discuss irrationality in belief and action in a later chapter, and I indirectly return to the subject in this one through remarks about the principle of charity. But here, very briefly, are a number of ways in which emotional irrationality might be seen: the belief which is constitutive of the emotion may be incompatible with other beliefs one holds, or with the evidence one has easily available; the constitutive desire may be a holdover from a previous period in one's life, and out of keeping with one's present, more overriding desires; cause and reason may come apart, as when one is frightened of the snake in the path, but does not believe (even unconsciously) that snakes, or something they symbolize, are dangerous; one is (more or less intentionally) feeding the beliefs or desires that constitute the emotion in order to put oneself into a state one holds desirable (the soldier who reminds himself of his enemy's atrocities in order to feel angry, the man who fears impotence imagining what he has to in order to feed his lust).[14]

It may help to clarify the view I am proposing if we look at what is wrong, and right, with some rival theories.

EMOTION AS 'FEELING'

I have been using these terms interchangeably, as we often do in ordinary speech. But in the context of theories of emotion a traditional view holds that a feeling is by definition entirely inner, consciously experienced, and similar to sensations like a chill or a prickle, as in the 'shiver' of fear and the 'heat' of lust. To have an emotion just is to experience such a feeling.

On this view a study of the emotions would presumably consist in a systematic introspective description of certain states.

James developed a species of this view, placing it however in a biological frame. Darwin's classic work *The Expression of Emotions in Man and Animals* (1896) studied concomitants of emotions, not the emotions themselves. But James thought that the following line remedies that defect while acknowledging the rightness of Darwin's orientation: A perception of an event causes a physiological change of the sort Darwin had been studying; emotion per se then arises when the physiological change is registered in consciousness. Note that on this view the perception of the event plays no *constitutive* role in the emotion; it is a cause and not a reason.[15]

Freud also aligns himself with 'feeling' theories in holding—as in the passage quoted earlier—that an emotion is by definition something of which we are aware. Since Freud's own interpretive procedure lends itself most readily to an interpersonal view of the mental, the subject of the emotions is yet another important juncture at which Freud is torn between third-person and first-person or subjectivist intuitions.

What is right with feeling theories is that an actively present emotion, as distinguished from a disposition, for example to be afraid when snakes are around, contains an element of felt pleasure or pain, comfort or discomfort, though one need not know what the feeling is about.[16] Furthermore, there is sometimes a visceral feeling that seems peculiar to an emotion of that sort.

Yet clearly pain and pleasure are not by themselves sufficient to identify any emotion; for what differentiates this painful feeling from that one? Moreover, the same visceral phenomena can even characterize emotions of very different types (Cannon, 1929; MacLean, 1970).[17] In any case, feelings are not always present: One can be proud that one solved the puzzle, worried that it may rain, ashamed about the lie one told, without any accompanying sensation. So 'feeling' does not accomplish the primary task of a theory of emotion, which is to tell us how to identify both individual emotions and emotion types. In fact, feeling theories can account for none of the features of emotion which we have already seen to be essential:

(1) Intentionality. One might try to serve Intentionality by positing some kind of accompaniment, perhaps in the form of a mental image. It would be the image, on this suggestion, that would identify the emotion's content. But recall from Chapter 1 the argument that images, mental or otherwise, do not carry their meaning on their face. Here is an implication of that argument: if the anger is one thing, and the image another, then it must be possible for the wrong image to come before the mind; but if it is the image that gives the anger its meaning or content, then one must necessarily be angry about whatever one's image is of. Yet surely my anger

may be about Jones's remark whether or not there happens to be an image in my mind of my favorite dress.[18]

(2) The sense in which emotions are reasonable and unreasonable. One might answer that this is a function of what has caused the emotion. So it is. But only causes that are also reasons can account for the irrationality of what they cause, and only effects that have a logical structure can have causes of this sort.

(3) The respect in which emotions can be unconscious, for this can only be explained by the embedding of emotion in belief and desire, first of all, and second, by a theory of the mental according to which consciousness is not a necessary feature of mental content.

(4) The role that emotions play in our third-person explanations of behavior. People who are jealous are apt to behave spitefully toward those they believe to be their rivals; people who are ashamed may hide their heads. Emotions are more public than feeling theories can allow. They must be so, furthermore, if children are able to learn to talk about their emotions in the first place.[19] Anger, pride, guilt, and so on are not names for some private, inaccessible mental sensations, but concepts referring to complex mental states that are essentially relational in nature and complexly related to each other.[20]

How do we know what someone else is feeling? It's often not easy; but here too interpretation requires being guided by the principle of charity or the assumption that by and large the creature we are interpreting is rational in a general sense of that word, then locating that holistic network in the light of which we can see the reason in her behavior.

INNATISM AND THE QUEST FOR PRIMARY MOTIVES

Are all emotions derivable from a few basic building blocks? The cognitivist answer is clearly No, no more than all intentions are. Though Spinoza (and Freud) were right to think that emotions are grounded in pleasure, pain, and desire, or something like desire, perhaps a pre-volitional striving as when the baby tries to grab the mobile wheeling above its head.[21] Only a creature who can experience pleasure to begin with can be pleased to have won the lottery, proud of having learned to tie her shoes, grateful for the favor done. Only a creature who can experience pain can feel ashamed of his rude remark, or sad because he's going away. If every emotion is a positive or negative attitude of some sort toward some idea or other, then it is pleasure, pain, and volition that become articulated in an endless number of ways by cognitions and beliefs.

But the quest for primary motives claims far more than this. S. S. Tomkins (1981), for example, holds that there are nine primary affects—

he calls them interest, enjoyment, surprise, fear, anger, distress, shame, contempt, and disgust—which are a function of "inherited programs that . . . control facial muscle responses, automatic blood flow, respiratory, and vocal responses" (p. 323).[22] All affects are variants on these few. Consistently, he also claims that "feeling and thinking are two independent mechanisms" (p. 316); that "affective judgments precede cognitive judgments in time" (ibid.); and that an adequate account of affects will require us to give up assumptions like mine, that affect is "necessarily cognitively activated" and necessarily *about* something. Tomkins' particular version of this innatist view says, furthermore, that differences in affect can be accounted for by three variants of a single principle, the density of neural firing.

The problem with such a theory emerges when one asks how the experimenter collecting data knows what to count in the first place as instances of shame or contempt. How does he know to call the infant experiences by these names? How has the experimenter himself mastered these concepts? Infants have inclinations and wants, pains and pleasures; when frustrated or in pain they are apt, like us, to flail and hit; they make faces that can be universally recognized as expressions of 'surprise', 'anger', 'fear', and so on. But if we ask how we know to describe their expressions in these particular ways, we see that we have acquired the concepts of surprise, anger, guilt, and gratitude in that same complex process through which we learned to become interpreters of each other and to have any of our concepts in the first place. We clothe the infant's behavior in garb that would be appropriate to us, and it is this that allows us to identify his expressions in the ways we do, lending him much else in the process that will truly become his in time.

It might be—though I very much doubt it—that all those states that are picked out by our folk-psychological criteria as instances of sadness, for example, correspond to a certain range of neural firings, unique for sadness. Even so, this would not establish the dispensability of cognitions in the causal story. To see that this is so, take a look at Tomkins' own explanation of humor. "It is the sudden unexpectedness of the punch line that both surprises and terminates further increasing information processing," he writes; and although he grants that these are cognitive processes, he claims that "it is the direction and rate of neural firing that mediate the triggering mechanism rather than their meaning or content" (p. 319). That's a remarkable thing to say. If I understand it, it implies that even if you don't understand the punch line, your neural mechanisms will be fired, followed by laughter.

What affects, then, does it make sense to attribute to animals? to babies? Not ones with propositional content. We can attribute to them a certain sort of fear, rage (perhaps not anger), startlement (perhaps not surprise), and pain and pleasure; but we do not attribute to them fear *that* the house will fall down or *that* one is about to become ill. Fear needn't have a propositional content, though it may. I hesitate about anger, because typically it has an object (though one may not be aware of what it is) in the form of a belief that 'makes' one angry. And I hesitate also about 'surprised' as distinct from 'startled', since the latter only presumes some adaptive mechanism that responds to certain sorts of situations, while *being surprised* (by *x*) seems to presume a belief that *x* calls into question.

In this vein Robert Gordon suggests that we speak of contentless fear as the state of fear rather than fear per se:

> The *state of fear* appears to have been a complex evolutionary experiment, perhaps universal among mammals, involving physiological (especially autonomic) arousal, the riveting of attention, readiness for flight, and a disposition to flee . . . Since mammals of other species clearly exhibit [this] syndrome, one might say that they are subject to (states of) *fear* . . . It may sometimes be useful to attribute such fears in explaining as well as in predicting the animal's behavior, but it is important to do so with an understood *qualification:* that the attributed fear contents do not have anything *remotely* like the set of inferential connections such contents would be expected to have in a standard attribution, particularly an attribution to ourselves or to most other human beings. Thus one should not suppose a mouse to infer from its being hurt that it may be *wounded* or otherwise *injured,* or even that *a mouse* is hurt. (1987, pp. 71–72)

Once again, as with the language of mind in general, something is served by using the language of emotions to talk about animals and infants. But how much richer is this language than it needs to be to capture what we see, and how many are the usual implications of such talk that are inapplicable here.

I suggest that we think of 'affect' as an umbrella term covering phenomena wider than the emotions per se, spanning a continuum that reaches back not only to the infant but also to other animals, and including states that have propositional content as well as states that lack it: Lear's anger over Cordelia's imagined insult and Sophie's guilt, but also the pleasure a monkey feels when a certain part of its brain is stimulated, human aggression that is caused by nothing but a charge of adrenaline or testosterone, the infant's pleasure in seeing his mother, raw anxiety, and so on. Contentless rage, pleasure, delight, agitation, tension, contentment, and so on are not strictly speaking emotions; yet all have clear affinities with states that are: depending on a number of variables, pleasure or contentment in the presence of other people may in time become love, or kindness, or sympathy; pleasure in one's own activity, pride; curiosity, a passion to know about the physical world.

THE 'CONSTRUCTIVIST' VIEW

While Tomkins thinks that emotions are independent of culture and learning, others hold that by and large emotions are 'social constructs'. K. R. Averill (1980) writes:

> It might be said that emotions have a 'grammar'; and like the grammatical structures studied by linguists, emotional systems cannot be identified with any specific set of behaviors. For example, there are an indefinite number of ways in which a person may express his anger, just as there are an indefinite number of ways in which any particular proposition may be expressed in language. (p. 39)

My first response to this is to point out that 'emotional systems' cannot be identified with any specific set of behaviors simply because behavior is only one criterion for an emotional state. Constitutive features are belief and desire, which in turn cause people to behave as they do. Granted, people may express their anger in a variety of ways, and the customs of a family or a culture have a hand in determining what these ways are. The question we have been asking, however, is a prior one: What determines a state to begin with as anger?

Averill comes closer to arguing that emotions are themselves culturally determined when he goes on to say that the Japanese have fashioned from attachment an extremely fundamental emotion they call *amae,* for which there is no Western equivalent. Now it is true that since emotions are partly constituted by belief, and since beliefs differ both from individual to individual and culture to culture, so do emotions. But note that the general claims about interpretation and the mental made in the first few chapters also hold here: a response which we were able to recognize as a mental state in the first place must be one which is in principle open to interpretation; and interpretation presumes considerable agreement both in belief and attitude. On this ground, the continual widening of the community in which there is mutual understanding is always possible.

This brings us now to what is right about both the constructivist and the innatist views. It will even give a key importance to something like feeling. Recall the argument in Chapter 1 that for Intentionality to appear on the scene there must be communication. The Cartesian says, first there is mental content, then the communication of mental content. We have said that mental content is constructed only on a base of interpersonal communications and does not exist prior to them. So there is then an important sense in which all mental states, emotions included, are socially constructed.

Communication in turn requires, first, a common world which the communicants share and can sometimes presume to be the common focus of their words and thoughts. (This is why I remarked a moment ago that interpretability rests on there being considerable agreement.) And it requires, second, that the communicants share some fundamental traits and concerns, dispositions to find certain sorts of patterns in the world salient, and importantly, apropos of emotions, the capacity for pleasure, pain, and volitionally directed behavior. So the mental requires something in the way of innate species-shared dispositions.

Just what is innate is a matter for empirical investigation. Attachment behavior seems to be, for example, and our ability to recognize facial expressions as expressive of certain emotions; startle and fear responses, and generally the tendency to express our feelings in characteristic behavioral ways, for example crying when we feel pain and smiling when we have what we want; responsiveness to the human voice, face, and eye, and so on. All this built-in affective behavior is in the public domain. If it were not, there would be no way for the baby to communicate her needs. Given how dependent she is on members of her kind, an in-built capacity for affective communication is necessary to the survival of the species.[23] Thus it is not surprising that the human creature is susceptible to emotions like embarrassment, shame, guilt, affection, pride, gratitude, anger, and indignation, all of which have as a necessary condition our dependency on the good will of others. If the mental rides on communication, affective communications in particular are where the tracks begin. So while emotions are shot through with beliefs and desires, belief and desire themselves are anchored in affective habits and patterns which are often very old.

My view of the mental has claimed that interpretability is not something to which the mind may or may not be subject, since the conditions which make interpretation possible are the very conditions for the mind itself. They include not only a shared world and shared salience patterns, but also shared norms of rationality: meaning attaches to ideas only as constituents in a network of ideas; and if the lines between ideas did not conform in a very general way to a normative pattern that guides us all, we could make sense neither to ourselves nor of each other. It is because these norms must be shared for meaning to get going in the first place that I have insouciantly associated rationality with intelligibility.

Now it seems to me that apropos of emotional rationality a new element enters in. The rationality of belief is described by logical relations defining the notions of evidence, the true and the false, and so on. The rationality of action is described by the maxims of practical reasoning: If Sam wants x and believes y is the way to get it, then he will think it reasonable to do y, all other things being equal. But are these sufficient to explain my ability to understand why someone feels pride, or anger, or shame, in a situation that would strike me very differently? Once I have understood how he sees his situation, is there nothing left for our analysis to say? I believe there is, though perhaps it only makes explicit something already implicit in my earlier remarks about shared affective dispositions. It is this:

For any creature whose emotions I am able to find generally intelligible, there will be some situation to which he would respond with a generically similar emotion to mine—shame, or embarrassment, or anger, or fear. It is easy to think what such situations might be for some emotions: for envy, perhaps a playmate's getting the toy John wanted for himself; for jealousy, perhaps the new sibling in the mother's arms; for pride, perhaps being able for the first time to tie one's own shoe. My understanding another's alien emotional response depends, I am speculating, on my being able to assume that he has some responses in the same emotional family as this alien one that I would not find strange. About this 'paradigm' situation it would also be possible for me to say why it appropriately evokes the response it does: 'Of course John feels jealous. He sees someone else occupying the place he feels is his, and he feels left out'. Explanation here could go no further, and someone unable to understand why John feels jealous in this situation would likely not understand many of John's other emotional states. Freud delineated for us a number of such paradigm scenarios, allowing us to discern their outlines in apparently remote behaviors.[24]

It may be that children have affective responses to such paradigm situations before they have a complex of mental states and emotions per se, that before they feel jealousy, exactly, they are pained by situations that will later cause them jealousy. If so, the later emotions may be shaped by the behavioral habits set in motion by those earlier responses, shaped and given a certain color. Indeed it seems that more behavior is built in relating specifically to the development of emotion than to belief. If this is so, then emotions have a central place in any story about the advent of mind.

In any case, the child's early interpersonal relations are crucial determinants of his attitudes toward the world, and through them of his character traits and emotions, which are often themselves embedded in traits of character. (Think of the way that someone may chronically resort to anger as a means of control, or the feeling of helplessness as a defense against the fear of failure.) An infant whose parents are attuned and responsive to her needs is apt to develop an attitude of self-confidence and trust, one whose antic parents laugh with her at the funniness of things will likely come by a sense of humor, and so on. Such attitudes precede emotions as such. But they set the stage for them, determining how the infant looks at the world and what she sees.[25]

Take moods, for example, which unlike emotions do not necessarily have 'intentional objects'. Someone may feel depressed because he believes he's a failure, or that he is mortally ill. But the cause may also be some physiological condition, or a response to what is going on around him that doesn't have specific content, as neglected babies may begin to be depressed. And depression, whatever its cause, in turn predisposes one to see the world in muted shades: the depressed person is more disposed than the cheerful person to note the worm in the apple, or to think the task at hand too hard.

Some insist that the pre-verbal infant must have mental states; that to put the flag of the mental only over what has been colonized by language is to concede to language too much; that there must be a mental vocabulary which is clearly appropriate to the more complex animals and infants as well as adults. I would rather settle for a gray area in which affects, moods, and pre-intentional strivings have pride of place, since they play so important a causal role in shaping the infant into the more sophisticated psychological creature he will become.

In closing this chapter I want to make some remarks that bear on belief as well as emotion, and that will return us to a relative of that concept of 'feeling' I earlier found unhelpful. As I have already noted, the concepts of emotion, belief, and desire are all abstractions. Belief is an attitude toward a proposition; it isn't the proposition itself. There is always a context in which one holds a proposition true, and the context includes other beliefs, worries, conjectures, desires, hopes, values, memories, and so on, that give this belief a certain quality. The same is true of desire. One can only desire in a condition of felt lack, uncertainty, a particular anticipatory attitude toward the future, and a vast network of beliefs. To listen to someone's account of his beliefs and desires just *is* to hear a story in which emotion is implicit. Consider Freud's account of the beginning of his treatment of the Rat Man:

> He had a friend, he told me, of whom he had an extraordinarily high opinion. He used always to go to him when he was tormented by some criminal impulse, and ask him whether he despised him as a criminal. His friend used then to give him moral support by assuring him that he was a man of irreproachable conduct, and had probably been in the habit, from his youth onwards, of taking a dark view of his own life. At an earlier date, he went on, another person had exercised a similar influence over him. This was a nineteen-year-old student (he himself had been fourteen or fifteen at the time) who had taken a liking to him, and had raised his self-esteem to an extraordinary degree, so that he appeared to himself to be a genius. This student had subsequently become his tutor, and had suddenly altered his behavior and begun treating him as though he were an idiot. At length he had noticed that the student was interested in one of his sisters, and had realized that he had only taken him up in order to gain admission into the house. This had been the first great blow of his life. (1909, pp. 159–160)

This vignette is shot through with emotion; yet none of the paradigm emotion words figures in it. Instead we hear of the man's "high opinion" of his friend; his "tormenting criminal impulse"; his "question" about whether or not his friend despised him; the "moral support" he was given; the "dark view" he took toward his own life; and so on. One of the difficulties for a theory of the emotions is that often the best we can do by way of defining any particular emotional state is to bring out the fine grain of all its constituent attitudes. A superb poem, for example, renders an emotion as no other words could. We speak of the language of emotions, but it is rather that the language which describes human beings as motivated by beliefs and desires is necessarily an emotional language.

And this is where feelings come in. If emotions, and the valuings and appraisals of various sorts that are constitutive of them, are inextricable in this way from desires and beliefs, inextricable both in the activity of third-person interpretation and in the mind itself, then it may be arbitrary not to grant emotions a fitness to the world, a kind of truth, similar to that of beliefs. Think of emotions then as feelers, part of our human equipment for discerning certain properties in reality that bear directly on our well-being. The baby sees the mother's smiling face, and feels her pleasure in the baby, or her disapproval, her tension or her anxiety. As the baby grows, the situations that bear on its well-being are more and more complex, since feelings are increasingly refined by cognitions. I suspect, incidentally, that just here is where a gap typically opens between what we know, in the sense of feel, and what we can say about what we know; first, because what feeling discerns may outrun our verbal articulations; second, because what we are allowed or encouraged to recognize by those around us may be at odds with what we feel.

If feeling is discerning, then in the ideal case one would feel afraid when truly in the presence of danger, ashamed when having done something shameful, grateful when given a gift, and so on. Arguing this would require showing that shamefulness and generosity, for example, are objective properties of actions and situations in the world. (It would also require developing a notion of well-being or human flourishing that would include not only the health of the body and the sanity of the mind but also the welfare of what moral philosophers used to call the soul.) The argument would grant that fearfulness, shamefulness, and so on are subjective in the following sense: What it is for an object to have such a property is intelligible only in terms of its capacity to modify in an appropriate way a human sort of sensibility. But subjectivity in this sense is not incompatible with an object's really having such a property independently of how it is experienced on any particular occasion. David Wiggins offers an analogy for this suggestion:

> We may see a pillar-box as red because it is red. But also pillar-boxes, painted as they are, *count* as red only because there actually exists a perceptual apparatus (e.g. our own) that discriminates, and learns to group together, all and

only the actual red things. Not every sentient animal that sees a red postbox sees it as red. But this in no way impugns the idea that redness is an external, monadic property of a postbox. (1987, p. 107)

To change the example: it would be foolish to try to construct a concept of amusingness which was intelligible otherwise than in terms of characteristic human responses to what is amusing; but within that human framework some things truly are amusing (McDowell, 1983). Once again there are both causes and reasons, for what we find amusing as well as for what we believe; for often one can explain to someone who doesn't get the joke what he's missing. On such a view, a training of the feelings is at the same time a training in the discernment of complex properties of the world.

If something like this is right, then Freud was mistaken in thinking that an emotion so central in human affairs as guilt can be explained through an entirely psychological process in which the self turns in on itself, (falsely) projecting value properties onto the world in the process. We might instead read the Oedipal Complex as telling us more about the human sensibility on which emotions depend, as providing the mise-en-scène for its flowering. I will return to this issue in the final chapter.

We are now in a position to see some interesting interrelations between a number of important Freudian themes—the theory of instincts or drives, the nature of thinking, the role of external reality in the mind, and the unconscious—and to see also how an internalist view of mental content often underwrites them all. Let's look again at the passage from Rapaport which I quoted in Chapter 1:

Philosophical psychology, the ancestor of scientific psychology, was a subsidiary of epistemology. Its major query was: How do we acquire our knowledge of the world of reality? . . . For the theory of thinking, it may be of some advantage to note that [Freud's] manner of facing the problem [of adaption to reality] . . . shows some similarity to Leibniz' formulation of the problem of epistemology. Leibniz asked: How is it possible that reasoning arrives at conclusions which coincide with the outcome of processes occurring in reality? . . . Freud's problem was: How can the apparatus regulated by the pleasure-principle (drives) be also adapted to reality? (1951, pp. 316–317)

This formulation of Freud's problem is exactly right: Freud is not surprised that the ego is adapted to reality; in fact on one of his models the advent of the reality principle is what begins to mold the ego from the id. But he is surprised that the drives might be so adapted; yet surely for reasons of evolutionary adaptation this must also to some degree be so. What is Freud assuming that leads him to be surprised by one and not the other? To get at this, let me cast his surprise a little differently: It is not surprising that belief (the ego) has something to do with the truth (reality). Granted, just how to view the relation between them is no easy matter; this is why philosophers have been so concerned with questions of epistemology. But that some relation exists, and necessarily, is a philosophic fact. For if belief is divorced altogether from the real, there can be no such thing as true belief; if true belief is excised from the mind, then there is no such thing as mind, certainly no such thing as a biologically viable mind-body organism. (The relations between belief, true belief, and the external world were what my theory of meaning addressed in the first chapter.) But it is surprising, Freud thinks, that the passions might also have something to do with truth.

Freud is surprised by this because he thinks that passion and belief have no essential relation to each other, and because his internalist view of the mental occludes the roles of other people and external reality in the mind generally. If instead we assume the positions I have been arguing, first that passions (wishes, and desires) are fully mental and logically inextricable from belief, and second that mental content is constituted out of inter-relations between organism and external world, organism and other organisms, then we will expect it to be the case that passions, desires, and interests are also in some general way adapted to external reality, no matter how much they stray here and there.

Freud is surprised also because he is struck by the capacity of the unconscious to erect a world of phantasy that flies in the face of reality, struck by the causal power of what he thinks of as instinctual wishing to affect both mind and behavior. I will take account of this in what follows, showing how phantasizing is inflected like any other mental state by the external world, and substituting for Freud's grounding of irrationality in pre-rational drives an analysis that traces irrationality to certain sorts of fissures in a largely rational fabric.

Part Three

Irrationality

8   Primary Process

Ernest Jones called the concept of primary process functioning Freud's most revolutionary contribution to psychology (1946, p. 436). The kinds of clinical data that led Freud to the concept are the following: thinking which, like dreaming, but also like unconscious phantasy, is often visual, typically tolerant of contradiction, out of touch with the world and reason; motivation closer to wishful thinking than to the forming of realistic beliefs about how to achieve gratification; a kind of 'slippage' of meaning (particularly in dreams and neurotic symptoms) such that one idea is confused with another on the basis of superficial similarities, or a number of different ideas are compressed into one (Freud called such phenomena 'condensation'); and displacement, in which an emphasis or a feeling belonging to one idea appears to belong instead to another.

But primary process is more than shorthand for such data. It is a theoretical construct which posits, as we saw in Chapter 2, an ontological order midway between body and mind, an order of the 'mental'—call it the proto-mental—prior to concept formation, knowledge of the external world, and the so-called laws of logic. Said to characterize early childhood and to persist throughout mental life, above all in unconscious mental processes like repression, primary process is 'primary' in being temporally first, the most direct psychological expression of instinct; it is also more primitive structurally, showing its disorganized character in dreams, psychosis, and neurotic symptom formation. Finally, from what Freud calls the 'economic' point of view of mental functioning, primary process refers to the free flow of psychic energy from one idea to another—'mobility of cathexis'—whereas in secondary processes psychic energy is 'bound'. (In the first case, one "cathects" an idea as answer to a wish, for example, on the basis of some superficial similarity to an idea of previous gratification, or even because of a resemblance in the sounds of the associated words; in the second case one posits a goal through processes requiring reality testing and judgment. Condensation and displacement in particular are meant to explain the first sort of case, or mobility of cathexis.)

There are many themes here—schizophrenic thought, the concept of psychic energy, dream thinking, various associative rather than logical thought processes—most of which I am going to neglect in order to concentrate on the concepts of meaning and motivation, in preparation for the discussion of repression and irrationality in the next two chapters. For Freud's own writings provide a better account of at least a large class of symptomatic and irrational behaviors than the theory on which 'primary process' rides. Furthermore, the central idea in this theory, that there is a sort of instinctual 'wishing' which is prior to a knowledge of reality, concept formation, and the rest of what Freud calls 'secondary process', rests on and encourages a mistaken view of human thought and motivation.[1]

Freud's ideas about primary process have two extra-clinical sources. Discussing these will lead me again to the subject of children's thinking, then to some remarks on condensation and metaphor.

I   The Sources

The first source lies in certain of Freud's views about the origins of language, the second in his early neurological conception of the mind. Let's take these in turn.

In "The Antithetical Meaning of Primal Words," Freud repeats a remark he had made in *The Interpretation of Dreams*:

> The way in which dreams treat the category of contraries and contradictories is highly remarkable. It is simply disregarded. 'No' seems not to exist so far as dreams are concerned. They show a particular preference for combining contraries into a unity or for representing them as one and the same thing. Dreams feel themselves at liberty, moreover, to represent any element by its wishful contrary. (1910, p. 155)

He goes on to say that a pamphlet by the philologist Karl Abel (1881) has now given him the clue to this peculiar character of dreamwork. Abel purports to show that in ancient Egyptian, earlier even than the first hieroglyphic inscriptions, there were a number of words with opposite meanings. Freud's idea, then, was that unconscious processes preserve, in a Lamarckian fashion, some universal, archaic language in the history of the human race, a language in which certain important words had an antithetical sense. Freud ends this paper by remarking:

In the correspondence between the peculiarity of the dream-work mentioned at the beginning of the paper and the practice discovered by philology in the oldest languages, we may see a confirmation of the view we have formed about the regressive, archaic character of the expression of thoughts in dreams. And we psychiatrists cannot escape the suspicion that we should be better at understanding and translating the language of dreams if we knew more about the development of language. (p. 161)

Emile Benveniste (1971) has shown that Abel's and Freud's work involved etymological mistakes. But my objection is a deeper one. To see what is wrong with Freud's idea one should ask what could show, in the sense Freud has in mind, that one word expresses two opposite meanings. As David Archard (1984) points out, a single phoneme can communicate different ideas; but we can say this is so only if it is possible, perhaps from accompanying gestures or context, to say what in any given case these different ideas are. Think how a non-English speaker might find out that by 'pān' I sometimes mean a pain in the head, sometimes a pane of glass, and so on. If there is no way, then he has no reason to call my word ambiguous; if there is, then a distinction exists to be marked, even if the word alone doesn't do it. Another example: in different contexts the word 'fair' can mean 'just' versus 'unjust', 'light' versus 'dark', or 'unblemished' versus 'marred'. It would be wrong to claim that therefore one and the same concept covers a range of different oppositions.

Similarly, one may say or think 'No' when he means 'Yes'. But this doesn't imply that to him 'No' and 'Yes' mean the same thing. If it can be said of John that he misleadingly says one for the other, then he must himself be able to recognize the difference.[2]

In *The Interpretation of Dreams* Freud writes that "the system *Ucs.* is characterized by: *exemption from mutual contradiction, primary process* (mobility of cathexis), *timelessness,* and *replacement of external by psychical reality*" (1915a, p. 187). It should be said first with respect to contradiction that desire doesn't raise the problems belief does. Of course one could not simultaneously *do x* and not-*x*, nor consistently have the all-out intentions to do them at the same time. But no logical contradiction is involved in desiring on the one hand that it will rain today because otherwise I'll have to go on the hike that I'd like to skip, and on the other that it won't because rain would spoil the new coat of paint on the house; or in wanting to be a better writer than my father, while feeling guilty at the thought of what such a defeat would mean for him. A desire is typically not an all-out sort of thing, but a disposition qualified in various ways— 'insofar as *x* would achieve *y* I would like to do *x*', and so on, though such qualifications are often not apparent prior to conscious reflection. Nor is there any logical contradiction involved in hating and loving the same person at the same time; though I suspect that typically one hates him under one description and loves him under another, or loves her at one moment, hates her at another.

There are subtleties here about motivational conflict that are not germane to my point, which is that beliefs can be straightforwardly contradictory, and that when they are they obviously pose a problem verging on paradox. Of course someone can believe *p* at one time, and not-*p* at another, or 'in another part of her mind', as we sometimes say. What interpretation won't tolerate is the idea that someone believes *p and not-p;* for to attribute such a 'belief' would deny sense not merely to him but to ourselves. This is one of the intuitions at the heart of Freud's concept of primary process as a special mental operation, prior to thought per se. He should then have concluded, however, not that there is a special sort of thought to which contradiction is irrelevant, but, as he sometimes did, that certain kinds of tension in belief require our positing a mind divided within itself.

Yet might there not be a sort of thinking to which our constraints of rationality are irrelevant, a thinking characteristic, perhaps, of some primitive peoples, or schizophrenics, or children? If we say No, aren't we—like someone who, knowing only Bach and Mozart, dismisses jazz as *music*—imposing our (parochial) standards and values on others? So Jonathan Lear supposes:

> Throughout philosophical anthropology there runs the axiom that the possibility of interpreting others—as thinking, saying, doing anything—depends on interpreting them as being, more or less, like us. This 'principle of humanity' is a priori and non-optional: without it, an interpretation cannot get off the ground. However, although the principle may be a priori, its content is not. We do not know a priori what it is like to be *like us,* and we do not know and cannot set limits to the behavior in others that we will come to recognize as intelligible. There has been a tendency in the philosophical study of interpretation to slide from 'interpreting others as like us' to 'interpreting others as rational.' For instance, it has been argued that for interpretation to get started, we must find a way of imposing 'our logic' onto the natives' utterances. That is why, allegedly, we could never properly translate a native's utterance as saying '*p and not-p*'. (1990, pp. 191–192)

Lear is right that we may come to find sense in utterances and behavior which we had thought unintelligible. This is one of Freud's lessons. His interpretive procedure, however, is not to set reason aside, but to find it where we had thought it lacking, a theme I will develop in the next chapter. For now, take a famous clinical example: a man experiences a 'senseless' suicidal compulsion to cut his own throat, then thinks 'absurdly' as he goes to fetch the razor: 'No, it's not so simple as that. You must go and kill the old woman' (Freud, 1909). Freud advises us to look for the story from which these pieces have been abstracted, or torn free.

When we find it in this case we see that the man thought the old woman an impediment to his desire, that he therefore wanted her out of the way, and that the 'senseless' suicidal desire was motivated by guilt. The absurdity belongs to the abbreviated conscious thoughts, not to the unconscious text that interpretation restores.

The principle of humanity (or 'charity') advises that we must interpret others as more or less like us. But that advice has to be pitched at the right level of generality, at maxims which constrain not the content of belief but the process of interpretation itself. I may think your belief that the earthquake was caused by a demon, or that Haile Selassie was a saint, and so on, is false, even in some sense 'absurd'. But neither is literally absurd. And nothing in their content entitles me to say that you cannot truly hold them.

What might someone then mean by a 'mental' process *exempt* from contradiction? One possibility is that he confuses the idea that 'primary process' or the unconscious—perhaps in the form of instinct—is alogical with the idea that it is illogical. But this is just a confusion. Irrationality and illogicality are vicissitudes of mind; we can predicate them only of processes that are in some general sense rational in the first place. Yet something like this confusion characterizes Freud's idea of primary process wishing—as I will say in a moment—and it can be seen as well in the following passage: "What sort of language should we use when talking about the unconscious? . . . To use any psychophysiological language is to establish an analogy with a reductive physio-chemical model: to use everyday language is to establish an analogy with a conscious linguistic model" (Benassy and Diatkine, 1964, pp. 171–172).

Of course some human behavior can *only* be described in a language that combines talk about affective behavior and physio-chemistry, the behavior, for example, of neonates, who do not yet have any truly *psychological* states. To describe their behavior in such a language is not then to reduce it to something other or less than it is. Mental states *are* bodily states. But bodily states as such do not have *content* as beliefs and desires do; they cannot be said to be true or false, consistent with each other or inconsistent. They are 'exempt' from contradiction in the sense that the concept is inapplicable.

Are there no mental states which are non-propositional? Of course: mental images, feelings of elation or fatigue, pains and pleasures, melodies going through the head—the list goes on. But Freud assigns to primary process the task of *wishing,* and of *representing* wishes as fulfilled; and whether it makes sense to attribute such activities to a creature lacking concepts, including a concept of reality, is questionable. Which brings us to the *Project* (1950 [1887–1902]), the second of Freud's sources for the idea of 'primary process'.[3]

As described in chapter VII of *The Interpretation of Dreams,* hallucinatory wish fulfillment is the very model of primary process functioning, the mode to which the organism regresses, Freud thinks, in dreams, in neurosis, in unconscious phantasy. As a quasi-psychological state, wishing is born when the infant experiences a need and on the basis of a remembered experience of satisfaction, 'hallucinates' the object for which it longs. Freud means this model to exemplify a reflex arc, a conditioning which requires for its explanation none of the conceptual acquisitions of secondary process thought. Earlier (in Chapter 2) I argued that Freud's use of the psychological term 'wish' *(Wunsch)* to describe the 'primary' processes he tells us about is not justified. My thesis was this: a creature that can represent to itself, via a 'hallucinatory' image, the object *for* which it longs is a creature that is capable of making judgments about reality, whether or not it exercises that capacity fully in any given case of wishing.

Freud needs the concept of wishing to explain what he calls repression, acting out, and phantasy; for on his theory libidinal wishes are the first target of repression; and it is such repressed, libidinal wishes that are acted out in symptoms, or enacted in phantasy. The concepts 'wish' and 'desire' are different, furthermore, in ways that serve his purpose. Compared to desire, wishing can seem to operate in relative freedom from the constraints of time, space, and reality generally. One can wish that the past had been different, that she were in two places at once, that things were in this moment other than she knows them to be; and for the having of things she believes it impossible to have. But one does not 'desire' that the past had been different, and so on. (This is a grammatical fact about wishing and desiring: that the one, but not the other, can be counterfactual. Aristotle distinguishes wish from desire in ways similar to these in Book III of *The Nicomachean Ethics.* He is of course talking about conscious wishes.) Freud needs also the idea that some wishing is not verbalized but takes instead the form of envisioning or imagining; so he calls it 'hallucinatory'.

In the next chapter I will show how Freud developed such a concept— 'phantasy'—which I want to free from its moorings in the metaphysics of primary process. For now, I'll note that none of the features of wishing mentioned so far suggests that it can occur prior to the formation of *some* beliefs and a considerable knowledge of reality.[4] When we consider wish and belief, belief and desire, in their guise as first-person introspectable states, each can seem autonomous. But if we think about wish, desire, and belief as concepts that have their home in describing and explaining what people do, it is clear that the concepts presuppose each other. To desire that p is to be predisposed to act in a way that would bring p about, if one's relevant beliefs about the world were true and there were no conflicting desires. To believe that q is to be disposed to act in a way that would satisfy those desires that mesh with q in the right way. These are not merely empirical generalizations about how people act, but conceptual remarks about the meaning of belief and desire. Concepts, and a knowledge of reality, then, are as necessary a constituent of the one as of the other.

Yet while wishing presupposes some conceptual sophistication, it may be true that phantasies and wishful thinking of all kinds flourish particularly in childhood. If so, the reasons might be that need and wish are more imperative then than they will be later, and that children are more under the sway of the idea that desire magically effects its object.[5] We might then want to posit a state of agency appropriate to a developmental period in which concepts are relatively fluid, beliefs rudimentary, and in which the creature has not yet learned the limits of its will, the fact that human 'desiring' does not magically realize itself but requires instrumentality. In the learning of this lesson, Freud is surely right to suppose frustration the indispensable teacher. One achieves the capacity for full-fledged agency as one learns the hard distinction between *what is* and *what might be,* and as one's beliefs about the world become more finely articulated.

To come back now to the passage from Benassy and Diatkine: they say that if we use "the everyday language" to talk about the unconscious we draw a false analogy with "a conscious linguistic model." My response is that the language of belief and desire which Freud uses to talk about the unconscious is simply the language of *mind,* any mind, conscious or unconscious; and it presupposes what that language presupposes. They continue:

> It is language which builds up time and contradiction. Without spatial, verbal, and social bearings, comparisons of time length are uncertain. Outside language there are no *contradictory* terms or relationships, but different terms, different relationships, and that is why there is no time and no contradiction in the unconscious. (1964, p. 172)

But notice that 'outside language' there are neither contradictory nor different 'terms'; there are simply *things,* waiting to be conceived, named, sorted out. So let me use this fact to make the opposite point from theirs: Where there are terms, ideas, and wishes, so also are there language and some grasp of temporal and logical relations.

II   Children's Thinking, Condensation, and Metaphor

Does what Freud calls condensation point to a fundamentally different mental order? Again I think not. Let's look at two different sorts of things one might have in mind as examples of 'condensation', the first an aspect of a difference between a child's articulation of the world and ours, and the second, metaphor.

Children are on the way to their first concepts, our concepts; and on the way, theirs are bound to be looser. Things will be lumped together between which adults make distinctions. Since it will often be hard for us in interpreting a child to know what he means by a word, we are apt—Lear argues (1990)—to attribute to him a more determinate concept than he has, drawing the lines of his along the same as ours.

In Lear's example, Freud assumes that by 'widdler' Little Hans means what we do by 'penis', since 'widdler' is what he calls his own penis and also a lion's in the zoo. So when Hans says that his seven-day-old sister's 'widdler' is quite small, Freud assumes that Hans is making a kind of mistake in terms of his own concept. That is, finding the idea of a creature like himself without a penis too threatening, Hans theorizes that his sister has a very small penis which will grow.

The problem is that Hans also refers to a cow's udder and the hose of a fire engine as a widdler. He remarks that if his widdler were cut off he would widdle with his bottom. And he says, seeing a pan filled with blood after the delivery of his baby sister, "But blood doesn't come out of *my* widdler." In virtue of what, Lear asks, "are we to say that Hans has made a mistake about the cow? Or his sister? Why aren't udders and vaginas and, indeed, bottoms that widdle also widdlers?" (p. 100). For Hans to have made a mistake he must have a determinate concept. And for us to know just what that concept is, we must know how Hans would go on, that is, just what else he would sort under this concept. It is not enough to know that he calls penises 'widdlers'; for he might call many other things 'widdlers' as well which we exclude from the category 'penis'. Indeed, 'widdler' may just mean 'protuberance from which liquid comes'.

Getting the hang of a child's concepts does present an interpreter with two special difficulties. The first is that since the child is eager to join us in our use of words, there seems no way to investigate his use without simultaneously risking the possibility of altering it. The second is that the child may group together things—fire hoses, penises, bottoms, perhaps elephant trunks and garden hoses—that we classify differently. Of course we can see similarities between them. But for us they are not the salient similarities. Given the way Hans groups things, furthermore, his thoughts about 'widdlers' may slip along a chain of associations, eliding ideas that to our minds seem different and even opposed, substituting a hose for a penis, fusing them all into a single 'idea'. It is quite possible that such early associations remain locked away in an adult mind, providing a store of unconscious resonances from which we later draw, in dreams, symptom-formation, the creative process, all those things in which Freud thinks we see the work of primary process.

Note, however, that our difficulties in interpreting Hans stem not from the fact that Hans's mind is ineffable, or lacking in concepts, or that it is subject to mechanisms of a different mental order from our conscious adult thought, but that his concepts reflect somewhat different interests from ours, while being at the same time more 'concretistic' (Werner, 1973).

What about Lacan's construal of condensation as another name for metaphor? This is so central a theme in his work—crucial to his view that the unconscious is 'structured like a language'—that an adequate answer would require a work in itself. I will only make some highly schematic remarks.[6]

What is metaphor? A crude beginning of an account might say that it is calling something by another name than the one we usually use. We say that a flower stem is 'a fuse', a woman 'the sun', the Church 'a rock'. We say something that is literally false, and in doing so—if the metaphor is good—we inspire a kind of revelation. So what is going on? Any answer will clearly depend on some theory of meaning, of how words come to mean what they do.

On Lacan's theory, meaning is a function of signs, and signs exist only in the context of a language. Following Saussure, Lacan holds that a sign is the essentially arbitrary linking of a signifier—say the sound or the inscription 'tree'—and a signified. (I'll postpone discussion for a moment of the 'signified'.) In calling this link arbitrary, Saussure meant first that any other sound could just as well have signified trees; and second, that any sign has the value it does only through its relations to other signs in the language: the meaning of a 'signifier' is given by its place in a chain of signifiers, specifically by its differences from them. Over time, furthermore, the meaning of a word can change. (Saussure did *not* mean, as Lacan suggests, that this could happen at any moment.) Now Lacan takes the fact that the link between signifier and signified is arbitrary, in all these senses, to mean that signifiers are inherently open to slippage; and it is just this slippage, he thinks, which is metaphor.

One of the problems with Saussure's account—and Lacan inherits it—is that Saussure blurs the distinction between a concept—say 'tree'—and the class of things which the concept nets: mental images and pictures of trees, but also actual trees in the world. Is the signifier the word plus the concept, and the signified, then, the class of things the concept picks out (its reference)? Or is the concept part of what is signified? The point matters because what sound or inscription we use to mark the concept 'tree', or to refer to trees, *is* arbitrary, in the sense that any other would have done just as well. But this is not true of the relationship between the concept 'tree' and the class of things to which it refers. Because of the way we sort things in the world, that is, because of the properties that we have come to think essential to trees, 'tree' picks out elms, oaks, willows, and so on, and not roses, or unicorns, or mineral water, or dogs.

Couldn't we sort things differently? Isn't what we call the 'essence' of trees a function of what matters to us? And can't our criteria change? Of course. Concepts do change. But not overnight. They change in response to discoveries we make about the world, or shifts in our own values, in the characteristics we think salient, and why. We used to think that whales were fish, before we discovered how whales nourish their young; that males, and only males, could be 'presidents' and 'breadwinners', before we began to question some of our ideas about men and women. Concepts mean what they do only in a particular context of use. But given this context, what objects in the world any concept selects is not arbitrary.

This tells us, furthermore, that the interrelation between concepts is an important but not the only constraint on meaning. The meaning of 'tree' is determined partly by its logical connections to other concepts such as bush, growing thing, and so on, and partly by the interrelation between words and speakers, and between words, speakers, and world. Lacan wants to think of language as an impersonal system that exists independently of speech and speakers, a system into which each of us is born as a thinking creature and which alienates us from ourselves in the process. But language can't be separated from speech, concepts from concept users, in this way.

Of course not all concepts are exemplified by real material objects, for example, 'unicorn'. Science itself is generous with more complex problems along this line. But any theory of signs (and language) must include a theory of reference, of how words hook onto the world. It must be able to tell us how meaning or language gets going in the first place. There are many different ways of trying to tell this story. But all need that venerable distinction between concept and things that instantiate it, or connotation and denotation, or sense and reference, that Lacan blurs. (These pairs of terms are not interchangeable; but all have been used to mark something like the distinction in question.) So a theory of meaning needs at least three critical terms: sound or inscription, concept, and referent of the concept. By neglecting the distinction between the last two, Lacan can say that there is no extra-linguistic reality to which words refer, and that, as he darkly puts it, "the world of words creates the world of things."[7]

In ignoring the connections between external world and concepts, and between concepts and speakers, Lacan also ignores the distinction between the meaning of a term and its use. But just this is crucial to an understanding of metaphor.[8] If on being told how babies are born Little Hans refers to his baby sister as a 'lumf', is he speaking metaphorically? It depends. If he means by 'bottoms' and 'lumf' and 'babies' just what we do, then perhaps he is. But chances are either that he's making a mistake about bottoms, or—and this was Lear's point—that Hans doesn't quite have a grasp of these concepts yet. Or suppose the child calls the stem of the flower its fuse. Has the child spoken metaphorically? Not if he is still learning the concepts of 'stem' and 'fuse' and thinks that *we* put them in the same class. Of course that doesn't prevent *us* from suddenly being struck by the image of an explosive force dynamiting the flower through its stem; in which case metaphor happens, so to speak, in us.

So how does metaphor work? I think like this. When we speak metaphorically, we use words and concepts in an unfamiliar way, one which trades for its effect on established meanings, on a relatively fixed way of classifying things. Dylan Thomas' "the force that through the green fuse drives the flower / Drives my green age" astonishes precisely because flower stems are not literally fuses; which is to say that we don't normally put them in the same class. A metaphoric use of language depends on there being prior meanings, and so inspires us to see one thing in new ways, which we can do only if we have articulated them differently to begin with.

I have argued that neither metaphor nor a certain relative fluidity in children's thinking points to the existence of a pre-conceptual mental order. But this is true: sometimes thoughts follow each other in ways that are simultaneously causal and rational, as when the wish to build a bird-cage leads me to look for appropriate materials, or when the thoughts that all men are mortal and that Socrates is a man prompt the thought that Socrates is mortal. The first is paradigmatic of practical reasoning, the second of syllogistic. It is just such connections that Freud was a master sleuth at detecting, beneath a play of surface absurdities or non sequiturs. Yet without question the mind has other ways of working as well which are, by contrast with the ones just mentioned, mechanical or quasi-mechanical: on the basis of resemblance, or contiguity in space or time, and so on, one idea reminds me of another: an apple of the globe, or snakes, or yesterday's picnic. Such causal relations between thoughts are neither rational nor irrational. Yet their entry into thought processes that are of an essentially rational sort can account for various ways in which thinking may go astray. If Alan believes his father is a threat to his very existence, Alan has reason to be afraid of him. But if superficial resemblances between Jack and his father cause Alan to fear Jack, Alan's fear is no longer rational. Associations like these point to different mental processes from the ones we variously call reason, but not to ones that are temporally prior. (See Dorpat and Miller, 1992.)

Metaphor, concept formation, condensation and displacement, all rely on a fundamental way in which world and mind are made to fit each other: the one offering variety but also order, the other able to find similarities and also to mark differences. If this were not so, there could be no concepts. That we find phenomena classifiable and cross-classifiable in endless ways is a condition of there being a world for us, one which is endlessly discoverable. There is, as I see it, a kind of dialectic between world and concept, concept and perception, perception and new concept, and so on. Prior to concept formation we interact with the world in myriad ways. The world moves and stimulates us, making patterns on our retinas, triggering the release of hormones, engaging us in ever more complicated interactions with other creatures like ourselves. Out of all this slowly come language and thought, and in the beginning, ways of categorizing things which, relative to an adult's, are loose and fluid. As we acquire ever more articulate concepts, we become able to take account of things and reflect on them. And as we do, our beliefs may change. With such changes come new ways of behaving and perceiving. New things become salient, new concepts are born. This is one of the things that happens in the psychoanalytic process: the patient acquires new ways of seeing things, and so new and somewhat different concepts; new concepts and so new ways of seeing things.

Philosophers sometimes talk as if what they are doing is a matter of clarification, which suggests something already there—the concept—waiting to be clarified. Often it is. One can point out, for example, that when we say a thing is 'determined' sometimes we mean it is caused, sometimes forced, sometimes that it has a determinate nature. Then we can go on to distinguish between the notions of cause and force, to call to mind the different senses of force, and so on. Or to take other examples: an art student may not yet quite have the hang of the distinction between renaissance and baroque in architecture, or a biology student of 'molecule' and 'cell'. It's not that these concepts are crystal-clear; just clear enough for many purposes.

Since our concepts will always lag behind the world and what we are capable of noticing in it, all concepts are potentially open to change. Philosophers have not had the last say about the concepts of freedom and determinism; nor art historians and biologists about styles and cells. In the first chapter I sketched a view of meaning according to which concepts are not laid up in a Platonic heaven waiting to be discovered, but formed in a process of human interaction. To an extent, then, adults and children are in the same boat. Children's concepts are obviously fluid and in the process of catching up with ours. Ours, while fixed enough for communication to happen more or less successfully, are nevertheless on the move.

And this suggests that belief as well is more fluid than we sometimes consider it. Think of belief as sometimes the conclusion of an activity, one which rests on having other desires and beliefs. Then we may want to say that apropos of p one may have ideas that do not yet have the status of belief. Some beliefs are neat, like those about cats on mats. Others are not.

Ideas often remain unformulated because arriving at the belief would be painful. But this doesn't necessarily mean that the formulated belief is hiding in 'the unconscious'.

In his short story "The Death of Ivan Ilyich," Tolstoy writes of his hero:

> It occurred to him that what had seemed utterly inconceivable before—that he had not lived the kind of life he should have—might in fact be true. It occurred to him that those scarcely perceptible impulses of his to protest what people of high rank considered good, vague impulses which he had always suppressed, might have been precisely what mattered . . . (1981 [1886], pp. 126–127)

When Ivan suppressed those 'scarcely perceptible impulses', did he know what he now knows on his deathbed, or what he would have known had he attended to them at the time, that his values are false, his affections shallow, his life devoid of pleasure? There is no reason to assume so. We speak of recognitions, of ac-knowledgments. But what is recognized or acknowledged may have been to some extent indeterminate prior to the recognition.

What goes on in some instances of repression may be rather like the following: I catch out of the corner of my eye something happening across the street; I see enough to find it unpleasant and avert my head; so then I genuinely do not know the details of what is happening. Yet as Freud said, repression takes energy, the energy of avoiding something within the range of one's vision about which one is curious. Furthermore, what one now imagines may be far worse than what one would have seen; so the imaginings themselves may trigger a second act of avoidance, and so on.

But aside from the potential painfulness of the yet unformulated belief, there can be other causes as well. The belief—say about the kind of life you want, or what sort of person you are, or what matters most to you—might require synthesizing a number of different beliefs, or looking at a number of things in different lights, or acquiring a specific know-how. Or the belief might be one that would be available to you only if you had a concept that you don't yet have. For example, you may have noticed aspects of a building you will later come to recognize as a fine example of Italian baroque. Having acquired that concept now makes yet other aspects newly apparent to you.

Such reflections lead me to suggest that what Freud calls the unconscious is both more articulate than he sometimes says it is, and less.[9] He himself was of two minds on the matter, viewing primary process as chaotic, and repressed mental contents not only as perfectly rational but also as containing just those thoughts that will emerge after repression has been overcome. He writes:

> We are driven to conclude that two fundamentally different kinds of psychical process are concerned in the formation of dreams. One of these produces perfectly

rational dream-thoughts, of no less validity than normal thinking; while the other treats these thoughts in a manner which is in the highest degree bewildering and irrational . . . *they have been transformed into the symptom* [the dream] *by means of condensation and the formation of compromises, by way of superficial associations and in disregard of contradictions, and also, it may be, along the path of regression.* (1900, p. 598)

Here he assumes that primary process simply provides the matter for disguise, and that the perfectly rational text which is the result of reconstruction and interpretation existed in the unconscious all along. This is the assumption, I think, that leads him to ask:

> When a psychical act (let us confine ourselves here to one which is in the nature of an idea) is transposed from the system *Ucs.* into the system *Cs.* (or *Pcs.*), are we to suppose that this transposition involves a fresh record—as it were, a second registration—of the idea in question, which may thus be situated as well in a fresh psychical locality, and alongside of which the original unconscious registration continues to exist? (1915a, p. 174)

It seems more likely that, as Freud acknowledges (1937), what analyst and patient together construct by way of a 'memory' or an earlier understanding was in many cases not thought of even unconsciously in just that way at the time. For one may be engaged in a process which might normally culminate in belief, more or less true belief, if one's goal were the truth. Of course in repression it is not. But to say that someone is not oriented to the truth, even that she is in flight from it, does not necessarily imply that she already has those beliefs she might otherwise have come to hold. I am not denying that often there are fully formed unconscious beliefs which are consciously repulsed, but suggesting a spectrum along which 'beliefs' take different shapes.

Nor does the fact that certain of a person's mental states are relatively inchoate in the ways suggested imply that she is in the grip of a mental process which preceded thought per se. Freud notes that repression is inarticulate; but it does not therefore point to a mental order that is in principle inarticulable. Children's thought rests on the same general conditions as adult or 'secondary process' thought: acquaintance with reality, a grasp of the distinction between 'how things seem to me' and 'how things are', and those very general principles of rationality that are constitutive of belief, no matter what the content.

The most obvious criticism of Freud's views about primary process is that they don't do justice to the cognitive character of the unconscious which his own accounts presume. He holds that, in the form of condensation and displacement, primary process is responsible for such highly complex, and complexly linguistic, activities as joking and punning. They are the means, furthermore, by which the ego in its censoring capacity disguises unconscious thoughts so as to make them presentable to consciousness. It would seem then that primary process does not precede secondary process but requires it; and that Freud will have a hard time explaining just how a 'primitive' mental process can interact in such sophisticated ways with one from which it is said categorically to differ.[10]

To come back, now, to Little Hans: What *was* he anxious about? Castration? What do we mean by castration? Or is that our word for worries which were both more global and less specific than the word normally suggests? And if we were to make the interpretation 'fear of castration' to Hans as an adult, what might we mean?

It would of course depend on the situation. We might be suggesting, for one thing, that as a child Hans was anxious about his adequacy to satisfy another's needs, hence to keep her love; and that in his mind this was related in ways inarticulable by him at the time to worries about his bodily integrity and the sources of his pleasure, to admiration for his father, to the desire to be a grown-up man in the world at the same time as he has a child's need for his mother, and so on. Our word 'castration' is a kind of metaphor for all this.

We might also be suggesting, for another, that those earlier unarticulated worries now echo in his adult concerns about potency and autonomy. This is not to say that they are necessarily present in all such adult concerns. Or that even where they are, such concerns are 'reducible' to the childhood situation. But those earlier worries may remain, coloring Hans's adult perceptions now. So we would be inviting him to see his adult self in the light of the world of his childhood as the analytic dialogue has so far created it, to put things together which he has seen as separate, or which he has been able to keep separate.

Freud thought the two great discoveries of psychoanalysis were the dynamic unconscious and infantile sexuality. Though the poets had long known about the first, he remarked, he credited psychoanalysis with developing a theory of the unconscious that implies a radically new model of the mind. It is a theory which underwent a number of major revisions. But throughout the writings of his middle period—culminating in 1923 with *The Ego and the Id*—Freud's theory of the unconscious makes a number of related yet different claims. I will group them as follows: (1) Primary Process: There is a primary mental order, characteristically different from ordinary or 'secondary' thought processes, that we need in order to account for dreams, neurotic symptoms, and the sorts of irrational thoughts and behaviors that psychoanalysis investigates. Primary process is primary in that it is the earliest mental process and the most primitive in form, remaining as a substrate of even the most adult and normal mind. (2) The Dynamic Unconscious: Many of our memories, beliefs, and desires, including the ones that move us to action, are not merely outside of present awareness, but inaccessible to it under ordinary circumstances, as distinct from ideas which simply happen to be out of conscious awareness at the present. An idea is 'dynamically' unconscious if the lack of conscious awareness is motivated, and the product in particular of repression. (3) The Legacy of Childhood: This is my name for the idea that childhood events, or rather unrevised childhood readings of events, together with childhood beliefs and passions, may be preserved as a motivating force in the adult mind in the form of a kind of split-off self, or even a plurality of such selves.

These are separable claims, whether Freud thought so or not. Of the first I am critical. But I believe that (2) and (3) are importantly right. Showing how they can be accommodated to the picture of the mind I have drawn so far is part of the task of the next two chapters.

9 Reasons, Repression, and Phantasy

Freud's originality as an interpreter does not lie in his charting of a new mental terrain, but the ingenuity with which he applied a familiar explanatory model: where common-sense understanding often fails in the face of seemingly incoherent utterances and behavior different from one's own, Freud assumes that given the right circumstances, 'nonsense' reveals sense; an apparently idle and free-floating idea discloses a recognizable attitude like belief or desire; an action which is puzzlingly contrary to the agent's conscious reasons shows its motivation in reasons that are unconscious. Finally, thoughts may themselves have a structure resembling that of actions, as when a 'memory' or a 'forgetting' or an act of phantasizing is the product of desire.

Consider the following clinical vignettes:

A man reports deliberately removing a stone from the middle of a road in the belief that it may constitute a danger to his 'lady', whose carriage will pass that way. After a few moments he decides that what he had done was foolish; but instead of leaving well enough alone, he compounds the folly by putting the stone back where it had been. On Freud's interpretation the conscious reasons for both removing and replacing the stone were only part of the story, which turns out to contain as well an angry wish to harm the lady and a denial of this conflict (Freud, 1909).

On the basis of an anonymous letter a woman has formed the torturing belief that her husband is unfaithful to her. She reports having confided to her maid that her husband's infidelity would make her unhappy, and she knows the maid has motives for punishing her. The woman has some reason then for attributing the letter to the maid and for skepticism about its contents. Yet she unwaveringly persists in her (delusional) belief. In the course of her analysis she confesses her erotic feelings for her son-in-law and is stricken with guilt. Freud suggests that she had preferred believing in her husband's infidelity to acknowledging her own, and that this wish prompted her to look for, even to invite, the painful 'evidence' (1933 [1932]).

A child recalls having seen his parents engaged in an act of anal intercourse, a recollection with which he seems unduly preoccupied. Freud explains the preoccupation by saying that the memory served to block out memories or thoughts of his mother's vagina, with accompanying thoughts of possible castration. So the memory may not be a memory at all but a phantasy, a wish-fulfilling belief, or a memory that has been distorted by such a wish (Freud, 1918 [1914]).

Criticism of Freudian theory often consists either in denying the coherence of its explanations of symptomatic actions, or in noting Freud's vacillation between the languages of mind and body, his inappropriate insertion of mechanism into the language of Intentions and Intentionality (see Ricoeur, 1970). We'll come to the second point later. Let's begin with the first.

A case much discussed in this context is that of the 'table-cloth lady',[1] the middle-aged woman, long separated from her husband, who obsessionally runs every day into the room next to her bedroom, takes up a very particular position beside a table, rings the bell for the maid, and then runs back into her own bedroom, behavior as unintelligible to the woman herself as it is at first to Freud (Freud, 1916–1917 [1915–1917]). As her story unfolds, the symptom is linked to her husband's impotence on their wedding night years before. Many times he had come from his bedroom to hers to try again, but without success. The next morning he had said angrily that he would feel ashamed in front of the housemaid when she made the bed and had poured a bottle of red ink onto the sheet, but unfortunately not exactly on the spot where a blood-stain might have been appropriate.

As Freud and his patient reconstruct her 'reasoning' she is repeating this traumatic scene, only in the repetition the tablecloth represents the bed, and she is imagining that it is stained, as it would ideally have been, with her blood. Her repetition is then a kind of imaginative correction: correcting in doing so the placement of the stain; for if she calls the maid in to observe it, then it must, as it were, be in the right place; and she is correcting her husband's impotence as well. Freud writes: "So the obsessional action was saying: 'No, it's not true. He had no need to feel ashamed in front of the housemaid; he was not impotent'. It represented this wish, in the manner of a dream, as fulfilled in the present-day action" (1916–1917

[1916–1917], p. 263). The woman's phantasy, then, was that her husband had not been impotent; and her obsessive action is explicable as the acting out of this phantasy.

Here is the problem some have found with such explanations: If what the woman did (as described by Freud) counts as an action, as fully intentional behavior, then it seems we must impute to her a particular desire to revise her wedding night, a particular belief that running to the table and so on is a way of satisfying that desire, and some very odd general beliefs such as that the past can be redone, that one can redo it by acting as if it had been the way one wishes it had been, that objects which (like tablecloths and bedsheets) resemble each other in some ways are therefore functionally equivalent. And that someone might have such beliefs and desires, these critics say, is just not plausible. It is one thing to ascribe a mental attitude to someone of which she is not aware at the time but which she would nevertheless find perfectly intelligible. If I believe I have told you a hurtful truth out of concern for your welfare and someone suggests that I was retaliating for an injury I believe you have done me, I accept that as a possible motive, whether or not I think it mine in this instance. If you have in fact misled me and I believe you have done so intentionally, my belief may be unfounded and in that sense irrational; yet it is understandable to you as a belief. It is another thing, however, to ascribe to someone beliefs and desires so fundamentally odd, not only by our standards but also by hers, that neither we nor she would think they provided a reason for doing anything whatever. So either what the woman has done is not an action, or Freud's explanation of it must be wrong, the criticism concludes.

I think the criticism is apt, but that it points to some needed qualifications in the reason-explanation model. What is interesting about the behaviors that caught Freud's attention is how hard they press the language of intentions while at the same time resisting it.[2] Freud is right that even before we slip off the field of the mental and onto that of the strictly neurophysiological, there is a limbo in between the fully intentional and the purposive in some weaker sense. How should we describe it? For reasons discussed in the last chapter, 'primary process' cannot be the solution. Nor is it to abandon the language of mind for neurophysiology. Freud claims that the psychological hypothesis about the Unconscious resembles theories in physics about what lies behind the phenomenal appearance of things. But the parallel won't hold: physics is not constrained to describe this 'unknowable' realm in the language of everyday experience, while this 'everyday' language of mind, Freud himself says, is just what we must use for talk about the Unconscious.

The solution is to see if we can't do justice to the clinical phenomena without departing too far from this everyday language. Taking them in the reverse order, I want to explore in this chapter Freud's concepts of unconscious phantasy and repression. Repression is the test case, since it is the dynamic unconscious, the activity of willfully banishing a thought from conscious awareness, that Freud thought demands a major revision in our thinking about mind. The key to a solution lies in the important changes in Freud's own views; for his last revisionary work on repression and related matters—*Inhibitions, Symptoms and Anxiety* (1926 [1925])—builds squarely on a reason-explanation model.

I *Repression*

From early on, clinical data had led Freud to see an intimate connection between inhibition of the sexual instinct, anxiety, and neurotic symptoms. Anxiety, Freud says in his *Introductory Lectures on Psycho-Analysis,* is at "the very center of our interest in the problems of neurosis" (1916–1917 [1915–1917]), p. 404). What then are the connections between repression, anxiety, and symptom-formation? Between neurotic and normal anxiety?

In line with his reductionist wishes, prior to 1926 Freud viewed anxiety as a chemical transformation of inhibited libidinal energy. First there is repression, and then anxiety as its direct consequence: neurotics suffer from anxiety because they have repressed their sexual impulses. This early view of repression attempts to dispense with beliefs and desires as part of the causal story.

So how is this story supposed to go? Repression, Freud says, is a three-stage process. What the layman calls 'repression' is only the second stage, which Freud describes as "turning something away . . . from the conscious." (Elsewhere he remarks that what Schopenhauer says "about the struggle against accepting a distressing piece of reality coincides with my concept of repression so completely that once again I owe the chance of making a discovery to my not being well-read" [ibid., p. 15]. Freud is speaking here of repression in its second stage.) In the first stage, called primary repression, the 'repressed' idea never reaches consciousness in the first place; for, like primary process, primary repression is supposed to characterize the psyche prior to the formation of an ego, and so prior to the formation of judgment, the sense of self, the ability to assess reality and to recognize danger. Primary repression is marked by some release of anxiety, then a more or less successful containment of it. In the second stage there is 'a return of the repressed' in the form of a re-evocation of the repressed impulses. Now there is repression proper, that is, repression as the layman understands it, together with a fresh release of anxiety. Then in the third stage, as an attempt to contain or 'bind' this anxiety, the organism 'displaces' it through some kind of psychic mechanism onto an external situation. Hence the formation of symptoms in which a fear of one's own libidinal impulses presents itself, for example, as a phobic fear of horses.

Both anxiety and repression are problematic on these accounts. For the idea that anxiety is simply the conversion of inhibited libido does not square with Freud's conviction that anxiety is a response to danger. In normal anxiety the danger situation is said to be external and more or less realistically perceived: anxiety triggers a flight-response, or preparedness for flight, or whatever other behavior might be appropriate in the situation. In neurotic anxiety, which is what primary repression is supposed to explain, the danger situation is internal—one's own libido. But how can the organism's own libido constitute a danger? (Freud answers, as he often does when painted into a corner by his penchant for instinctual mythologizing, that there must be some kind of phylogenetic inheritance. That is, he wants to construe repression as a genuinely psychological process; but since his positing of a primary repression that precedes judgment and belief rules such a process out, he sneaks it in the back door via a sort of blood 'remembrance'.) And if repression is a response to danger, mustn't there be some agent or agency, like the ego, which somehow assesses it?

Inhibitions, Symptoms and Anxiety solves both problems by viewing anxiety, normal and neurotic, as the accompanying and more or less appropriate affect of a perception of danger, which is at once motive for and the cause of repression. Earlier Freud had distinguished normal from neurotic anxiety by saying that the first corresponds to 'external', the second to 'internal' dangers. He had held that the ego needs to defend itself against the id, which it does through primary repression. Phobias had been explained as replacing "an internal, instinctual danger with an external, perceptual one." Now he acknowledges that "an instinctual demand is . . . not dangerous in itself; it only becomes so inasmuch as it entails a real external danger . . . Thus what happens in a phobia in the last resort is merely that one external danger is replaced by another" (1926, p. 126). That is, the child has various desires which were previously unconflicted; but he comes to have reason to fear that the penalty for gratifying them, perhaps even for having them, is something dreadful. Freud now analyzes childhood phobias as a 'displacement' of castration anxiety, itself understandable given the child's desires and his beliefs about the world. The child's apparently irrational fear yields to interpretation once we understand his situation as he sees it. It is how anxiety is handled, whether it is acknowledged or denied, displaced, repressed, and so on, that makes it 'normal' or 'neurotic'.

Psychoanalysts describe this decisive change in Freud's theories as a shift from instincts and 'the id' to an emphasis on ego. A plainer way of putting it is that Freud's views about anxiety and repression are now consistent on the one hand with his earliest clinical intuition that more behavior than we had thought is intelligible in terms of reasons, and on the other, with his growing understanding of the role of our real relations with other persons in unconscious thought structures. The emphasis on psychic reality has in no way been relinquished; but psychic reality is now viewed as dependent on knowledge of the external world.

Freud opens his investigation of anxiety in *Inhibitions, Symptoms and Anxiety* by recounting briefly the story of Little Hans and his phobia of horses. Freud writes:

> It takes a little time to find one's bearings and to decide which the repressed impulse is, what substitutive symptoms it has found and where the motive for repression lies. 'Little Hans' refused to go out into the street because he was afraid of horses. This was the raw material of the case. Which part of it constituted the symptom? Was it his having the fear? Was it his choice of an object for his fear? Was it his giving up of his freedom of movement? Or was it more than one of these combined? What was the satisfaction which he renounced? And why did he have to renounce it? (1926, p. 101)

Freud answers as follows:

> Here, then, is our unexpected finding: in both cases [Little Hans and the Wolf Man] the motive force of the repression was fear of castration. The ideas contained in their anxiety—being bitten by a horse and being devoured by a wolf—were substitutes by distortion for the idea of being castrated by their father. This was the idea which had undergone repression. (p. 108)

Freud goes on to say that Little Hans's castration fear is not a manifestation of neurotic anxiety, nor is it symptomatic. The symptom consists rather in the 'displacement' of the anxiety onto horses. The child unconsciously believes, with good reason given his age and experience, that he might be castrated. What are these reasons? They include his belief that women have been castrated; his inference that castration is therefore a genuine possibility; his wish for physical intimacy with his father as well as with his mother; his belief that such intimacy presupposes his being castrated as he believes his mother to be. So Hans fears castration as both the precondition and the consequence of gratifying his incestuous desires, in fact even of having them; for like all children, in Freud's view, Hans invests desire itself with the power of overt physical action and believes his thoughts to be as visible as his body. Once Freud had thought of castration fears as some kind of inherited legacy; now he sees them as the child's response to an essentially interpersonal situation. (Of course Freud may continue to hold the earlier view as well; but it no longer has any explanatory value.)

So now how should we view symptom-formation, and what is its relation to repression? As Freud had asked in his 1915 essay "Repression," are they coincident or divergent processes? answering that they are divergent. First there is repression, achieved by what agency and for what reason we do not know, which generates anxiety. Then there is symptom-formation as a more or less purposeful activity designed to avoid or minimize the anxiety. In light of Freud's later theory, however, it seems that repression and symptom-formation are phases of one and the same process. The various defense mechanisms specify the nature of the symptoms, the different ways in which an act of repression is made effective over time.

How is a symptom formed? Hans has a warning experience of anxiety, for example, which he handles by doing perhaps the only thing he can, namely 'repressing' his awareness of his beliefs and desires, or perhaps his awareness of the situation itself. Anxiety, that is, more particularly what Freud calls 'signal anxiety', occasions repression; and repression is the attempt to avoid greater anxiety by somehow blinding oneself to the situation that occasions it, or blurring or disguising it, or attributing it to something less fearful. For example, the woman in our earlier example nurtures belief in her husband's infidelity because it allows her not to acknowledge her guilty lust for her son-in-law. Or a boy (the Wolf Man) wants to be intimate with his father as his mother is; but since that would seem to require that he be castrated (as he believes her to be), he imagines anal intercourse instead. One wishes that the world were different in a certain way from the way one has reason to think it is, or different in a way which would render innocuous, or false, the beliefs which make one anxious; and in consequence one imagines that it is.

Freud's new understanding of the relationship between repression and anxiety connects symptoms to gratification in a way that is also new in his theory, and casts a different light on the concept of a wish.[3] In his earliest models of repression there is a wish on the one hand, and some inhibiting or censoring force on the other. Symptoms are the substitute and displaced gratification of a repressed libidinal wish. In the later model, the primary wish that symptoms gratify is itself the product of conflict: it is the wish to avoid acknowledging one's own beliefs, or making one's perceptions explicit. Though Freud continues to speak of the repression of instincts, his model in *Inhibitions* implies that repression acts primarily on perception or awareness: one 'knows' and one 'doesn't know', Freud will often say. One 'knows' (unconsciously); and it is because one does that one represses, so comes (consciously) 'not to know'. In the process one typically acquires a belief which is itself psychically painful—for example Hans's phobic belief about horses, or the woman's belief about her husband's infidelity—yet less painful than the one against which it is a defense.

The symptom is then only partially successful. Hans has an inhibiting fear of horses, which are yet more easily avoided than fathers. (Why horses in particular? Freud suggests a number of associations that make them a natural focus of the child's fears.) And he reaps the 'secondary' or unintended gain that he is allowed to stay home with his beloved mother, a gain that then reinforces the phobic phantasy. Yet the true danger situation—Hans's libidinal desires, which threaten, he thinks, both his penis and his father's love—persists unchanged. Symptom-formation is an exchange not so much of gratifications as of anxieties: one anxious state of mind defends against another, the more disturbing of the two. The fact that the symptomatic state is itself painful helps the agent not to recognize it as the product of his own wish.

The question is: How do these acts of self-blinding, of imaginative recreation of the world 'in the service of defense', take place? If we were trying to force repression to reason's bed, we would take Freud at his sometime word, construing repression as a fully intentional process. Then it might look like this: Wanting not to believe that (or think about, or be aware or mindful of) p, and thinking that a certain activity of selective focusing, or of pretending or imagining that q might do the trick, one sets oneself to focus, or pretend, or imagine in the relevant ways. I have no doubt this sometimes happens. Nor need intentions require forethought or deliberation. Consider the woman who runs into a burning building to save her child. She doesn't think about what she is doing or why. Yet she does what she does because she wants to save her child, who she believes is in the building; she believes also that she may save him by acting as she does. Her action is unpremeditated yet fully intentional. Another example: A man who looks away from the scene of an accident because he doesn't want to see it may believe that looking away serves that end, and say so later if he is asked. Yet he is undoubtedly unaware of such a belief at the time; and he may not know what it is exactly that he fears to see. If these two are unaware of their motives it is not because they are extraordinary, repressed, or darkly unconscious, but so very ordinary.

The reason that neither Hans's phobic avoidance in particular, nor the imaginative or focusing activity involved in repression in general, can be understood as intentional is that a crucial element is missing, namely the instrumental belief that one might fulfill his desire by doing what he does.[4] If I do x intentionally, then I have a desire, and a belief that I can realize it by doing x, whether this desire and this belief are conscious or unconscious.[5] We can tell Hans's story so as to provide the desire: he would like to feel less anxious. But it is absurd to suppose that he believes he may lessen his anxiety by phantasizing the fearfulness of horses; and without such a belief there is desire but not intention. Or to return to the example of the tablecloth lady: under the description 'putting ink on the sheet' her behavior is an action, and intentional; but under the fuller description which makes reference to the phantasy, 'putting ink on the sheet as a way of envisioning the past undone', it is not. This latter description, furthermore, implying as it does that she believes putting ink on the bed, and so on, is a way of redoing the past, is misleading. She does not have such beliefs. Phantasy requires a different kind of accounting.

An anxious wish itself, I suggest, may cause a defensive activity of envisioning in the absence of any instrumental belief. The wish causes an imagining, and when it does, *it is as if*—Richard Wollheim says—*the desire were gratified*. Wollheim characterizes phantasy as an instance of 'iconic imagining', an activity or a state caused by wish or desire in which we represent the world as it might be if our wish or desire were fulfilled (1984, chaps. 3 and 4). Desire characteristically expresses itself in imaginative acts, Wollheim adds, which tend to leave the imaginer in a condition appropriate to what they represent. Angry and wishing to express one's anger in a violent form, one imagines doing so and feels to some extent gratified in the process.

In the next chapter I endorse a use of 'mental mechanism' which refers to an intention of a certain sort. In this chapter I am proposing another use according to which a mental mechanism is a mental cause, namely a wish, that is not embedded in a full intentional structure. In *Jokes and Their Relation to the Unconscious* Freud had claimed an important characteristic of unconscious thinking to be that "no process that resembles 'judging' occurs. In the place of rejection by judgment, what we find in the unconscious is 'repression'. Repression may, without doubt, be correctly described as the intermediate stage between a defensive reflex and a condemning judgment" (1905, p. 175). Perhaps we have saved what is right and important in this passage while rejecting Freud's notions of primary process and primary repression as activities which are intrinsically prior to judgment.

In psychoanalytic theory the concept of unconscious psychic functioning typically refers to mental contents, like Hans's anger toward his father, his fears of retaliation, his worries about bodily integrity, his desire to have his mother to himself—all those mental contents which 'lifting repression' brings to consciousness.[6] As Michael Moore says (1988), this is a 'pre-theoretic' concept in the realm of reasons. It includes the pre-conscious, and much of the repressed, dynamic unconscious. Nevertheless, it belongs to folk psychology, and did so before Freud came along to widen its domain. But sometimes the concept refers instead to processes that are by definition beyond consciousness. Psychoanalysts may on occasion want to use 'repression', for example, to refer to events of which it is not possible even in principle to be aware.[7]

Wittgenstein blurs this distinction in comparing talk about unconscious thoughts, volitions, and so on, to the practice we might adopt of calling a certain painless state of decay in a tooth 'unconscious toothache' (1958, pp. 22–23). The comparison holds for what I am calling the theoretical unconscious, but not for those thoughts and volitions of which one might become aware. Benjamin Rubinstein (1976) blurs it as well in arguing that unconscious processes can only be construed as neurological; that in talking about unconscious processes the psychoanalyst is talking about his patient not as a person but as an organism. And on the same basis I disagree with Michael Basch when he writes: "The recognition that brain function is what we should mean by 'mind' relieves us of the burden of hypothesizing a mythical mental apparatus whose nature, essence, and function must then be established" (1977, p. 249).[8] We don't need or want to hypothesize such an apparatus. But we do want to distinguish dropping a glass *simply* because of a nervous tremor, and dropping it out of a hostile wish, or a desire to provoke attention.

No one model will fit all the cases of repression, any more than it will self-deception. At one end of a spectrum will be intentional attempts to distract oneself, to turn one's attention to something else, or to deny one's own feelings or agency, and fully-formed recognitions that are the object of such attempts; at the other, processes that go on below the level of recoverable mental contents.[9] In between is the species on which I've focused, for I think it is the one most characteristic of what is recovered or 'created' through the activity of psychoanalytic interpretation.

II Phantasy

I have said that the concepts of repression, symptom formation, and phantasy are linked as follows: repression is accomplished through an imaginative activity of a certain sort which Freud calls phantasy; the symptomatic behavior is then an acting out of the phantasy in something like the way that the actor playing Polonius enacts the scenario of *Hamlet* when he hides behind an arras. A full discussion of Freudian phantasy would require a treatise on the imagination. I want to say just enough to prepare the notion of psychic division elaborated in the next chapter, and to defend another of the ideas to which Freud's talk about primary process and hallucinatory wish-fulfillment points: when the mind in trouble short-circuits reason, repressing and phantasizing instead of acknowledging conflict, mental attitudes form that are relatively immune to correction by experience. They tend to persist, sometimes organizing themselves into split-off mental sub-structures that retain an infantile character.

In "Writers and Day-Dreaming," Freud speaks of phantasy as follows:

> Might we not say that every child at play behaves like a creative writer, in that he creates a world of his own or, rather, re-arranges the things of his

world in a way that pleases him? It would be wrong to think he does not take that world seriously . . . The opposite of play is not what is serious but what is real. In spite of all the emotion with which he cathects his world of play, the child distinguishes it quite well from reality; and he likes to link his imagined objects and situations to the tangible things of the real world. This linking is all that differentiates the child's play from 'phantasying' . . .

As people grow up . . . they cease to play, and they seem to give up the yield of pleasure which they gained from playing. But whoever understands the human mind knows that hardly anything is harder for a man to give up [than] a pleasure which he has once experienced . . . What appears to be a renunciation is really the formation of a substitute or surrogate. In the same way, the growing child, when he stops playing, gives up nothing but the link with real objects; instead of *playing,* he now *phantasies.* He builds castles in the air and creates what are called *day-dreams.* (1908 [1907], pp. 144–145)

It's clear enough what Freud has in mind by 'the playing child': he pretends that the broom is a horse, the rock a lion, knowing all the while that he is dealing with brooms and rocks. He is like the poet, calling a flower stem a fuse. But how are we to understand the phantasizing adult who 'gives up the link with real objects'? Does Freud mean merely that the adult pretends without the aid of props? That wouldn't be an interesting difference, for the writer of fiction and the rehearsing actor can forgo props too; and Freud sees 'phantasy' as occupying a slightly different place on the spectrum of imagining from either of these activities. Does he mean that the adult phantasy makes no reference to objects, some of which are 'real'? That is obviously false. Words do not lose their normal ties to things in the world when they are employed in the making of a fiction; if they did they would change their meaning. Or does he mean that although the adult also knows that rocks aren't lions, and so forth, still in phantasizing he brackets off a part of what he knows, holding apart incompatible recognitions and beliefs, some of which he would have to revise or give up were he to put them all together? I suggest this as the best reading of what Freud has in mind; and it fits in nicely with what he means by 'the splitting of the ego', an idea we come to in a moment.

The passage just looked at makes clear that Freud thinks of 'phantasy' as an extension of the folk-psychological concept of daydreaming. What the passage doesn't bring out are the peculiar 'Freudian' changes. For these, consider the following early note on 'the architecture of hysteria': "The aim seems to be to arrive [back] at the primal scenes. In a few cases this is achieved directly, but in others only by a roundabout path, *via* phantasies. For phantasies are psychical facades constructed in order to bar the way to these memories" (1897, p. 248).

Now it seems clear that, as I noted earlier, the wish that spurs phantasy is typically born of anxiety; it is an anxious wish, or rather, a wish to escape an awareness of some sort that makes one anxious. The imaginative act is defensive and deceiving in nature: one imagines that the world is other than one knows, or could easily know, it is. It is, in short, the sort of imaginative act we have linked to repression. As for 'screen memory', sometimes Freud means merely a memory that is preternaturally vivid through having become a kind of filter or emblem for a number of genuine memories; more often he has in mind here too a fiction which is itself anxiety-provoking yet which manages to screen from view a still more anxious thought.

In the following passage from a late essay, "The Splitting of the Ego in the Process of Defence" (1940 [1938]), Freud puts together the ideas we have articulated so far:

> He [the child] replies to the conflict with two contrary reactions, both of which are valid and effective. On the one hand, with the help of certain mechanisms he rejects reality . . . on the other hand, in the same breath he recognizes the danger of reality, takes over the fear of that danger as a pathological symptom and tries subsequently to divest himself of the fear . . . But everything has to be paid for in one way or another, and this success is achieved at the price of a rift in the ego which never heals but which increases as time goes on . . . The two contrary reactions to the conflict persist as the centre-point of a splitting of the ego. The whole process seems so strange to us because we take for granted the synthetic nature of the processes of the ego. But we are clearly at fault in this. The synthetic function of the ego, though it is of such extraordinary importance, is subject to particular conditions and is liable to a whole number of disturbances. (pp. 275–276)

To accommodate the sort of process Freud describes here, the philosophy of mind requires a notion of division, for which I will give an argument in the next chapter.

Freud was working toward articulating a number of ideas that are new in philosophical psychology. 'Phantasy' is part of a network of concepts which includes 'repression', 'repetition', 'acting out', 'screen memory', and 'memory', gathering together Freud's discoveries both about the use of the imagination in defense and about psychological time: the past is 'remembered' in the light of phantasy, which may be taken for memory; the present is (unconsciously) seen, or rather enacted, as a repetition of the past. And the very fact of acting *as if* a certain story were true, itself begins in the mind of the agent to lend some credence to the idea that it is true.

In a passage quoted earlier (1914), Freud writes:

> We may say that the patient does not *remember* anything of what he has forgotten and repressed, but *acts* it out. He reproduces it not as a memory but as an action; he *repeats* it, without, of course, knowing that he is repeating it . . . [The physician] celebrates it as a triumph for the treatment if he can

bring it about that something that the patient wishes to discharge in action is disposed of through the work of remembering. (1914a, pp. 150–153)

In the case of the 'table-cloth lady', for example, repression allows the past to be remembered, but not *as* memory. This protects her from the pain of realizing that *as* past there is nothing to be done about it; and it allows her to act *as if* she thought she might now redo the past in the present.

In discussing how phantasy manages to form early mental structures that are relatively immune to correction, we should note the way in which imaginative activity in general sets other imaginings going of which one may not be conscious. Think of Cinderella, consciously daydreaming of her prince. This carries in its wake thoughts of rescue, of turning the tables on her sisters, of winning her father's total love, thoughts which may be neither repressed nor conscious, generating a gaiety that she herself cannot explain. Kendall Walton (1990) puts the point this way:

> After Fred has occurrently imagined himself becoming a millionaire by winning a lottery and has gone on to think about his political career and retirement, he doesn't cease imagining that he won a lottery. His imagining this is a persisting state that begins when the thought occurs to him and continues, probably for the duration of the daydream. After the initial thought is a nonoccurrent imagining which forms a backdrop for later occurrent imaginings . . . (An effect of this background imagining might be a vague gnawing feeling, as the fantasy progresses, that his successes are unearned and undeserved . . .)
>
> It is a mistake to think of a daydream as simply a disconnected series of individual mental events . . . The various imaginings are woven together into a continuous cloth, although only some of the strands are visible on the surface of any particular spot. (p. 17)

Freud bespeaks a similar insight in the following passage: A patient asks: "'But in that case the phantasy that has transformed itself into these childhood memories would not be a conscious one that I can remember, but an unconscious one?'" To which Freud responds: "Unconscious thoughts which are a prolongation of conscious ones. You think to yourself 'If I had married so-and-so', and behind the thought there is an impulse to form a picture of what the 'being married' really is" (1899, p. 116).[10]

But unconsciousness of a different sort enters the picture when the imaginative process is defensive in nature; for then it begins to mask and isolate the initial anxiety against which the phantasy was a protection, sealing off the initial desires, increasingly putting them beyond recognition, and falsifying other aspects of reality in the process. By its nature, Hopkins (1982) points out, phantasy must falsify reality in two ways: it misrepresents inner reality or the state of the agent, and it misrepresents outer reality or what he is doing in the world. Take so simple an example of a wish-fulfilling envisioning as the following: One dreams of drinking from a cool stream, and awakens in a state of thirst. While thirsty the dreamer portrays himself as gratified, and while suffering a desire he portrays himself as gratifying it. Intrinsic to the condition of phantasy is that it obscures what one is experiencing and doing, keeping both from awareness. The wish remains unrecognized, ungratified, and unmodified. And while it may disturb others of one's mental attitudes, it does not qualify their content. Such conscious thoughts, for example, as the Rat Man's 'I love and admire and wish to honor my father' do not take into account the angry wish to dishonor and defy him, and the latter is not tempered by the man's real love.

Furthermore, because the wish of phantasy is rooted in anxiety, in time it becomes for that reason as well scarcely identifiable as a wish. The thought of having the wish provokes anxiety; for example, the Wolf Man's childhood longing for intimacy with his father would require him, he imagined, to be 'castrated' as he believed his mother was. Or the wish takes the particular form it does by answering an anxious thought, which is nevertheless still present in inchoate form. So the child imagines anal intercourse, which does not require castration. The wish becomes further unrecognizable through the work of condensation and displacement.

Freud says that condensation serves the purpose of disguise but that it is not necessarily motivated by that purpose. It is simply the way the mind works in certain of its states: in dreaming, in the creative process, and in phantasy. Condensation, displacement, and the revisionist nature of memory are all illustrated in the phantasy told to Freud by four different female patients in which a child is being beaten. Is this a memory, a belief, a worry? It is not clear, except that in each case the thought is accompanied by intense sexual excitement, which suggests that the thought is somehow related to desire. The terms of the phantasy are also unclear. Was the child being beaten the one producing the phantasy, or another? Was it always the same child? Who was beating the child? "Nothing could be ascertained," Freud writes, "that threw any light upon these questions—only the hesitant reply: I know nothing about it: a child is being beaten . . ." (1919, p. 181).

As the phantasy is slowly spelled out, it is seen to reflect wishes and anxieties interacting with others from different periods of the phantasizer's life, all preserved in the structure of the phantasy. It expresses, and condenses, a number of transformations: in the first instance, the child who is being beaten is a rival (brother or sister) for the father's love, and the beating is proof that the phantasizer is his preferred love object. Then under the influence of the guilt which the child came to feel—through omnipotence of thought—for her incestuous wishes, the child being beaten becomes the girl herself, and the motive for the transformation is punishment for the guilty wish. This does not mean, however, that the first motive is replaced. The phantasy expresses the jealous wish, and simultaneously the punishment for it, and something else as well, though Freud does not explicitly say so here: a symbolic representation of the act of intercourse as understood by a child and colored by her feeling of guilt. The layering in this phantasy illustrates the narrative way in which the mind naturally works: catching up the past and weaving it into the fabric of the present, telling the present in the figures of the past.

We have seen that some of the wishes around which a phantasy forms are childhood wishes; as such, they may no longer be even identifiable as wishes, and one's own. How, for example, can a grown man recognize being buggered by his father as something he or anyone might want? So one may ask: 'But if the desires which spun the phantasy are no longer even recognizable, then how is one finally able to break the thread? How can one work through a phantasy, and so be released into the present?' Wollheim illuminatingly suggests an analogy with the process of coming to understand a work of art. In one conception, the wrong one he thinks, we start with perception of the work. Next, we acquire background information, details about how the work was put together, what it represents (if anything), and so on, that lead us to a number of beliefs about it. And then on that basis we arrive at conclusions, which are to be regarded as our best interpretation. On another conception there are not three phases but two: we begin with beliefs about the work which we may arrive at in any number of ways, including perception itself; and then with all this information in hand we arrive at an understanding. Understanding the work just is perceiving it in the light of all the information we have gained. Some of this understanding can be put into words, but no more than the painting itself (or the piece of music, or the poem) can all of it be.

The lifting of repression works, then, by bringing the hidden wishes to conscious light and finding the right description for them, and by making clear, in doing so, how inappropriate they are; for the wishes that phantasy gratifies are often rooted in situations of childhood, and it is only in the world of the child that they might have been thought to bring gratification. Since a wish can be felt and acknowledged as a wish only if it is not gratified, Freud therefore insisted that analysis must take place in a condition of abstinence. He had in mind the gratification not only of acting out but also of phantasy itself, which will ideally be replaced by imaginings of other sorts and by wishing acknowledged as such.

Freud thought wishing a more primitive state than desiring. Yet in a sense, things go just the other way around: When we recognize that one of our desires is outweighed by another, or when we come to believe that gratifying it is not merely unlikely but impossible, then we *desire* it no longer; but the wish does not necessarily go away.[11]

10 Dividing the Self

So far we have taken the concept of irrationality for granted. It's time, at last, to specify a crucial sense of irrationality toward which I have been heading and which interests Freud as well as philosophers. In this sense an act or a belief is 'internally' irrational if it is inconsistent or undesirable in the agent's own terms, by criteria or in light of facts he or she implicitly acknowledges. The Rat Man's belief that his midnight escapades were witnessed by his father was irrational in this sense, since the man knew his father was dead. By contrast, if I falsely think that the ravage in my garden was caused by lions, yet have good reason for thinking so, I am mistaken or deceived, but my belief is not internally irrational. Nor is a belief which strikes us as bizarre—for example, that the world was formed from worms and cheese—but which makes sense in the context of the believer himself.

Internal irrationality is interesting because it presses hard on the nature of the mental; for 'holism' tells us that something can be construed as a belief or an intention only if it is linked to other such states in generally rational ways. Of course Mary can, like a parrot, utter the sounds 'It's raining and it's not raining today, here, now'. But were we to take her to believe that it's raining, then—it goes almost without saying—we would expect her not to believe at the same time that it's not. Yet something like this paradoxical holding of incompatible beliefs seems to occur, for example when we are self-deceived, or repressing awareness of something we know.

The paradoxicality has two aspects, one concerning the state of the person who is said to believe both *p* and not-*p*, the other, the process of deceiving oneself. Why the first is paradoxical is self-evident. The second turns in part on the assumption that self-deception is intentional in the same way as deceiving another: when John *deceives* Mary, as distinct from merely saying something to her which is false in fact but which he sincerely holds to be true, John intends that Mary be taken in by a belief he knows he thinks is false. If self-deception is analogous, then John, setting out to believe something that he does not, must know he does not. The obvious problem is that this knowledge would seem to undermine the intention itself.

Some philosophers deny that self-deception is analogous in these ways to deceiving others.[1] They may be right for many cases. Even about others we surely have put the matter too starkly; for we are seldom certain both that a proposition is true and that it is not. More likely we have evidence inclining us on the whole to believe that *p*, but, moved by the hope that it is false, we disregard the evidence, or emphasize that which points in another direction. Yet even so, self-deception seems to sin against a normative 'principle of total evidence' which enjoins us in a situation of conflict to hold the belief that is best supported. Think of this normative principle not as something that we were *taught,* or that we always observe, or as a constraint that we would or could consciously avow, but as a conceptual necessity in distinguishing between internal irrationality and 'irrationality' of other kinds, between, on the one hand, being deceived or in error, or changing one's mind, and, on the other, being self-deceived. Irrationality is a failure, not an absence, of rationality; and the 'principle of total evidence' is one of the things we need to clarify this failure. If someone simply fails to see the evidence that goes against her, or has no idea what it is to be conflicted because some evidence goes one way and some another, then she is like Mary deceived by John; she is not self-deceived. Self-deception is a state of holding incompatible beliefs on the part of someone capable of recognizing, however dimly, that they are.

Freud also recognizes the need for something like this normative principle in describing irrationality. It is because he does that he is moved in *The Ego and the Id* (1923) to revise his topography of the mind. His first model had drawn a line between consciousness and the system Unconscious, the latter consisting primarily of the repressed. He had envisioned internal or intra-psychic conflict as taking place between these two systems, one 'self' knowing but not wanting to know, the other genuinely ignorant, with 'the censor' located more or less on the side of consciousness. But he came to see that such a model doesn't picture either the fact that the agency doing the repressing is typically itself unconscious (if not explicitly repressed), or that the unconscious knows more than it says.

So partly for this reason, Freud introduces, with his second topographical theory, the structures 'id', 'ego', and 'superego' to cut across the conscious/unconscious divide. Much of the ego *(das Ich)* is repressed; but the ego is also that center of mental agency which acknowledges and attempts to reconcile conflicting beliefs and desires, and which in doing so sometimes represses. Freud's 'ego' is that agent who—because he or she implicitly acknowledges such principles of rationality as we have posited—can be said to repress and to 'split'.

This change recognizes the internal character of irrationality, but at the cost of reviving the paradoxes implicit in it. Freud attempts to avoid them by assigning deceived and deceiver to different structures or systems; but as Sartre (1956) rightly argues, in positing an unconscious 'repressing' Ego, unaware of its own act of repression, Freud reinstates the unity of deceived and deceiver now on the side of the unconscious. And it is just this unity which drives the paradoxes. Both self-deception and repression, then, pose the problem of constructing a model of the mind that acknowledges a certain degree of internal irrationality without jeopardizing the mind's intelligibility overall. The strategy I want to explore, despite its problems, is the Freudian one of mental partitioning. Our question will be how to draw the boundaries in a way that doesn't merely give us new names for old problems.

Let's begin by thinking of the mind as a network of interlocking desires, beliefs, memories, and so on, in which there may be sub-divisions or partitions that largely but not entirely overlap with the whole. David Pears (1984) suggests the following picture. Prior to partitioning the mind contains all the agent's beliefs and desires that are holistically implied by any one. Call this 'mind' S. S also contains the wish to believe that p, the belief that not-p, and something Pears calls the cautionary belief that q, namely that it would be irrational to believe that p, since the evidence inclines against it. The cautionary belief is what I earlier called the principle of total evidence.

Now what happens, Pears suggests, is that the wish to believe that p creates the belief that p *in O*, a sub-structure of S. That is, the wish creates O, which contains the wishful belief:

> The sub-system [S] is built around the nucleus of the wish for the irrational belief and it is organized like a person. Although it is a separate center of agency within the whole person, it is, from its own point of view, entirely rational. It wants the main system to form the irrational belief and it is aware that it will not form it, if the cautionary belief is allowed to intervene. So with perfect rationality it stops its intervention. (1984, p. 87)

The model saves Freud from Sartre's criticism, Pears remarks, since S's wish to believe that p creates p not in S but in O. S does not foster the inconsistent belief in itself but in a sub-division of itself. Pears's description suggests to an unfortunately literal degree, however, an idea of little persons within the person, a complaint I'll return to later. But first let's look at a similar model, one in which 'partitioning' names a certain way in which reasons fail to mesh with causes.

Davidson defends the following three claims, all of which he thinks can be found in Freud:

> *First,* the mind contains a number of semi-independent structures, these structures being characterized by mental attributes like thoughts, desires, and memories.
>
> *Second,* parts of the mind are in important respects like people, not only in having (or consisting of) beliefs, wants and other psychological traits, but in that these factors can combine, as in intentional action, to cause further events in the mind or outside it.
>
> *Third,* some of the dispositions, attitudes, and events that characterize the various substructures in the mind must be viewed on the model of physical dispositions and forces when they affect, or are affected by, other substructures in the mind. (1982, pp. 290–291)

It is this last point, Davidson says, which justifies Freud's use of metaphors from hydraulics and mechanics to describe certain kinds of psychological phenomena.

Davidson argues for the third claim as follows: While typically the mental causes that explain an action are also reasons for doing it, this is not always so. In such a case there may be a fully mental cause which is not a reason for what it causes, and which is therefore in a sense mechanical. As an example of an action which is irrational in this sense, Davidson cites an incident told by Freud in a footnote to his case history of the Rat Man. A man walking in a park stumbles on a branch. Thinking it may be dangerous to others, he removes the stick and throws it in a hedge beside the path. On his way home, however, it occurs to him that the branch may be dangerously projecting from the hedge, so he returns to the park and replaces the branch in the road. Both actions are rational in and of themselves, for in each the man acts in light of a reason, a belief-desire complex which is necessary to explain the action. If he had not had these reasons he would not have done what he did; so the reason in each case is also a cause.

The irrationality consists not in doing either of these actions, nor even both, but in the fact that in returning to the park to replace the stick the man intentionally ignores not only his own initial reasons for removing it but also the principle of continence, or doing that action he thinks best, all things considered. (The principle of continence is to weakness of the will as the principle of total evidence is to self-deception.) He has a motive for ignoring it, namely that he wants—perhaps for very strong unconscious reasons—to restore the branch to its original position. Presumably he believes he will feel less anxious or will somehow be happier if he does. But this motive enters his reasoning twice over, as Davidson says, first in overruling his own reasons for removing the stick, and second in overruling the principle of continence. There can be good reason to seek out evidence for beliefs we don't yet have, even for downplaying evidence for some we do. For example, thinking she might be happier if she learned to focus on her strengths and stop brooding over her weaknesses, Tanya may have good reason to look for evidence to support more 'positive' thinking. But the principles of continence and of total evidence aren't on a par with other 'beliefs'; against these principles there can be no evidence since— like the principle of induction (that the past is some sort of guide to belief about the future), or the law of non-contradiction—they are constitutive of rationality itself. To return now to the man in the park: the wish not to believe, or not to do, what reason counsels, causes him to neglect the principle of total evidence. This cause is his reason. But in the nature of the case there cannot be a *good* reason for neglecting it.

Often in human action the fabrics of reason and cause are so interwoven that we fail even to discern their different textures; but occasionally they come apart. Where they do the cause is like a quasi-mechanical force; and it draws a boundary between the conflicting beliefs. The boundary Davidson and Pears postulate is not available to introspection; nor is it to be thought of necessarily as a line between conscious and unconscious mental states. It is rather a "conceptual aid to the coherent description of genuine irrationalities" (Davidson, 1985b, pp. 91–92).

According to Davidson, it can be the case both that one intentionally ignores the principle of continence and that what causes one to do so is, in a sense, mechanical. In the previous chapter I suggested another kind of mental mechanism which is at work particularly in phantasizing and repression and which does not have the structure of intention. Yet I agree with Davidson that where there are mental phenomena, holism and rationality must more or less prevail; and that this is reason to postulate division in cases of internal irrationality. Considering an argument of Mark Johnston's against both Pears and Davidson will help separate the issue of mental mechanisms from the larger issue of mental holism.

Johnston (1988) argues that the idea of mental partitioning as construed by both Pears and Davidson posits a homuncularist community of selves within selves, and is on that account alone unacceptable. But as we will see, Johnston is after bigger game than this, namely an explanation of irrationality that calls for a quite different conception of the mental than Davidson's.

As I do, Johnston holds that often mechanisms are at work in cases of Freudian irrationality that render the behavior less than fully intentional.

But from this point on Johnston and I diverge. For his strategy is to unhinge the notions of belief and evidence, thereby undermining the idea that rationality is constitutive of the mental. He argues that we can provide an analysis of self-deceptive sorts of phenomena via the idea of operant conditioning: we have a belief about the future which lessens anxiety, and which is then reinforced by this reduction of pain. The belief is not arrived at on the basis of any sort of evidence, but in what Johnston calls a 'tropistic' manner; once in place the very fact that the belief is reinforced keeps unwelcome evidence at bay. If such a strategy were successful, it is true that irrationality would no longer require partitioning.

The problem, however, is that Johnston's analysis ignores just those facts about belief which he himself calls to our attention. He quotes the following from Bernard Williams:

> If I could acquire a belief at will, I could acquire it whether it was true or not; moreover I would know that I could acquire it whether it was true or not. If in full consciousness I could will to acquire a 'belief' irrespective of its truth, it is unclear that before the event I could seriously think of it as a belief, *i.e. as something purporting to represent reality.* (1973, p. 68)

A belief is by definition something we hold true, something that purports to represent the way things *are*. It is tied to evidence in such a way that, according to H. H. Price (1973) whom Johnston also quotes, what we describe as belief in the absence of evidence is not strictly speaking belief but something else. It is because this is so that self-deception is the seeming paradox it is. Once one has a belief, then operant conditioning, as well as evidence, can reinforce it. But how does one acquire the belief to begin with? What constitutes it as belief, if not the very sort of tie to evidence that Johnston wants to sever? One can indeed set out to acquire a belief one doesn't have, to put aside a belief one does, as in my earlier example about Tanya, who wants to bolster her self-confidence. But she will accomplish this, if she does, precisely through a different sorting of evidence. So, as the new belief becomes lodged in her mind, it cannot help affecting the weave of a large area of her other beliefs and desires. I could rest my case against Johnston here. But a closer look at his argument is illuminating of the concepts of belief and reasoning as I want them to be understood.

What is involved in calling a mental process rational? Johnston asks. Simply that causal relations hold "between mental states one of which is in fact a reason for the other" (p. 87). So Davidson also says. How then does Johnston get from this the anti-Davidsonian conclusion that he wants? The following passage points the way:

> Suppose that what is required over and above causation by states that are in fact reasons for the states or changes they cause is as follows. First the agent

must recognize that he has reasons that support the drawing of a certain conclusion or the performance of an intentional act; second, the agent must will
the drawing of the conclusion or will the performance of the act; and third, as
a result of the willing, draw the conclusion or perform the act. The special
something extra distinguishing rational causal processes from the mere
mental tropisms that constitute irrational changes in belief is then supposed
to be an intervening act of will. (1988, p. 88)

Something like this might occasionally take place, Johnston remarks; but it
cannot be a general condition on a connection's being rational. For if it
were, then every time there was a causal connection between someone's recognizing that he has reasons to perform an act, and his willing or forming
the intention to perform the act, there would also have to be the forming of
an intermediate "willing to will"; and this would launch us on an infinite
regress. So "at some point we must recognize an intentional act that is constituted merely by attitudes causing activity that they rationalize."

This is right. Johnston has so far given a familiar argument that an
account of intentional acts does not—in fact, cannot—require an act of
willing, construed as something separate from the agent's recognizing an
appropriate relation between his beliefs and desires. In other words, it
cannot be that rational thought processes require a homuncular sub-agent
who sees the rational connection and then wills to draw it. One of
Johnston's primary objections to partitioning as a way of dealing with
irrationality is that it entails just such a homuncularist idea. He complains
that partitioning is credible only

so long as we do not allow its advocates the luxury of hovering noncommit-
tally between the horns of a dilemma: either take the subsystem account literally, in which case it implausibly represents the ordinary self-deceiver as a
victim of something like multiple personality, or take it as a metaphor, in
which case it provides no way to evade the paradoxes while maintaining that
intentional acts constitute self-deceptions and wishful thinking. (1988, p. 82)

To avoid homuncularism—a danger then, Johnston thinks, as much for
an account of reason as of unreason—he proposes the following:

So . . . the case of intentionally drawing the logical conclusion from one's
beliefs must ultimately turn on the operation of tropisms connecting the attitudes in question . . . If we are to be able to draw any conclusions at all we
must in the relevant sense draw some conclusions blindly, which is not to say
unintentionally but rather to say without there occurring in us anything more
than an automatic response to those reasons. (p. 88)

What is right about this is that at some point explanation comes to an
end. If I see that p is true and I hold that if p is true, q must also be, then
normally I conclude, without more thought or deliberation, that q. There

is no further question to ask about why I do. This is the only sense in which I 'automatically' and 'blindly' draw conclusions. But to think it automatic in any other sense would lump the rat's 'choosing' the right door because it has been conditioned to do so with your choosing to give up coffee when the doctor has told you it's the cause of your indigestion; it would sort Rubinstein's beginning a fast arpeggio in E flat with his index finger (without thought at the time, but after much thought and practice) with the reflexive jerk of your knee at the tap of the doctor's hammer. The concept of a 'trope', as I believe Johnston intends it (he leaves it unanalyzed), derives from biology, where the paradigm is a sunflower's turning toward the sun. If all human behavior could be explained on such a pattern, there would be no need for reasoning as an explanatory category. This isn't, I think, what Johnston means to argue. While attacking the claim that rationality is constitutive of the mental, he wants nevertheless to mark off a domain of agency from which sunflowers are excluded. He wants clear-eyed choices and rational intentions. But it is precisely in defining such a domain that rationality and holism play their part.

How, then, if we don't go along with Johnston's argument that reasoning is 'blind', are we to avoid homuncularism? A different concept of trope gives a lead. Nathalie Sarraute (1957) uses the term to refer to subtle activities of the psychological life that usually go unnoticed. William James (1890) suggests a similar idea in speaking of the "transitive" rather than the "substantive" parts of the stream of experience, things like feelings of activity or the process of reflecting or drawing a conclusion. Models of syllogistic or practical reasoning capture the premises, the conclusions, even the structure of an argument as a whole; but by their nature they cannot reflect the temporality of the reasoning as a psychological activity.[2] Now since, unlike desires and beliefs, such transitive activities don't turn up as contents of consciousness, we can easily be led to the idea of a homunculus, a self outside of awareness who is the source of reasoning. Instead we should think of the reasoning that moves us from desire to the forming of intention not as some other thing over and above desire and belief, but as an activity that normally lies below the level of phenomenology and so escapes the philosopher's attention. Part of our problem in talking about these matters is that, as I've remarked before, the concepts of belief and desire are abstractions, from each other and from temporal processes more complex and messy than the propositions that philosophers pick out as instances of belief and desire— 'There is a tree in front of the window', 'I want an apple'—suggest.

Some work in cognitive psychology draws a similar distinction between, on the one hand, 'declarative' knowledge, or knowledge of the world and ourselves that is available to consciousness, and, on the other, "the procedural knowledge repertoire of skills, rules, and strategies that operate on declarative knowledge in the course of perception, memory, thought, and action" (Kihlstrom, 1987). Perhaps this is what Johnston has in mind. But if so, it doesn't tell against the idea of mental holism. And this is what gives content to the idea that rationality is constitutive of the mental.

I conclude, then, that neither partitioning nor reasoning, as Davidson understands it, presumes little agents within the mind; that rationality is constitutive of the mental; and that we are forced to posit partitioning whenever holism is violated to a significant degree, as it surely is in some cases of self-deception and even in repression. For on the view proposed in the last two chapters, the phantasizing that is often a part of repression takes place unhindered by a distinction the agent is perfectly capable of making in general, between belief and make-believe. On my view phantasizing is triggered by a wish, it serves a defensive purpose, but it takes place without the intermediary belief that would give it the structure of an intentional act. Yet in ignoring the principle of total evidence, it calls for the model of the divided mind.

What, if anything, does this model explain? Have we simply given the problem of internal irrationality another name? Yes and no. No, because the picture both acknowledges the problems implicit in the phenomena of irrationality and avoids the paradoxes they seem to generate. Yes, because neither Pears nor Davidson thinks he is enlightening us about the psychological stratagems at work, or characterizing the mental sub-divisions, or showing us just how splitting takes place and how the partitions are kept apart. They are not *explaining* anything in that sense, but drawing an abstract picture of the mind as they think internal irrationality requires it to be drawn. Davidson's picture puts the principle of continence (along with other such principles of rationality) in the dominant part of the mind together with some but not all of the premises in the agent's reasoning that generate the inconsistency or the contradiction; in the exiled structure go the premises that have been left out. The model gives no details about what other beliefs and so on go where; it says nothing about the endurance of sub-structures over time. Partitioning is a bare logical notion, nothing more. And just this bareness is its virtue. It travels light, requiring no particular theory of psychological development. Yet it can be fitted out with whatever empirical story one thinks is true.

Earlier I remarked that Davidson's tale of the man and the stick comes from a footnote to a case of Freud's. Let us look at the case itself and at Freud's own description of the irrational behavior:

One day, when he was out with her [his lady] in a boat and there was a stiff breeze blowing, he was obliged to make her put on his cap, because a command had been formulated in his mind that *nothing must happen to her.* This was a kind of *obsession for protecting,* and it bore other fruit besides this . . . On the day of her departure he knocked his foot against a stone lying in the road, and was *obliged* to put it out of the way by the side of the road, because the idea struck him that her carriage would be driving along the same road in a few hours' time and might come to grief against this stone. But a few minutes later it occurred to him that this was absurd, and he was *obliged* to go back and replace the stone in its original position on the road. (Freud, 1909, pp. 189–190)

The Rat Man's narrative begins with a tale of dreadful punishment by which he is obsessed—rats boring into the victim's anus—and which he vividly imagines happening to his father and his 'lady'. At first this obsession presents itself as 'just a thought'; but the fact that his feelings about this 'thought' are fascination and anxious guilt suggests that he is envisioning this torture as a punishment that he would like himself to inflict on his father and his lady, and that for him it is as if what he envisions were about to come true. Freud links the incident of the stone in the road to the rat obsession, to others of the man's obsessively violent thoughts, and to his bizarre compulsion to work until late at night, followed by his masturbating in front of the mirror. This last compulsion Freud analyzes, in part, as the acting out of a phantasy that the father he knows is dead is alive, and properly horrified by the man's defiantly exhibitionistic behavior.

What are the beliefs and desires in terms of which these phantasies are intelligible? None—on Freud's analysis—that are acknowledged or acknowledgeable by the Rat Man's grown-up self. They include, among others, very early feelings of hatred toward his father; perceptions of him as very powerful; a 'projection' of his own anger onto his father, perhaps misperceived as angry toward the child; self-deceptive feelings of his own innocence; certain early beliefs (for example, that his thoughts are visible to others and endowed with a kind of magical power); and the tendency to see other persons as either objects of his desire or impediments to it, a tendency which has presumably governed his relations with the world from early childhood.

In sum, the process of interpretation leads Freud from the episode in the park to a much earlier mental structure of the man's, to beliefs and desires that are alien to his conscious, adult self, and that are partial cause of his present behavior. The structure is characterized as a whole by confusions between past and present, between what is and what one wishes there were, even between what are genuinely pleasurable thoughts and what are rather thoughts that are 'pleasurable' only in that they help ward off anxiety.

Recall that on Davidson's analysis the irrationality of the man's behavior with the stick/stone enters at the point at which he ignores the principle of continence, or his own best all-things-considered judgment. I suggest that a split very much like this one—involving closely related beliefs, desires, memories, phantasies, and so on—took place much earlier, creating a kind of psychological fault that has persisted through time. In the typical cases of 'Freudian' irrationality the split-off mental structures are formed by relatively early anxiety and around phantasy, as described in the previous chapter. For imagine, now, that the anxiety situation is chronic—for example, a threatening ever-present father and a seductive mother—and that the phantasy which forms around it and which bails the child out is one on which he comes habitually to rely. Then habits of misperception may begin to settle; the exiled structure begins to crystallize and consolidate.

Thus early on the 'split' takes on character, dividing fragmentary impressions, together with phantasies modeled as a defense against them, on the one hand, from more occurrent perceptions in potential conflict with the phantasy structure, on the other. Increasingly there is a split between the past, as now both embedded and rewritten in phantasy, and the present. What started out as a wishful belief acquires the force and structure of a habit, a way of acting, a way also of perceiving, that reinforces the initial avoidance. Old fears, old memories both veridical and false that might have a very different meaning now if one reflected on them, are preserved. Furthermore, given that the imagination works in the associative way it does, more and more situations may come to remind the person of what he doesn't want to confront: If I avoid reflecting on x because it makes me anxious and x reminds me of y, then I avoid thoughts of y as well. So in that sense new thoughts are drawn into the structure that is split off, a process Freud attempted to explain with the notion of primary repression as a kind of magnet in the depths of the mind.

We can now see how a mental sub-structure with some of the characteristics of 'primary process' might begin to crystallize: timelessness (or imperviousness to the passage of time), exemption from mutual contradiction (holding on to beliefs which are inconsistent with other beliefs one has, or with the evidence available to one), replacement of external reality by internal reality (phantasy itself). Repression seeds the sub-structure; but there is nothing in the way of some 'primary repressed' material in which this sub-structure is grounded. (Any act of repression, however, may build on a sub-structure formed in the wake of a prior act of repression; repression may tend to burgeon in something like this way.)

Freud saw a crucial link between infantile anxiety and repression. So there may be, simply because in childhood one is so vulnerable, and unable to deal with dangers in the world by taking the appropriate actions. A kind of psychic flight, or looking away, together with hallucinatory wish-fulfillment, may be the only defenses at the child's disposal. Furthermore, the child has not articulated many of his own thoughts, not because he is in the grip of a symbolic process that is intrinsically different from the one inflected in language, but because he hasn't yet acquired the techniques of spelling them out.

Davidson's account of self-division supports the Freudian story. But as applied to the episode of the stone in the road, and others like it, the account doesn't do justice to the fact that the divisions of the self are not of the same temporal order: in the main structure, occurrent beliefs and desires that are open to evidence and subject to revision in the ordinary way; in the sub-structure, beliefs and desires that are embalmed, increasingly alien to those of the present, and inappropriate in light of present experience. Just how these older structures impinge on behavior, and the extent to which, when they do, they modify the agent's responsibility for his activity, are complicated questions which I have only begun to answer in these chapters.

Let me be clear about two things. First, my defense of Freud's view on this issue is not an apology for his tripartite structure of id, ego, and superego. Second, my proposals about the nature of partitioning in cases like that of the Rat Man have an entirely empirical character. I claim that we are led to them by the process of interpretation itself, and that whereas often we can explain an action well enough by staying fairly close to the agent's immediate beliefs and desires, neurotic actions typically will make sense only in a context that is much more complex than usual and that reaches further back into the agent's life. Such a context is what I have called the Legacy of Childhood. Phantasy interferes with other mental structures, then, not as counter-argument to argument, or desire to contrary desire, but as hallucinatory wish-fulfillment interferes with realistic appraisal of reality and its modifying effect on one's desires and beliefs.

Dewey describes the process of forming aims as

> beginning with a wish, an emotional reaction against a state of things and a hope for something different. Action fails to connect satisfactorily with surrounding conditions. Thrown back upon itself, it projects itself in an imagination of a scene which if it were present would afford satisfaction. This picture is often called an aim, more often an ideal. (1922, p. 234)

Dewey is describing imagination in the service of rationality, where it connects with belief to yield an appraisal of the present and a program for the future. This is not how phantasizing works. If we think of rationality as that ideal condition in which one acts in the light of all her beliefs and desires, and in which every mental attitude is spontaneously revised in the light of all the rest, then phantasy is inimical to rationality and to learning from the past. (I take this to be a part of what Freud means in speaking of a 'repetition compulsion'.) It is inimical to the forming of intentions in the sense in which an imagined future state serves as an end for one's present activity, since a condition for forming such ends is precisely that one recognize the imagined future state as something to be striven for, something not present now. Phantasizing, on the contrary, feeds the dream that the world is as one wishes it were, or is not as one is capable of seeing it is.

On one of Freud's models the rational mind, the mind that can say 'I think that . . .' and 'I doubt that . . .', is a lonely outpost against a bestial unconscious. But on the model that I favor the concept of 'the unconscious' rather calls attention to the ways in which earlier mental states, scarcely intelligible to the adult mind, can be preserved, stunted, and isolated. The adult uncovers her 'unconscious' as she learns to hear the voice of the child she harbors.

And now, said Socrates, are we agreed upon the following conclu-
sions? One, that love is always the love of something, and two, that
something is what he lacks?

Conclusion: Valuing and the Self

"Under what conditions did man construct the value judgments *good* and
evil?" Nietzsche asks (1956, p. 151). In the beginning, he suggests, the
language of value was an invention of those in power. More or less synon-
ymous with 'noble', 'beautiful', and 'strong', 'good' was the Greek aris-
tocracy's description of itself. There was no concept of 'evil', and no self-
hatred in the form of bad conscience. 'Bad' simply discriminated those
beyond the pale, the weaklings, the Others.

In this first stage in the history of values, warrior and priest composed a
single ruling class. But as culture developed these groups diverged; and in
a struggle between them the priests lost. Nietzsche asks us to imagine that,
over an indeterminate period of time, an inversion of values was effected
through which the powerful warriors whom the priests admired and
envied, and so in a way loved, were reviled as sinners. Not only did the
powerful, or formerly powerful, now think themselves 'bad', but the
priests, identifying with the warriors whom they desperately wanted to
replace, thus seeing themselves in the warriors' eyes, despised what was
'good' in themselves. Under the banner of Christian love, weakness
sought to mortify strength, and accepted, even glorified, its own humili-
ation. "In the earliest phase," Nietzsche writes, "bad conscience is
nothing other than the instinct of freedom forced to become latent, driven
underground, and forced to vent its energy upon itself" (p. 220). The
invention of guilt, which the Judeo-Christian tradition proclaims its
greatest spiritual treasure, represents rather the ignoble triumph of
repressed envy, resentment, and self-disgust.

Nowhere is Freud's debt to Nietzsche more apparent than in his views about valuing, particularly as Freud states them in *Civilization and Its Discontents* (1931 [1929]). In the climactic fifth chapter Freud says that the clue to mankind's discontents under the yoke of civilization is supplied by "one of the ideal demands . . . of civilized society. It runs: 'Thou shalt love thy neighbour as thyself'" (p. 109). What could the source of such a strange and impossible demand be, Freud asks, other than the need to counter an aggressive instinct so violent that it threatens to destroy both individual and society? Whereas Nietzsche had laid guilt at the door of the Judeo-Christian tradition, Freud tracks it further back to aggression deep in the heart of the human creature, and to the species' need to handle aggression in a way that allows communal life to continue. The unhappy solution, he thinks, so far a tenable but costly compromise in the cosmic war between Eros and Thanatos, is that aggression, in the form of guilt, is directed backward onto the self.

Like Nietzsche, Freud sees the moral sense as the uneasy resolution in a dialectic between impotence and power, love and hate. In Freud's story the roles of strong and weak are played, of course, not by social classes but by parent and child. The dependent child rages against the powerful adult whom the child hates and resents, but also loves and admires, resolving his conflict finally by identifying with the one he would like to replace and whose retaliatory vengeance he fears. The child borrows the father's 'You must not do *x*' (take your mother to bed) and makes it his own, deriving the strength for compliance from the combined motives of fear of the father and rage, whose target he has now himself become.

For both Nietzsche and Freud the final outcome is the same: resentment and aggression, flourishing secretly in the dark of the mind behind a mask of love; self-hate fueled ever more by the inhibition of instinctual energy; repression, and the creation of a mortal enemy within the self, in the shape for Freud of a special agency or structure he calls the superego. The Oedipal complex is Freud's version of the Fall, for he thinks that moral values can bloom only in the opening of a fissure between child and father, self and self, a divide across which the Unconscious speaks in a strange language unintelligible to the conscious mind.[1]

Nietzsche and Freud both reveal perversions to which conscience is subject. I have no doubt, furthermore, that the process of psychological splitting—self malevolently turned against self in identification with a fearfully loved aggressor—which Freud postulates goes some way toward accounting for these perversions, and describes in any case some prevalent pathologies. But I don't think he has given us good reason to accept this process for what he thinks it is, a genealogy of the moral sense and the emotion of guilt in general.

Freud himself is of two minds on a number of issues related to this: he holds, on the one hand, that other persons are an imposition on a pre-existing self, that the moral self is, necessarily, the split self, that genuine object love is an illusion; on the other, that the moral self derives from just those developmental events that constitute the self in the first place, events which are necessarily interpersonal and affective in nature. The latter is the view I will defend in part II of this chapter, as needed companion, furthermore, for the interpersonal view of the mind developed in the first chapter of this book. But let's begin by charting the evolution of some of the conflicting strands in Freud's moral philosophy.

I Ambiguous Objects, Narcissism, and the Superego

We recall that in *Three Essays on the Theory of Sexuality* (1905) Freud had drawn a distinction, modeled on the difference between hunger and love, between the instincts of self-preservation and the libidinal instincts. At the beginning hunger alone holds the field. Then with the infant's first cradling at the breast, libido comes into play: in the process of satisfying hunger the infant makes a rudimentary discovery of other persons, and with them the pleasures of relations to an 'object'.

Unfortunately Freud didn't have the concept of an *Intentional* object clearly in mind, something at which an act of thought, and only an act of thought, is directed. So he is often unclear whether the gratifying 'object' is meant to signify another person, perceived and desired as such by the child, or whether it is the 'extensional' object, the thing in the world, whatever it is, that will satisfy an itch. That is, in talking about libidinal desire, is Freud talking about specifically mental states, or the chemical processes that underlie them? If the first, then the object that matters for the child is the object he sees under some description or other; and other persons presumably play an essential role in the child's psychological development. But of course other persons *seen as such* play no role in a strictly neurophysiological account. Some of the continuing debate between 'drive' theory and 'object relations' theory arises from insufficient attention to this distinction.

The Three Essays comes down more or less on the 'Intentionalist' side. By way of introduction Freud alludes to Aristophanes' fable, reported in Plato's *Symposium*, in which the genealogy of love is described this way: Our first ancestors were spherical creatures whom the gods punished for defiance by cutting each one into two halves. Love is our doomed attempt to achieve a wholeness which once was ours and which can never in this world be ours again. Freud is clearly talking here about psychological experience. So also is he when, defining an instinct in terms of its *aim* and its *object,* Freud says that the sexual object is *"the person* [my italics] from whom sexual attraction proceeds" (1905, p. 135).

Later in the essay he goes on to say:

> At a time at which the first beginnings of sexual satisfaction are still linked with the taking of nourishment, the sexual instinct has a sexual object outside the infant's own body in the shape of his mother's breast. It is only later that he loses it, just at the time, perhaps, when he is able to form a total idea of the person to whom the organ that is giving him satisfaction belongs. As a rule the sexual drive then becomes auto-erotic . . . The finding of an object [later, after the latency stage] is in fact a re-finding of it. (p. 222)

Here Freud seems to say that sexuality comes into its own with the loss of the real object, known as such by the child, and with a compensatory turn—I imagine Freud thinking—toward an imaginary object, a phantasy in which the lost object figures. Self-love in the form of autoerotism arises as a response to object loss, and only when the child is able to conceive of another person as a real object separate from himself.[2]

But by the time of "Instincts and Their Vicissitudes" (1915c), Freud has changed his emphasis. Now 'the object' that figures in mental development is only incidentally another person. He writes: "The object [*Object*] of an instinct is the thing in regard to which or through which the instinct is able to achieve its aim. It is what is most variable about an instinct and is not necessarily connected with it, but becomes assigned to it only in consequence of being peculiarly fitted to make satisfaction possible" (p. 122). *Three Essays* reads as a profound essay on the nature and varieties of love; but love as such does not appear in "Instincts." It cannot, since Freud's language here is primarily his reductivist neuropsychology.

Both the concepts of an 'object' and of 'libido' become yet murkier in "On Narcissism" (1914b), in which Freud postulates a primary or 'normal' narcissism in everyone. Whereas before ego instincts differed from libidinal partly in the fact that the latter are more or less directed to other persons, now Freud introduces the idea that libido itself has a dual aspect, that it should be divided into ego-libido and object-libido. Earlier the concept of the libidinal object wavered between an Intentional and an extensional sense of 'object'; now there is a further vacillation, between a Jungian notion of 'ego-libido' or self-love which is indistinguishable from an instinct of self-preservation, and self-love as a particular kind of mental state.

What is this mental state like? In answer Freud draws a distinction between primary and secondary narcissism. He reminds us that we have long regarded narcissism as more than a particular perversion in which a person treats his own body in the way he might treat the body of a sexual object; for we have recognized the narcissistic attitude in homosexuals and in schizophrenics. There its features are megalomania and a turning inward, away from interest in the external world. What happens then to this withdrawn object-libido? Assuming that the total sum of energy must remain constant, Freud answers that the object-libido is directed back onto the self, giving rise to the attitude we recognize as narcissism:

> The megalomania itself is no new creation; on the contrary, it is . . . a magnification and plainer manifestation of a condition which had already existed. This leads us to look upon the narcissism which arises through the drawing in of object-cathexis as a secondary one, superimposed upon a primary narcissism that is obscured by a number of directed influences . . . An extension of the libido theory . . . receives reinforcement from yet a third quarter, namely, from our observations and views on the mental life of children and primitive people. In the latter we find characteristics which, if they occurred singly, might be put down to megalomania. (1914b, p. 75)

The 'megalomania' Freud has in mind consists in overestimating the power of one's wishes and mental acts, and magical thinking.

The suggestion then is that pathological narcissism is secondary, resting on a primary and 'normal narcissism', "a complement to the egoism of the instinct of self-preservation, a measure of which may justifiably be attributed to every living creature" (p. 74).[3] There is an original libidinal cathexis of the ego, "from which some is later given off to objects, but which fundamentally persists and is related to the object-cathexis much as the body of an amoeba is related to the pseudopodia which it puts out" (ibid., p. 75).

In the second and third sections of the essay Freud says that the erotic life provides one of three approaches to the study of narcissism. He distinguishes two kinds of object-choice, anaclitic and narcissistic. The first, generally characteristic of men, Freud says, is modeled after the child's attachment to its first object, its mother, and is a genuine or true object-choice; the second (more 'feminine') kind is modeled after the child's primary narcissistic choice of itself.[4]

The question then arises: If regardless of which path they take all lovers draw from a reservoir of self-love to which genuine object love may always retreat, what happens to the ego-libido in those who love according to the anaclitic type? (Note that in describing this type Freud wants us to understand by 'object' another person, for the directedness to such an object is the mark of 'genuine object love'.) Does all of it pass into 'object-cathexis'? No; it becomes self-love at another level, love for the ideal self one would like to be, or perhaps phantasizes one is. Presumably not all object-libido derives from ego-libido; otherwise there would be no reason for positing the two kinds. But Freud is clear that the object love which expresses itself in moral ideals is apparent only:[5]

The same impressions, experiences, impulses and desires that one man indulges . . . will be rejected with the utmost indignation by another . . . The difference between the two . . . can easily be expressed in terms which enable it to be explained by the libido theory. We can say that the one man has set up an *ideal* in himself by which he measures his actual ego, while the other has formed no such ideal . . . This ideal ego *(idealich)* is now the target of the self-love which was enjoyed in childhood by the actual ego . . . What he projects before him as his ideal is the substitute for the lost narcissism of his childhood in which he was his own ideal *(Ideal)*. (ibid., pp. 93–94)

What prompts "the subject to form an ego ideal *(Ichideal)*, on whose behalf his conscience acts as watchman, arose from the influence of his parents (conveyed to him by the medium of the voice)," to which, Freud remarks, other voices are added in time. So other persons enter this genealogical story only by way of explaining how what may look like other-directed behavior in the form of altruism or moral principles is really a circuitous routing of self-love.

What evidence is there for the idea of this primary narcissistic state? Very little in the way of observations of infant behavior, Freud acknowledges:

The primary narcissism of children which we have assumed and which forms one of the postulates of our theories of the libido, is less easy to grasp by direct observation than to confirm by inference from elsewhere. If we look at the attitude of affectionate parents towards their children, we have to recognize that it is a revival and reproduction of [the parents' own] narcissism, which they have long since abandoned. (ibid., p. 91)

The attitude of parents toward their children may often be narcissistic; but the assumption that its source must be the very primary narcissism which is unobservable in infants is clearly unwarranted. Furthermore, there is a decisive argument against it: to say that the infant takes himself as his own ideal, that he thinks of himself as perfect, is necessarily to attribute to him a concept of 'self'; it posits just the cognitively sophisticated duality between thinker and object which primary narcissism is said to precede.

In saying that "a unity comparable to the ego cannot exist in the individual from the start," Freud himself seems to see the problem. So he hypothesizes a state even prior to primary narcissism which he calls auto-erotism. What then marks the transition from one to the other? He doesn't say. But an earlier passage suggests the direction of an answer:

As regards the differentiation of psychical energies, we are led to the conclusion that to begin with, during the state of narcissism [I believe this should read 'autoerotism' if Freud were true to his own distinctions], they exist together and that our analysis is too coarse to distinguish between them; not

until there is object-cathexis is it possible to discriminate a sexual energy—
the libido—from an energy of the ego-instincts. (ibid., p. 76)

The implication seems to be that prior to "object-cathexis" we have no
reason for speaking of either libidinal or ego-instincts. Since as an
observable phenomenon 'object-cathexis' can only mean love for real
other persons, we can now put Freud's hypothesis in a way that answers
my objection that self-love makes sense only for a creature who has a
concept of the self: this concept arises in the same (logical) moment as the
concept of an object. If this is so, then self-love is the reverse side of love
for an Other; and we have no reason for saying that either the 'ego ideal'
or the ideals of 'the ego' arise from self-love, and every reason for positing
their source in love for the other.

As for parental attitudes toward the infant, these are more easily understood as deriving from adult longings and phantasies than from recollections of infancy. From our point of view, with all we now know about
lack and limit, the infant's ignorance is enviable; so it can seem that once,
like them, we *were* perfect. Again Freud almost acknowledges as much.
He says:

> They [parents] are under a compulsion to ascribe every perfection to the
> child . . . The child shall have a better time than his parents; he shall not be
> subject to the necessities which they have recognized as paramount in life.
> Illness, death, renunciation of enjoyment, restrictions of his own will, shall
> not touch him; the laws of nature and of society shall be abrogated in his
> favour; he shall once more really be the centre and core of creation—'His
> Majesty the Baby', as we once fancied ourselves. (ibid., p. 91)

That the infant is perfect is then our phantasy, or the phantasy of an older
child who knows he does not have the strength and power of the adults he
loves.

One may ask: What difference does it make whether we say that the
infant thinks of himself as complete at birth and greets the growing recognition of his smallness and dependency with shock, or that he forms the
phantasy of himself as complete only later? Isn't the point in either case
that the recognition is so painful as to motivate self-deceptions which
warp the growing child's relations with itself and others for ever after?
The answer may not make a difference to a psychoanalyst's interpretations in any particular clinical situation. But it might have subtler and
more far-reaching effects, coloring one's views of the nature of the mind,
and particularly of the imagination. For why does Freud, in the absence of
corroborating evidence, and armed with a theory that warns of our tendency to project our phantasies onto infants, still insist that the child is a
narcissist like us? I think it must be, in part, because he reductively

assumes that whatever thoughts we are capable of entertaining have been present in us somehow from the beginning;[6] that phantasy is memory, or distorted memory; that the limits of the human imagination are given by what is already in the mind at the start; that all the materials for one's moral ideals, as well as for one's Ideal Self, are in place prior to the discovery of other persons and the external world *as* external world; that there is a self from the first.

Along with the relations between self-love and other-love, another key idea in Freud's genealogy of values begins to sound in "Mourning and Melancholia" (1917 [1915]), namely that morality arises out of a division in the self. In this work Freud postulates melancholia as the pathological counterpart of mourning. Where mourning is the acknowledgment of the loss of a loved object, melancholia is the refusal of such acknowledgment. The melancholic *takes the lost object inside himself* in a regressive move to the oral stage in which identification takes the form of oral incorporation or devourment. That is, the melancholic constructs a phantasy in which the object is literally a part of himself, or in which he imagines himself to be the lost object, an object he both loves and hates. The ironic consequence is that the melancholic heaps on himself (as this object) the reproaches he has silently directed toward the ambivalently loved object. In one of his most evocative passages, Freud writes:

> Let us dwell for a moment on the view which the melancholic's disorder affords of the constitution of the human ego. We see how in him one part of the ego sets itself over against the other, judges it critically, and, as it were, takes it as its object . . . Thus the shadow of the object fell upon the ego, and the latter could henceforth be judged by a special agency, as though it were an object, the forsaken object. In this way an object-loss was transformed into an ego-loss and the conflict between the ego and the loved person into a cleavage between the critical activity of the ego and the ego as altered by identification. (1917 [1915], pp. 247–249)

"What we are here becoming acquainted with," he remarks, "is the agency commonly called 'conscience'" (p. 247).

This is the view on which Freud builds in elaborating the concept of the super-ego in *The Ego and the Id* (1923). But whereas he speaks in "Mourning" of diseases of conscience of which melancholia is said to be one, in the later work conscience itself is the disease; more accurately, it is the product of those unconscious defensive processes, centrally repression, which the Oedipal complex names. For the details of that account I return to *Civilization and Its Discontents*.

What is the origin of the sense of guilt? Freud asks in chapter 7. Perhaps we will say, he offers, that "a person feels guilty . . . when he has done something which he knows to be 'bad'." But this begs the question, which is how we distinguish bad from good in the first place: "We may reject the existence of an original . . . capacity to distinguish good from bad. What is bad is often not at all what is injurious or dangerous to the ego; on the contrary, it may be something which is desirable and enjoyable to the ego" (1930 [1929], p. 124). Notice that according to this passage, the ability to distinguish bad from good and to inhibit one's actions accordingly, where the criterion is injury or benefit, pain or pleasure, to the self, presents no particular problem. So presumably the puzzle is that we sometimes judge actions and wishes 'bad' because of what they portend to others.[7] Freud concludes that there must therefore be "an extraneous influence at work" which decides "what is to be called good and bad" in this other-regarding and peculiarly moral sense. How 'external' metamorphoses into 'internal' is what the Oedipal complex attempts to explain. Freud is drawing a sharp line between self-regarding and other-regarding motives; and as he earlier derived object-libido from narcissistic libido, so now he will attempt to derive conscience and the moral sense from self-love.

The motive for submitting to this extraneous impulse, Freud suggests, is provided by the child's helplessness, his dependency on other people, which amounts to fear of the loss of their love. "At the beginning, therefore, what is bad is whatever causes one to be threatened with loss of love. For fear of that loss, one must avoid it." In Freud's genealogical picture, 'guilt' is at first nothing more than a fear of external punishment in the form of a loss of love or approval. Call this stage in the development of the moral sense 'proto-guilt'. The decisive change comes "when the authority is internalized," when one refrains from doing something 'bad' not because one is afraid of being found out, or of punishment inflicted from without, but because one thinks it bad on one's own. Here is conscience proper, and the capacity for guilt as distinct, presumably, from regret. At this point the difference between doing something bad and merely wishing to do it disappears entirely, Freud says, "since nothing can be hidden from the super-ego, not even thoughts."

He adds that moral feeling now exhibits a new and peculiar feature: the more virtuous the individual or the more he inhibits instinctual satisfaction, the guiltier he feels. Whereas earlier conscience was appeased by renunciation, now conscience battens on it. The reason, Freud speculates, has to do with the fact that what is renounced is not sexuality but aggression. The Oedipal child must indeed inhibit his sexual desire for his mother; but it is the renunciation of aggression against the father, whose retaliation and punishment he fears, that brings the child to genuine guilt. For in the way sketched in "Mourning and Melancholia," the child accomplishes this renunciation by identifying with the authority, the loved and hated father, turning his aggression toward the father back against himself.

> The relationship between the super-ego and the ego is a return, distorted by a wish, of the real relationships between the ego, as yet undivided, and an external object . . . But the essential difference is that the original severity of the super-ego does not—or does not so much—represent the severity which one has experienced from it [the object] . . . it represents rather one's own aggressiveness towards it. (ibid., pp. 129–130)

What we call conscience, we would agree with Freud in saying, includes the capacities to judge that an action is bad because it is potentially harmful to others; to censor thoughts, inhibit impulses, and refrain from actions that are bad by this standard; to feel pained when one violates it, even if one thinks he will not be caught out.

Freud thinks these capacities call for a special accounting, over and above that required for the formation of the ego, that is, of beliefs and desires, the concepts of truth and reality, the faculty of judgment. And it is to give this special accounting that he posits a mental structure he calls the super-ego (Über-Ich), formed after the ego is in place, and through the kinds of Oedipal identifications just sketched. A part, at least, of this special structure is repressed, and split off from the mental structure as a whole. But whatever the stage of moral development, one's motive for refraining from an action one considers 'bad' is fear. The difference between proto-guilt and guilt proper is that the object of fear in the first case is loss of the other's love, or punishment at his hands, and in the second, loss of self-love. Guilt is the pain of this second loss, often magnified by the motive of punishing oneself.

I think there is a fundamental error at the heart of this analysis. Freud is right that what looks like love is often self-love, as it is also often hate, and that both are nowhere more evident than in self-righteous love of principle. (This was Nietzsche's ferocious insight.) But only a familiar confusion would lead one to say that all love is necessarily self-love. The confusion is that any interest I take in whatever object is of course an interest of mine; and I wouldn't pursue the interest, or voluntarily undertake to do what I do on the object's behalf, unless I expected or hoped the doing would gratify some value of mine. In this sense it is necessarily the case that whatever I do voluntarily I do 'out of self-interest'. But this sense is virtually tautological; it is not the sense we normally have in mind in speaking of 'self-interest' or prudence; and it admits values of many kinds, along with love of the other for his own sake as well as concern for him because he serves some interest of mine. To say that all action is self-interested in this broad tautological sense tells us nothing about the character of either our interests or their objects. And the difference remains, between refraining from doing *x* because one doesn't want to feel guilty and because *x* threatens something or someone that one values.

While the super-ego may explain various neurotic forms of self-punishment, precisely what it doesn't explain, nor even make room for, is the moral point of view, which demands just what Freud's reduction of all interests to self-interest won't allow: valuing something because one holds it to be valuable in itself. This is a process neither of projecting something entirely subjective in character onto the world, nor of discovering some new and mysterious quality, but of adopting a certain objective viewpoint in which one sees oneself as one person among others, and understands that what one takes to be a reason for one's own activity is potentially, therefore, a reason for others' behaving in relevantly similar ways.[8] A constitutive feature of guilt as it regards our actions and intentions toward other persons is, I suggest, a certain kind of love, namely love for the other as a separate person from oneself, with values of his own that one values just because they are his. Such love has to be distinguished from valuing another as means to one's own ends, because of some service he performs for the self, or because in his reflected light one can love one's self better. Freud speaks about the difference between these two kinds of love indirectly, when he distinguishes narcissistic love from genuine object love. But the theory of primary narcissism tends to see 'genuine' object love as illusory, which is perhaps why Freud's theory about valuing simply ignores it.

The internalizing that, according to Freud, marks the end of the Oedipal complex and constructs the super-ego is modeled by the *phantasy* of incorporating the other described in "Mourning and Melancholia" in which the internalized other becomes the eye ('I') of self-regard. As Freud describes it, the 'new' attitude which Oedipal identification affords is not a looking outward, an extension of sympathy toward another, but a looking backward at the self. Furthermore, the Other who figures in this Oedipal identification, the castrating father whom the Oedipal child (in phantasy) installs inside himself, is a distorted other, the father perceived or imagined in the light of the child's own rage against the father. Call this an inward-looking identification.

Identification of another outward-looking sort takes place, I suggest, when one begins to comprehend another's interests as one's own, or, simply, when one acknowledges her as another person. Whereas in Oedipal identification as described in *Civilization and Its Discontents* two persons collapse into one, in the outward-looking identification there are, and necessarily, two persons acknowledged as two by the identifier, with identification spanning the distance between them. And one's awareness of the other as Other demands that one try to see him more or less as he is. It is such an awareness, not the rising of an 'ideal I' from the ashes of infantile narcissism, which is needed to describe the moral point of view. And in the accounts given earlier in this book, it is something like this sort of awareness, in the form of communication with another by whom one wants to be understood, that founds the mind itself. (The root of 'responsibility' is *respondeo*, 'I answer', for myself, and to you.)

As for the emotion of guilt, has Freud illumined its constitutive strands? I don't think so, and Freud himself seems to have his doubts. His moral genealogy in *Civilization and Its Discontents* goes on to remind us of the extraordinary story of the Primal Horde which he told in "Totem and Taboo" (1912–1913). The sons banded together to slay the father, who was in fact, not merely in the sons' perception, terrible. The sense of guilt was first born in that actual killing long ago, Freud says, and is part of our phylogenetic legacy.

He anticipates objections. First, if an act of actual aggression explains the sense of guilt, then we seem not to need the theory just developed, that guilt results rather from the inhibition of aggression. Second, the Primal Horde story would be an instance of someone's feeling guilty because he has really done something which cannot be justified; and for this feeling, Freud says, calling it remorse, psychoanalysis has no explanation:

> If the human sense of guilt goes back to the killing of the primal father, that was after all a case of 'remorse'. Are we to assume that [at that time] a conscience and a sense of guilt were not, as we have presupposed, in existence before the deed? If not, where, in this case, did the remorse come from? There is no doubt that this case should explain the secret of the sense of guilt to us and put an end to our difficulties. And I believe it does. This remorse was the result of the primordial ambivalence of feeling towards the father. His sons hated him, but they loved him, too. After their hatred had been satisfied by their act of aggression, their love came to the fore in their remorse for the deed. It set up the super-ego by identification with the father; it gave that agency the father's power, as though as a punishment for the deed of aggression they had carried out against him, and it created the restrictions which were intended to prevent a repetition of the deed. (1930 [1929], p. 132)

Freud takes the capacity for remorse, then, as a given in that it is an emotion which no special psychological machinery is needed to explain. Granted, a careful account of guilt might want to distinguish it from remorse; but remorse takes us most of the way. And it's hard to see how Freud's story takes us the rest. Just what is it that this super-ego structure, presupposing as it does the capacity for acknowledging with suffering a wrong done, might explain? Not the fact that we formulate rules and principles designed to protect us from doing things that will cause us pain. For these belong with maxims of prudence; and Freud does not think that prudence, or refraining from "what is injurious or dangerous to the ego," needs explaining. Thinking generalizes, remembers, anticipates; it is capable of imagining ways in which the world might be different from what it is and how one might feel if one were to do things one hasn't done. It warns against actions one may regret.

Nor do we need the super-ego to explain the anxiety we feel even about our impulses, not only about our deeds. The nature of impulse or desire is to motivate action unless it is inhibited, either by the external world or by stronger desires or motivations of one's own. This is something that even a child understands at some level. So we would expect a creature who is aware of impulses that jeopardize things he values to become anxious.

Nor do we need the super-ego to account for the fact that we take ourselves as objects. For such self-reflexivity comes with thought itself. Any creature who can entertain a belief, or desire that something be the case, can also, on occasion, know that he does. Self-reflexive awareness, awareness in which oneself is the object, is part of the fabric of the mind. The sense in which self-reflection makes the mind a duality is not a sense that calls for a partitioned mind. Nor, by the same token, does judging that one has done wrong, ruing what one has done, wishing to make amends, even punishing oneself. So far we have only been talking about capacities intrinsic to thought itself, not ones that are added on and that need special accounting.

Nor is the super-ego required to tell why it is that every child takes on some version of the values of his culture. Identification with the parent alone accounts for that.

Moral philosophy does need to understand how the moral sense extends itself not only to those we know and love, but also to those we don't, even to those we have reason to fear and to hate. This is the paradox that sets Freud thinking in *Civilization and Its Discontents*. But the Oedipal complex doesn't attempt to resolve it. It doesn't explain how the internal inhibition against aggression toward the father generalizes to all others. Freud now descends to another explanatory level, namely his latest version of the dual instinct theory, that all organic processes are driven by the forces of life working against the forces of death (1920a). But even if the theory were plausible, it wouldn't give any weight to the *psychological* account of guilt that Freud offers, an account he obviously wants to stand on its own ground.

Throughout this book I have contrasted two lines in Freud's thinking. One tends to reduce mind to body, values to mechanisms, all interests to self-interest. It sees subjectivity as prior to objectivity, the self as theoretically isolable, from the external world and from other selves. This is the line that leads Freud to view morality as a fancy name for self-interest.

The second line takes mind to be an irreducible explanatory category; and it sees the connection between minds not as an imposition from without but as constitutive of the mental. On this line, moral judgment is no more extraneous to the ego or the self than belief. And no more than belief does morality presuppose a divided self. In the best case there comes to be a change in the child's relations to others such that it is able to imagine the world from the Other's point of view and to care about it as one cares for her. And this is a change that, rather than rending the self, expands it. The character of love, again at its best, just is to make this outward-looking sort of identification. In a process we commonly describe as 'identifying with the values or interests of another', one regards oneself, some of the time, as part of a community defined by shared interests, goals, values, and principles. Typically the process requires inhibition and suppression of hostile impulses toward the love object, but not necessarily repression; and it does not at all presuppose partitions in the self. Granted that valuing has a social history, we can nevertheless imagine a person whose values are thoroughly 'hers'.[9]

In Chapter 1 I said that what we call the mind is constituted in a process of triangulation, the three apexes of which are my mind, other minds, and external world. The 'Freudian' triangle is of course 'daddy-mommy-me' (Deleuze and Guattari, 1983). I want in the next section of this chapter to press Freud's implicitly intersubjectivist view, taking 'the Oedipal complex' as a compass which, like ours, situates the mind in a triangle connecting child to other persons, and persons to external world. Freud is right that there must be extraneous influences at work for the child to acquire moral values, and that these influences are specifically interpersonal in character. But the Freud I turn to now suggests that this same 'Oedipal' process is required for thinking. Freud's triangulation story is more passionate than the one we explored earlier, and in being so gives our own some needed detail.

Since Lacan also reads the Oedipal complex as founding not merely the moral sense but also the mind, I should again say what distinguishes my view from his. According to Freud, repression and the phantasies involved in Oedipal identification cause a split in the self. Lacan understands the split as riving the language-learning child from its immediate, that is unmediated, experience; the 'Symbolic Order' from the 'Imaginary'; the thoughts that become possible for the child through language from its earlier, pre-linguistic and pre-symbolic images. In the process, the unconscious is created. Among the child's pre-symbolic images are those in which it sees or senses itself as fragmented or in pieces. The mirror stage stands for those perceptions of itself as whole, perceptions which assuage the sense of fragmentation. (Such perceptions may arise either from the child's encounter with actual mirrors, or from identifying with the physical person of the mother.)

The libidinal desire for union with the mother is not rock-bottom (I am still speaking for Lacan), but rests on the child's inchoate memory of its unmediated union with mother and world. (So Freud might say; this is the

importance of the concept of primary narcissism.) The union is inter-
rupted by the advent of language, which both severs child from world and
partially substitutes for the loss, since with language one gains some
control over the world, and so regains the world, albeit in a distanced
way. Lacan calls this advent the Name-of-the-Father, which brings with it
culture. The Oedipal child learns culture and rules in learning a language.

On Freud's view, the Oedipal child fears castration at the hands of the
father. On Lacan's, the language-learning child discovers that it is already
'castrated', that is, cut off from immediate experience and from union
with the world. But the child longs for union and wholeness, and it is this
wholeness that the 'phallus' comes to signify. (Lacan reserves the name
'penis' for the literal bodily part, 'phallus' for the phantasy that the penis
symbolizes.) The phallus is then something that both boys and girls want
and that neither ever had.

Echoing the story of the expulsion from the Garden, Lacan's reading of
Freud powerfully voices a number of complex adult feelings and phantasies. My objection to this reading, very briefly, is that it sees culture as
an overlay on a pristine experiencing self which must divide in the
process. And just this is the central question raised by Freud's moral genealogy: Are communal relations extrinsic to the self, or rather essential to
its very fabric? Our answer will affect what we count as an imposition on
the self, how we distinguish what is 'internal' and 'intrinsic' to it from
what is 'external' and 'extrinsic'.

So let's begin a moral genealogy anew, which I am suggesting is at the
same time a genealogy of the mental and of the self.

II Triangulation Revisited

In "Formulation on the Two Principles of Mental Functioning" (1911)
Freud imagines an initial infantile condition of psychic rest, from time to
time disturbed by the peremptory demands of internal needs, which the
infant organism immediately 'satisfies' for itself in the form of hallucinatory wish-fulfillment. Freud describes such a creature as governed by
the pleasure principle, a condition which in a pure form is as mythical as
the one Hobbes called 'the state of nature', and which cannot in any case
last for long. Freud writes:

> It was only the non-occurrence of the expected satisfaction, the disappointment
> experienced, that led to the abandonment of this attempt at satisfaction by
> means of hallucination. Instead of it, the psychical apparatus had to decide to
> form a conception of the real circumstances in the external world and to
> endeavor to make a real alteration in them. A new principle of mental func-
> tioning was thus introduced; what was presented in the mind was no longer
> what was agreeable but what was real, even if it happened to be disagreeable.

In a footnote Freud remarks:

> It will rightly be objected that an organization which was a slave to the pleasure principle and neglected the reality of the external world could not maintain itself alive for the shortest time, so that it could not have come into existence at all. The employment of a fiction like this is, however, justified when one considers that the infant—provided one includes the care it receives from the mother—does almost realize a psychical system of this kind. (1911, pp. 219–220)

The usual way of reading these passages is to say that hallucination is how the baby briefly handles the absence of the mother and the gratification she brings. This reading suggests a view of the infant as solipsist, self-sufficient and uninterested in the external world. But the provision that "one include the care it receives from the mother" suggests that the baby is not an isolated, self-enclosed organism but a part of an interpersonal field.[10] From a god's-eye point of view, what the baby 'hallucinates' will often be the real object or mother.

On either reading, Freud's thought experiment makes the logical point that for a creature who experienced no gap between desire and fulfillment, for whom gratification appeared as soon as desire arose, there could be no distinction between appearance and reality. Until there is frustration there is no way the child can distinguish himself from the world, and no way for him to have concepts with which to think the world. The crisis that propels him to a new principle of mental functioning is the absence of the mother.

Many philosophers have held that it is just the concept of a public reality, as something that may be distinct from a merely private appearance, that provides for Intentionality, the feature of being about something that is the hallmark of the mental. If this is so, then Freud's view—which seems to me surely right—is that the mental has a necessary connection to desire, to the experience of need and lack. The concept of an object as a real thing in the world is dependent on pain and impotence, on frustration and dependency, and more specifically, on real other persons, who will also be the child's first objects.

Speculating in *Civilization and Its Discontents* on the origins of the sense of self, Freud writes:

> The infant at the breast does not as yet distinguish his ego from the external world as the source of the sensations flowing in upon him. He gradually learns to do so, in response to various promptings. He must be very strongly impressed by the fact that some sources of excitation, which he will later recognize as his own bodily organs, can provide him with sensations at any moment, whereas other sources evade him from time to time—among them what he desires most of all, his mother's breast—and only reappear as a result of his screaming for help. In this way there is for the first time set over

against the ego an 'object', in the form of something which exists 'outside' and which is only forced to appear by a special action. (1930 [1929], p. 67)

The reciprocal concepts of self and other are acquired, Freud suggests, in completion of the following circuit: a condition of felt need; a scream of pain; and in response the appearance of an object, specifically a person, that relieves the pain.

Inspired by these passages, Ferenczi suggests that there are "stages in the development of the sense of reality" (1956). The first, he says, describes the fetus, whom we may imagine as having, in its state of plenitude, a sense of omnipotence; the second, the infant who achieves temporary satisfaction through hallucinatory wish-fulfillment; and the third, the infant who has learned that some of its wants will be answered if it makes the right signals. Ferenczi's story implies, as Freud also sometimes does, that the child knows what it wants prior to making its 'signals', that the infant whose mother 'magically' arrives at the moment of his need believes that he has produced her out of his own omnipotent power. Let me amend Ferenczi's account by saying instead that prior to its communications with others the infant is neither solipsist nor believer, for the reason that he has no real concepts at all; nor, for the same reason, does he have phantasies.

But Ferenczi has something important right, which might be put this way: The infant is biologically programmed to do things that other people will interpret as meaningful signals for help. His cries are meaningful to us, but not to him.[11] What is initially a cry without meaning to the crier, not a sign intended to be understood in a particular way, becomes meaningful in part through the behavior it produces in another. The child then begins to acquire concepts through that intercourse with other persons through which it acquires language. And it is these very same processes which allow the child to distinguish between appearance and reality, to have the sense of reality, and with it to become a 'thinker'. Psychoanalysis contributes to the idea that thought is necessarily interpersonal, a reminder that these communications are emotionally laden; that first speech occurs in the context of demand, gratitude, and anger.

In a passage from "Beyond the Pleasure Principle" (1920) made famous by Lacan, Freud muses on the meaning of his eighteen-month-old grandson's game with a cotton-reel. Again and again the child casts the spool away from him with a syllable that sounds like 'fort' (gone) and reels it back with a joyful 'da' (here). Freud links the game to the child's attempt to master the painful experience of its mother's departure. Playing with the cotton-reel, Freud thinks, allows the child to repeat an experience in which he was painfully passive, the one left, making it tolerable by reversing the active and passive roles.[12] But in light of the importance that

Freud gives to the processes of separation and individuation in such works as "Mourning and Melancholia" (1917 [1915]), we might rather interpret the child's activity as an attempt to take in his discovery of interpersonal reciprocity: if his activity in relation to the mother consists in his ability to summon her to him, her ability to answer him is a function of a principle of activity that is not his but hers. And this implies that just as it is by her initiative that she comes, so by that same initiative can she go. His power over her, he has discovered, is limited; for the one who answers my call can do so only because she is not part of me, nor is she, like my own limbs, at the end of my will. And as she is someone who can leave, so I am someone who can be left; she is not here, but I discover that she is somewhere, there where I am not.

The concept of objective reality, then, has an inescapably interpersonal dimension: it is that which is neither exclusively yours nor mine but the common field for our different points of view. The sounds 'fort', 'da' mark places in a game which is essentially both spatial and erotic and in which language and thought are together in the making, along with the discovery of other minds. "Writing," Freud says in *Civilization and Its Discontents*, "was in its origin the voice of the absent person; and the dwelling-house was a substitute for the mother's womb" (1930 [1929], p. 91). Whether or not there will one day be machines that can think in the sense we do may be an empirical question. Freud supports a conceptual claim to the effect that 'thinking' in this sense has necessary connections to desire and love.

Acknowledging the otherness of other minds is one of the organizing principles of psychological development, Freud thinks, and also its principal stumbling block. He examines some vicissitudes of the process of separation in "Mourning and Melancholia," where he traces a certain form of depression to conditions in which, rather than accepting object loss, one attempts, in phantasy, to incorporate the lost object into himself, on the model of the baby at the mother's breast. Mourning is the normal way in which one registers the real loss of a loved object, not only a loss of the object's presence through death or absence but also of the object's esteem or love, or a loss in the form of disappointment in the object as a suitable target for one's esteem and love. A pathological counterpart of mourning, melancholia is caused by the attempt to avoid acknowledging the loss that would normally elicit mourning. Melancholia is mourning's shadow, mourning that has been resisted or subverted. Melancholic introjection is to be understood as such an attempt at subversion, one which distorts the agent's views of both external and internal world, for it causes a split within the subject's own self.

> So we find the key to the clinical picture: we perceive that the [melancholic's] self-reproaches are reproaches against a loved object which have been shifted

away from it on to the patient's own ego . . . In this way an object-loss was transformed into an ego-loss and the conflict between the ego and the loved person into a cleavage between the critical activity of the ego and the ego as altered by identification. (1917 [1915], pp. 248–249)

Melancholia gives us a view, Freud says, of the constitution of the human ego in which one part sets itself over against another part, "judges it critically, and, as it were, takes it as its object." This is of course how Freud describes the super-ego or conscience, of which melancholia, he says, is a disease. We might infer, then, that whereas melancholia is mourning forestalled, producing a split self in the process, the healthy conscience, evolving from mourning undergone, is whole.

Many of Freud's remarks about the Oedipal complex support such a reading. He says: "These [Oedipal] identifications are not what we should have expected [from the earlier account of oral introjection], since they do not introduce the abandoned object into the ego" (ibid., p. 32). (But of course the Oedipal child can phantasize identifications of the earlier sort. If I am right that phantasy comes only with thinking in the sense we have been talking about, then only the child who knows others as other is able to phantasize himself as somehow fused with them.) And the shifts that are said to take place during the working out of the Oedipal complex are just those that mark the child's acknowledgment of his separate state. He acknowledges that his mother is not his alone and that she has interests apart from him. He identifies with his father, but, crucially, only in some respects: he is *like* his father, not one with him.

Oedipal 'identifications' are of many sorts on Freud's view. Some are by definition distortions of reality, that is of the child's own perceptions of reality; for example, identifying with the parent who has been idealized, or whose aggression has been exaggerated, perhaps in a denial of one's own hostility. And at the edge of pathology, though an inevitable one, Freud seems to say, Oedipal identifications are less a modeling of oneself after another than a blurring of identities. But if the healthy conscience— which perhaps exists only as an ideal—evolves from an acknowledgment of loss, then what distinguishes Oedipal identifications is that the object is recognized as *other* than or separate from oneself. The identifications constitutive of the "ego Ideal" or the healthy "over-I" (Freud uses the terms interchangeably in *The Ego and the Id*) are then of the sort that characterize mourning, not melancholia.[13]

I take Oedipal identification, then, to be not a blurring but a full awareness of individuation. To identify with someone in this sense is, as I suggested earlier, simply to imagine the world from the perspective of the beliefs and desires one attributes to him, knowing that some are different from one's own. This identification attends the knowledge that one's own point of view is partial; that one may be an outsider in the dialogue of others; that one is but one person among many, each with his or her own beliefs and desires and claims on the world. Identification of this sort is the ground of dialogue, which presumes awareness of both similarity and difference. If I cannot assume that you and I mean more or less the same things by some of our words and that we share some beliefs in common, there is no way I can begin to understand you. But if at the same time I don't know that I sometimes need to make an effort to be understood and to understand, I will simply hear in your words an echo of my own.

Dialogue presumes a tolerance for disagreement and difference, and a capacity, furthermore, for acknowledging that some differences are not a matter of 'good' and 'bad', 'better' and 'worse', 'superior' and 'inferior'. Not all differences in quality are necessarily differences also in intrinsic worth. Sex is prototypical of this kind of difference, though anxieties related to questions of sex can ready one to perceive any difference as occasion for battle and conquest. The concept of Oedipal resolution might be seen as delineating an ideal of dialogue (and of mind) according to which differences—in generation, in gender, in social role—are accepted. It is an ideal because finding the common ground one shares with others at the same time as one recognizes and tolerates disagreement, acknowledging as well that not all disagreements are matters of right and wrong, makes interpretation and dialogue at their best possible. One is asked to acknowledge simultaneously his dependency on others and the fact that he can lose them, to remain connected to them while exercising a certain independence. (There may then be a strong temptation to try to make oneself self-sufficient by denying the need for others or their intrinsic value.)

For Descartes, space and time are essential characteristics of physical reality; they are not attributes of mind. But if the idea of one's self as a self is the other side of Oedipal triangulation, then that self cannot be abstracted from space-time as a condition of mourning lived through in time, any more than space and time, as we now know them, can be abstracted from each other. One's first approaches to the concepts of space and time must be through the experiences of movement, willing and wanting, and increasingly of absence, hope, and return.

In exploring the constraints on human knowledge, philosophers typically discuss the implications of the fact that necessarily every knower's viewpoint is spatially and temporally partial: one sees the front of the apple, but not, at the same time, its other sides; one is immediately acquainted only with the present, and must recall the past and make inferences about the future. The epistemological constraints that psychoanalysis explores are of a different kind: the ways in which desire and anxiety subvert perception and belief. Knowledge of objects of all sorts is vulnerable, but none more so, for the child at least, than those 'objects' which are other people, since it is they on whom she must depend, whose love she most needs, whose anger and displeasure she most fears. The introjective phantasies characteristic of melancholia are motivated, Freud tells us, by such desires and anxieties.

Melanie Klein's developmental account (1984) picks up from Freud the theme of mourning as constitutive of the human self. From the very beginning, Klein thinks, the infant has some rudimentary idea of other persons as psycho-physical entities or 'objects'. But he does not understand other persons as whole and as separate from himself in ways that adults take for granted. Klein takes the breast as emblematic of objects for the infant. Such objects may be parts of persons from our point of view; from the infant's they can be physically incorporated or introjected, also spat out or projected.

In the first few months of life, according to Klein, the infant occupies a 'paranoid-schizoid' position in which he is subject to rage and extreme anxiety. He experiences these painful emotions, along with the frustrations which are to some degree the cause of them, as intrusive quasi-material objects, against which he defends himself by projecting them, in imagination, into other persons. The infant is also subject to splitting—imagining the one object, himself or the other, as two, the all-good and the all-bad, need-gratifying and need-frustrating; idealization—imagining the object as all-good as a denial of the infant's bad rage; projection and introjection.

But if the object of desire that the child, in phantasy, takes in is in reality truly and sufficiently gratifying—and more or less reliably so—the infant's rage becomes less. The tendency to envy 'the withholding breast' is tamed, and the infant can feel gratitude instead. He enters the depressive position, which Klein thinks occurs in the second quarter of the first year. In the depressive position the infant is capable of recognizing the wholeness both of the object and of himself as subject. That is, the infant realizes that the same object of desire can be both good and bad, both gratifying and frustrating; and recognizes that he is himself the same creature whether feeling grateful toward the object or willing its destruction. This realization leads to guilt in relation to the object and to the wish to repair the harm done, or the harm that he phantasizes having done. Hence the infant's depression, an analogue of mourning.

On my view, and that of most psychoanalysts, gratitude and mourning presume a degree of cognitive development that a very young infant does not have. But we can leave aside the question of when this development occurs and focus rather on Klein's very interesting thesis that gratitude and mourning are emotions which register crucial developmental changes. The thesis is not only psychological but also philosophical, implying as it does that certain moral emotions play a constitutive role in the human self. Gratitude and mourning are key developmental moments because among the conditions for them are some fundamental acknowledgments about oneself and about the external world. I use the word 'acknowledge' to indicate a recognition of facts—for example, that what one wants and thinks one needs is in a given case simply not available—that bear directly on desire and disappointment. With such acknowledgment, then, comes the need sometimes to escape into phantasy.

Because of its relation to desire, one would expect that acknowledgment could take place only in an emotional state like sadness, dismay, anxiety, frustration, or mourning. If belief is often subverted by anxiety and desire, nevertheless knowledge of reality begins in such affective states. (Some facts can only be known—acknowledged—through feeling: if someone says that she has willfully and maliciously harmed another and that she believes such harm to be wrong, yet truly feels no guilt, we suspect her of insincerity. If someone professes love for another whom he believes now lost to him forever, yet feels no sadness or grief, at best we find his love shallow.)

What are the acknowledgments in the case of gratitude? My answer depends on the view of the emotions sketched in an earlier chapter, that in the typical case an emotion is caused by beliefs and desires or pro-attitudes of some sort. These beliefs and desires cause the emotion; they provide the reasons why someone has the emotion that she does; and they identify it as the particular emotion it is, gratitude, say, rather than simply relief or pleasure. (Klein does not put the point this way; she does not specify that among the conditions for gratitude and mourning are certain beliefs that identify them as these particular emotions.) An analysis of gratitude like the one I gave in Chapter 7 will then consist in locating the network of beliefs and desires which have this function.

First of all, I take gratitude to be an essentially interpersonal emotion. If there is such a thing as an impersonal gratitude to no one in particular (say for being alive, even though one does not believe in God), it is derivative from the more typical interpersonal case in which one feels gratitude with regard to *x* to someone. Beyond this, I have said that gratitude depends on acknowledging that one has been given something; that one did not procure it for oneself; that the giver gave the gift intending it as such; that what one has been given is something one wants and values. So gratitude toward another person depends on acknowledging the limitations of one's own will in relation to its objects; acknowledging the existence of another person as an agent who has beliefs and intentions, some of which are benevolent toward oneself; and acknowledging a degree of dependency on that person.

Mourning, at least as described by Klein, requires all this and more: a recognition that persons, both the mourned and oneself as the mourner, are 'whole' persons in the sense defined earlier (I am the same person whether I am feeling anger or love toward you, as you are the same 'object' of my different passions).[14] This true belief about the nature of persons is then among the conditions of mourning. Another, again on Klein's account, is that one values a person not as a means to some end of one's own (or not only), but for herself, perceived as unique and irreplaceable. Winnicott makes this condition more explicit than Klein. He speaks of an essential stage in object love as marked by "the subject's perception of the object as an external phenomenon, not as a projective entity, in fact recognition of it as an entity in its own right" (1971, p. 89).

In sum, the creature that can be said to feel gratitude must acknowledge that he has been given something real, and something that is valuable— valuable, of course, to the creature. But also: acknowledging this just is the feeling of gratitude. And there is no reason to call this a projection of anything onto either the object received or its giver. The creature that mourns loves the 'giver' for her sake, values her for what she is, not for what she has given; and he knows also that the mourned 'object' is herself a source of valuing. The 'object' is valuable not only to the child but also to herself. And she herself holds objects valuable, among them, the creature (the child). What, then, does the mourner know? And what is his relation to reality? He is a lover of a part of it. And he knows that the things one loves are irreplaceable; that the time of human life moves in one direction only.

A venerable question in moral philosophy asks, Are values out there, or only in us? Do we discover the valuable, or do we project it onto the world, mistaking a merely subjective experience for an objective fact about reality? The second view sees an incommensurable split between fact and value. Fact is what the mind mirrors, or what it discovers to be the case; value is what the mind brings from itself, or what we want or would like to be the case. So Hume said (1951), arguing that to consider something 'good' is merely to have a certain pleasurable feeling toward it. And arguing along Kleinian lines, Wollheim takes a similar approach. Valuing originates, he says, "in the projection of bliss satisfied," remaining thereafter no more than a psychological fact about us (1984, p. 215).

Valuing originates in love, certainly. The conclusion I have been moving toward, however, is not Wollheim's, but this: when the child has come to love someone in the way Klein's concepts of mourning and gratitude suggest, he has *discovered* something that is of value outside himself.[15] Moreover, that the child loves is a fact about the child; but if it's true that only the child who has, in Winnicott's famous phrase, been given 'good enough mothering' can love, then the fact that the child loves tells us, and eventually him, something about the world beyond himself.[16]

Rather than saying that morality is superimposed on a pre-existent thinking subject, the lesson to be found in the Oedipal story is that thought itself is more passional than we sometimes take it to be. The human infant requires something extrinsic or external to it, something from outside its brain and skin in the way of interaction with an external world, before it can have or be anything we can call a self. A crucial part of this external world is other creatures to whom the child is libidinally attached. Through its interactions with them the child learns a language and comes by a sense of Self and Other, acquires the capacities to generalize, to frame scientific hypotheses as well as more homely everyday generalizations, to formulate maxims of prudence and moral principles. With thought also comes self-reflective awareness, the ability to imagine things, including oneself, different from the ways one finds them, to form ideals, to take oneself as an object. And if there is thought only where there are question and answer, need and response, interpersonal activities and communications of a variety of sorts, then love is not external to mind but its very condition.

One may complain that my version of the Oedipal complex is a far cry from Freud's passionate family romance. The complaint is just. I take the tack I do because my aim in these pages is primarily not psychological but philosophical. Neglecting much that one might want for other purposes, I have borrowed from Freud's account of the Oedipal complex what I think philosophers need for their account of mind, any mind that at all resembles ours.

Carol Gilligan has been writing of the different ways in which boys and girls think about moral issues (1982). Boys seem to be guided more by abstract considerations of rules and principles, girls by concern for the feelings of particular individuals. Gilligan's descriptions for these ways of thinking are meant to capture different emphases rather than mutually exclusive viewpoints; all of us are familiar with both. The psychoanalyst might attempt to account for this divergence in something like the following way: in a society in which infants are tended primarily by women, boys, in identifying themselves as 'boys', must sever the connection with the woman who has nurtured them and take on a set of values that distance them from her. This may lead them to under-value connectedness to particular others and to over-value abstract principles. Girls, on the other hand, in identifying themselves as 'girls', remain close to their first love object, and in consequence may over-value connectedness and under-value abstract principles. Where moral theory and theory of moral development have been largely in the hands of men, then theory too may reflect the masculine bias.

Gilligan's point is that the female emphasis on the feelings of particular persons, rather than on what is right as measured by some abstract principle, is the result not of a moral defect—as it has seemed to psychologists who, like Freud, take masculine development as the paradigm—but of moral perception. Turn this point a little and it becomes the idea that thinking begins in attachment to others, which of course is the priority of neither sex; and that under the right conditions such attachment just is an opening to the moral dimension.

Earlier I commented on passages in Freud that link the idea of an object to the recognition of something which is given to us, something which is in that sense external to our will. It is in this light that I read the following passage from Heidegger:

> The Old English *thaencan,* to think, and *thancian,* to thank, are closely related; the old English word for thought is *thanc* or *thonc*—a thought, a grateful thought, and the expression of such a thought . . . The things for which we owe thanks are not things we have from ourselves. They are given to us. (1968, p. 142)

Let's now return to Freud's *Three Essays,* in which he alludes, we remember, to the fable Plato reports in the *Symposium,* describing love as originating in a kind of ludicrous Fall. Freud does not refer to Plato's own view, presented through the figure of Socrates, that while love indeed originates in lack, most lovers misconstrue what they lack. Aristophanes' comic fable illustrates this misconstrual: we think that we long for another creature, necessarily as incomplete and insubstantial as ourselves, when what we truly want transcends particularity, embodiment, and lack itself. Knowledge begins in desire, which is by definition an unstable state; it culminates in an absorption of the knower into a realm of Being that is timeless and incorporeal and that is at once the fulfillment of desire, reality, and goodness. Ordinary, sexual, embodied love is the first step toward reunion, but of an order not glimpsed by Aristophanes.

Though he protests that love must be left to the poets, Freud nevertheless has a good deal to say on the subject. He agrees that love originates in an experience of lack, and that we were once a part of what we lack. It is apropos of this theme that he alludes to Aristophanes. (For Freud, of course, the longed-for reunion is with the mother, whom one begins to know as 'an object' in the very experience of deprivation.) Freud also holds that there is typically, and always at first, a misconstrual, both of the object of love and of that happiness which possession of the beloved aims to achieve. Child or narcissist, focused as each is on his own needs, seeing the beloved as some kind of reflection of himself, misconstrues both self and loved object. Perhaps one remains forever prey, furthermore, to phantasies that deny the facts of separation, that imagine a lost union more perfect than any one ever knew, as answer to a present pain.

But like Plato, Freud also holds that without desire there can be no knowledge. As love motivates various misperceptions of reality, so for

Freud it also provides the route, the only route, by which reality in its fully human dimension can be perceived. In the form of communication with others, love is the condition for language and thought. Beyond that, it instructs us in the limits of our power, the nature of ourselves and our relations with other persons, and space and time as dimensions that define loss and separateness. Finally, love yields that knowledge of other minds without which neither dialogue nor the idea of an intersubjective truth would be possible.

We may ask: What must reality be like in order for us to know it, and to know ourselves as minds knowing it? The Platonic view that goodness, truth, and beauty are names by which we crudely discriminate aspects of a Being that is One, responds: Only if the ultimately desirable and the real are identical, only if what one loves is what one wants, or could be said to want if one knew one lacked it, only then can there be for us objects of knowledge. This is the condition on which something is sufficiently attractive and recognizably akin to us to be known. This is the condition on which we know ourselves as minds, related to objects.

Here too, as I earlier suggested, one can find an odd similarity to a prevailing psychoanalytic view. The child who is able to mourn has learned that the real includes not only the good and the desirable, but also the bad and the undesirable. The same object is seen to be both bad and good; and bad and good objects are integrated into the conception of a single reality. Perhaps more important, the infant discovers that much that is objectively real and desirable is not of his own making. He knows himself therefore to be dependent on it for his gratification. This understanding is part of the developmental period that, following Klein, I have called *gratitude*.

Of course Freud's conception of reality is vastly different from Plato's. Whereas Platonic epistemology distinguishes belief, which is ensnared in the sensible world, from knowledge, which transcends it, Freudian epistemology distinguishes a minimal sort of knowledge—knowledge denied, or repressed, or shorn of its emotional significance (another minimal sort of knowledge he calls the preconscious)—from an acceptance of what is here and now. For Freud, reality is not what we would know if we were free of our human constraints, but what we would know if we acknowledged them; and valuing another embodied person as real and separate from oneself is the very model of such acknowledgment.

I began this book by invoking Descartes. Against him I have argued that not all our beliefs can be false; but of no particular belief may we say that come what may we will judge it true. This is not because reality forever withholds itself from us, but because knowledge accrues through a process of dialogue which in principle has no end, and which will typically cause us to change our minds about some of the things we believe, value, and desire. In the anti-subjectivist view, skepticism about other minds and the external world generally amounts to no more than the obvious fact that there will always be more to know than we know now; cultural relativism to the fact that cultures do not share all the same beliefs, practices, and values. This makes mutual understanding difficult but not impossible.

Implicit in psychoanalytic theory as I would reconstruct it are views that are broadly similar. To summarize them briefly: We need to account neither for our knowledge of other minds nor for that of a real, shared, material world, since such knowledge is a condition of mind itself. What needs explaining are rather certain kinds of confusions about other minds, and certain kinds of flight from reality. However uneasy, knowledge is the norm, and certain sorts of failure of knowledge the pathology. Psychoanalysis as well as philosophy has no use for the idea of a noumenal reality from which we are hopelessly cut off, and might seek the genesis for such an idea in conflicts and fantasies about separation (Hamilton, 1982).

As the idea of what the mind knows when it knows, 'reality' has traditionally pointed toward a number of distinctions: between what I see from this vantage point and what I would also see from others; between what I think I see under distorting circumstances and what I might see under ones that are other and better; between what *I* see and what *we* see. It opposes thoughts about things to the things themselves, and (for a Cartesian or a Kantian) appearances of things for creatures who know the world in a mediated, sensual way, to what we might see if we could see without eyes. To these Freud adds distinctions that have more to do with the will: between what I wish were so, and what it gives me pain to recognize is so; between what is within the reach of my will, and what is not.

Like Descartes in a way, Freud was concerned with the problem of error, and his meditations on that problem led him to a view both surprisingly similar and interestingly different. Descartes asks why, since we are made in the image of God and by His perfect and benevolent hand, do we fall into error? Because, Descartes answers, I am something intermediate between God and nought. My will, like His, is infinite; but the scope of my ideas is not. Will and imagination together are the root of error: I let my imagination run away with me and I judge things to be so or not so even where I do not perceive clearly and distinctly.

Freud's question is why, given that we are creatures with a mind (an etymological cousin of 'memory') which has evolved in the service of survival, are we so often irrational, failing to learn from the past, subverting our own best interests? His answer too invokes a collaboration between will and imagination: We are unwilling to acknowledge the ways in which we are less potent and less complete than we would like to be; so we deny what we know, or easily could know. We construct phantasies designed to protect us against pain that often serve rather to make us stupid. Insofar as there is a concept comparable to that of the thing-in-itself in Freud, it is not what God sees, nor what we would see were we God, but what we might see if we could bear it.

Again like Descartes, Freud thinks that the mind has built into it an ideal of its own functioning. I know myself as myself, Descartes claims, through "the image and similitude which God has placed upon me." But where Descartes translates that ideal 'Self' into an ontological reality—God—for Freud it is an unachievable limit of integration according to which we work unwelcome beliefs and uncomfortable, conflicted desires through the mental structure. Not the limit itself, but our capacity to progress toward it, defines the 'normal' as a range of functioning which is 'mental health'.

Notes · Bibliography · Index

Notes

1. Meaning and Mind

1. O'Shaughnessy (1980) makes this point in the Introduction to *The Will*, vol. 1.
2. The arguments against such reduction are made in Chapter 6.
3. Intentionality in this sense has little to do with the sense of intention in which we say that someone spilled his coffee intentionally. To distinguish these two senses, I will always capitalize the first.
4. I wonder if the psychoanalytic idea of 'the representational world' doesn't depend on such an idea. In their classic paper on this subject, Sandler and Rosenblatt speak of "our knowledge that perception of objects in the external world cannot take place without the development, within the ego of the child, of an increasingly organized and complex set of representations of external reality" (1965, p. 131). One would have to look carefully at the way 'representation' is being used here, as well as in Piaget, whom the authors cite, to know just what work the concept of representation is doing.
5. According to Stroud (1989), Walker gives a modern version of Descartes' argument for the existence of God: "Walker draws the truly astonishing conclusion that our confidence in our system of beliefs is tantamount to a commitment to belief in a non-deceiving God."
6. More specifically, functionalism claims that the mind thinks its thoughts in *mentalese*, which is context-invariant and the same across cultures, and then translates these thoughts into a natural language (see Fodor, 1987). Though he was himself the first to formulate functionalism, Hilary Putnam now calls it yet another misguided attempt to make meaning scientific by reducing it to something else that it isn't. The reasons for Putnam's change of heart have in large part to do with his turn to an externalist view of meaning. He writes:

"Propositional attitudes are not 'states' of the human brain and nervous system considered in isolation from the social and nonhuman environment" (1988, p. 73). We think that "the mind (or brain) thinks (or 'computes') using representations [because] all the thinking we know about uses representations. But none of the methods of representation that we know about— speech, writing, painting, carving in stone, etc.—has the magical property that . . . the representations *intrinsically* refer to whatever it is they are used to refer to. All of the representations which we know about have an association with their referent which is contingent, and capable of changing as the culture changes or as the world changes" (ibid., pp. 21–22).

7. For an excellent discussion of Mind-Body Dualism and the issues surrounding it, see Donagan (1970). This is a good overview of many of the topics under discussion here.

8. See Hanly (1990).

9. Kohut's view (1959) that introspection and empathy are the only tools the psychoanalyst needs is to this extent Cartesian, and so an exception to what I take to be the dominant view among psychoanalysts generally.

10. The terms 'internalism' and 'externalism', used in this way, are relatively recent additions to philosophical jargon. But I think it's nevertheless fair to characterize Wittgenstein as an externalist about mental contents.

11. Bilgrami cited this remark of Austin's in a lecture on Davidson at the NEH summer institute, "Perspectives on Anti-Cartesianism: Heidegger and Davidson," University of California at Santa Cruz, summer 1990.

12. Wittgenstein's *Tractatus* had considerable influence on the logical positivists. But there are big differences: the positivists did not hold a picture theory of propositions, and Wittgenstein never hinted at a verification theory of meaning.

13. For the formulations in these last two sentences I am once again indebted to Bilgrami's lectures on Davidson.

14. The argument is of a type Kant called 'transcendental'. One begins with something one takes to be a crucial assumption about human experience, then asks what else must be the case if this assumption is correct. Of course it has to be forfeited if the question cannot be answered in a plausible way. Kant's assumption is that we do have some knowledge of the world. He asks what the world and the mind must be like if they can have this relation to each other. This question leads him, for example, to a refutation of Hume's analysis of causality. Hume thought that our assumption that every event has a cause is an inductive generalization, one for which we can provide evidence only by assuming the very thing we are trying to prove. Hume bit the bullet and said our supposed knowledge of the external world is not knowledge at all, but just stubborn animal belief. Kant turns the whole thing around, saying that we do have some knowledge of the external world, and that therefore the basic assumption of causal reasoning cannot itself be inductive. Rather the mind has built into it certain assumptions and ideas, among them the idea that every event has a cause; and these assumptions then mould our experience, rendering it knowable. Kant should not be seen as simply denying Humean skepticism, or as saying 'I prefer my intuition that we do

have knowledge to Hume's conclusion that we don't'. There would be no philosophical interest in that. Rather Kant illumines certain interdependencies between the concepts of knowledge and cause that had been obscure. Similarly, though he does not accept Kant's idea that the mind models the world after itself, Davidson's argument reveals certain interdependencies between philosophical subjects that had previously been treated as independent, among them meaning, truth, the mental, and knowledge of other minds.

15. Ramberg notes (1989, pp. 81 and 82) that Davidson gives no argument in support of this assumption. If we rejected it we would either have to deny that interpretation is possible, or come up with an alternative theory of it.

16. Kripke's externalist arguments (1972) apply primarily to proper names. Putnam's arguments (1988) turn on the meaning of words for natural kinds. The use of the word 'water', for example, has a causal history which enters into its meaning: it is that clear liquidy stuff which we drink, in which we swim, and in whose presence we were first taught to say 'water'. Putnam argues that the reference of such words is fixed by what he calls 'a linguistic division of labor'. That is, reference is established socially, over time.

   Davidson's arguments for the social character of thought are more general in scope. They don't depend on puzzle cases, indexicals, or words for natural kinds, but are part of a general theory of concept formation and the mind.

17. Davidson's inspiration is Tarski's theory of truth. But whereas Tarski is after an elucidation of that notion, Davidson is after meaning.

18. The reader might want to look at the elaboration of this idea in Putnam (1988).

19. Crediting the phrase to N. L. Wilson, Quine used the phrase 'the principle of charity' (1969, p. 46) before Davidson.

20. See "Telling Stories" (Chapter 4) for the application of this discussion to Hanly (1990).

21. This is of course the issue of the irreducibility of the mental, which I will tackle in Chapter 3. And as I will say later, Freud never truly abandoned his reductivist hopes.

22. For an overview of recent work on what is 'built in', as well as on early infant-mother interactions, see Lichtenberg (1983); also Emde (1981). Neonate researchers envision the neonate and the caretaker as a developing interactional system, in which "each partner is viewed as having separate competencies which affect the other's behavior and as initiating and reinforcing the behavior of the other" (Emde, 1980, p. 89). Lichtenberg comments that many of the observations of early infant-mother interactions imply that "from the beginning both the newborn and the mother are primed to participate in a social interaction rather than to act as two individuals sending discrete messages ... The picture that emerges is one of two partners, each prepared to act on and react to the other" (1983, p. 18). Summarizing recent infant research, Lichtenberg says that young neonates respond differently, and in specific ways, for example to the mother's voice, face, and smell, to the father, to a toy.

23. The argument here is similar to one of Wittgenstein's against the possibility of a private language.

24. Some critics of this view contend that externalism is incompatible with that first-person authority which earlier I cited as a hallmark of the mental. For a refutation, see Davidson (1987).

25. In recent writings Davidson has argued that they are inseparable also from desire. I will not present that argument here; but the basic idea is that speech is intentional behavior, and that all intentional behavior is a vector of beliefs and desire, what one thinks is the case, and what one wants to be the case.

26. Gedo (1981, chap. 8) points out that there are two different meanings of the term 'object relations' as psychoanalysts have used it. In the first, it refers to actual interpersonal relations and their importance in development. In the second, it refers to intrapsychic relations, to memories of and phantasies about important persons in the child's world.

2. Minding the Frontier

1. The editors of the *Standard Edition* regularly translate Freud's word *Trieb* as 'instinct'. I generally follow their practice. They note, however, that Freud has in mind something more mental than 'instinct' usually conveys. What this something more can be is one of my subjects in this chapter.

2. Freud was not the first to make this claim. As Malcolm (1959) pointed out, many of the major philosophers have also. Descartes, for example, says that "all the same thoughts and conceptions which we have while awake may also come to us in sleep." In fact it is because he assumed that in sleep a man may have beliefs like any other, make judgments, be deceived, that Descartes can use dreams to support his skepticism about the adequacy of the mind to know the external world. If it is right to say that in dreaming we can judge we are sitting before a real fire, yet be deceived, then surely we may be deceived whether the fire is real or no. So Freud also speaks of dreams as a state in which we can be said to have beliefs. They are a kind of hallucination, Freud says, "an experience [to which] . . . we attach complete belief" (1900, p. 50). This is one of the respects in which he thinks that dreams, though occurring in normal as well as abnormal people, are on a spectrum occupied by unconscious phantasy and psychotic delusion. (Malcolm argues that we do not make judgments in dreams; that judgments come into the picture only when there is the possibility of checking up to see whether what we judge is true or false.)

3. Freud amends this thesis slightly as a result of the new instinct theory formulated in "Beyond the Pleasure Principle" (1920a). The consequence of this revision for his theory of dreams is that while many dreams can still be understood as hallucinatory wish-fulfillments, the dreams of patients suffering from traumatic neuroses are rather to be understood as attempting "to master the [anxiety-provoking] stimulus retrospectively" (1920, p. 32).

4. Gedo helpfully suggests (1979) that we distinguish *need* from *wish*, reserving the latter for mental states that are potentially available to consciousness.

For a cogent criticism of Freud's assumption of hallucinatory wish-fulfillment in the neonate, see Basch (1976a).

5. See Dorpat and Miller (1992, chap. 1) for a discussion of Freud's model of
   cognition and the experimental evidence against it.
6. On Freud's notion of 'word presentation', see Wollheim (1971, pp. 191–193).
7. O'Shaugnessy has another interpretation of this concept. He argues that
   there is a sub-propositional kind of knowledge in animals and infants, for
   example of the whereabouts of one's own foot or knee. "Yet this knowledge
   is a peculiar variety of knowledge in that, until brought to one's notice . . . it
   is . . . *sub-propositional* . . . in a sense akin to that which Freud employed
   when in characterizing The Unconscious, he said of its contents that they
   were not yet linked with 'word presentations'" (1980, vol. 2, p. 65).
8. For a discussion of the history of this concept in Freud's writings and how it
   might be understood now, see Frank (1969).
9. Eagle (1988) makes the same point. He writes that "the definition of id
   involves a conflation of meanings: id as impersonal through disavowal and
   id as instinct and therefore *inherently* alien ('it') and impersonal" (in Clark
   and Wright, 1988, pp. 93–94).
10. Hartmann (1939) claimed that 'ego functions' like perception and reality
    testing are autonomous in the sense that they do not develop from instinct.
11. As I understand it, this is what Millikan proposes (1984).
12. The analogy is Davidson's (private communication).
13. See my discussion of Intentionality and the mental in Chapter 3, section II.
14. There is a different sense in which meaning can be said to be indeterminate
    that I will discuss in Chapter 4.
15. See my discussion of metaphor in Chapter 8, section II.
16. See also Gedo's discussion (1984, particularly chaps. 9, 11, and 12) of Lich-
    tenberg. Lichtenberg notes that Basch places the onset of representational
    thought even later. In Basch's own words: "The relatively late onset of asso-
    ciational thought suggests that so-called infantile fantasies may represent
    the working over of earlier experiences and their interpretation by the more
    mature mind of the child" (1976b, p. 162).
17. Isaacs' views here may be based on the now discarded biological notion that
    the grown form of an organism is preformed from the beginning.
18. Because I am often misunderstood on this point, I must emphasize both that
    we obviously cannot say exactly *when* there is thought in the most literal
    sense, and that it is relatively early. The child of two and a half who is inter-
    acting with the analyst in play therapy can have phantasies in every sense of
    the word.

3. Mind, Body, and the Question of Psychological Laws

1. For what this sense is, see the discussion of Freud (1940a [1938]) in the previous chapter.
2. The concept of an 'action' is sometimes used, particularly by psychologists
   and psychoanalysts, in a more extended sense. Piaget, for example, speaks of
   'action schema' in infants. O'Shaughnessy himself argues that 'action'

includes pre-intentional doings. I have no quarrel with such uses. But I am using 'action' in the more conventional philosophical way, to specify doings which are intended.

3. See, for example, Anscombe (1959), Hampshire (1959), Kenny (1963), and Melden (1961).
4. See also MacIntyre (1958) and Peters (1958).
5. These objections are all dealt with by Davidson in "Mental Events." His essay "Action, Reasons, and Causes" is the *locus classicus* for the argument that reasons are causes. Both essays are in Davidson (1980).
6. The example is Dennett's (1978).
7. See Davidson, "On the Very Idea of a Conceptual Scheme," in Davidson (1984); see also Putnam (1988).
8. Freud is speaking here not of the prediction of action but of traits of character. His point affects both equally.
9. See Davidson, "Mental Events," also "Causal Relations," both in Davidson (1980).
10. The literature on the concept of psychoanalytic 'metapsychology' is enormous. Rapaport (1959) divided psychoanalytic theory into a clinical part and a general part, and debates about how the distinction should be drawn, whether or not it is useful, and whether or not psychoanalysis needs a metapsychology at all, have been raging ever since. In addition to the works I have already cited on this subject, see Rubinstein (1967, 1976); all the essays in Gill and Holzman (1976); and Moore (1980).
11. Drive theory has been well and roundly criticized by, among others, Guntrip (1971), Basch (1976a), Holt (1976), Eagle (1987).
12. See Moore (1980) for an account of functional explanations, and a criticism of the way in which Freud conflates them with explanations via reasons.
13. Ricoeur (1970) endorsed the reason-cause distinction, claiming that because psychoanalytic explanations are interpretations via reasons, therefore they are not causal. Grünbaum points out (1984, p. 73) that under the influence of Sherwood (1969), Ricoeur (1981) came to have second thoughts on this matter.
14. For criticisms of Grünbaum, each along different lines, see Cioffi (1988) and Sachs (1989).
15. I discuss this in "Reasons, Repression, and Phantasy" (Chapter 9).
16. This is a variation on an example of Grünbaum's (1990).
17. See the discussion of similar points in Neu (1976).

4. Telling Stories

1. In a brooding article on the future of psychoanalysis, Rangell (1988) describes the following case presentation. An analyst tells his colleagues of a patient who came to his Monday hour depressed. The patient connects his depression to the death of his dog over the weekend, which he thinks was his fault. The analyst reports that he interpreted the patient's sadness as caused by his separation from the analyst. No one in the audience demurs, even though they had already been informed of the patient's lifelong guilt over a childhood accident

of his brother's for which the patient had also felt responsible. Rangell's complaint that something has gone terribly wrong here raises some of the questions considered in this chapter about just what the psychoanalyst's task is.

2. There is another possibility I take up later, namely that the primal scene took place, but prior to the patient's capacity for articulate observation and thought. So it must be constructed, or re-constructed, in terms that make it intelligible now.

3. See Farrell's criticisms of the view that the psychoanalyst aims only at the telling of an intelligible story (1981, particularly chapter 3).

4. The first example comes from Freud (1954); the second from Fenichel (1945).

5. I am indebted to a very interesting article by Meehl (1983) for bringing this passage to my attention.

6. This is a line of thought I owe to Hampshire (1982).

7. See Sharpe (1988) for a discussion of similar ideas.

8. See, for example, Freud, *Introductory Lectures on Psycho-analysis* (1916–1917), Lecture 28; also "From the History of an Infantile Neurosis" (1918 [1914]), chap. 6.

9. For a development of this view of metaphor, see Davidson, "What Metaphors Mean" (in Davidson, 1984a).

10. See 1991a and 1991b, in the latter, particularly "Wittgenstein, Heidegger, and the Reification of Language."

5. Behind the Veil of Language

1. This formulation is Nagel's in a highly influential paper, "What Is It Like to Be a Bat?" (1979). I discuss its theme later in this chapter.

2. Many psychologists have taken the child's recognition of itself in the mirror as a criterion of its having a self-concept. This recognition seems to occur somewhere between 21 and 24 months. See Zazzo (1975) for a survey of this literature, and a very interesting discussion of the anxieties which such recognition seems to inaugurate.

3. Lichtenberg (1983) suggests that it may not make sense to attribute to an infant a sense of self prior to its having a concept of self, together with the capacity for symbolic thought, which comes much later. See also Southwood's review (1988) of Stern.

4. See the discussion of this concept in Chapter 3.

5. See Williams (1973b) for a development of this point.

6. I have made no attempt here to summarize even those of Lacan's views that are relevant to the matter at hand. I have not mentioned, for one, his Saussurian idea that the basic unit of meaning is the word, nor the distinction, also from Saussure, between 'langue' and 'parole'. 'Langue' is the name for language as a synchronic structure, independent of speakers; 'parole' is speech and so is tied to particular occasions in time, particular speakers and their intentions. Readers of my earlier chapters will know that on the view I

am putting forward the basic unit of meaning is not the word but the sentence, and that the concept of meaning is tied to the concept of truth via the notion of truth conditions. The conditions under which a sentence is held to be true by the speaker are partially constitutive of its meaning. They are not wholly constitutive because the meaning of any one sentence is a function of the meaning of all the other sentences with which it is implicated. Lacan is sympathetic to this idea of meaning holism. In fact, so far as I can see, it is the primary content of his concept of "the floating signifier." But the connections Davidson finds between meaning and truth are no part of Lacan's theory. And Lacan's idea of language as a structure independent of speakers is no part of Davidson's or mine.

I also have said nothing about the connections Lacan finds between the advent of language and the discovery of one's separation from others. Language is a system of signs, Lacan says, which are such just because what they represent is absent. Language is then, he thinks, peculiarly suited to represent the condition of separateness itself. In giving the child the power of speech, language is also peculiarly suited to make up for the loss, and to allow the child to 'repress' knowledge of its own incompleteness. My question to Lacan is this: Does the child know of its separateness and lack prior to language and the Symbolic order? If not, how are we to conceive of the loss for which language compensates? If so, how is this knowledge different, *as knowledge,* from the knowledge which is peculiar to "the Symbolic order"? (This question arises in myriad forms apropos of Lacan.)

7. One can arrive at the idea of a vision uncontaminated by language and society either through imagining backwards in time, or forwards. The forward-looking idea goes something like this: I know that my perspective on the world is partial, and that I might have a view of things clearer and more complete than the one I have at present if I were to adopt a standpoint less narrowly concerned with my own interests, less self-delusive, more informed by the world and more imaginative about it. Again, so far so good. But now the idea continues: All my beliefs and desires are *mine* in that they are all the beliefs and desires of someone who occupies a particular point in space and time. I see that no matter where I stood, my beliefs could never represent things as they really are, just because they would be *my* beliefs, beliefs formed from the perspective that is me. The only hope, then, is to have beliefs from no perspective at all, or as Nagel ironically puts it, "the view from nowhere" (1986). Nagel admits that the idea is scarcely coherent, but that he finds it nonetheless compelling.

8. Dennett (1991) makes this point at much greater length in *Consciousness Explained.*

9. See Dennett (1991, pp. 441–448) for further discussion of this point.

10. In a letter on recent philosophical treatments of consciousness, Danto (1991) remarks that the concept of consciousness will be intractable so long as philosophers think they must answer Nagel's question, 'What is it like to be a bat?' Think how hard it would be, Danto asks, to answer the question what it is like to be us. "To believe consciousness a mystery is to have allowed the problem of mind to have been usurped by the Problem of Other Minds."

11. For a lengthier discussion and criticism of this idea, see Malcolm (1984, the chapter titled "The Subjective Character of Experience").

6. Baby Talk

1. I am eliding distinctions which for other purposes than mine at the moment it would be necessary to draw. For example, there are at least three different sorts of intentions at work in all speech acts. First, as speaker you intend that your words 'There is a mouse in the corner', for example, be interpreted as true just in case there is a mouse in the corner. We often speak of these intentions as the utterance's 'literal meaning'. Second, you intend that your utterance should be taken as a command, a question, an assertion, and so on. (Note that grammar does not accomplish this. Something inscribed or even spoken as a question may in the context have the force of a command—'You call that a clean room?'—an assertion may have the effect of an exclamation, and so on.) We can refer to intentions of this second sort as the *force* with which something is said. Finally, there are ulterior intentions which are beyond the production of words: You say 'There's a mouse in the corner' with the intention of getting your hearer to look, or pick up her skirts, or of frightening her, and so on. (See Davidson, "Moods and Performances" and "Communication and Convention," in Davidson, 1984a. John Austin [1962] tried to mark similar distinctions with the terms 'locutionary', 'illocutionary', and 'perlocutionary' acts.) Talking about the 'pragmatic' dimension of language conflates the second and third sorts of intentions.

   It is important to note that intentions of the third sort are always present; they do not pick out a special class of utterances, but are a function of the ways in which language is inextricably bound to our larger lives as agents in the world. Furthermore, any speech act will of course have multiple, often ambiguous, intentions. Metaphor enters here; it is a function of the way words are used, the purposes to which literal meaning is put. (See my discussion of metaphor in Chapter 8, "Primary Process.") It is not itself a special kind of meaning.

2. Bruner discusses what he calls "the dark issue" of whether rules of grammar can "somehow be inferred or generalized from the structure of our knowledge of the world" in chapter 2 of *Child's Talk* (1985).

3. I am told that in the *Project* (1950 [1887–1902]) Freud himself includes motor sequences in infantile memory, though I have not yet found the reference.

4. For a discussion of the various modes of communication, see Levin (1991, chap. 7). There is an interesting discussion of the relations between the work of Piaget and psychoanalysis in Basch (1977).

5. Winnicott acknowledges that he has been influenced by Lacan's paper "Le Stade du Miroir," but remarks that what Lacan means by the mother's face as a mirror is different from what he means.

6. The idea of 'the Background' is Searle's. He defines it as "a set of nonrepresentational mental capacities that enable all representing to take place." To form

the intention to open the refrigerator door, for example, I must know how to walk, to move my arm, to move it differently from the way I would move it if I were opening a book or a bottle. "I can, for example, intend to peel an orange, but I cannot in that way intend to peel a rock or a car, and that is not because I have an unconscious belief, 'you can peel an orange but you cannot peel a rock or a car' but rather because the preintentional stance I take toward oranges (how things are) allows for a completely different range of possibilities (how to do things) from that which I take toward rocks or cars." To have beliefs and to form intentions, "I must know how things are and I must know how to do things, but the kinds of 'know-how' in question are not, in these cases, forms of 'knowing that'" (1983, pp. 143–144).

Searle's question, about what the Intentional logically presupposes, is logical in character. I have cast it in the form of a genetic or developmental question. The difficulties I point to about how, in either case, to flesh out the notion of a pre-intentional understanding are difficulties Searle himself acknowledges. But he holds to the idea of the Background anyway.

7. This suggestion comes from Stroud's criticism (1990) of Searle's idea of the Background.

8. This, incidentally, is one way an externalist might respond to Searle. He claims that the content of any mental state is entirely internal to it; and because he has cut the mental loose from the external world, he now needs to restore the ties via the notion of the Background.

9. A number of authors have explored this possibility, among them Laing (1964, 1969), Bateson (1972), and Palazzoli et al. (1978). There is now substantial evidence of a genetic predisposition to schizophrenia. The kinds of facts that I and these authors adduce might supply other conditions.

7. The Subject of Emotion

1. See Lester (1982) for a discussion of recent developments in the psychoanalytic theory of affects.

2. Brenner (1974) argued that ideas are essential to the constitution of affect, which arises early in life when ideas are associated with pleasure and unpleasure. This was a move in the right direction. One needs next to specify the nature of this 'association'.

3. The following is only a partial list of recent philosophical works which, despite differences on a number of issues, exemplify this view: Hampshire (1959, 1982), Kenny (1963), Bedford (1964), Thalberg (1964), Pitcher (1965), Davidson (1976), Solomon (1976), Neu (1977), Marks (1982), Taylor (1985), de Sousa (1987), Gordon (1987), Greenspan (1988).

4. I owe this way of putting the point to Neu (1977).

5. For agreement on this point among psychoanalysts, see Basch (1976a), Emde et al. (1976), and Lichtenberg (1983).

6. This is a topic I take up in Chapter 10, "Dividing the Self."

7. Philosophical analyses of emotion disagree over whether the belief component should be put more vaguely in terms of apprehending or imagining *that*, as the thought might occur to one that a man is untrustworthy though

one doesn't necessarily believe in the ordinary sense that he is (see Greenspan, 1988). Similarly, there is disagreement over whether to call the evaluative component evaluation, or wish, or desire, or simply some pro-attitude. These differences may matter for a full-fledged theory; but I believe I can ignore them here.

8. Sachs (1982) discusses Freud's idea that emotions are always appropriate to their occasions, if we only knew what those were, and that the occasions are causes which are beliefs. He doesn't take the next step, however, of saying that the causes are reasons.

9. For a long time philosophers thought that since a cause must be a real event or state of affairs while the object of an emotion may be a falsely imagined state of affairs, therefore the object of an emotion cannot be its cause. The remedy is to say that the cause of an emotion is always a belief, or something in the world *as seen* under some description or other. See Williams (1959), Davidson (1976), and Neu (1977) for discussion of this point.

10. De Sousa (1987) discusses this point.

11. For analyses of just how emotions are constituted out of beliefs and desires, again see de Sousa (1987), Gordon (1987), and Greenspan (1988).

12. Both Gordon (1987) and de Sousa (1987) think the latter.

13. Hampshire (1982) develops a very interesting view of the emotions on this basis.

14. Taylor (1985), Gordon (1987), de Sousa (1987), and Greenspan (1988) discuss at length the ways in which emotions can be irrational. There are briefer discussions in Pitcher (1965) and Davidson (1976).

15. Gordon (1987) suggests amending James's theory as follows so as to take account of the logical role of beliefs: beliefs and desires cause an underlying state of anger, say. This causes a bodily reaction which in turn gives rise to angry feelings.

16. This is a point on which Greenspan (1988) insists, I think rightly.

17. For a similar reason, Schachter and Singer (1962) suggested a modified Jamesian view according to which an emotion is a visceral activity in combination with cognitive factors. Visceral arousal alone is not enough, since the very same arousal may accompany emotional states which the subject interprets as very different emotions. It is the subject's cognitions, they concluded, which determine how he labels his state. Note that this is not a genuinely cognitive view in the sense I have outlined, since the beliefs enter only into the subject's labeling of his emotion, not the constitution of the emotion itself.

18. See Pitcher (1965) for an elaboration of this argument.

19. As Bedford (1964) puts it, being angry is logically prior to feeling angry; that is, only someone who understands the first can understand the second. For if it were the other way around, how would the adult explain the meaning of 'feels angry'? She would have to do something to make the child angry, and then say 'Anger is what you're feeling'. But how would the adult know he had it right, that anger is what the child feels? Instead the learning process must go rather like this: Something has happened which the adult imagines might make the child angry, and in fact the child behaves in an angry way. So

the adult makes a remark like 'Are you angry because I took the toy away from you?' 'Anger' here refers to a whole situation shared by adult and child and to observable behavior in the child.

20. De Rivera (1977) proposes in his *Structural Theory of the Emotions* that each emotion has its own structure and that all the emotions are interrelated in complex ways. I think something like this is right. But to articulate it clearly one needs to talk, as he does not, about the logical relations between beliefs, desires, and emotions. Furthermore, he assumes, I believe mistakenly, that an inquiry into the essence of any emotion is an exercise in phenomenology (p. 78).

21. For interesting discussions of the relations between Spinoza and Freud, see Hampshire (1956) and Neu (1977).

22. See also Izard (1977).

23. See Emde (1980) for a discussion of affective communication between infants and caretakers.

24. The notion of 'paradigm scenarios' with regard to emotions is de Sousa's (1987), though I am not at all sure he means what I do.

25. Lear (1990) speaks of "proto-emotion" as "an infantile orientation to the world," de Sousa (1987) of emotions as "setting the stage for belief and desire."

8. Primary Process

1. As this book was about to go to press, I read Dorpat and Miller's *Clinical Interaction and the Analysis of Meaning* (1992). They are critical of the traditional views about primary process in ways that complement my own. At the same time they suggest an interesting reinterpretation of primary process according to which it *is* a fundamentally different kind of cognition, one, however, that is not temporally prior to 'secondary process' and that is equally in touch with reality, though in different ways. This may well be right.

2. This too is Archard's point (1984, p. 29).

3. Sulloway remarks that "no other document in the history of psychoanalysis has provoked such a large body of discussion with such a minimum of agreement as has Freud's *Project* . . . The *Project* has even prompted some students of Freud's to make elaborate comparisons between it and more recent achievements in the kindred field of cybernetics" (1979, p. 118). Yet more recent writers see the *Project* as an anticipation of connectionist thinking about the brain (see P. M. Churchland, 1991).

4. One cannot make too much of arguments from ordinary language; still, it is interesting that we ordinarily attribute wishes only to a creature who has reasons for not doing as he might otherwise like to do, who in virtue of the capacities for self-awareness and self-reflection has not only dispositions to behave in certain ways—as all animals do—but also the capacity to inhibit his behavior. Wishes are typically desires upon which we might like to act but know we can or will not. The idea of a repressed wish, then, also presupposes knowledge, or some articulate and articulable beliefs. I take the following to be familiar examples of how 'wishing' gets used in daily life. The

mother may say to the child who is looking sadly out the window at the rain, 'I know you wish you could ride your new bike. It's a shame it's raining'. Or the child may say to the mother dressing to go out for the evening, 'I wish you wouldn't go', indicating his knowledge that she is going and that he is more or less resigned to the fact. Depending on our views about the mind, we might speak of animals as desiring; but only in play do we speak of them as wishing. For wishing seems precisely to presume awareness of reality under some description or other, and an awareness that one cannot have what one wants, or that it is not what one *really* wants, all things considered.

5. Wollheim (1984) speaks of the omnipotence of thought as a primitive theory that the mind entertains about its own functioning.
6. For critical discussions of this idea in Lacan, see Archard (1984), Locke (1987), and Wollheim (1979).
7. See Archard (1984, chap. 3) for a discussion of this point.
8. See Davidson's "What Metaphors Mean" (in Davidson, 1984).
9. Lear (1990, chap. 3) says that Freud under-rationalized primary process and over-rationalized the unconscious.
10. For a much longer criticism of Freud's idea of primary process, see Archard (1984, particularly chap. 1 and the Conclusion).

9. Reasons, Repression, and Phantasy

1. See, for example, Alexander (1962) and Mischel (1965).
2. For an elaboration of this point, see Mullane (1971, 1983).
3. Before his revisions of instinct theory in "Beyond the Pleasure Principle" (1920a), Freud had postulated a basic polarity between the sexual instincts and the ego-preservative instincts. Now that polarity is said to be between 'Eros' and 'Thanatos'. Struck by the fact that often people repeat painful or traumatic situations, Freud suggests that something other than a desire for gratification—namely, a compulsion to repeat—is at work. Freudian metaphysics aside, the following seems right: a creature is in no position to think about gratifying its desires so long as it is overwhelmed by anxiety. This is the sense in which 'binding' or mastering anxiety is 'beyond' the pleasure principle. Freud's important new vision—mentioned earlier in connection with 'wishing'—is that his former view of symptoms as deviously gratifying repressed sexual or aggressive desire was too simple; more typically they are an attempt to avoid the anxiety that satisfying a desire would cause (because of the punishments or pains imagined to be attendant on it, or the undesirable things it would seem to presuppose). Incidentally the symptom may gratify a libidinal wish: in Hans's case, to stay home with his mother. But this is not its primary motive. The idea now is that anxiety plays a unique and critical role in mental development. Defensive mechanisms are a response to anxiety, and are put into play, perhaps, by situations unique to creatures like us.
4. Wollheim (1993) discusses a number of ways in which Freud extended reason-explanations and suggests the term 'activity' rather than 'action' to cover cases where there is desire but no instrumental belief. What takes its place in phantasizing, Wollheim says (1984), is instinct.

5. Hampshire (1959) holds that unlike purposes, intentions can never be said to be unconscious. In the fullest sense of the word, 'intention' should be reserved, he argues, for purposes of a certain sort that are fully conscious and explicit.

6. Mullane (1983) distinguishes material that is repressed from the repressing activity. He writes: "Little Hans was afraid of his ill-tempered father, and *that* fear was unconscious. Later he became aware of this; the fear and the associated beliefs, which also underwent repression, became conscious. That 'material', like material in (nonrepressed) memory, is 'there' to be recovered. Hans *really did* have certain false beliefs which, along with the fear, were repressed; he never believed, however, that if he substituted horses for father he could avoid conscious anxiety by avoiding contact with horses" (p. 200).

7. For a neurophysiological account of repression see Basch (1983), Levin (1991), and McKinnon (1979).

8. Lichtenberg comments: "My own opinion is that unless issues such as the relationship between consciousness and the dynamic unconsciousness and the timing of the origin of fantasy are addressed, the gap between the bedrock of psychoanalysis and neonate research will remain relatively wide" (1983, p. 32). I agree with the spirit of this response; but it is interesting to note how readily even the psychoanalyst equates consciousness and the mental.

9. Recent work in cognitive psychology has shown that a great deal of complex cognitive activity can go on outside conscious awareness, provided the skills required for the task have been automatized (see Kihlstrom, 1987). We can reach conclusions about events without being able to articulate our reasoning for them; we can be aware of information below the threshold of consciousness on which we are nevertheless able to act. For a long while critics of the idea of subliminal perception argued that it is not possible to endow stimuli with meaning unless they have been consciously identified, a criticism to which recent experiments give the lie.

10. The tendency in psychoanalysis to think of phantasy as necessarily unconscious is a carryover from the idea that the child's first phantasizing activity, prior to the development of the ego and consciousness, is hallucinating the breast.

11. Grünbaum says that the wish supposedly disappears. See my discussion of this in "Mind, Body, and the Question of Psychological Laws" (Chapter 3).

10. Dividing the Self

1. The literature on the subject of self-deception is enormous. My suggestions for further reading would include Elster (1986), Mele (1987a, 1987b), and A. O. Rorty (1988).

2. I am indebted to Sass (1987) for this point and these references, though they turn up in his writing in quite a different connection.

Conclusion: Valuing and the Self

1. Brown says that St. Augustine "produced a singularly comprehensive explanation of why allegory should have been necessary in the first place. The need for such a language of 'signs' was the result of a specific dislocation of the human consciousness. In this, Augustine takes up a position analogous to that of Freud. In dreams also, a powerful and direct message is said to be deliberately diffracted by some psychic mechanisms, into a multiplicity of 'signs' quite as intricate and absurd, yet just as capable of interpretation, as the 'absurd' or 'obscure' passages in the Bible. Both men, therefore, assume that the proliferation of images is due to some precise event, to the development of some geological fault across a hitherto undivided consciousness: for Freud, it is the creation of an unconscious by repression; for Augustine, it is the outcome of the Fall" (1969, p. 261).
2. See Laplanche (1976, chap. 2).
3. Freud is now de-sexualizing the libido and sexualizing the self-preservative instincts in a way that brings him dangerously close to Jung's instinctual monism. Borch-Jacobsen (1987) has a very interesting discussion of this and other difficulties arising out of Freud's views on narcissism.
4. Gilligan (1984) has an interesting discussion of Freud's views about female narcissism.
5. The idea that primary narcissism is the source for our moral ideals is taken up and defended by Chasseguet-Smirgel. She notes that although by 1923 Freud has absorbed the concept of the ego ideal into that of the superego, they are different. Whereas the superego is heir to the Oedipal complex, the ego ideal is heir to primary narcissism. Quoting Freud, she writes, "Whoever understands the human mind knows that hardly anything is harder for a man than to give up a pleasure which he has once experienced," and comments: "When the infant took himself as his own ideal there was no unsatisfaction, no desire, no loss, and this time remains with us as an example of perfect, unending contentment. Freud thus gives us to understand . . . that whilst man may chase endlessly after this lost perfection, he can never actually achieve it. It is this quest, it seems, that lies at the base of the most sublime achievements, but also the most baleful errors, of the human spirit" (1985, p. 5). The infant thinks of himself as perfect, complete, needing nothing and no one; or he thinks of himself as fused with the one he does need and love, namely his mother. He attempts by every means to recover this lost perfection, even as experience humiliatingly separates him from it "by a gulf, a split that man is constantly seeking to abolish" (p. 5).

   On this basis Chasseguet-Smirgel conjectures that the child wants to think of himself as his mother's perfect partner in a union that will not admit nor ever has admitted any other person. Encouraged, as it may be where the father is absent or passive and the mother is strong and seductive, this wish may lead the child to deny that the mother has a vagina, not so much because (as Freud thought) it proves that she has been castrated and that castration is possible for the child, as because her vagina is humiliating evidence of the genital relationship between his parents. It proves the generational distance that separates him from them. "If his mother has a penis, she has no need of the father—the adult male—and he, the little boy, can satisfy his mother with his pregenital sexuality" (p. 16). Such denial and such phantasy may then provide the structure for fetishism, for example, in male perversion.

My comment on these views is that while such phantasies may exist in children old enough to have phantasies to begin with, for the reasons I am about to give they do not support the thesis of primary narcissism.

6. Compare the discussion of the assumption of genetic continuity in Chapter 2.

7. See Williams (1972) for a discussion of issues related to this distinction.

8. A number of moral philosophers have been developing a notion of moral objectivity according to which it is not essentially different from objectivity in relation to belief. See, for example, Nagel (1970, 1986), McDowell (1985), Hurley (1985), and Wiggins (1987).

9. Some current views of identification, as distinct from introjection, do not presume a split self. Sandler writes: "If one *identified* with some aspect of a parent, then one would duplicate that perceived aspect in oneself and become more like that parent. If one *introjected* the parent, then the introject would not modify one's self-representation but would become an internal companion, a sort of back-seat driver" (1990, p. 865).

10. This is suggested in Laplanche (1976).

11. Since Kleinians attribute very complex phantasies to infants, they would presumably hold that the infant's communications are meaningful to the infant as well as to us. Its cries are expressive of phantasies in which it thinks, for example, that it is spitting out its 'badness' into another. Depending on how early Kleinians think such phantasizing occurs, I may part company with them on this issue.

12. Lacan writes: "This reel is not the mother reduced to a little ball by some magical game . . . it is a small part of the subject that detaches itself from him while still remaining his . . . The activity as a whole symbolizes repetition, but not at all that of some need that might demand the return of the mother . . . It is the repetition of the mother's departure as cause of a *Spaltung* in the subject—overcome by the alternating game, *fort-da* . . . whose aim, in its alternation, is simply that of being the *fort* of a *da,* and the *da* of a *da*" (1981, pp. 62–63).

13. Why, one might ask, does the mourning constitutive of the self require acknowledging the separateness of not just one other, but two others? I'm not sure I can give a philosophical defense of this. But here's a try: staying fairly close to Freud, we might say that it requires identifications with two because to know myself as an I, I must know myself also as a second and as a third person, both as a 'you' for someone when I am with her and as a 'her' when we are apart, or when I am not the focus of her attention. The third-person point of view means knowing that as the object of my desire remains herself even when she is with someone other than me, so I remain myself whether I am in relation to her or to others, or am by myself. A third person is needed through whom the fact of relationship itself is represented (Abelin, 1975). Jealousy is the inscription in feeling of the discovery of one's self as

both separate from and related to others. (A Wittgensteinian answer to the question 'Why three?' might say that thought requires a mastery of words and concepts; and that such mastery presupposes community practice.)

If one asks the biological question: How many persons must there already be in the world for one more person to be conceived? the answer of course is, at least two. A more interesting question is psychological: How many other persons must one believe there to be, and acknowledge *as persons,* if one is to conceive of oneself as a self and as a person? Freud's answer is again, at least two. Right or wrong, one of his most original thoughts is that the human organism is such that the fundamental fact of sexual reproduction has a psychological correlate in the mind.

14. Wisdom notes that whereas according to Klein integration of the subject is parallel to integration of the object, the first must rather be "the presupposition of ambivalence towards one object. For suppose that the nucleus [of the self] is composed of two unrelated halves . . . and suppose further that one of them values an object as good and the other repudiates the object as bad. It is then one object that is regarded as both good and bad, but there is no ambivalence—any more than there is when Mr. Smith approved of Gladstone and Mr. Brown disapproved. Hence integration in the subject must come earlier . . . than ambivalence towards the object" (1962, p. 121).

15. If gratitude and mourning have the importance in the development of valuing—indeed, in the development of the person—that Klein suggests, then the categorical distinction that Wollheim draws between obligation and valuing would seem to be misguided. He writes: "Whatever may be the content of obligation, obligation itself is primarily self-directed. It is self-directed, though it may be other-regarding. For it expresses itself in a thought that a person has about what *he* ought to do . . . It is also true that a person may well have thoughts about what others ought to do, but my conviction is that either these thoughts do not express obligations or they require some circuitous interpretation. For they have no clear root in our psychology" (1984, p. 224). But if a certain stage in the genealogy of valuing that I have called mourning represents, in part, a sort of Kantian recognition that some 'objects' are valuable not only as means but also as ends, and that they are real objects in a real and public world, then it is not a wide step to the further idea that these objects are entitled to respect from others as well as from oneself. So I see no reason for saying either that obligation is primarily self-directed, or that third-person ascriptions of obligation have no root in our psychology.

16. I wrote these passages and the later ones comparing Freud and Plato long before reading Jonathan Lear's *Love and Its Place in Nature* (1990), so I was quite struck to find a similar idea there. Lear argues that a chaotic world could not give rise to human valuing; so there is valuing, and knowledge, only because in this sense the world is valuable, or lovable. This is, he points out, a kind of transcendental argument for the idea that the valuable is found—not, or not only, made.

Bibliography

Abelin, E. 1975. "Some Further Observations and Comments on the Earliest Role of the Father." *International Journal of Psycho-analysis* 56: 293–302.

Aldrich, V. C. 1973. "On What It Is Like to Be a Man." *Inquiry* 16: 355–366.

Alexander, P. 1962. "Rational Behavior and Psychoanalytic Explanation." *Mind* (July): 326–341.

Alexander, P., and F. Cioffi. 1974. "Wishes, Symptoms and Actions." *Proceedings of the Aristotelian Society Supplement* 48: 97–134.

Anscombe, G. E. M. 1959. *Intention.* Oxford: Blackwell.

Archard, D. 1984. *Consciousness and the Unconscious.* La Salle, Ill.: Open Court.

Arlow, J. 1986. "The Concept of Psychic Reality and Related Problems." *Journal of the American Psychoanalytic Association* 3: 27–44.

Armstrong, D. M., and N. Malcolm. 1984. *Consciousness and Causality.* Oxford: Blackwell.

Augustine, Saint. 1961. *The Confessions.* London: Penguin.

Austin, J. 1961. *Philosophical Papers.* Oxford: Oxford University Press.

——— 1962. *How to Do Things with Words.* Cambridge: Cambridge University Press.

Averill, J. R. 1980. "Emotion and Anxiety, Sociocultural, Biological, and Psychological Determinants." *Explaining Emotions.* Ed. A. O. Rorty. Berkeley: University of California Press.

Barrett, R., and R. Gibson. 1990. *Perspectives on Quine.* Oxford: Blackwell.

Basch, M. F. 1976a. "Theory Formation in Chapter 7: A Critique." *Journal of the American Psychoanalytic Association* 24: 61–100.

——— 1976b. "Psychoanalytic Interpretation and Cognitive Transformation." *International Journal of Psychoanalysis* 62: 151–175.

———— 1977. "Developmental Psychology and Explanatory Theory in Psycho-analysis." *The Annual of Psychoanalysis* 5: 229–266. New York: International Universities Press.

———— 1983. "The Perception of Reality and the Disavowal of Meaning." *The Annual of Psychoanalysis* 11: 125–154.

Bateson, G. 1972. *Steps to an Ecology of Mind.* San Francisco: Chandler.

Baxendall, M. 1985. *Patterns of Intention.* New Haven: Yale University Press.

Bedford, B. 1964. "Emotions." *Essays in Philosophical Psychology.* Ed. D. F. Gustafson. New York: Doubleday Anchor.

Benassy, M., and R. Diatkine. 1964. "Symposium on Fantasy." *International Journal of Psychoanalysis* 45: 171–179.

Benveniste, E. 1971. "Remarks on the Function of Language in Freudian Theory." Trans. M. E. Meck. *Problems in General Linguistics.* Miami: University of Miami Press.

Beres, D., and J. Arlow. 1974. "Fantasy and Identification in Empathy." *Psychoanalytic Quarterly* 43: 155–181.

Bilgrami, A. 1989. "Realism without Internalism: A Critique of Searle on Intentionality." *The Journal of Philosophy* 86: 57–73.

Bion, W. 1974. *Seven Servants.* New York: Aronson.

Blight, J. G. 1981. "Must Psychoanalysis Retreat to Hermeneutics? Psychoanalytic Theory in the Light of Popper's Evolutionary Epistemology." *Psychoanalysis and Contemporary Thought* 4/2: 147–205.

Borch-Jacobsen, M. 1987. *The Freudian Subject.* Trans. C. Porter. Stanford: Stanford University Press.

Boudreaux, G. 1977. "Freud on the Nature of Unconscious Mental Processes." *Philosophy of the Social Sciences* 7: 1–32.

Bouveresse, J. 1991. *Philosophie, Mythologie et Pseudo-Science: Wittgenstein Lecteur de Freud.* Paris: Éditions de l'Éclat.

Bowlby, J. 1969. *Attachment* (vol. I, *Attachment and Loss*). New York: Basic Books.

Brenner, C. 1957. *An Elementary Textbook of Psycho-analysis.* New York: Doubleday Anchor.

———— 1974. "On the Nature and Development of Affects: A Unified Theory." *Psychoanalytic Quarterly* 43: 532–556.

Brentano, F. 1924. *Psychology from an Empirical Standpoint.* Ed. O. Kraus. New York: Humanities Press.

Brown, P. 1969. *Augustine of Hippo.* Berkeley: University of California Press.

Brown, R. 1977. "Introduction." *Talking to Children: Language Input and Acquisition.* New York and Cambridge: Cambridge University Press.

Bruner, J. 1985. *Child's Talk.* New York: W. W. Norton.

Burge, T. 1979. "Individualism and the Mental." *Midwest Studies in Philosophy,* vol. 4. Ed. P. French, T. Uehling, and H. Weinstein. Minneapolis: University of Minnesota Press.

Cannon, W. B. 1929. *Bodily Changes in Pain, Hunger, Fear and Rage,* 2nd ed. New York: Appleton.

Cavell, M. 1988a. "Interpretation, Psychoanalysis, and the Philosophy of Mind." *Journal of the American Psychoanalytic Association* 36: 859–881.

—— 1988b. "Solipsism and Community: Two Concepts of Mind in Psycho-analysis." *Psychoanalysis and Contemporary Thought* 11: 587–613.

—— 1989. Book Review of *The Structure of Emotions,* by R. M. Gordon, and *The Rationality of Emotion,* by R. de Sousa. *The Journal of Philosophy* 86: 493–504.

Cavell, S. 1969. *Must We Mean What We Say?* New York: Charles Scribner's Sons.

—— 1987. *Disowning Knowledge in Six Plays of Shakespeare.* New York and Cambridge: Cambridge University Press.

Chasseguet-Smirgel, J. 1985. *The Ego Ideal.* New York: W. W. Norton.

Chisholm, R. 1956. "Sentences about Believing." *Aristotelian Society Proceedings* 56: 125–148.

—— 1957. *Perceiving: A Philosophical Study.* Ithaca, N.Y.: Cornell University Press.

Chomsky, N. 1975. *Reflections on Language.* New York: Random House.

Churchland, P. M. 1981. "Eliminative Materialism and the Propositional Attitudes." *The Journal of Philosophy* 78: 67–90.

—— 1991. *Neurocomputational Perspective: The Nature of Mind and the Structure of Science.* Cambridge, Mass.: MIT Press.

Cioffi, F. 1969. "Wittgenstein's Freud." *Studies in the Philosophy of Wittgenstein.* London: Routledge and Kegan Paul.

—— 1988. "'Exegetical Myth-Making' in Grünbaum's Indictment of Popper and Exoneration of Freud." *Mind, Psychoanalysis and Science.* Oxford: Blackwell.

Clark, P., and C. Wright. 1988. *Mind, Psychoanalysis and Science.* Oxford: Blackwell.

Collingwood, R. G. 1938. *The Principles of Art.* Oxford: Oxford University Press.

Danto, A. 1991. Letter in *The London Review of Books,* July 25.

Darwin, C. 1896. *The Expression of Emotion in Man and Animals.* New York: Appleton Press.

Davidson, D. 1976. "Hume's Cognitive Theory of Pride." Davidson, *Essays on Action and Events.* Oxford: Oxford University Press (1980).

—— 1980. *Essays on Actions and Events.* Oxford: Oxford University Press.

—— 1982. "Paradoxes of Irrationality." *Philosophical Essays on Freud.* Ed. R. Wollheim and J. Hopkins. New York and Cambridge: Cambridge University Press.

—— 1984a. *Inquiries into Truth and Interpretation.* Oxford: Clarendon Press.

—— 1984b. "First Person Authority." *Dialectica* 38: 101–111.

—— 1985a. "Incoherence and Irrationality." *Dialectica* 39/4: 245–354.

—— 1985b. "Deception and Division." *The Multiple Self.* Ed. J. Elster. New York and Cambridge: Cambridge University Press.

—— 1986. "A Coherence Theory of Truth and Knowledge." *Truth and Interpretation: Perspectives on the Philosophy of Donald Davidson.* Ed. E. LePore. Oxford: Blackwell.

—— 1987. "Knowing One's Own Mind." *Proceedings and Addresses of the American Philosophical Association:* 441–458.

—— 1989a. "The Conditions of Thought." *Le Cahier du College International de Philosophie.* Paris: Éditions Osiris.

—— 1989b. "The Myth of the Subjective." *Relativism: Interpretation and Confrontation.* Ed. M. Krausz. Notre Dame, Ind.: University of Notre Dame Press.

—— 1990. "Meaning, Truth and Evidence." *Perspectives on Quine.* Ed. R. Barrett and R. Gibson. Oxford: Blackwell.

Deleuze, G., and F. Guattari. 1983. *Anti-Oedipus, Capitalism and Schizophrenia.* Minneapolis: University of Minnesota Press.

Dennett, D. 1978. "Current Issues in the Philosophy of Mind." *American Philosophical Quarterly* 15: 249–261.

—— 1987. *The Intentional Stance.* Cambridge, Mass.: MIT Press.

—— 1991. *Consciousness Explained.* Boston: Little, Brown.

De Rivera, J. 1977. *A Structural Theory of the Emotions. Psychological Issues,* Monograph 40. New York: International Universities Press.

Descartes, R. 1984. *Meditations on First Philosophy. Philosophical Writings of Descartes,* vol. 1. Trans. J. Cottingham, R. Stoothoff, and D. Murdoch. New York and Cambridge: Cambridge University Press.

De Sousa, R. 1987. *The Rationality of Emotion.* Cambridge, Mass.: MIT Press.

Dewey, J. 1922. *Human Nature and Conduct.* London: Allen and Unwin.

Donagan, A. 1970. "Review of the Encyclopedia of Philosophy." Ed. P. Edwards. *Philosophical Review* 79: 83–138.

—— 1987. *Choice: The Essential Element in Human Action.* London: Routledge and Kegan Paul.

Donaldson, M. 1978. *Children's Minds.* New York: W. W. Norton.

Dorpat, T. L., and M. L. Miller. 1992. *Clinical Interaction and the Analysis of Meaning.* Hillsdale, N.J.: The Analytic Press.

Eagle, M. 1980. "A Critical Examination of Motivational Explanation in Psychoanalysis." *Psychoanalysis and Contemporary Thought* 3: 329–380.

—— 1987. *Recent Developments in Psychoanalysis.* Cambridge, Mass.: Harvard University Press.

—— 1988. "Psychoanalysis and the Personal." *Mind, Psychoanalysis and Science.* Ed. P. Clark and C. Wright. Oxford: Blackwell.

Elster, J. (Ed.). 1986. *The Multiple Self.* New York and Cambridge: Cambridge University Press.

Emde, R. N. 1980. "Toward a Psychoanalytic Theory of Affect." *The Course of Life: Psychoanalytic Contributions toward Understanding Personality Development.* Vol. 1: *Infancy and Early Childhood:* 63–112. Ed. S. I. Greenspan and G. H. Pollock. Rockville, Md.: NIMN.

—— 1981. "Changing Models of Infancy and the Nature of Early Development: Remodeling the Foundations." *Journal of the American Psychological Association* 29: 179–219.

Emde, R. N., T. J. Gaensbauer, and R. J. Harmon. 1976. *Emotional Expression in Infancy.* New York: International Universities Press.

Evans, G. 1986. Comments on Fodor's "Methodological Solipsism as a Research Strategy." *Collected Papers.* Oxford: Clarendon Press.

Farrell, B. A. 1981. *The Standing of Psychoanalysis.* Oxford: Oxford University Press.

Fenichel, O. 1945. *The Psychoanalytic Theory of Neurosis.* New York: W. W. Norton.

Ferenczi, S. 1933. "Confusion of Tongues between Adults and the Child." *Final Contributions to the Problems and Methods of Psychoanalysis*. New York: Brunner/Mazel, 1980.

—— 1956. "Stages in the Development of the Sense of Reality." *Sex in Psychoanalysis*. Trans. C. Newton. New York: Dover.

Fodor, J. 1985. "Fodor's Guide to Mental Representation." *Mind* 94: 76–100.

—— 1987. *Psychosemantics*. Cambridge, Mass.: MIT Press.

Forrester, J. 1980. *Language and the Origins of Psychoanalysis*. New York: Columbia University Press.

Frank, A. 1969. "The Unrememberable and the Unforgettable." *The Psychoanalytic Study of the Child* 24: 48–78.

Frankfurt, H. 1976. "Identification and Externality." *The Identities of Persons*. Ed. A. Rorty. Berkeley: University of California Press.

Freud, S. 1966–1974. *Standard Edition of the Complete Psychological Works of Sigmund Freud*. Trans. and ed. J. Strachey et al. London: Hogarth Press.

—— 1892. "Sketches for the 'Preliminary Communication' of 1893." *S.E.* 1.

—— 1894. "The Neuro-Psychoses of Defence." *S.E.* 3.

—— 1897. "Draft L. Notes I (May 2, 1987)." *S.E.* 1.

—— 1899. "Screen Memories." *S.E.* 11.

—— 1900. *The Interpretation of Dreams*. *S.E.* 4 and 5.

—— 1905a. *Three Essays on the Theory of Sexuality*. *S.E.* 7.

—— 1905b. *Jokes and Their Relation to the Unconscious*. *S.E.* 8.

—— 1908 [1907]. "Creative Writers and Day-Dreaming." *S.E.* 9.

—— 1909. "Notes upon a Case of Obsessional Neurosis." *S.E.* 10.

—— 1910. "The Antithetical Meaning of Primal Words." *S.E.* 11.

—— 1911. "Formulation on the Two Principles of Mental Functioning." *S.E.* 12.

—— 1912–1913. "Totem and Taboo." *S.E.* 13.

—— 1914a. "Remembering, Repeating, and Working Through." *S.E.* 12.

—— 1914b. "On Narcissism: An Introduction." *S.E.* 14.

—— 1915a. "The Unconscious." *S.E.* 14.

—— 1915b. "Repression." *S.E.* 14.

—— 1915c. "Instincts and Their Vicissitudes." *S.E.* 14.

—— 1916–1917 [1915–1917]. *Introductory Lectures on Psycho-Analysis*. *S.E.* 15.

—— 1917 [1915]. "Mourning and Melancholia." *S.E.* 14.

—— 1918 [1914]. "From the History of an Infantile Neurosis." *S.E.* 17.

—— 1919. "A Child Is Being Beaten." *S.E.* 17.

—— 1920a. "Beyond the Pleasure Principle." *S.E.* 18.

—— 1920b. "The Psychogenesis of a Case of Homosexuality in a Woman." *S.E.* 18.

—— 1923. *The Ego and the Id*. *S.E.* 19.

—— 1925. "Negation." *S.E.* 19.

—— 1926 [1925]. *Inhibitions, Symptoms and Anxiety*. *S.E.* 20.

—— 1930 [1929]. *Civilization and Its Discontents*. *S.E.* 21.

—— 1933 [1932]. "New Introductory Lectures on Psychoanalysis." *S.E.* 22.

—— 1937. "Constructions in Analysis." *S.E.* 23.

—— 1940a [1938]. "An Outline of Psycho-Analysis." *S.E.* 23.

—— 1940b [1938]. "The Splitting of the Ego in the Process of Defence." *S.E.* 23.

—— 1950 [1887–1902]. *Project for a Scientific Psychology. S.E.* 1.

—— 1954. *The Origins of Psychoanalysis.* Ed. M. Bonaparte, A. Freud, and E. Kris. London: Imago.

Gedo, J. 1979. *Beyond Interpretation.* New York: International Universities Press.

—— 1981. *Advances in Clinical Psychoanalysis.* New York: International Universities Press.

—— 1984. *Conceptual Essays in Psychoanalysis, Essays in History and Method.* Hillsdale, N.J.: The Analytic Press.

Gill, M. M. 1967. "Primary Process." *Motives and Thought: Psychoanalytic Essays in Memory of David Rapaport.* Ed. R. R. Holt. *Psychological Issues,* Monograph 18/19. New York: International Universities Press.

Gill, M. M., and P. S. Holzman. 1976. *Psychology versus Metapsychology: Psychoanalytic Essays in Memory of George S. Klein. Psychological Issues,* Monograph 36. New York: International Universities Press.

Gilligan, C. 1982. *In a Different Voice.* Cambridge, Mass.: Harvard University Press.

—— 1984. "The Conquistador and the Dark Continent: Reflections on the Psychology of Love." *Proceedings of the American Academy of Arts and Sciences* 113: 75–95.

Ginzburg, C. 1980. *The Cheese and the Worms.* Baltimore: Johns Hopkins Press.

Glover, E. 1931. "The Therapeutic Effect of Inexact Interpretation." *International Journal of Psychoanalysis* 12: 397–411.

Glymour, C. 1991. "Freud's Androids." *The Cambridge Companion to Freud.* Ed. J. Neu. New York and Cambridge: Cambridge University Press.

Goldberg, A. 1976. "A Discussion of the Paper by C. Hanly and J. Masson, 'A Critical Examination of the New Narcissism.'" *International Journal of Psychoanalysis* 57: 67–70.

Gordon, R. M. 1987. *The Structure of Emotions.* New York and Cambridge: Cambridge University Press.

Greenberg, J. R., and S. A. Mitchell. 1983. *Object Relations in Psychoanalytic Theory.* Cambridge, Mass.: Harvard University Press.

Greenspan, P. 1988. *Emotions and Reasons.* New York: Routledge and Kegan Paul.

Grice, P. 1957. "Meaning." *The Philosophical Review* 66 (3): 377–388.

Grünbaum, A. 1990. "Meaning Connections and Causal Connections in the Human Sciences: The Poverty of Hermeneutic Philosophy." *Journal of the American Psychoanalytical Association* 38: 559–579.

—— 1984. *The Foundations of Psychoanalysis.* Berkeley: University of California Press.

Guntrip, H. 1971. *Psychoanalytic Theory, Therapy, and the Self.* New York: Basic Books.

Habermas, J. 1978. *Knowledge and Human Interests.* London: Heinemann.

Hacking, I. 1975. *Why Does Language Matter to Philosophy?* New York and Cambridge: Cambridge University Press.

Hamilton, V. 1982. *Narcissus and Oedipus, The Children of Psychoanalysis.* London: Routledge and Kegan Paul.

Hampshire, S. 1959. *Thought and Action.* London: Chatto and Windus.

——— 1982. "Disposition and Memory." R. Wollheim and J. Hopkins, *Philosophical Essays on Freud.* New York and Cambridge: Cambridge University Press.

Hanly, C. 1990. "The Concept of Truth in Psychoanalysis." *International Journal of Psychoanalysis* 71: 375–383.

Harlow, H. F., and M. K. Harlow. 1965. "Social Deprivation in Monkeys." *Scientific American* 207 (5): 136.

Hartmann, H. 1939. *Ego Psychology and the Problem of Adaptation.* New York: International Universities Press.

Heidegger, M. 1968. *What Is Called Thinking?* Trans. and Intro. by J. G. Gray. New York: Harper and Row.

Holt, R. R. 1965. "A Review of Some of Freud's Biological Assumptions and Their Influence on His Theories." *Psychoanalysis and Current Biological Thought.* Ed. N. Greenfield and W. Lewis. Madison: University of Wisconsin Press.

——— 1967. "The Development of Primary Process: A Structural View." *Motives and Thought: Psychoanalytic Essays in Honor of David Rapaport. Psychological Issues,* Monograph 18/19. New York: International Universities Press.

——— 1976. "Drive or Wish? A Reconsideration of the Psychoanalytic Theory of Motivation." *Psychology versus Metapsychology. Psychoanalytic Essays in Memory of George S. Klein. Psychological Issues,* Monograph 36. Ed. M. M. Gill and P. S. Holzman. New York: International Universities Press.

——— 1989. *Freud Reappraised.* New York: The Guilford Press.

Hopkins, J. 1982. Introduction to *Philosophical Essays on Freud.* Ed. R. Wollheim and J. Hopkins. New York and Cambridge: Cambridge University Press.

——— 1988a. "Epistemology and Depth Psychology: Critical Notes on the Foundations of Psychoanalysis." *Mind, Psychoanalysis and Science.* Ed. P. Clark and C. Wright. Oxford: Blackwell.

——— 1988b. "'Exegetical Myth-Making' in Grünbaum's Indictment of Popper and Exoneration of Freud." *Mind, Psychoanalysis and Science.* Oxford: Blackwell.

Hopkins, J., and A. Savile. 1992. *Mind, Psychoanalysis and Art: Essays for Richard Wollheim.* Oxford: Blackwell.

Hume, D. 1951. *A Treatise of Human Nature.* Oxford: The Clarendon Press.

Hurley, S. L. 1985. "Objectivity and Disagreement." *Morality and Objectivity.* Ed. T. Honderich. London: Routledge and Kegan Paul.

Isaacs, S. 1952. "The Nature and Function of Phantasy." *Developments in Psychoanalysis.* Ed. J. Riviere. London: Hogarth Press.

Izard, C. E. 1971. *The Face of Emotion.* New York: Meredith and Appleton-Century Crofts.

Jacobson, E. 1953. "The Affects and Their Pleasure-Unpleasure Qualities in Relation to the Psychic Discharge Process." *Drives, Affects, Behavior.* Ed. R. Lowenstein. New York: International Universities Press.

James, W. 1884. "What Is an Emotion?" *Mind* 19: 188–204.

——— 1890. *The Principles of Psychology,* vol. 1. New York: Henry Holt.

Johnston, M. 1988. "Self-Deception and the Nature of the Mind." *Perspectives on Self-Deception.* Ed. A. Rorty. Berkeley: University of California Press.

Jones, E. 1953, 1955, 1977. *The Life and Work of Sigmund Freud,* vols. 1, 2, and 3. London: Hogarth Press.

Kagan, J. 1972. "Do Infants Think?" *Scientific American* 226: 74–82.

Kant, I. 1965. *The Critique of Pure Reason.* Trans. Norman Kemp Smith. New York: St. Martin's Press.

Kenny, A. J. P. 1963. *Action, Emotion and Will.* London: Routledge and Kegan Paul.

Kernberg, O. 1982. "Self, Ego, Affects, and Drive." *Journal of the American Psychoanalytic Association* 30: 893–917.

——— 1983. *Internal World and External Reality: Object Relations Theory Applied.* New York: Jason Aronson.

Kihlstrom, J. F. 1987. "The Cognitive Unconscious." *Science* 237: 1445–1451.

Klein, G. S. 1976. "Two Theories or One?" *Psychoanalytic Theory: An Exploration of Essentials.* New York: International Universities Press.

Klein, M. 1984. *Envy and Gratitude and Other Works, 1946–1963.* London: The Hogarth Press.

Kohut, H. 1959. "Introspection, Empathy, and Psychoanalysis." *Journal of the American Psychoanalytic Association* 92: 459–483.

Kripke, S. 1972. "Naming and Necessity." *Semantics of Natural Language.* Ed. D. Davidson and G. Harman. Dordrecht: Reidel.

Lacan, J. 1977. *Écrits.* Trans. A. Sheridan. New York: W. W. Norton.

——— 1981. "The Transference and the Drive." *Four Fundamental Concepts of Psycho-analysis.* Ed. J. A. Miller. Trans. A. Sheridan. New York: W. W. Norton.

Laing, R. D., and A. Esterson. 1964. *Sanity, Madness and the Family: Families of Schizophrenics.* London: Tavistock.

——— 1969. *The Divided Self.* London: Tavistock.

Laplanche, J., and B. Pontalis. 1973. *The Language of Psycho-Analysis.* Trans. D. Nicholson-Smith. New York: W. W. Norton.

——— 1976. *Life and Death in Psychoanalysis.* Ed. and Trans. J. Mehlman. Baltimore: Johns Hopkins.

Lear, J. 1990. *Love and Its Place in Nature.* New York: Farrar, Straus and Giroux.

LePore, E. (Ed.). 1986. *Truth and Interpretation: Perspectives on the Philosophy of Donald Davidson.* Oxford: Blackwell.

LePore, E., and B. McLaughlin (Eds.). 1985. *Actions and Events: Perspectives on the Philosophy of Donald Davidson.* Oxford: Blackwell.

LePore, E., and R. van Gulik. 1990. *John Searle and His Critics.* Oxford: Blackwell.

Lester, E. 1982. "Panel: New Directions in Affect Theory." *Journal of the American Psychoanalytical Association* 30: 197–212.

Levin, F. M. 1991. *Mapping the Mind.* Hillsdale, N.J.: The Analytic Press.

Lewin, B. 1950. *The Psychoanalysis of Elation.* New York: Norton.

Lewis, C. I. 1946. *An Analysis of Knowledge and Valuation.* La Salle, Ill.: Open Court.

Lewis, D. 1983. *Philosophical Papers,* vol 1. New York: Oxford University Press.

Lichtenberg, J. D. 1983. *Psychoanalysis and Infant Research*. Hillsdale, N.J.: The Analytic Press.

Lock, G. 1987. "Analytic Philosophy, Psycho-Analytic Theory and Formalism." *Revue de Synthèse* 4/20: 157–176.

Locke, A. (Ed.). 1978. *Action, Gesture and Symbol: The Emergence of Language*. London: Academic Press.

Locke, J. 1961. *An Essay Concerning Human Understanding*. London: J. W. Yolton.

Lovibond, S. 1983. *Realism and Imagination in Ethics*. Minneapolis: University of Minnesota Press.

Lussier, A. 1991. "The Search for Common Ground: A Critique." *International Journal of Psychoanalysis* 72: 57–62.

MacIntyre, A. 1958. *The Unconscious: A Conceptual Analysis*. London: Routledge and Kegan Paul.

MacLean, P. D. 1970. "The Triune Brain, Emotion, and Scientific Bias." *The Neurosciences Second Study Program*. Ed. F. O. Schmitt. New York: Rockefeller University Press.

Mahler, M., F. Pine, and A. Bergman. 1975. *The Psychological Birth of the Human Infant*. New York: Basic Books.

Malcolm, N. 1959. *Dreaming*. New York: Humanities Press.

——— 1984. "The Subjective Character of Experience." *Consciousness and Causality*. Ed. D. M. Armstrong and N. Malcolm. Oxford: Blackwell.

Marks, J. 1982. "A Theory of Emotion." *Philosophical Studies*. Oxford: Oxford University Press.

McDowell, J. 1983. "Aesthetic Value, Objectivity, and the Fabric of the World." *Pleasure, Preference and Value*. Ed. E. Schaper. New York and Cambridge: Cambridge University Press.

——— 1985. "Values and Secondary Qualities." *Morality and Objectivity*. Ed. T. Honderich. London: Routledge and Kegan Paul.

——— 1989. "Scheme-Content Dualism, Experience, and Subjectivity" (unpublished).

McKinnon, J. 1979. "Two Semantic Forms: Neuropsychological and Psychoanalytic Descriptions." *Psychoanalysis and Continental Thought* 2: 25–76.

Meehl, P. E. 1983. "Subjectivity in Psychoanalytic Inference: The Nagging Persistence of Wilhelm Fliess's Achensee Question." *Minnesota Studies in the Philosophy of Science*. Vol. 10: *Testing Scientific Theories*: 349–411. Minneapolis: University of Minnesota Press.

Melden, A. I. 1961. *Free Action*. London: Routledge and Kegan Paul.

Mele, A. R. 1987a. "Recent Work on Self-Deception." *American Philosophical Quarterly* 24: 1–17.

——— 1987b. *Irrationality: An Essay on Akrasia, Self-Deception and Self-Control*. Oxford: Oxford University Press.

Michaels, R. 1985. "Introduction to Panel: Perspectives on the Nature of Psychic Reality." *Journal of the American Psychoanalytic Association* 33: 516–521.

Millikan, R. G. 1984. *Language, Thought, and Other Biological Categories: New Foundations for Realism*. Cambridge, Mass.: MIT Press.

Mischel, T. 1965. "Reply to Alexander." *Mind* (January 1965): 71–78.

Monk, R. 1990. *Ludwig Wittgenstein: The Duty of Genius.* New York: The Free Press, Macmillan.

Moore, Michael. 1980. "The Nature of Psychoanalytic Explanation." *Psychoanalysis and Contemporary Thought* 3 (4): 459–543.

——— 1988. "Mind, Brain and Unconscious." *Mind, Psychoanalysis and Science.* Ed. P. Clark and C. Wright. Oxford: Blackwell.

Mullane, H. 1971. "Psychoanalytic Explanation and Rationality." *The Journal of Philosophy* 68: 413–426.

——— 1983. "Defense, Dreams and Rationality." *Synthese* 57: 187–204.

Nagel, T. 1965. "Physicalism." *Philosophical Review* 74: 339–356.

——— 1970. *The Possibility of Altruism.* Oxford: Oxford University Press.

——— 1979. "What Is It Like to Be a Bat?" *Mortal Questions.* New York and Cambridge: Cambridge University Press.

——— 1986. *The View from Nowhere.* Oxford: Oxford University Press.

Neu, J. 1976. "Thought, Theory, and Therapy." *Psychoanalysis and Continental Science* 3: 103–144.

——— 1977. *Emotion, Thought and Therapy.* London: Routledge and Kegan Paul.

Nietzsche, F. 1956. "The Genealogy of Morals." *The Birth of Tragedy and the Genealogy of Morals.* Trans. F. Goffing. New York: Doubleday.

Nisbett, R. D., and T. D. Wilson. 1977. "Telling More than We Can Know: Verbal Reports on Mental Processes." *Psychological Review* 84: 231–259.

O'Shaughnessy, B. 1980. *The Will,* vols. 1 and 2. New York and Cambridge: Cambridge University Press.

Palazzoli, M. S. L. Boscolo, G. Cecchin, and G. Prata. 1978. *Paradox and Counterparadox.* Trans. E. V. Burt. New York: Jason Aronson.

Pears, D. 1984. *Motivated Irrationality.* Oxford: Oxford University Press.

Peters, R. S. 1958. *The Concept of Motivation.* London: Routledge and Kegan Paul.

Piaget, J. 1952. *The Origins of Intelligence in Children.* New York: International Universities Press.

——— 1958. *The Child's Construction of Reality.* London: Routledge and Kegan Paul.

——— 1962. *Play, Dreams, and Imitation in Childhood.* New York: Norton.

Pitcher, G. 1965. "Emotions." *Mind* 74 (July 1965): 326–346.

Plato. 1952. *The Phaedo.* Trans. R. Hackworth. New York: Library of Liberal Arts.

Polanyi, M. 1958. *Personal Knowledge.* Chicago: University of Chicago Press.

Price, H. H. 1973. *Perception.* London: Methuen.

Putnam, H. 1975. *Mind, Language and Reality. Philosophical Papers, 2.* New York and Cambridge: Cambridge University Press.

——— 1981. *Reason, Truth and History.* New York and Cambridge: Cambridge University Press.

——— 1988. *Representation and Reality.* Cambridge, Mass.: MIT Press.

Quine, W. V. O. 1964. *Word and Object.* Cambridge, Mass.: MIT Press.

——— 1969. *Ontological Relativity and Other Essays.* Cambridge, Mass.: Harvard University Press.

——— 1970. "On the Reasons for Indeterminacy of Translation." *The Journal of Philosophy* 67: 178–183.

—— 1974. *Roots of Reference.* La Salle, Ill.: Open Court.

—— 1975. "The Nature of Knowledge." *Mind and Language.* Ed. S. Gutenplan. Oxford: Clarendon Press.

—— 1980. *From a Logical Point of View,* 2nd ed. rev. Cambridge, Mass.: Harvard University Press.

Ramberg, B. T. 1989. *Donald Davidson's Philosophy of Language: An Introduction.* Oxford: Blackwell.

Rangell, L. 1988. "The Future of Psychoanalysis: The Scientific Crossroads." *Psychoanalytic Quarterly* 57: 313–340.

Rapaport, D. 1950. "On the Psychoanalytic Theory of Thinking." *International Journal of Psychoanalysis* 31: 161–170.

—— 1951. *Organization and Pathology of Thought: Selected Sources.* New York: Columbia University Press.

—— 1959. "The Structure of Psychoanalytic Theory: A Systematizing Attempt." *Psychological Issues.* Monograph No. 6. New York: International Universities Press, 1960.

Ricoeur, P. 1970. *Freud and Philosophy.* New Haven: Yale University Press.

—— 1981. *Hermeneutics and the Human Sciences.* Trans. J. B. Thompson. New York and Cambridge: Cambridge University Press.

Rorty, A. O. 1972. "Belief and Self-Deception." *Inquiry* 15: 387–410.

—— 1980. *Explaining Emotion.* Berkeley: University of California Press.

Rorty, A. O., and B. P. McLaughlin (Eds.). 1988. *Perspectives on Self-Deception.* Berkeley: University of California Press.

Rorty, R. 1979. *Philosophy and the Mirror of Nature.* Princeton, N.J.: Princeton University Press.

—— 1985. "Solidarity or Objectivity." *Post-analytic Philosophy.* Ed. J. Rajchman and C. West. New York: Columbia University Press.

—— 1991a. *Objectivity, Relativism and Truth. Philosophical Papers,* vol. I. New York and Cambridge: Cambridge University Press.

—— 1991b. *Essays on Heidegger and Others. Philosophical Papers,* vol. II. New York and Cambridge: Cambridge University Press.

Rovane, C. 1986. "The Metaphysics of Interpretation." *Essays on Truth and Interpretation.* Ed. E. Lepore. Oxford: Blackwell.

Rubinstein, B. 1967. "Explanation and Mere Description: A Metascientific Examination of Certain Aspects of the Psychoanalytic Theory of Motivation." *Motives and Thought: Psychoanalytic Essays in Honor of David Rapaport. Psychological Issues,* Monograph 18/19. Ed. R. R. Holt. New York: International Universities Press.

—— 1976. "On the Possibility of a Strictly Clinical Psychoanalytic Theory: An Essay in the Philosophy of Psychoanalysis." *Psychology versus Metapsychology: Psychoanalytic Essays in Memory of George S. Klein. Psychological Issues,* Monograph 36. Ed. M. Gill and P. Holtzman. New York: International Universities Press.

—— 1981. "Address to the New York Psychoanalytic Society," quoted in E. Ticho (1982), "The Alternate Schools and the Self." *Journal of the American Psychoanalytic Association* 3: 849–863.

Rubovits-Seitz, P. 1988. "Kohut's Method of Interpretation: A Critique." *Journal of the American Psychoanalytic Association* 36: 933–959.

Russell, B. 1940. *An Inquiry into Meaning and Truth.* London: Allen and Unwin.

Sander, L. 1975. "Infant and Caretaking Environment: Investigation and Conceptualization of Adaptive Behaviors in a Series of Increasing Complexity." *Explorations in Child Psychiatry.* Ed. E. J. Anthony. New York: Plenum.

Sandler, J. 1983. "Reflections on Some Relations between Psychoanalytic Concepts and Psychoanalytic Practice." *The International Journal of Psychoanalysis* 64: 35–45.

——— 1990. "On Internal Object Relations." *Journal of the American Psychoanalytic Association* 38: 859–880.

Sandler, J., and B. Rosenblatt. 1965. "The Concept of the Representational World." *The Psychoanalytic Study of the Child,* 17. New York: International Universities Press.

Sandler, J., and A.-M. Sandler. 1983. "The 'Second Censorship', the Three Box Model and Some Technical Implications." *The International Journal of Psychoanalysis* 64: 413–425.

——— 1984. "The Past Unconscious, the Present Unconscious, and Interpretation of the Transference." *Psychoanalytic Inquiry* 4: 367–399.

Sarraute, N. 1957. *Tropisms.* Trans. M. Jolas. New York: Braziller.

Sartre, J. P. 1956. *Being and Nothingness.* Trans. H. E. Barnes. New York: Philosophical Library.

Sass, L. A. 1987. "Introspection, Schizophrenia, and the Fragmentation of the Self." *Representations* 19: 1–34.

Scaife, M., and J. S. Brune. 1975. "The Capacity for Joint Visual Alteration in the Infant." *Nature* 253: 265–266.

Schachter, S., and J. E. Singer. 1962. "Cognitive, Social and Physiobiological Determinants of Emotional States." *Psychological Review* 69: 379–399.

Schafer, R. 1976. *A New Language for Psychoanalysis.* New Haven: Yale University Press.

——— 1983. *The Analytic Stance.* New York: Basic Books.

——— 1990. "The Search for Common Ground." *International Journal of Psychoanalysis* 71: 49–52.

Searle, J. R. 1983. *Intentionality.* New York and Cambridge: Cambridge University Press.

Sellars, W. 1956. "Empiricism and the Philosophy of Mind." *Minnesota Studies in the Philosophy of Science,* 1. Ed. H. Feigl and M. Scriven. Minneapolis: University of Minnesota Press.

Sharpe, R. 1988. "Mirrors, Lamps, Organisms and Texts." *Mind, Psychoanalysis and Science.* Ed. P. Clark and C. Wright. Oxford: Blackwell.

Sherwood, M. 1969. *The Logic of Explanation in Psychoanalysis.* New York: Academic Press.

Shoemaker, S. 1963. *Self-Knowledge and Self-Identity.* Ithaca, N.Y.: Cornell University Press.

——— 1968. "Self-Identity, Self-Reference, and Self-Awareness." *The Journal of Philosophy* 65: 339–356.

Snow, C., and C. Ferguson. 1977. *Talking to Children: Language Input and Acquisition.* New York and Cambridge: Cambridge University Press.

Solomon, R. C. 1976. *The Passions: The Myth and Nature of Human Emotions.* New York: Doubleday.

Southwood, H. M. 1988. "*The Minds of Young Infants.* A Book Review." *Adelaide Review* (May).

Spence, D. P. 1982. *Narrative Truth and Historical Truth.* New York: W. W. Norton.

Stern, D. 1977. *The First Relationship: Infant and Mother.* Cambridge, Mass.: Harvard University Press.

———— 1984. *The Interpersonal World of the Infant: A View from Psychoanalysis and Developmental Psychology.* New York: Basic Books.

Stich, S. 1983. *From Folk Psychology to Cognitive Science: The Case against Belief.* Cambridge, Mass.: MIT Press.

Stolorow, R. D., B. Branchaft, and G. E. Atwood. 1987. *Psychoanalytic Treatment: An Intersubjective Approach.* Hillsdale, N.J.: The Analytic Press.

Stoutland, F. 1970. "The Logical Connection Argument." *American Philosophical Quarterly: Monograph Series,* No. 4. Oxford: Blackwell.

Stroud, B. 1989. "Review of *The Coherence Theory of Truth: Realism, Antirealism, Idealism,* by R. C. S. Walker." *Times Literary Supplement,* July 7.

———— 1990. "The Background of Thought." *John Searle and His Critics.* Ed. E. LePore and R. Van Gulik. Oxford: Blackwell.

Sulloway, F. 1979. *Freud, Biologist of the Mind.* New York: Basic Books.

Taylor, G. 1985. *Pride, Shame and Guilt.* Oxford: Clarendon Press.

Thalberg, I. 1964. "Emotion and Thought." *Philosophy of Mind.* Ed. S. Hampshire. New York: Harper and Row.

Tolstoy, L. 1981 [1886]. *The Death of Ivan Ilyich.* Trans. L. Solotaroff. New York: Bantam Books.

Tomkins, S. S. 1981. "The Quest for Primary Motives: Biography and Autobiography of an Idea." *Journal of Personality and Social Psychology* 41/2: 306–329.

Trevarthen, C. 1978. "Secondary Intersubjectivity: Confidence, Confiding and Acts of Meaning in the First Year." *Action, Gesture and Symbol: The Emergence of Language.* Ed. A. Lock. New York: Academic Press.

———— 1987a. "Sharing Makes Sense: Intersubjectivity and the Making of an Infant's Meaning." *Language Topics: Essays in Honor of Michael Halliday.* Philadelphia: John Benjamins.

———— 1987b. "Infants Trying to Talk: How a Child Invites Communication from the Human World." *Plenary Lecture, Fourth International Congress for the Study of Child Language.* Lund, Sweden.

Trevarthen, C., and K. Logotheti. 1987. "First Symbols and the Nature of Human Knowledge." *Cahiers des Archives Piaget,* Geneva.

Viderman, S. 1979. "The Analytic Space: Meanings and Problems." *Psychoanalytic Quarterly* 48: 257–291.

von Wright, G. E. 1971. *Explanation and Understanding.* Ithaca, N.Y.: Cornell University Press.

Vygotsky, L. S. 1978. *Mind in Society: The Development of Higher Psychological Processes.* Cambridge, Mass.: Harvard University Press.

Wallace, E. 1989. "Pitfalls of a One-Sided Image of Science: Adolf Grünbaum's Foundations of Psychoanalysis." *Journal of the American Psychoanalytic Association* 37: 493–529.

Wallerstein, R. 1964. "The Role of Prediction in Theory Building in Psychoanalysis." *Journal of the American Psychoanalytic Association* 12: 675–691.

———— 1985. "Psychoanalysis as a Science: A Response to the New Challenges." Freud Anniversary Lecture, New York Psychoanalytic Institute.

———— 1988. "One Psychoanalysis or Many?" *International Journal of Psychoanalysis* 69: 5–21.

———— 1990. "The Search for Common Ground." *International Journal of Psychoanalysis* 71: 49–52.

Walton, K. L. 1990. *Mimesis as Make-Believe.* Cambridge, Mass.: Harvard University Press.

Weiss, J. H. Sampson, and the Mount Zion Psychotherapy Research Group. 1986. *The Psychoanalytic Process: Theory, Clinical Observation, and Empirical Research.* New York: Guilford Press.

Werner, H. 1973. *Comparative Psychology of Mental Development.* New York: International Universities Press.

Whorf, B. L. 1956. "The Punctual and Segmental Aspects of Verbs in Hopi." *Language, Thought and Reality: Selected Writings of Benjamin Lee Whorf.* Ed. J. B. Carroll. Cambridge, Mass.: The Technology Press of Massachusetts Institute of Technology.

Wiggins, D. 1987. "Truth, Invention and the Meaning of Life." *Needs, Values, Truth.* Oxford: Oxford University Press.

Wilkes, K. 1988. *Real People.* Oxford: Clarendon Press.

Williams, B. 1959. "Pleasure and Belief." *Philosophy of Mind.* Ed. S. Hampshire. New York: Harper and Row, 1966.

———— 1972. *Morality: An Introduction to Ethics.* New York: Harper and Row.

———— 1973a. "Deciding to Believe." *Problems of the Self.* New York and Cambridge: Cambridge University Press.

———— 1973b. "Imagination and the Self." *Problems of the Self.* New York and Cambridge: Cambridge University Press.

Winnicott, D. W. 1971. *Playing and Reality.* New York: Basic Books.

Wisdom, J. 1953. *Philosophy and Psycho-Analysis.* Berkeley: University of California Press.

———— 1962. "Comparison and Development of the Psycho-Analytical Theories of Melancholia." *International Journal of Psychoanalysis* 43: 113–132.

Wittgenstein, L. 1953. *Philosophical Investigations.* Ed. G. E. M. Anscombe. Oxford: Blackwell.

———— 1958. *The Blue and Brown Books.* New York: Harper and Brothers.

———— 1967. *Lectures and Conversations.* Berkeley: University of California Press.

———— 1972. *On Certainty.* New York: Harper and Row.

Wollheim, R. 1971. "Sigmund Freud." *Modern Masters.* Ed. F. Kermode. New York: Viking.

———— 1979. "The Cabinet of Dr. Caligari." *The New York Review of Books,* January 25.

———— 1984. *The Thread of Life.* Cambridge, Mass.: Harvard University Press.

———— 1987. *Painting as an Art.* Princeton, N.J.: Princeton University Press.

———— 1993. "Desire, Belief, and Professor Grünbaum's Freud." *The Mind and Its Depths.* Cambridge, Mass.: Harvard University Press.

Wollheim, R., and J. Hopkins. 1982. Introduction to *Philosophical Essays on Freud.* Ed. R. Wollheim and J. Hopkins. Cambridge: Cambridge University Press.

Zahn-Waxler, C., and M. Radke-Yarrow. 1982. "The Development of Altruism: Alternative Research Strategies." *The Development of Prosocial Behavior.* Ed. N. Eisenberg. New York: Academic Press.

Zazzo, R. 1975. "La genèse de la conscience de soi (La reconnaissance du soi dans l'image du miroir)." *Psychologie de la Connaissance de Soi: Symposium de l'association de psychologie scientifique de la langue française.* R. Angelergues, D. Anzieu, E. E. Boesche, Y. Bres, J. B. Pontalis, and R. Zazzo. Paris: Presses Universitaires de France.

Index

Abel, K., 162–163
Action: beliefs and desires in, 9, 20, 58–60, 62–64; descriptions of, 58–59, 62, 64–65, 72, 77–79, 91–92; causes of, 61–62; rationalization of, 63–64; thoughts as, 177. *See also* Reason-explanation
Affects, 138, 144, 150–151, 153–154; in animals, 150–151. *See also* Emotions
Agency, 62, 76–77. *See also* Freedom; Responsibility
Aggression, 75, 76, 151, 208, 215–219, 225
Aldrich, V., 129
Anxiety, 83, 84, 93, 109, 114, 133, 139, 140, 151, 156, 180–185, 187–191, 202–203; signal anxiety, 183
Archard, D., 163
Aristotle, 58, 166
Augustine, Saint, 22, 24, 208n1
Austin, J., 25, 121n1
Averill, J. R., 152

Background, pre-intentional, 131–132
Basch, M. F., 128, 186
Baxendall, M., 92
Belief: and meaning, 9–10, 39–40; and desires in explaining action, 20, 58–66, 69–70; as caused, 29–31, 87–88, 198; and truth, 38–40, 198; 'hard' sense of, 38, 40; as abstraction, 155; fluidity of, 172–173.

See also Mental States; Practical reasoning; Propositional attitudes
Benassy, M., 165, 167
Benveniste, E., 163
Bilgrami, A., 20, 39
Bouveresse, J., 60
Bowlby, J., 76, 122
Brenner, C., 75, 76
Brentano, F., 66, 78
Bruner, J., 123–125

Cartesianism, 14–16, 18–19, 21, 40–41, 43, 60, 73, 102, 111, 152, 233
Causal explanations, 57–59; of action, 61–62; of emotions, 143–144
Causal relations and causal laws, 59, 61, 66–74, 71–73
Cavell, S., 130
Charity, principle of, 32, 68, 147, 149, 165
Chasseguet-Smirgel, J., 211n5
Chisholm, R., 67
Chomsky, N., 121
Cioffi, F., 60
Concept formation: in children, 37–38, 123–124; in adults, 102, 172. *See also* Infants, language acquisition
Conceptual schemes, relativity of knowledge to, 33–34, 88–89. *See also* Scheme-content

Condensation, 161, 162, 167, 169, 171, 174, 190
Conscience, 207, 208, 212, 214–216, 218, 225. *See also* Moral sense

Darwin, C., 148
Davidson, D.: theory of meaning, 27–41; and Quine, 27–30; radical interpretation, 27–28, 36; on conceptual relativism, 33–34; triangulation, 36–41; on irrationality, 196–205; on divided mind, 196–197
Denial, 16, 177, 197, 225, 227, 234. *See also* Phantasy; Self, self-deception
Dennett, D., 71
Derrida, J., 129
Descartes, R., 11–18, 20, 21, 24, 30, 40–41, 71, 97, 116, 226, 232–234, 237. *See also* Cartesianism; Internalism; Skepticism
de Sousa, R., 50, 51
Determinism, 59, 62, 82, 172
Dewey, J., 2, 26, 27, 204
Displacement, 139, 161, 162, 171, 174, 181, 182, 190
Dream-work, 163. *See also* Condensation; Displacement; Primary process
Drives, 44–45, 55–56, 75–76. *See also* Id; Instincts

Eagle, M., 66
Ego, 4, 47, 49, 50, 75, 120, 137, 139, 157, 174–175, 180–181, 187–188, 194–195, 204, 210–219, 222, 223, 225; splitting of, 187–188, 202–203, 208, 214, 219–220. *See also* Self
Emde, R. N., 122
Emotions: rationality (cognitive nature) of, 138–147, 149–150, 153–154, 157–158; unconscious, 139–140, 149–151; causes of, 143–148; compared to actions, 143, 145–146; Intentionality of, 141–142, 144, 148, 150, 154; objects of, 144; as propositional attitudes, 146, 153; irrationality of, 147; as feeling, 147–148, 155–158; innatist view, 149–152; constructivist view, 152; paradigm scenarios in, 154; adaptation to reality, 157–158. *See also* Affects; Infants
Empathy, 34, 111–112
Externalism, 13, 17, 29–30, 39, 46, 49. *See also* Interpreter's perspective

Ferenczi, S., 133, 134, 223
First-person authority, 10, 39n24
First-Person View, 11–20. *See also* Cartesianism; Descartes, R.; Internalism; Subjectivity
Fliess, W., 89
Fodor, J., 12, 17n6
Folk psychology, 57, 72, 185
Frankfurt, H., 93
Freedom, 62, 91, 95–96; Freud on, 82
Freud, S.: interpersonal view of the mental in, 2, 148; Cartesianism in, 14, 18–19; externalism in, 21, 46, 221–226; internalism in, 46–47; word-presentation vs. thing (object)-presentation, 46–47; representation, instinctual, 48–49; reductivism in, 46, 48–49, 75–76, 82, 213; on judgment, 49–50; primal scene, 83–84; therapeutic goals of, 94; folk-psychological explanations in, 177–179. *See also* Ego; Id; Instincts; Oedipal complex; Primary process; Primary repression; Structural theory; Super-ego.
CASES
Little Hans, 72, 112, 168–171, 175, 182–185, 249, 250
Rat Man, 52–53, 58, 69, 77, 88, 99, 100, 137, 139–141, 143, 155, 177, 190, 193, 196, 201–204
"table-cloth lady," 178–180, 189
Wolf Man, 83, 84, 101–102, 178, 183, 190
WORKS
"Beyond the Pleasure Principle," 44n3, 183n3, 219, 223
"A Child Is Being Beaten," 190–191
Civilization and Its Discontents, 115, 120, 208, 214, 217–219, 222–223, 224
"Constructions in Analysis," 84
The Ego and the Id, 47, 175, 194, 214, 225
Inhibitions, Symptoms and Anxiety, 180–182
"Instincts and Their Vicissitudes," 49, 210
The Interpretation of Dreams, 44, 162, 163, 166
Introductory Lectures on Psycho-Analysis, 178–180
Jokes and Their Relation to the Unconscious, 185
"Mourning and Melancholia," 214, 217, 224–225

"On Narcissism," 210
"Negation," 49–50
"An Outline of Psycho-Analysis," 48
Project for a Scientific Psychology, 69, 138, 165–166
"The Psychogenesis of a Case of Homosexuality in a Woman," 68
"Remembering, Repeating, and Working Through," 98–99, 188–189
"Repression," 183
"The Splitting of the Ego in the Process of Defence," 188
Three Essays on the Theory of Sexuality, 209–210, 231
Totem and Taboo, 218
"The Unconscious," 18–19, 140, 174
Functional explanations, 17n6, 58
Functionalism, 3, 17–18

Gedo, J., 75, 101
Genetic continuity, principle of, 54
Gilligan, C., 230
Ginzburg, C., 88, 89, 92
Glymour, C., 18
Gordon, R. M., 146, 151
Gratitude, 142, 227–229, 231–232
Grice, P., 122
Grünbaum, A., 57, 79–82
Guilt, 207–208, 214–215, 218

Habermas, J., 79
Hacking, I., 20
Hallucinatory wish-fulfillment, 45–46, 133, 166, 183, 203–204, 221–223. *See also* Phantasy; Wishing
Hanly, C., 87, 89, 95
Harlow, H. F., 76
Harlow, M. K., 76
Heidegger, M., 41, 103, 231
Hermeneutics, 1, 32, 61, 79, 95
Hobbes, T., 20, 221
Holism, 26, 28, 30–32, 35, 69, 73, 193, 197, 200, 201
Holt, R., 46, 74, 76
Homuncularism, 199–200
Hopkins, J., 81, 189
Hume, D., 11, 43, 50, 135, 229
Hysteria, 138, 187

Id, 4, 47, 48n9, 137, 157, 175, 181, 194, 195, 204, 214, 225. *See also* Drives; Instincts

Ideas (thought): as mental 'objects', 13–14, 17–18, 47; as preceding language, 20–21, 23–25, 47–49, 110–111, 115–116. *See also* Primary Process; Subjectivity
Identification, 133–135, 217–219, 225. *See also* Empathy
Imagination, 1, 34, 98, 110, 186, 188, 203, 204, 213, 214, 227, 233. *See also* Phantasy
Infants: mother-infant interactions, 37n22, 122–129; built-in responses, 37n22, 51, 122–123, 153; 'mental' life of, 51–56, 131–132, 155; phantasies in, 53–55; sense of self in, 107–113, 132; mental images in, 120, 123; non-verbal communications with, 122–129, 132; memory in, 123; language acquisition of, 124–131; egocentricity of, 129–130; emotions in, 137, 138, 147, 155. *See also* Bruner, J.; Lichtenberg, J. D.; Piaget, J.; Trevarthen, C.; Winnicott, D. W.
Inner world, 19, 42, 49. *See also* Ideas, as mental 'objects'; Representational world; Subjectivity
Instincts, 18, 44, 46, 48–50, 54, 55–56, 75, 76, 140, 157, 161–162, 180–181, 183n3, 207–211, 213, 219; psychical representatives of, 48, 53–54; Intentional character of, 50–51. *See also* Id; Drives; Primary process
Intentionality, 10, 20, 38, 39, 46, 50, 51, 66–67, 75, 77, 78, 89, 109, 131, 141, 144, 148, 152, 178, 222; as essential characteristic of the mental, 45–46, 66–68; of emotions, 148–149
Intentions and goal-seeking behavior, 21, 38, 45, 52, 60, 64, 72, 77–78, 91–92, 131, 132, 179, 204; discovery of in others, 92–93, 97–98; in repression, 184–185. *See also* Action; Folk psychology; Practical reasoning
Internalism, 12–14, 17–18, 20, 24, 29–30, 35, 43, 46–47, 119–120, 124, 157–158. *See also* Cartesianism; Descartes, R.
Interpersonal view of the mental, 2–3. *See also* Interpreter's perspective; Triangulation
Interpretation: in Davidson, 27–34; of dreams, 44–45; as construction, 83–85; truth of, 86–90; metaphorical nature of, 96–98. *See also* Psychoanalytic interpretation

Interpreter's perspective, 2, 20–41. *See also* Davidson, D.; Externalism; Wittgenstein, L.

Irrationality, 4, 33, 139, 147, 149, 158, 162, 165, 193–199, 201–203

Jacobson, E., 137

James, W., 81, 143, 148, 200

Johnston, M., 197–201

Jones, E., 149, 161

Kant, I., 11, 14–16, 28n14, 116

Kihlstrom, J. F., 201

Klein, G., 74, 79, 128

Klein, M., 227–228, 229n14, 232

Knowledge. *See* Other minds; Truth

Kohut, H., 21n9

Lacan, J., 5, 38, 39, 113–115, 118, 121, 169, 170, 220, 221, 223

Language: publicity of, 20–21; private language, 24–26; learning, 27, 36–39, 110, 121, 124–127, 129–131; semantics, 28, 121–122; syntax, 121; and the unconscious, 165, 167. *See also* Davidson, D.; Lacan, J.; Meaning; Quine, W. V. O.; Wittgenstein, L.

Laplanche, J., 5

Lear, J., 100, 140, 145, 151, 164, 168, 171, 229n16

Legacy of Childhood, 4, 176, 203–204

Leibniz, G. W., 16, 157

Lewin, B., 53

Lewis, C. I., 58–59

Lewis, D., 32

Lichtenberg, J. D., 51, 53, 112, 123

Locke, J., 11, 14, 50

Love, 100; object love, 209–211, 213–217, 228–229, 231; self-love, 211–216

Mahler, M., 113, 135

Malcolm, N., 118, 44n2

McDowell, J., 116, 157

Meaning: theories of in Freud, 2; and belief, 9; publicity of, 20–21, 26, 29–34, 36–40, 124; in Wittgenstein, 21–25; and use, 22; as function of mental images, 23–24; and Austin, 25, 121n1; constraints on, 25–26, 31–33, 36; and truth, 25, 29–31, 35–36, 39–40; in Quine, 25–30; holism of, 26; in Davidson, 27–41; as entities, 28; indeterminacy of, 28, 33, 52, 89–90; causal determinants of,

29–31; normativity of, 32, 89–90, 97; related to conceptual scheme, 33–34; privacy of, 35; literal, 121n1; natural vs. non-natural, 122. *See also* Charity; Externalism; Ideas; Internalism; Language; Metaphor

Memory, 43, 45, 49, 60, 75, 77, 86, 87, 90, 98–100, 101, 119, 123, 133, 188–190; 220, 233; retroactive nature of, 53–55, 83–84, 191; as truth or phantasy, 83–85; in infants, 101–103; screen, 188. *See also* Repetition

Mental illness, 132–135. *See also* Schizophrenia.

Mental mechanisms, 75, 185, 196–197. *See also* Condensation; Displacement; Irrationality; Phantasy

Mental states: representational character of, 12–14, 17, 19, 23–24, 46–47, 48, 50–51, 53, 131; as essentially unconscious, 14; interpersonal character of, 36–41, 219 (*see also* Externalism; Interpreter's perspective; Triangulation); anomalous nature of, 66–74; non-propositional, 98, 165; avowability of, 144–145. *See also* Emotions; Intentionality; Internalism; Reasons

Mental verbs, 67

Metaphor, 26, 30, 33, 96, 97, 114, 128, 162, 167–171, 175, 199

Metapsychology, 57, 74–75

Michaels, R., 19

Mind as structure, 195–196, 234. *See also* Holism; Self, divided

Mind-body: dualism, 17–18, 71; frontier, 49, 55–56, 131, 161; problem, 55–56, 57; reductionism, 70–74, 219; token-token identity, 71; supervenience of mental on physical, 73

Moore, M., 185

Moral genealogy, 207–209, 218, 221

Moral ideals, 211–212. *See also* Valuing

Moral sense, 215–219. *See also* Guilt; Oedipal complex; Super-ego; Valuing

Motives. *See* Action; Folk psychology; Intentions

Motives, primary, 149–150

Mourning, 214, 215, 217, 224–229, 225n13, 229n15

Nagel, T., 11, 115n7, 117–119

Naive realism, 14

Narcissism, 209–212, 217, 221; primary and secondary, 210–212, 217
Narrative: psychoanalytic, 83–86, 98; historical, 88–89, 92; nature of the mental, 90, 191. *See also* Psychoanalytic interpretation
Nietzsche, F., 207, 208, 216
Non-verbal communications, 112; with infants, 122–129

Objectivity: concept of as necessary to thought, 38; of psychoanalytic interpretation, 86–89
Object relations theory, 5, 40, 76
Oedipal complex, 214–221, 225–226
O'Shaughnessy, B., 9n1, 47n7
Other minds: knowledge of, 18–19, 40–41, 111–112; acknowledgment of, 224. *See also* Empathy

Pears, D., 195–197, 201
Perception, 12–14, 18, 19, 45–47, 95, 117–118, 135, 144, 156–157, 172, 181, 183, 191
Phantasy, 45–46, 53, 54, 84, 166–167, 183–191, 202–205, 234; in infants, 53–55. *See also* Hallucinatory wish-fulfillment; Primary process
Phobias, 181–184
Piaget, J., 46, 123, 124
Plato, 14, 40, 66, 97, 102, 209, 231, 232
Polanyi, M., 53
Practical reasoning, 58–59, 153, 171, 200. *See also* Action; Reason-explanations
Price, H. H., 198
Primal scene, 83–84, 187. *See also* Freud, Wolf Man case
Primary process, 4, 45–46, 102, 103, 161–167, 168, 173–175, 179, 180, 185, 186, 203
Primary repression, 4, 47, 48, 56, 69, 75, 80–82, 86, 94, 95, 97, 101, 102, 114, 134, 139, 161, 162, 166, 173, 174, 176, 177, 180–186, 188, 189, 191, 195, 197, 201, 203, 208, 214, 220
Principle of continence, 196, 197, 201, 202
Principle of total evidence, 194–197, 201
Projectivism. *See* Empathy
Propositional attitudes, 98, 146; defined, 10. *See also* Belief; Intentionality
Psychic reality, 16, 18, 19, 43, 77, 86–87, 94, 182

Psychoanalysis: as 'hard' science, 48, 57–74; theories of as metaphorical, 55; as 'hermeneutic' science, 61; therapeutic goals of, 80–81, 94
Psychoanalytic interpretation, 32, 34–35, 55, 87–90, 94–103; of dreams, 44–45; as construction, 83–86, 96–98, 101–102; truth of, 86–90; metaphorical nature of, 96–98; as analogous to parent-child relation, 102. *See also* Transference
Psychoanalytic situation, peculiarities of, 100–101
Putnam, H., 12, 21, 23, 26, 124

Quine, W. V. O., 21, 25–30, 33, 89

Radical interpretation, 28–38. *See also* Davidson, D.
Radical translation, 27–28
Rapaport, D., 16, 157
Rationality, 89, 153, 164, 174, 194, 195, 204; as constitutive of the mental, 32–34, 197–201; of emotion, 138–145; imagination in service of, 204. *See also* Irrationality; Reason-explanations; Reasons
Reason-explanations, 57–66, 58, 62, 64, 66–68, 72, 81, 179, 180; normativity of, 68, 93–94. *See also* Action; Folk psychology
Reasons: unlawfulness of, 59 (*see also* Mental states, anomalous nature of); as causes, 59–63, 65, 90, 95–96; avowability of, 60–61; in justification, 62, 93–94
Repetition, 98–99, 178, 188–189. *See also* Memory
Representation, symbolic, 53–54, 99, 112–113, 119, 221
Representational world, 10n3
Repression, 47, 75, 79–80, 86, 95, 97, 161, 166, 180–181, 183–186, 188, 194–195, 201; lifting of, 81–82, 94, 191. *See also* Primary repression
Responsibility, 76–79, 91–93
Ricoeur, P., 79, 178
Rorty, R., 28, 103, 110
Rubinstein, B., 57, 70, 73, 74, 186, 200
Russell, B., 11
Ryle, G., 21

Sander, L., 125
Sandler, A.-M., 55
Sandler, J., 55

Sarraute, N., 200
Sartre, J. P., 195
Sass, L., 135
Saussure, 121, 169
Scaife, M., 123
Schafer, R., 18; on action and agency, 76–79; on psychoanalytic narrative, 85–103
Scheme-content, 33, 116
Schizophrenia, 47, 118, 135, 162, 164, 211
Schopenhauer, A., 180
Searle, J., 11, 131n6
Seduction theory, 43
Self: self-understanding, 94–96; self-deception, 97, 193–194; divided (split mind, split ego), 99, 196–197, 201–204, 214, 219–220; sense of in infants, 107–109, 113, 132; and narrative, 117; self-love, 211–216 (*see also* Narcissism); ideal self, 211, 214; origin of sense of, 222–223; as structure, 234 (*See also* Mind, as structure)
Sellars, W., 110
Sexuality, 75, 76, 209–210, 212–213, 215; infantile, 128, 175
Skepticism, 11, 15, 19, 40, 41, 178, 233. *See also* Cartesianism; Descartes, R.
Skinner, B. F., 21
Socrates, 65, 66, 171, 207, 231
Southwood, H. M., 128
Spence, D. P., 18, 83, 90
Spinoza, B., 62, 146, 149
Stern, D., 108, 111, 113–115, 118, 120, 122, 125, 127, 128, 132, 135
Structural theory, 137–138, 195, 204
Subjectivity, 38–40, 43, 117–119, 121; in infants, 11; prior to language, 113–115; as relational property, 117; ineffability of, 117–119; prior to objectivity, 219
Sulloway, F., 165n3
Super-ego, 216–219, 225
Symbolization, 1, 23, 25, 110, 119, 174, 203–204, 220. *See also* Representation, symbolic
Symptom-formation, 45, 47, 80, 82, 102, 138, 161, 166, 168, 174, 175, 178, 180–188

Teleological explanations, 58
Tomkins, S. S., 149, 150, 152

Transcendental arguments, 28n14, 229n16
Transference, 26, 84, 85, 94, 98–100, 102, 133
Trevarthen, C., 125–127
Triangulation: in Davidson, 27–38, 220; in Freud, *see* Oedipal complex; Oedipal, 220–221; in Davidson and Freud compared, 220–227
Tropisms, 199–200
Truth: consistency vs. correspondence theories of, 17–18, 35–36; as constraint on meaning, 31–36; in psychoanalytic interpretation, 86–89. *See also* Belief; Interpretation; Meaning; Memory

Unconscious, the, 14, 38, 39, 44–46, 99, 114, 158, 165, 167, 169, 173–175, 179, 185, 194, 195, 205, 208, 220; as unknowable, 14; as prior to consciousness, 48; linguistic, 114; cognitive character of, 165, 167, 174; analogous to concepts in physics, 179; theoretical unconscious, 186. *See also* Id; Instincts; Primary repression

Valuing, 207–208, 214–216, 217, 220, 229–231. *See also* Guilt; Moral ideals; Moral sense; Super-ego
Viderman, S., 101
Vygotsky, L. S., 124

Waelder, R., 70
Wallerstein, R., 18, 26
Walton, K. L., 189
Weakness of the will, 196
Whorf, B. L., 33
Wiggins, D., 156
Wilkes, K., 118
Williams, B., 80, 198
Winnicott, D. W., 55, 127, 128, 229
Wisdom, J., 96, 97, 229n14
Wishing, 100, 166–167; in *The Interpretation of Dreams*, 44–46. *See also* Hallucinatory wish-fulfillment; Phantasy; Primary process
Wittgenstein, L., 2, 21–26, 28, 36, 39–40, 46, 52, 59–61, 63, 71, 73, 96, 102, 103, 110, 121, 123, 129–131, 185, 225n13
Wollheim, R., 118, 119, 185, 191, 229